HARLEM'S GLORY

HARLEM'S GLORY

BLACK WOMEN WRITING

1900–1950

EDITED BY

Lorraine Elena Roses

Ruth Elizabeth Randolph

Harvard University Press

Cambridge, Massachusetts, and London, England

First Harvard University Press paperback edition, 1997

Library of Congress Cataloging-in-Publication Data

Harlem's glory : Black women writing, 1900–1950 / edited by Lorraine
Elena Roses, Ruth Elizabeth Randolph.
p. cm.
ISBN 0-674-37269-7 (cloth)
ISBN 0-674-37270-0 (pbk.)
1. American literature—Afro-American authors. 2. Afro-American
women—Literary collections. 3. Afro-Americans—Literary
collections. 4. American literature—Women authors. 5. American
literature—20th century. 6. Harlem Renaissance. I. Roses,
Lorraine Elena, 1943- . II. Randolph, Ruth Elizabeth.
PS508.N3H37 1996
810.8′09287′08996073—dc20   96-12342

To Wilhelmina and Rayfield Randolph

and to the memory of

Mollie and Herbert Silvershine
and
Velma "Aunt Jackie" Hoover

Acknowledgments

There are many individuals, too numerous to name, whom we would like to thank. Among them we count our supportive family members, especially Jonathan L. Roses, whose wise guidance and sharp editor's eye have been invaluable. Special thanks are extended to our research assistants, Wellesley College students, now all alumnae, Felicia D. Herman, Karima Atiyah Robinson, and Amanda Lebby. We also want to thank Professor Maryemma Graham for recommending Northeastern University students Sharon Pineault Burke and Renita Martin, our research assistants for the early stages of the project. Several grants from the Committee on Faculty Awards at Wellesley College made it possible for us to hire all of the aforementioned students and to pass on the torch to the next generation of researchers.

A number of colleagues have been supportive of our efforts, among them Selwyn R. Cudjoe, Mae G. Henderson, Doris Abramson, and Kathy A. Perkins. We also want to express our appreciation to the librarians and archivists who assisted us, including Charles Niles, Boston University Special Collections; Karen Jensen, Wellesley College Inter-Library loan; Esme Bhan and JoEllen El Bashir, Moorland-Spingarn Collection at Howard University; Betty Gubert, Diana Lachatanere, and Mary Yearwood at the Schomburg Collection, New York Public Library; and Mike Peterson, Library of Congress.

Contents

Part 3 · NATIVE DAUGHTER   *113*

Part 4 · LONGINGS   *175*

Part 5 · SPUNK   *205*

Part 6 · MY GREAT, WIDE, BEAUTIFUL WORLD   *239*

Part 7 · HARLEM'S GLORY: A WOMAN'S VIEW   *301*

Part 8 · IN THE LOOKING GLASS   *351*

Part 9 · CRISIS *397*

Part 10 · THE OFFERING *461*

HARLEM'S GLORY

Introduction

A flurry of interest surrounding African-American literature by women has brought widespread publicity and recognition to many writers. But this strong focus on such brilliant figures as Toni Morrison, Alice Walker, Gwendolyn Brooks, and Maya Angelou, among others, has had the odd effect of making it seem as if black women writers are anomalous, as if they emerged out of nowhere. In truth, they boast a venerable literary lineage that dates back to the eighteenth century. Lucy Terry, the first African-American poet, wrote "Bars Fight" in 1746; Phyllis Wheatley was the first African-American to write a volume of poetry, in 1773. Harriet E. Wilson's *Our Nig: or Sketches from the Life of a Free Black,* of 1859, was the first novel published by a black person in this country.[1]

To discover the more recent history of writing by African-American women, in 1985 we undertook extensive research aimed at identifying immediate predecessors, our assumption being that such talents as Morrison, Walker, Gloria Naylor, and many others, did not materialize out of thin air. If they could not be understood within mainstream American literary traditions, it should be possible to approach them from within black literature. As a first step we decided to review the sourcebooks on black women writing during the first half of this century.

We found a mysterious void. At that time sources on women writers made no mention of those who were black, and sources on black writers overlooked women. Even though the Harlem Renaissance that occurred between the two world wars was—and is—widely recognized as an

---

1. Ann Allen Shockley, *Afro-American Women Writers, 1746–1933* (Boston: G. K. Hall, 1988), p. 4.

unprecedented flowering of black artistic talent,[2] accounts of that period covered the contributions of only a small number of women. The field of African-American women writers active from 1900 to the close of World War II turned out to be virtually unexplored territory.

Alice Walker's rediscovery of one important writer of the period pointed the way to recovering the missing story. Walker's private investigation of Zora Neale Hurston's last years and her act of placing a tombstone on the author's weed-choked grave site in Fort Pierce, Florida, started a veritable "Zora renaissance."[3] This important beginning opened the question of who were Zora's "sisters," the other black women who must have challenged the barriers to authorship during the first half of the century. We became suspicious of the prevalent notion that Hurston was an exception to the unwritten rule that there was no worthwhile writing by black women from those years.

We began our research with a thorough review of the critical literature (including reference books, period anthologies, particularly work on the Harlem Renaissance), which produced a short list of "major" women whose names were scattered among the men's: Jessie Fauset, Nella Larsen, Dorothy West—all writers of prose fiction—and the poets Anne Spencer, Georgia Douglas Johnson, Gwendolyn Bennett, and Helene Johnson.[4] The available material on these women was not extensive, and this seemed to be a very small number. Many scholars characterized African-American literature, even during the Harlem Renaissance, as primarily a male event and mentioned women's participation only in passing. However, Bruce Kellner's *Harlem Renaissance: A Dictionary for the Era*[5] did mention a large number of women engaged in activities outside of the limelight. Kellner's book provided biographical sketches of female arts promoters,

2. See Nathan Irvin Huggins, *Harlem Renaissance* (New York: Oxford University Press, 1971) and *Voices of the Harlem Renaissance* (New York: Oxford University Press, 1976).

3. Robert Hemenway's biography of Hurston (*Zora Neale Hurston: A Literary Biography,* foreword by Alice Walker, Urbana: University of Illinois Press, 1977) and Walker's own articles ushered in the rediscovery of Zora Neale Hurston: the reissuing of her books, the establishment of a Zora Neale Hurston society, and the growth of the critical literature. See Alice Walker, "Zora Neale Hurston: A Cautionary Tale and a Partisan View," in *In Search of Our Mothers' Gardens: Womanist Prose by Alice Walker* (San Diego: Harcourt Brace Jovanovich, 1983).

4. See Margaret Perry, *Silence to the Drums: A Survey of the Literature of the Harlem Renaissance* (Westport, Conn.: Greenwood, 1976).

5. Bruce Kellner, *Harlem Renaissance: A Dictionary for the Era* (Westport, Conn.: Greenwood, 1984).

entrepreneurs, and writers on the Harlem scene, furnishing some more names for our growing list.

In all, these first researches yielded a bibliography of the work of more than one hundred forgotten writers. Fleshing out these writers' own stories, however, required a great deal more work. In some cases there was not so much as a birth date available, and our search entered the realm of historical inquiry and private investigation, complete with visits to nursing homes and cemeteries. Some of the writers were so undocumented that it was a challenge to verify that they had ever existed.

As more of the stories of forgotten individuals came to light, a remarkably complex and varied picture began to emerge—of women who didn't begin publishing until age sixty, and others who were quite precocious. Most of the writing was published between 1920 and the early 1940s, but earlier work could be seen as part of a continuous stream of novels, poems, essays, historical accounts, memoirs, and journalism. It emerged, too, that these enterprising African-American women had formed literary groups in many states, and beyond this country's borders as well. Some published their own "little" magazines, while the majority published in *The Crisis* and *Opportunity,* using those magazines as a sort of national network. After some five years of research, we completed our first work, *Harlem Renaissance and Beyond: Literary Biographies of 100 Black Women Writers, 1900–1945.* The response to that book—from reviewers, readers, researchers—made us realize that this anthology was needed.

In presenting these writings, we would like to place them in a theoretical context based on the phase theory of curricular "re-vision" developed by literary critic Peggy McIntosh.[6] McIntosh presents a thought-provoking theory of the shift away from monocultural ways of seeing. She describes racial or ethnic monoculturalism as "the assumption that we are all in the same cultural system together, and that its outlines are those which have been recognized by people who have the most ethnic or racial power" (1990, p. 1). Her statement applies quite well to the absence of black

---

6. Peggy McIntosh, *Interactive Phases of Curricular and Personal Re-Vision with Regard to Race,* Working Paper no. 219 (Wellesley, Mass.: Wellesley College Center for Research on Women, 1990). See also Peggy McIntosh, *Interactive Phases of Curricular Re-Vision: A Feminist Perspective* (Wellesley, Mass.: Wellesley College Center for Research on Women, 1983).

women's writing in curricula and even to anthologies that purport to be inclusive.[7] McIntosh's theory—which has informed and inspired our work from its inception—parallels theories developed by women's historians Joan Wallach Scott and Gerda Lerner while offering a model more attuned to race.[8] McIntosh describes five "phases" of awareness that apply to our project, and incorporates the fact that the experiences of African-American women are shaped by a complex web of race, gender, culture, and class.

In the first phase, "womanless and all-white history," the importance of people, places, things, and events is defined in terms of existing power structures, without reference to formative racial or gender elements. This is the traditional curriculum that excludes "types of knowledge that the privileged class does not share" (McIntosh 1983, p. 7). Here the writings of African-Americans are never considered.

In McIntosh's phase 2, "exceptional white women and people of color," women do appear when they are ambitious or fortunate enough to succeed in men's territory. In this phase, the few African-American women admitted as tokens to the annals of literary history are those who have achieved publishing successes analogous to those of black men. Such individuals, according to McIntosh's theory, "have gone far but not irrationally far in challenging existing male frameworks" (McIntosh 1990, p. 9).

Phase 2 is followed by a third phase in which "all women and men of color [are treated] as a problem, anomaly, or absence in history." Attention is paid to systemic oppression of groups, but not to individual voices. Women are included (or excluded) in terms of their value to those positioned at the apex of power at a given time. Difference is perceived as deprivation.

In phase 4, which McIntosh calls "women *as* history and the lives of people of color *as* life," the question is how to alter the discovery and presentation of knowledge in such a way that difference need not be perceived as deprivation. Here the right of African-American women to exist in the realm of their own experience is acknowledged and honored.

---

7. See, for example, David Levering Lewis, *The Portable Harlem Renaissance Reader* (New York: Viking, 1994).

8. See Joan Wallach Scott, *Gender and the Politics of History* (New York: Columbia University Press, 1988); and see Gerda Lerner, *The Majority Finds Its Past* (New York: Oxford University Press, 1979).

their own context and identified as a group apart
:rarchies of power, as "haves" instead of "have
ık is not, "Did the women write anything good?"
'n write?" (McIntosh 1983, p. 7). For the literary
necessitates first *finding* the pieces and reserv-
ɔr a future phase, and may as well necessitate
:nonical structures. McIntosh warns of the dan-
:: if the pain that systems of subjection inflict is
: sentimental celebration. To praise diversity as
that had prevented and continue to prevent
, misguided. But phases 3 and 4 must be linked
ɔower by keeping in place the sense that life is
fight for power.

.c 5, "history redefined or reconstructed to in-
.cIntosh sees the work toward phase 5 as taking
ring "a reconstruction of consciousness, percep-
Intosh 1990, p. 8). Since we can hardly envision
: future will look like, this phase is indescribable,
:w balance.

i\
a\
if\
on\

clud\
a full\
tion, a\
what a\
but it w

180 South Garrison Street ▼ Lakewood ▼ Color

Phase 4 is the setting for this anthology, a collection intended to place before contemporary readers and critics the African-American women writers of the first half of the twentieth century. It includes fiction, poetry, memoirs, plays, and essays written between 1900 and 1950—some never before published—by fifty-nine women. Some of these writers, like Zora Neale Hurston and Nella Larsen, are already well known, while others are virtually undiscovered and ripe for introduction to a reading public alerted to the strength and the uniqueness of African-American women's writing.

All African-American writers of the period faced a host of racial barriers on the path to publication: mainstream white publishers, save a few who favored black writing at the high-water mark of the Harlem Renaissance, were unreceptive. Often the only avenues for literary expression were the "race magazines," especially *Opportunity* and *The Crisis;* well over a hundred women answered the call to submit work to these journals. Some also turned to self-publication, to circumvent the formidable barriers of conventional discrimination. But black women writers faced additional constraints—what Mary Church Terrell called the "double cross" of color and sex, and the black community's expectation that they would play a supportive (and subordinate) role in the nurturing of rising male artists. Yet despite these and other constraints, African-American women lived extraordinary lives and created extraordinary literary texts.

It is difficult, almost daunting, to evaluate the quality of their writing at a time when literary criteria are in such flux, especially in light of the debates over cultural production and the literary canon, and our growing awareness of how specific ethnocentric values have worked to exclude the very writing we are trying to present. Consequently we have chosen, from thousands of pieces collected over the past ten years, those that strike us as vivid and memorable—not only for their social, cultural, and political content, but also for their overall effect. We made a point of including pieces that use language in varied and ingenious ways, whether that involves elaborate refinement or dialect. Though we two editors are of different generations and different ethnic and cultural backgrounds, we still found much to agree on in selecting the pieces here.

Our selections signal the diversity and complexity of the black women writers who preceded today's more celebrated figures. Taken together, the pieces—some quite sophisticated, others rough-hewn— allow us to repossess a sensibility we were not even aware of before. They display an infinite spectrum of black female commentary on the American experience. The writings hold meaning for us today insofar as they articulate, in another voice, a gendered voice, many issues that recur now in other guises and continue to elude resolution.

The contributions of black women to the literature of America have not been fully realized, let alone researched or appreciated. This collection is one modest attempt to bring to light an area of American literary life that has been so obscure that many thought it did not exist. It represents a legacy to be reclaimed by all Americans as part of our common heritage. We challenge the reader to experience the universality of the writings, and we hope that each reader will find something of him- or herself in the pages of this book.

BLACK AND WHITE
TANGLED THREADS

Black and White Tangled Threads was the title Zara Wright, an obscure Chicago writer, gave to her 1920 novel about true love thwarted by racial difference. Through a biracial heroine, the author offered a paradigm of what she saw as the complex entanglement of black and white lives in America, intimating the extraordinary burden that life in a stringently segregated society placed not only on African-Americans but on others as well.

The works in Part 1 address this same theme, whether it is seen in the events that occur as characters attempt to improve their lives, or, for some whose skin tone is very light, in their attempts to blend into white society. Also addressed is the usually taboo issue of genetic mixing—"tangling"—which grew out of the close contact between the races during slavery and over the centuries.

African-American female writers of the early twentieth century repeatedly addressed the difficulty of establishing healthy human relationships of any kind between blacks and whites in this peculiar context. Nella Larsen's story "Sanctuary," about a black mother in the South who is asked to shelter a young black man from the law, emphasizes the tension between personal ethics and racial solidarity. In Florida Ruffin Ridley's story "Two Gentlemen of Boston," a black mother, this time in the North, observes her son's seemingly ideal friendship with a white classmate. For Alvirah Hazzard, the social implications of a young black woman's presence at a white college become material for the stage.

The theme of distorted relationships in a context of racial tension is especially strong in the stories about the genetic intermingling of blacks

7

and whites, which had two distinct outcomes: children born outside of narrowly defined racial categories (Zara Wright's heroine), and others so light skinned that they could "pass"—that is, live and work among whites. Passing, a not uncommon strategy, is directly addressed in Gertrude Schalk's "Flower of the South," when an English guest learns from an elderly black woman about the frequency of the practice despite laws designed to draw hard and fast color lines. In a society that represented itself as being "pure," many families did not admit to black ancestry for fear of losing the social status and economic benefits of being white.

From those light-skinned characters who make the conscious decision to take on a white identity, the reader learns of the consequences of such action: a life of enforced secrecy, loss of ties with the black community, and the strain of living a double life. This dramatic situation is developed in Regina Andrews's "The Man Who Passed," about the effects of relinquishing ties to the black community. In Eloise Bibb Thompson's story "Masks," the anxiety about passing wreaks havoc on three generations. An essay by Mary Church Terrell analyzes and illuminates the phenomenon of passing from an anecdotal perspective. In contrast, some writers do resolve the tension of black and white dual heritage, as Aloise Barbour Epperson demonstrates in her celebration of her two grandmothers.

The writings included in this section speak not to race or gender as entities in themselves, but rather to the constructions of race and gender that rendered life exceedingly complex in the decades preceding the civil rights movement.

NELLA LARSEN

Sanctuary

I

On the Southern coast, between Merton and Shawboro,* there is a strip of desolation some half a mile wide and nearly ten miles long between the sea and old fields of ruined plantations. Skirting the edge of this narrow jungle is a partly grown-over road which still shows traces of furrows made by the wheels of wagons that have long since rotted away or been cut into firewood. This road is little used, now that the state has built its new highway a bit to the west and wagons are less numerous than automobiles.

In the forsaken road a man was walking swiftly. But in spite of his hurry, at every step he set down his feet with infinite care, for the night was windless and the heavy silence intensified each sound; even the breaking of a twig could be plainly heard and the man had need of caution as well as haste.

Before a lonely cottage that shrank timidly back from the road the man hesitated a moment, then struck out across the patch of green in front of it. Stepping behind a clump of bushes close to the house, he looked in through the lighted window at Annie Poole, standing at her kitchen table mixing the supper biscuits.

He was a big, black man with pale brown eyes in which there was an odd mixture of fear and amazement. The light showed streaks of gray soil on his heavy, sweating face and great hands, and on his torn clothes. In his woolly hair clung bits of dried leaves and dead grass.

Source: Forum 83 (January 1930): 15–18.
    *Fictional locations.

He made a gesture as if to tap on the window, but turned away to the door instead. Without knocking he opened it and went in.

II

The woman's brown gaze was immediately on him, though she did not move. She said, "You ain't in no hurry, is you, Jim Hammer?" It wasn't, however, entirely a question.

"Ah's in trubble, Mis' Poole," the man explained, his voice shaking, his fingers twitching.

"W'at you done now?"

"Shot a man, Mis' Poole."

"Trufe?" The woman seemed calm. But the word was spat out.

"Yas'm. Shot 'im." In the man's tone was something of wonder, as if he himself could not quite believe that he had really done this thing which he affirmed.

"Daid?"

"Dunno, Mis' Poole. Dunno."

"White man o' niggah?"

"Cain't say, Mis' Poole. White man, Ah reckons."

Annie Poole looked at him with cold contempt. She was a tiny, withered woman—fifty perhaps—with a wrinkled face the color of old copper, framed by a crinkly mass of white hair. But about her small figure was some quality of hardness that belied her appearance of frailty. At last she spoke, boring her sharp little eyes into those of the anxious creature before her.

"An' w'at am you lookin' foh me to do 'bout et?"

"Jes' lemme stop till dey's gone by. Hide me till dey passes. Reckon dey ain't fur off now." His begging voice changed to a frightened whimper. "Foh de Lawd's sake, Mis' Poole, lemme stop."

And why, the woman inquired caustically, should she run the dangerous risk of hiding him?

"Obadiah, he'd lemme stop ef he was to home," the man whined.

Annie Poole sighed. "Yas," she admitted slowly, reluctantly, "Ah spec' he would. Obadiah, he's too good to you all no 'count trash." Her slight shoulders lifted in a hopeless shrug. "Yas, Ah reckon he'd do et. Emspecial' seein' how he allus set such a heap o' store by you. Cain't see w'at foh, mahse'f. Ah shuah don' see nuffin' in you but a heap o' dirt."

But a look of irony, of cunning, of complicity passed over her face. She went on, "Still, 'siderin' all an' all, how Obadiah's right fon' o' you, an' how white folks is white folks, Ah'm a-gwine hide you dis one time."

Crossing the kitchen, she opened a door leading into a small bedroom, saying, "Git yo'se'f in dat dere feather baid an' Ah'm a-gwine put de clo's on de top. Don' reckon dey'll fin' you ef dey does look foh you in mah house. An Ah don' spec' dey'll go foh to do dat. Not lessen you been keerless an' let 'em smell you out gittin' hyah." She turned on him a withering look. "But you allus been triflin'. Cain't do nuffin' propah. An' Ah'm a-tellin' you ef dey warn't white folks an' you a po' niggah, Ah shuah wouldn't be lettin' you mess up mah feather baid dis ebenin', 'cose Ah jes' plain don' want you hyah. Ah done kep' mahse'f outen trubble all mah life. So's Obadiah."

"Ah's powahful 'bliged to you, Mis' Poole. You shuah am one good 'oman. De Lawd'll mos' suttinly—"

Annie Poole cut him off. "Dis ain't no time foh all dat kin' o' fiddle-de-roll. Ah does mah duty as Ah sees et 'thout no thanks from you. Ef de Lawd had gib you a white face 'stead o' dat dere black one, Ah shuah would turn you out. Now hush yo' mouf an' git yo'se'f in. An' don' git movin' and scrunchin' undah dose covahs and git yo'se'f kotched in mah house."

Without further comment the man did as he was told. After he had laid his soiled body and grimy garments between her snowy sheets, Annie Poole carefully rearranged the covering and placed piles of freshly laundered linen on top. Then she gave a pat here and there, eyed the result, and, finding it satisfactory, went back to her cooking.

III

Jim Hammer settled down to the racking business of waiting until the approaching danger should have passed him by. Soon savory odors seeped in to him and he realized that he was hungry. He wished that Annie Poole would bring him something to eat. Just one biscuit. But she wouldn't, he knew. Not she. She was a hard one, Obadiah's mother.

By and by he fell into a sleep from which he was dragged back by the rumbling sounds of wheels in the road outside. For a second fear clutched so tightly at him that he almost leaped from the suffocating shelter of the bed in order to make some active attempt to escape the horror that his capture meant. There was a spasm at his heart, a pain so sharp, so slashing, that he had to suppress an impulse to cry out. He felt himself falling. Down, down, down . . . Everything grew dim and very distant in his memory . . . Vanished . . . Came rushing back.

Outside there was silence. He strained his ears. Nothing. No footsteps. No voices. They had gone on then. Gone without even stopping to ask Annie Poole if she had seen him pass that way. A sigh of relief slipped from him. His thick lips curled in an ugly, cunning smile. It had been smart of him to think of coming to Obadiah's mother's to hide. She was an old demon, but he was safe in her house.

He lay a short while longer, listening intently, and, hearing nothing, started to get up. But immediately he stopped, his yellow eyes glowing like pale flames. He had heard the unmistakable sound of men coming toward the house. Swiftly he slid back into the heavy, hot stuffiness of the bed and lay listening fearfully.

The terrifying sounds drew nearer. Slowly. Heavily. Just for a moment he thought they were not coming in—they took so long. But there was a light knock and the noise of a door being opened. His whole body went taut. His feet felt frozen, his hands clammy, his tongue like a weighted, dying thing. His pounding heart made it hard for his straining ears to hear what they were saying out there.

"Evenin', Mistah Lowndes." Annie Poole's voice sounded as it always did, sharp and dry.

There was no answer. Or had he missed it? With slow care he shifted his position, bringing his head nearer the edge of the bed. Still he heard nothing. What were they waiting for? Why didn't they ask about him?

Annie Poole, it seemed, was of the same mind. "Ah don' reckon youall done traipsed way out hyah jes' foh yo' healf," she hinted.

"There's bad news for you, Annie, I'm 'fraid." The sheriff's voice was low and queer.

Jim Hammer visualized him standing out there—a tall, stooped man, his white tobacco-stained mustache drooping limply at the ends, his nose hooked and sharp, his eyes blue and cold. Bill Lowndes was a hard one too. And white.

"W'atall bad news, Mistah Lowndes?" The woman put the question quietly, directly.

"Obadiah—" the sheriff began—hesitated—began again. "Obadiah—ah—er—he's outside, Annie. I'm 'fraid—"

"Shucks! You done missed. Obadiah, he ain't done nuffin', Mistah Lowndes. Obadiah!" she called stridently, "Obadiah! git hyah an' splain yo'se'f."

But Obadiah didn't answer, didn't come in. Other men came in. Came in with steps that dragged and halted. No one spoke. Not even Annie Poole. Something was laid carefully upon the floor.

"Obadiah, chile," his mother said softly, "Obadiah, chile." Then, with sudden alarm, "He ain't daid, is he? Mistah Lowndes! Obadiah, he ain't daid?"

Jim Hammer didn't catch the answer to that pleading question. A new fear was stealing over him.

"There was a to-do, Annie," Bill Lowndes explained gently, "at the garage back o' the factory. Fellow tryin' to steal tires. Obadiah heerd a noise an' run out with two or three others. Scared the rascal all right. Fired off his gun an' run. We allow et to be Jim Hammer. Picked up his cap back there. Never was no 'count. Thievin' an' sly. But we'll git 'im, Annie. We'll git 'im."

The man huddled in the feather bed prayed silently. "Oh, Lawd! Ah didn't go to do et. Not Obadiah, Lawd. You knows dat. You knows et." And into his frenzied brain came the thought that it would be better for him to get up and go out to them before Annie Poole gave him away. For he was lost now. With all his great strength he tried to get himself out of the bed. But he couldn't.

"Oh, Lawd!" he moaned. "Oh, Lawd!" His thoughts were bitter and they ran through his mind like panic. He knew that it had come to pass as it said somewhere in the Bible about the wicked. The Lord had stretched out his hand and smitten him. He was paralyzed. He couldn't move hand or foot. He moaned again. It was all there was left for him to do. For in the terror of this new calamity that had come upon him he had forgotten the waiting danger which was so near out there in the kitchen.

His hunters, however, didn't hear him. Bill Lowndes was saying, "We been a-lookin' for Jim out along the old road. Figured he'd make tracks for Shawboro. You ain't noticed anybody pass this evenin', Annie?"

The reply came promptly, unwaveringly. "No, Ah ain't sees nobody pass. Not yet."

IV

Jim Hammer caught his breath.

"Well," the sheriff concluded, "we'll be gittin' along. Obadiah was a mighty fine boy. Ef they was all like him—I'm sorry, Annie. Anything I c'n do, let me know."

"Thank you, Mistah Lowndes."

With the sound of the door closing on the departing men, power to move came back to the man in the bedroom. He pushed his dirt-caked feet out from the covers and rose up, but crouched down again. He wasn't cold now, but hot all over and burning. Almost he wished that Bill Lowndes and his men had taken him with them.

Annie Poole had come into the room.

It seemed a long time before Obadiah's mother spoke. When she did there were no tears, no reproaches; but there was a raging fury in her voice as she lashed out, "Git outer mah feather baid, Jim Hammer, an' outen mah house, an' don' nevah stop thankin' yo' Jesus he done gib you dat black face."

FLORIDA RUFFIN RIDLEY

Two Gentlemen of Boston

Usually [the] homeward journey from school was a dignified process; it was decidedly fitting that thirteen-year-old ranking scholars of the eighth grade graduating class should have occasion for serious conversation. The closing half-hour of school, devoted to the consideration of "Gems from History and Literature," always left Arthur and Morton in a contemplative mood and ready for serious debates on the lives and deeds of Napoleon and King Arthur and Marmion* and all the others.

From my shaded seat on the porch I could see them from the time they left the school yard all the way up the tree-bordered street, and as I watched the straight, manly little figures, I took delight in imagining the course of their absorbed conversation, and in observing the companionship which seemed to promise so much in the way of mutual benefit and pleasure.

They were so markedly different in outward characteristics! There was always something happening to separate Arthur's blouse and trousers, or to snap his garters, and in the midst of the most intense discussion even of so vital a question as to "which you'd rather be the greatest orator in the world or the greatest football player in the world"—it was always necessary for him to make some clothing adjustment; to Arthur, clothes

Source: *Opportunity* 3 (January 1926): 12-13.
*Marmion: from the poem of the same name by Sir Walter Scott, published in 1808 and set in the early sixteenth century, about an English nobleman whose reputation as a brave knight was spotless (Frank Northen Magill, *Cyclopedia of Literary Characters* [New York: Harper and Row, 1963]).

at best, were only necessary accompaniments, and at worst, impediments to the pursuit of happiness; but these lapses from dignity and solemnity in the daily conversational intercourse of the two boys, were more than redeemed by Morton, who at thirteen years of age, reflected an indelible impress of three years contact with foreign salons—the reaction of an only child, accompanying parents of social and literary aspirations in their old-world journeyings. No intriguing considerations of "Horatius at the Bridge,"* could be great enough to upset the poise with which Morton would at once readjust a garter which dared to begin a false move.

Today, however, the approach of the boys was distinctly out of form— it was not that there [were] attendants, to the number of eight or ten; very often their debates were extended to include followers, who gave more life and vigor to the scene and the occasions by supplementing their points with side whacks at shrubbery and high leaps at curbs. I was used to this variation from the usual, but today the formation was entirely out of the ordinary, one striking feature being that the comrades walked apart and silent, the followers compact and in earnest conversation. As the groups drew near, I was startled by the sudden realization of what the scene meant. Without doubt Morton, the dilettante, and Arthur, the dreamer, had disagreed, had gone so far in the disagreement as to fight, and had had a bloody fight at that! There was no sign of belligerency in their attitudes, they walked quietly and apart; characteristically, Morton had restored his clothes to some order—his Norfolk jacket was tightly buttoned to hide the dust and mud left on the blouse from its contact with the earth, but his scratched and bleeding knuckles couldn't be hidden in his efforts to cover a blackening eye with a very grimy hand-kerchief. Arthur was frankly dishevelled, and seemed utterly indifferent to the fact that he was without hat or tie; his face carried some slight intensification of its inclination toward griminess, which for racial rea-sons, was never as readily discernible as upon his friend Morton; his lack of bruises and general bearing indicated quite clearly that he had been the victor in the fray.

I was rather sorry that I had disclosed myself by an involuntary move toward the approaching group, for it at once became evident to me that

*A reference to Horatius Cocles, a Roman who is said to have held back the Etruscans from the wooden Sublican Bridge until it could be demolished, and who then, despite his wounds, swam across the Tiber to safety (*Oxford Classical Dictionary* [Oxford: Clarendon Press, 1949]).

Morton had intended to pass without stopping (what more natural). On seeing me, however, he stopped and with the courtesy that was so charming and so marked an attribute, he tried to drag his cap from his disfigured head. "It's all right, Mrs. Allen," he said, "*merely* a little difference of opinion," and replacing his cap, he swung down the road alone, leaving me to recover, before turning to those who were left, the poise which the approach and his speech had rather upset.

I turned to my son who was evidently suffering under the disadvantage of having a "smooth talker" get in his work first. "I'll fight anybody that attacks my good name," he volunteered, with great emphasis, and then with the evident desires to level up intellectually in the eyes of the cortege, "he who steals my purse"* he began, and stopped short, whether from some budding sense of good taste, or from the realization that a hint to his meaning was all that was necessary to his followers, it was not clear, but he began to edge toward the screen door in silence.

It was plain that he had decided to say no more—Morton had offered no explanation, made no accusations—attempted no defense. Should he, Arthur, take advantage of the absence of his companion to make out a case for himself? I read in a flash their code, and was convinced that any explanation of the affair would have to come from others. I was clearly out of it, how [to] force the confidence of these gentlemen? How was it possible to chide a man for defending his good name? How call to order men who are adjusting "a mere difference of opinion" in their own way? The dignity of thirteen years must be sustained, its obligations respected, its ethics acknowledged. I accepted my evident limitations and confined myself to a meek suggestion to Arthur that it would be well to "bathe his hands in sulphur-naphthal solution." The round-eyed caravan dissolved, as Arthur passed through the screen door. I settled myself with more complacency than I felt to think over the situation. It was all so unlooked for! The companionship had been so smooth, so complementary, and then too, boys now-a-days were not in the habit of disfiguring each other as in the old days—what could have ruffled Arthur's good temper and thrown Morton out of his natural poise sufficiently to bring about a bloody row?

*From Shakespeare, Iago, in *Othello,* act 3, scene 3: "Good name in man and woman, dear my lord, / Is the immediate jewel of our souls; / Who steals my purse steals trash; 'tis something, nothing: / 'Twas mine, 'tis his, and has been slave to thousands. / But he that filches from me my good name / Robs me of that which not enriches him / And makes me poor indeed."

Only the day before, Morton had graciously accepted an invitation to stay to lunch, being largely influenced, I have no doubt, by the sight of the hot biscuits which were being taken from the oven as he came through the kitchen; he had conditioned his acceptance, however, upon the loan of a clean collar. We had sat at the table in the peace and contentment that accompany a satisfactory meal, eaten in congenial company. We had dallied over the meal even longer than it took the boys to demolish two large pans of biscuits with accompaniments; the day was warm and Morton was waiting for a telephone call. He began talking of France, his parents were going over again in a few weeks. "You ought to go to Paris, Art," he said, "why couldn't you send him over to join us, Mrs. Allen?" He tossed this remark casually, as he gracefully broke open another biscuit. "I'd rather go to Canada and raise silver foxes," Arthur had turned to say. "Well, if you came to Paris you would see where Napoleon lived— will you excuse me, Mrs. Allen, if I see what time it is, you know I have my violin lesson at two o'clock."

After so large and cordial an invitation, and so intimate an afternoon, it gave me some surprise to find that the friends at their very next meeting had engaged in battle.

The growth of their intimacy had been of great interest to me. In the big American public schools, democracy is most truly demonstrated in the freedom with which children make and develop friendships. Even the guiding hands of parents cannot always be effective here. Arthur and Morton were neighbors, but the fact of their difference in race kept the families apart as far as social contact is concerned; Arthur being the only one of his kind in the neighborhood, the children generally had played in and out of each other's houses. Not being dependent on close social contact, and entirely unconcerned about it, the limiting of social recognitions to courteous outdoor exchanges between us parents was entirely acceptable to me.

I had at first hesitated at encouraging the close companionship between Arthur and Morton which loomed inevitable. American standards of simplicity had been too strongly bred in me to accept whole-heartedly the polish with which Morton literally shone; still Arthur, with his inherited indifference to externals, could stand quite a little working upon, and I not only realized the benefits that Morton would bring Arthur, but also those that Morton would receive; in fact, I felt sure Morton had the advantage. Morton was never, as Arthur, so absorbed in a book that he overlooked offering a chair when necessary, but, although I worried and grieved over my young barbarian who would bring to the table along with his immaculate young guest a pair of hands that never should have left the cellar, yet I could not but warm to the fact that he had forgotten himself in seeing that his pets received their daily attention, and on time.

In the days that followed the battle, I kept "a weather eye" open for any hint or suggestion that would enlighten me as to its cause. There was some estrangement, Morton's missionary zeal had received a set-back, the two boys did not walk together on the homeward journey, neither [was] there any interchange of visits—it was impossible for them to keep entirely apart, their interests were too close—but there was a barrier and as I watched them in the week that followed, I became convinced that the barrier had been raised principally from the outside.

The time was drawing near for Morton's family to start upon the European trip and I was still in the dark. My enlightenment came suddenly, however.

I was at my kitchen window making out a batch of cookies that were great favorites with the young literati; two classmates of the duelling pair were lying upon the grass beneath the window and their voices came up to me. "Art and Mort had a fight last week, when you were absent." "Gee, I never saw Mort get into a fight." "Naw, he didn't want to this time, but Art made him!" "Who licked?" "O, Art." "Did he make his nose bleed?" "Yes, and blacked his eye!" "Gee, wish I'd been there," and, after a pause, "what'd they fight about?" "Well," with deliberation, "Mort attacked Art's good name, I'd fight for my good name, wouldn't you—Mort tried to talk out of it but all the fellas were on Art's side!"

"Sure, I'd fight for my good name—did he call him a liar?"

"Worse than that, he went to the guild and he had to report his good deed, and he said he had been 'elevating a little colored boy!'"

"'Elevating a little colored boy!' Gee, wish I'd been there—is that your dog—come on" and two pair of legs went scurrying across the lawn.

A little later, Morton came in with Arthur. "We're leaving tonight, Mrs. Allen, and I came to bid you good-bye and to wish you a very pleasant summer," and the little hand was extended with its usual grace. Our young Chesterfield* sailed for Europe three days later, leaving more questions in my mind than before. What had been his reaction from the fight? In his

*A reference to the son of Chesterfield, Philip Dormer Stanhope, fourth Earl of Chesterfield, a statesman and man of letters. Wrote "Letters to His Son" that render a classic portrait of an eighteenth-century gentleman (*Benet's Reader's Encyclopedia* [New York: Harper and Row, 1987]).

relations with Arthur, how much had he been influenced by adults? What were the parents' reactions? Were they possibly those of the rebuffed missionaries who only feel pity that the heathen do not know what is good for them? As for my little son—I never discussed the matter with him, I felt he had shown himself wiser than I. With instinctive wisdom, he had sensed a situation to which I was blind, and had met that situation adequately. I had not recognized the "patronizing pose," neither would I have had the directness and courage to reduce it to its lowest terms and deal it the "knock out" blow.

ALVIRA HAZZARD

Little Heads:
A One-Act Play of Negro Life

Bee and Joe (Twelve-Year-Old Twins)
Mrs. Lee (Their Mother)
Frances (Their Sister)
Edna (A Friend)

(The scene is a comfortable living room. There is a window, right, and an entrance from the front door and the rest of the house at the left. The arrangement of the furniture is optional. There should be a reading table in the room. Joe and Bee are discovered at opposite ends of the table, studying.)

JOE *(looking up)*: What's the good of studying, Bee. Let's quit.

BEE *(looking around cautiously)*: You know what mother said.

JOE *(in whisper)*: She wouldn't know.

BEE: But you know what Miss Perry said about your conscience!

JOE: When?

BEE: Oh, you were there. She says that a little voice inside worries us most awful if we do something wrong, whether anyone knows it or not.

Source: Saturday Evening Quill 2 (April 1929): 42–44.

JOE: How does she know?

BEE: Don't be a big silly! She's smart, like Frances. Mother says that Francie'll be a teacher some day, just like Miss Perry.

JOE *(chin in hands)*: Miss Perry's white.

BEE: All the same, Francie's just as smart.

JOE: She's smarter, I think—except when she reminds me about behind my ears and all that nonsense. *(Pauses.)* Say, Bee, wouldn't you like to be white sometimes?

BEE: No.

JOE: Aw, be yourself! I saw you almost cry the other day in geography. *You* saw Allen Farnsworth look and grin when they were saying about the black race havin' kinky hair and all that junk.

BEE: Well, anyway, I wouldn't be white.

JOE *(pointing finger)*: You're bein' stubborn!

BEE *(slapping finger)*: Get your finger out o' my face.

JOE *(catching her hand and laughing)*: Who'll make me?

BEE *(rising; he holds her tightly)*: Stop, Joe.

JOE: Make me.

(They come forward. Joe is pleasant and teasing, but Bee is getting cross. She cannot get away.)

BEE *(kicking)*: MOTHER! Joe's hurting me! *(Mrs. Lee enters.)*

MRS. LEE: Joe, what are you doing to your sister?

JOE *(letting go)*: Nothin'.

BEE: He hurt my wrist. *(She rubs it.)*

JOE *(quickly)*: She slapped me.

BEE: You started it.

JOE: I didn't.

MRS. LEE *(firmly)*: Stop it! *(They eye her, and are silent.)* Back to your books, both of you.

BEE: But mother . . .

MRS. LEE: Not another word. Frances is coming tomorrow night, and you won't want to study then.

JOE: Bee said . . .

MRS. LEE: Don't make me speak to either of you again.

(Slowly, silently, they flop into chairs again. They cast sly glances at each other, trying to keep sober. Finally both grin sheepishly.)

BEE *(softly)*: You didn't hurt me much.

JOE: Why'd you holler?

BEE: I wanted you to stop.

JOE: I'll squeeze you hard next time.

BEE *(hands behind her)*: Dare you.

JOE: Say it again, and see what happens.

BEE. Double dare.

(Joe jumps at her so suddenly that in evading him she falls over chair. He trips also. They are in awkward positions on floor when Mrs. Lee appears.)

BOTH *(giggling)*: It was Bee—Joe.

MRS. LEE *(entering and re-arranging things)*: March right off to bed, the two of you. Do you hear me?

(They get up and face left. At sound of door bell Mrs. Lee goes out. Voices are heard outside: "Frances!" "Hello, mother," etc. Children rush out. They come back immediately each with a bag. Frances and mother follow. Frances is the center of attention. She takes off hat

and coat and sits down. Mrs. Lee stands near table. The children
stand at a distance from Frances, eyeing her.)

MRS. LEE: Well, this is a surprise, Frances. How did it happen?

JOE *(to Bee)*:   I will!

BEE *(alarmed)*:   You needn't.

JOE *(teasing)*:   I will!

BEE: Don't, Joe, please . . .

JOE: Frances, she got a C in 'rithmetic.

BEE *(running out)*:   You mean, hateful boy!. I hate it, anyway.

FRANCES *(laughing)*:   Come back, Bee, it can't be helped. I hate it,
too.

(Bee comes back and hangs over Frances's chair. Joe sprawls near
his mother. They cast glances at each other.)

FRANCES: Oh, yes, you were asking me why I am ahead of time. Well,
you see, there is to be a most wonderful week-end party at Oak Manor
given by one of the wealthiest girls on the campus. Mary says that my
name is actually on the list. I had to get home and sort of get together.
I cut a class to do it, but the party is worth it.

MRS. LEE: We'll miss having you here.

FRANCES: I know it, but this time I'm not able to be sensible and
resist.

MRS. LEE: Of course you want to go. They are all white though, aren't
they?

FRANCES: Yes, but they are all so nice to me that I shall be quite at
home. Then, too, Palmer is going. We can be together, and I just know
it will be great.

MRS. LEE: Does everyone in the school go?

FRANCES: Indeed not. That's the thrill of it. Only a dozen or fifteen

couples are to be favored. No one but Mary could make me believe
that I'm actually included.

MRS. LEE *(trying to hide worry)*:   Won't it be expensive, Francie?

FRANCES: About a hundred dollars extra would do wonders. Isn't my
endowment policy due about now? You know I'm twenty-one. *(She
hugs her knees in anticipation.)*

MRS. LEE: We'll see about it. But run and rest a while now, and I'll get
you a bite to eat.

FRANCES *(rising)*:   Sounds good to me. I'm famished. But such oodles
of news as I still have to tell you. Don't bother fixing anything special,
for I could chew shingle nails. *(She goes out. Bee follows, making a
face at Joe as she reaches the door. Joe bolts after her.)*

MRS. LEE: Right back here, young man. I'll have no more fussing in
this house tonight.

*(A voice is heard outside. A pleasant young girl of about Frances's
age enters.)*

EDNA: Hello, folks. I walked right in, since the door was open.

MRS. LEE: Fine. Come right in, Edna.

EDNA *(coming in and ruffling Joe's hair; he frowns)*:   I saw Frances
come in, and couldn't wait to greet her. Isn't she ahead of time?

MRS. LEE *(blankly)*:   Yes, we were not looking for her until tomorrow.
It was a real surprise. She is upstairs, and will be right down. Make
yourself at home.

(Edna leans on the table and thumbs a book. Mrs. Lee rises.)

MRS. LEE: Edna, my dear—*(noticing Joe)*—Joe, mother wants to
speak to Edna. *(He scuffs out.)* I suppose I shouldn't bother you with
this, but, well, it's like this . . .

EDNA *(encouraging)*:   What is it?

MRS. LEE *(in an attempt to get it over with)*:   Frances had some money from an endowment policy. We spent it, and cannot replace it at once. I didn't think of Francie wanting it so soon. I had planned to give it to her in gold for her birthday. *(She sits down again and fingers her beads or scarf nervously.)*

EDNA: Do you think that Frances will really mind?

MRS. LEE: Oh, she won't mind, because I deposited it to Bob's account. He finishes Howard* this year, you know, and he is always broke. Poor Bob's pitiful pleas came with the check—the same mail. It was pampering him to send so much, but, as I told you, the money was handy, and I planned getting it in gold from the bank the first of the month. What worries me is that Francie has her mind set on a party for this very week-end. I'd rather do anything than spoil her fun.

EDNA: That is a shame. What can we do?

MRS. LEE *(leaning toward Edna)*:   I don't know, but I thought you might help me think. I'm rather upset about it. She wants new clothes, I'm sure.

(Edna gets up and walks to the window. There is an awkward silence.)

EDNA *(turning)*:   I'll tell you what, let's not tell her until the last moment—that is, let's wait a day and see if she decides to do without many new things. I'll try to talk her into making the trip as cheaply as possible.

MRS. LEE *(rising and going toward door)*:   All right, Edna, you do that, and we'll both sleep on it before we tell her. You just make yourself comfortable while I fix her something to eat. She ought to be down any minute now. *(She goes out.)*

EDNA *(coming down center and sitting on chair arm)*:   Just like a mother. A couple hundred—it must have been that much—to that spendthrift of a son. And to be paid back to a gem of a daughter from the interest of the family income. Well, Frances deserves it, there is no

*Howard University in Washington, D.C., one of the prestigious historically black universities.

doubt about that. *(She goes back to the window and looks out. Frances comes in on tiptoe, and surprises Edna. They hug each other. Edna whispers something.)*

FRANCES: Not really! Is he keen?

EDNA: You'll see him. How about yourself, heartbreaker?

FRANCES: No news here, except that the adorable Palmer Brennon is to be invited to Dolores's party, and Mary says she saw my name on her list. I hope the invitation comes tonight.

EDNA *(sitting, while Frances lounges on the arm)*: Your mother told me. Isn't it thrilling!

FRANCES: Positively! They evidently are asking *both* of us, to make it pleasant all around. We must shop tomorrow. I have an insurance that is most handy at this particular time. I really think mother has it already, but wants to be mysterious.

EDNA: Yes?

MRS. LEE *(from outside)*: Come on, girls. I'm all ready.

(They go out with their heads together. Joe comes in and sits down in deep thought, his head in his hands. He snaps his fingers as if an idea had struck him.)

JOE *(calling)*: Bee, O Bee! *(She enters.)* Listen, silly, I've got news.

BEE: Foolin'?

JOE: No, I'm not.

BEE *(going to window)*: Joe, the mailman is coming here. I can just see him.

JOE *(over her shoulder)*: Gee, Sis, I've a hunch it's that letter.

BEE: What letter?

JOE: You wouldn't understand, but wait. *(He runs out, coming back with a letter in his hand. Bee stays at the window.)* See, I was right. It's special for Frances. Can you keep a secret?

BEE: Of course.

JOE: Well, this is that letter inviting Frances to the party, and her money is spent, so she can't go.

BEE: I've got five dollars in my bank.

JOE *(with disgust)*: What's five dollars? The check was for ever so much over a hundred. Sit down. *(She does.)* Now, listen. If Frances does not get this, mother won't have to worry about sending her money to Bob. She'll think the rich girl forgot to invite her, after all.

BEE *(in alarm)*: Oh, Joe, we can't keep it.

JOE: Well, what shall we do?

BEE *(frowning)*: I can't think.

JOE *(fingering the letter)*: *We* might open it.

BEE *(covering her ears)*: Oh, Joe, never, never!

JOE *(with an air of importance and standing with feet apart, near her)*: Bee, remember you're a girl. I'm going to pry it open and read it to see if that helps.

BEE: How?

JOE: My jackknife.

(They bend eagerly over the table as Joe pries the letter open carefully. As it is done they both sigh heavily.)

JOE: Listen to this: "Dear Frances, I'm having a week-end party at the Oak Manor, and want you to come. Palmer, we hope, will come also. You are both so clever, we want you to help entertain. Haven't you some old things so that you can dress like—well, you know—sort of old-fashioned, and sing some of those delightful spirituals? Palmer will probably bring his sax. You will have some fun, besides serving your schoolmate, Dolores Page."

BEE: Then Frances won't need much money, after all.

JOE: Won't you ever grow up a little!

BEE: I'm as old as you are.

JOE *(strolling to window, and looking back at her in contempt)*: In years.

BEE: You're not so awful smart, see.

JOE *(coming back to the table)*: Well, we can't argue this time, and you can't ever tell, because you helped me. *(He tears the letter into bits and stuffs it into his pockets, while Bee looks on in wonder and amazement. She jumps up and runs to door to peep and see that no one has seen them.)*

BEE: Don't you feel most awfully wicked, Joe?

JOE *(with feeling)*: No, I don't, but I just hate that Dolores Page. Let's go now. *(Voices are heard.)* We'll feel guilty—a little bit—when they come in.

(They tiptoe out hand in hand.)

My Two Grandmothers

I had two royal grandmothers,
Long they have been gone,
One was black as the midnight
The other fair as the dawn.

One had hair like cotton,
Wooly as sheep have grown,
The other had hair like satin,
As silken as any have known.

My milk white grandmother was lovely,
Meticulous, elegant and grand,
My coal black grandmother was ugly
With broad features and toil roughened hand.

But between the two, believe me,
My heart will not declare
Which I loved the better
The dark one or the fair.

Fair and lovely grandmother
Was gracious in her ways,
And memory of her presence
Like an attar* stays.

*A fragrant essential oil, obtained from flower petals.

But oh! my coal black grandmother,
Who did not drink as she,
From wisdom's precious fountain,
Was a spreading green bay tree.

Source: Reprinted from Aloise Barbour Epperson, *Unto My Heart and Other Poems* (Boston: Christopher House, 1953), p. 49.

GERTRUDE SCHALK

Flower of the South

They had lunch on the veranda, the Senator, his daughter Betty, and their guest, the Hon. Hugh Stanhope Wiltshire of the Sussex Wiltshires. The splendidly green lawn swept coolly away from the huge white mansion perched on the gently sloping hill, and the weeping willow trees that lined the creek behind the house waved solemnly in the breeze.

"Your South is very beautiful," Hugh said more than once. To his typically English mind, the procession of fair, sunny days seemed miraculous. And the hospitable people, who called themselves the aristocrats of America, astounded the young Englishman with their drawling speech and odd ways.

The two weeks he had spent at the Manor as guest of the Lees had been one succession of things he should remember and things he should remember to forget. It seemed that there were more things to remember to forget than there were to remember.

That a people so charming, so beautiful, seemingly, in spirit, should have such ugly black pages in their history, seemed incredible. In all the murky haze of those two weeks only one thing stood clear and shining.

Betty Lee, the fairest of all southern beauties, a veritable flower of the South, was the sole reason for Hugh's visit to America. A mere glance from her sparkling dark eyes served to cause his usually staid and well-behaved heart to jump about like a skittish colt. From all the intrigues of this beautiful South, Betty alone stood clean and pure.

Source: Saturday Evening Quill 3 (June 1930): 70-72.

Hugh hadn't as yet recovered from the shock that had followed his discovery of the southern gentleman's two families. Even the Senator had, among his dark servants, three or four fair-skinned boys and girls who looked with knowing eyes at the old aristocrat whenever he came near them.

It seemed to be a well-established custom. Hugh had talked several times with one of the old mammies in the town of Dixville, which was just a few miles from the Manor, and her observations had amazed him to the point of stupefaction.

"Shuah, suh, we ain't none of us without de white streak. Chile, ah's old, mo's a hundred, an' Ah done had twelve chillun—all of um by my mahster."

Hugh had digested that.

"You mean, your white master?"

"Shuah." The old brown woman had cackled shrilly. "When Ah wasn't fifteen he come down an' took me up t' de big house. Ma mammy mighty nigh bit his han' off—"

"You mean you were taken against your will?" Hugh had interrupted.

"Cose! What dese white gen'men think o' nigger wimen? Dey jes walks up and takes yuh, an' yuh better not say nothin', neither, or dey flog yuh an' lynch yuh family."

"And you—you have children by—"

"Chile, Ah gots two datters who's married inter the bes' families in de South. Dey's so white dey's passin'. Chile, iffen dem white folks knowed dey was half colured . . .!" Again she cackled shrilly.

"Passing"—the word was strange to Hugh.

"Honey,"—the old mammy had leaned closer, her black eyes sparkling with secret humor—"Ah could tell yuh a heap 'bout dese high n' mighty families er de South. Dey's moah black blood in dem dan yuh could shake a stick at. Ca'se when a black 'oman gits a white baby, de mahster he takes it way and lets it grow up white sometime. An' de baby, he don't know nothin' 'bout hit. Dat's what dey did t' mine, but Ah knows my chillun." She had nodded wisely.

It had taken Hugh nearly a week to get over that. After that, he had found himself looking curiously at every fair-skinned Negro and had himself asking, "Who fathered that child?"

Betty alone stood beautifully fair above the muddy undercurrent of the South's vaunted chivalry. Gradually he had let Betty lull his disgust to an uneasy quiet.

Now Betty rose from the table, her dark beauty striking him afresh.

"Ah'm going to run into town," she said softly, dimpling at him. "Ah got a errand t' do."

Hugh never appreciated the southern drawl until Betty talked. Then he treasured each sound, each slow prolongation of syllable.

"Sure you don't want me along?" he begged.

"No. Yuh sit and talk to dad." Betty ran to her little roadster. "Ah won't be long."

The Senator and Hugh stood and watched her speed down the winding drive to the road.

"Fine gal," mused the Senator proudly.

"Beautiful!" Hugh choked over the word. Beautiful didn't begin to describe Betty.

The two men sat and smoked, talking intermittently. Between casual remarks Hugh thought of Betty. He'd propose tonight. He couldn't wait any longer. He could picture her as mistress of Wiltshire Abbey. His heart warmed. What a wonderful picture she would make standing in the vaulted hall greeting his guests!

He lost himself in dreams. Betty, riding to the hounds. Betty, gracing his table. Betty, bearing him beautiful, sturdy sons . . .

From inside the house the soft tinkle of the telephone disturbed his dream. With a muttered excuse the Senator went to answer it. The 'phone stood just inside one of the French windows and Hugh, lying lazily back in a cane chair, caught snatches of the one-sided conversation.

"What? Who? That Dousing gal? She ain't nothing but a whore . . ."

"Huh? What, a nigger? Means trouble . . ." The Senator swore.

Hugh squirmed uneasily. The Senator's bald wording often bothered his sensitive ear. In England one didn't call a spade a spade quite so glibly.

The Senator came back, his brow furrowed.

"Got t' go t' town," he said briefly. "There's been trouble an' Ah'm called t' help the jedge. Come along?"

Wonderingly Hugh followed the Senator to his car. He noticed that his host dismissed his black driver and took the wheel himself. And a last message to the puzzled black boy confounded the Englishman still further.

"Tell the niggers to keep quiet," he said quickly. "There's trouble in town."

The black boy turned almost pale then, and the last Hugh saw of him he was tearing down toward the servants' quarters like one demented.

"Er—what's the trouble?" Hugh wanted to know. The car was soaring down the road.

"A nigger's been accused of assaulting a white woman. Liable to lynch him."

Lynch him! Vaguely Hugh remembered the old black mammy's speaking of lynching. Farther back than that he remembered reading something in the papers about lynching, but like one who has never had the measles or come in contact with them, he didn't know anything about it.

The Senator began to talk grimly.

"We ain't had a lynching foah yeahs heah. Damn these whores—they come heah an' run aroun' with white and black alike an' then when they get caught up with, they blame it on some good nigger, and then there's hell to pay."

Hugh frowned. "You mean, it isn't the—the black's fault?"

"Oh, I ain't sayin' it ain't sometime, but Ah've lived heah all my life and nine times out of ten the gal is a whore like this Dousing gal who's yelling now. Everybody knows her in Dixville. Come heah las yeah and been cuttin' up evah since."

"Well, why will it cause trouble, if everyone knows?"

"Shucks, don't make no difference who the gal is, long's she white. If she says a nigger touched her, that's all these poah white trash want. Ah've had niggers in mah house evah since Ah was born. My daddy had befoah him, an' we always treated our niggers right. It ain't the gentleman who lynches; it's them poah white trash."

And then they were in town. The Senator headed straight for the square. Before the courthouse a sullen mob had gathered. Tense, white faces with angry, burning eyes turned toward the car. A low murmur rose and swelled.

"Won't take much to start 'em," muttered the Senator as he clambered out of the car, followed by Hugh. "Got t' get the nigger away or he won't be wo'th a cent."

What followed was strange and nightmarish to Hugh. First the slipping into the barred courthouse and the hurried whispering with the officials.

Then the prisoner, a brown youth whose face was ashy with fear. When he saw the Senator he began to cry.

"Ah didn't do hit, boss. Ah didn't do hit!"

"Hummmm." The Senator scratched his head. "Lizzie's boy. Good nigger."

He frowned. A constable came running up, his face pale.

"The mob's gittin' wild," he said hoarsely.

The Senator went over to talk to the quailing Negro boy.

Hugh stood alone in a corner listening to the rising tide of voices outside. It was like a slowly approaching sea, like the tide coming in. Finally the Senator came to him, slowly.

"Just as Ah thought," he said grimly. "The boy caught this gal with a white man an' she's gettin' back at him."

"What will you do?" Hugh found himself breathless.

"Try and git the boy away t' the next county, befoah the mob gits him." Briskly the Senator got into action. "Let's take him out the back way."

Cautiously they slid out the back door. They piled into two cars, the prisoner, the constables, and the Senator in one, Hugh and the county judge in another. They started. The first car sped around a corner . . .

A savage yell met Hugh's ears as his car rounded the curve.

"They got him!" The judge was bending forward. "They got the nigger!"

With sick eyes Hugh saw the white-faced mob swirling around the first car; saw snatching hands seize the terrified black boy and drag him from the grasp of the Senator and the constables. Shrill voices split the warm air.

"Lynch the nigger! Lynch him! Lynch him!"

A woman's voice, louder and more penetrating than the rest, led all the others. Standing in a stalled motor car, she goaded the maddened mob on.

"Burn the nigger! Burn him!"

Sick to his soul, Hugh stood and watched with fascinated eyes the hasty erection of a pyre. The trembling, pleading, crying Negro was bound to a stake and wood thrown about his feet. The woman sprang from her car and drew gasoline to fling on the wood.

There was a mist before Hugh's eyes. This, then, was the southern gentleman. This barbarous creature who boasted of being the flower of

American aristocracy; this *Thing* who burned men alive, yet preached freedom and culture.

There were women in the mob . . . Always the female of the species is deadlier than the male, more capable of fine cruelty. Hugh remembered that on a hunting trip in Africa the hunter would always rather come face to face with a lion than a lioness.

The first faint odor of burning flesh, accompanied by the shrill, tortured screams of the boy, made him ill. There was no way to escape it. Their car was hemmed in by screaming, gesticulating, blood-mad men and women.

And across that sea of waving arms and taloned hands Hugh saw the woman in the car urging them on, her voice cracked and shrill.

"Come on! Tear him!" She turned to wave the mob on.

Across the hazy space, Hugh's eyes, momentarily clear, leaped to meet the bloody gaze of Betty Lee. Her arm still aloft, her hair disarranged, her dress stained with the gasoline she had taken from the tank, she stood there in all her flaming southern beauty.

In that moment something died in Hugh; something that never again would blossom; something that would remain a cold lump in his breast until he died. Slowly, like one half asleep, he sat back in the car.

The mob surged away, leaving the car clear. Without emotion Hugh said to the driver:

"Will you drive back to the station, please?"

The car backed and turned. Across the widening space a woman's frightened voice reached him.

"Hugh! Hugh!"

The man in the car folded his arms. His ears were closed to the South, and his eyes were sick of its warmth and beauty, and his soul shrunk within him. God, he was ashamed.

ELOISE BIBB THOMPSON

Masks, a Story

Paupet, an octoroon and born free, was a man of considerable insight. That was because, having brains, he used them. The cause of Julie's, his wife's, trouble was no secret to him. Although it never dawned upon him fully until after she died. Then he dictated the words to be placed upon her tombstone. The inscription proved to be unique, but not more than the cemeteries themselves of old New Orleans. The motto written in 1832 read as follows: "Because she saw with the eyes of her grandfather, she died at the sight of her babe's face."

This grandfather, Aristile Blanchard, had been an enigma to the whole Quadroon Quarter of New Orleans. But he was no enigma to Paupet although he had never lain eyes upon him. Seeing him had not been necessary, for Paupet had heard his whole life's history from Paul, Julie's brother, whom he met in Mobile before he had known Julie. Paul, although a ne'er do well who had left the home-fires early, admired his grandfather immensely. Hence he had found delight even as a youth in securing from the old man those facts of his life which had proved so interesting to Paupet.

Now Paupet, among other things, was a natural psychologist albeit an unconscious one. He was accustomed to ponder the motives of men, their peculiar mental traits and their similarity to those of their parents whom he happened to know. No one was more interesting to Paupet than Julie, his wife. So of course he gave much thought to her. But the occasion is always necessary for the knowledge of a soul, and the opportunity for really knowing Julie came only when she was expecting her offspring.

Source: Opportunity 5 (October 1927): 300–302.

But even then Paupet would not have known where to place the blame for her peculiarity had he not known, as we have said, all there was to know about old Aristile Blanchard.

That Aristile was a man to be pitied Paupet felt there was no question. For what man does not deserve pity who sees his fondest dream fall with the swiftness of a rocket from a starlit sky to the darkness of midnight? No wonder that hallucination then seized him. With such a nature as his that was to be expected. But that the influence of such a delusion should have blighted Julie's young life was the thing of which Paupet most bitterly complained.

Aristile, Paul told Paupet, had been a native of Hayti. Coming to New Orleans in 1795 when the slave insurrection was hottest,* he had set up an atmosphere of revolt as forceful as the one he had left behind him. Of course when Julie entered the world, the revolution had long been over; Toussaint L'Ouverture had demonstrated his fitness to rule, had eventually been thrown in an ignominious dungeon and been moldering the grave some five years or more. But the fact that distressed Paupet was that Aristile lived on to throw his baneful influence over the granddaughter entrusted by a dying mother to his care.

Of all the free men of color in Hayti at the time none were more favored than Aristile. A quandroon of prepossessing appearance with some capital at hand, he had been sent to Bordeaux, France, by a doting mother to study the arts for which he was thought to show marked predilection. In reality he was but a dabbler in the arts, returning at length to his native land with some acquaintance with most of them, as for instance sculpture, painting, wood-carving and the like but with no very comprehensive knowledge of any one of them. There was one thing, however, that did not escape him—being there at the time when France was a hotbed of that revolt which finally stormed the Bastille—and that was the spirit of liberty. "Liberty, Fraternity, Equality" was in the very air he breathed. He returned from France with revolutionary tendencies far in advance of any free man in the island, tendencies that awaited but the opportunity to blossom into the strongest sort of heroism.

Although he burned to be of service to his race on returning to his native land he forced himself to resume his usual tenor of life. He sought apprenticeship to an Oriental mask-maker, a rare genius in his line where

*The Haitian revolution against French rule was one of the first anticolonialist uprisings in the history of the Americas.

the rich French planters were wont to go in preparation for their mas-querades and feast-day festivities. Masks had always had a strange fascina-tion for Aristile. He would often sit lost in thought beside their maker, his mind full of conflicting emotions. But when the French slave owners assembled at Cape Haitien to formulate measures against the free men of color to whom the National Assembly in France had decreed full citizen-ship, he forget everything and throwing down his tools immediately headed the revolt that followed.

With Rigaud, the mulatto captain of the slaves, he gave himself to the cause of France, offering at the risk of his life to spy upon the English when they came to the support of the native French planters bent upon re-establishing slavery upon the island.

Making up as a white man as best he could, he boldly entered the port of Jeremie where the English had but recently landed. His ruse would have succeeded had it not been for a native white planter all too familiar with his African earmarks, who standing by at the time readily spotted him out. Without warning, Aristile was seized, flogged unmercifully and thrown into a dungeon to die. But he was rescued after a time by a good angel in the form of an octoroon planter identified with whites all his life because of a face that defied detection; not only rescued but shipped with his daughter in safety to New Orleans. Then the octoroon rescuer took up the work of spy upon the English which Aristile had been forced to relinquish. That he was successfuly is manifested in the subsequent work of Toussaint L'Ouverture, who because of him was able before very long to drive in all the troops of the English, to invest their strongholds, to assault their forts, and ultimately to destroy them totally.

This incident had a lifelong effect upon Aristile. Full of despondency, disappointment over his failure in the work he had set himself to do with the enthusiasm and glow of a martyr, his mind dwelt wholly upon the facial lineaments that had brought about his defeat. "Cheated!" he would exclaim bitterly. "Cheated out of the opportunity of doing the highest service because of a face four degrees from the pattern prescribed for success. Fate has been against me. Nature has been against me. It was never meant that I should do the thing I burned to do.—O, why did not Nature give me the face of my father?—Then all things would have been possible to me. Other quadroons have been so blessed. Hundreds of them—thousands of them! Save for a slight sallowness of the skin there was absolutely nothing to show their African lineage. But Nature in projecting my lips and expanding my nose has set me apart for the contumely* of the world.—The ancients lied when they said the gods made man's face from the nose upwards, leaving their lower portion for him to make himself. Try as I may I will never be able to change the mask that Nature has imposed upon me."

Day and night these thoughts were with him. Paul described this state to Paupet, declaring that his mother had feared for Aristile's mind. At length this mood suddenly changed to one of exultation and he rose from his bed a new man.

"I have found the formula for greatness!" he told those about him. "It reads, Thou shalt be seen wearing a white man's face.—But only a fraction being able to carry out this prescription, it is left for me to create a symbol so perfect in its imitation of Nature that the remainder of mankind may likewise receive a place in the sun. My brothers and I shall no longer be marked for defeat. I shall make a mask that will defy Nature herself. There shall be no more distinct and unmistakable signs that will determine whether a man shall be master or slave. All men in future shall have the privilege of being what they will."

With this end in view he repaired to the Quadroon Quarter of New Orleans and set up a workshop that soon became the talk of the district because of the strange-looking objects it contained. Paupet could vouch for their strangeness for they were still in existence when he came to the place. Upon the walls of this room hung many attempts of the thing Aristile had set himself to do. There were masks of paper patiently glued in small bits together in a brave effort to imitate Nature in the making of a white man's face. Likewise masks of wood, of papier mache and of some soft, clinging, leaf-like material which it is very likely he discovered in Louisiana's wondrous woods. Interesting-looking objects they were, everyone of them, most of them, however, were far from the goal; but a few in their skin-like possibility of stretching over a man's face might have been made perfect—who knows—greater marvels have been seen—had their completion not been suddenly broken off. There was about the whole of this room an unmistakable depression, an atmosphere of shattered hope as if the maker of these objects had set out with high purpose toward their completion then suddenly been chilled by some unforeseen happening that filled him with despair. And so it really had been. While

*Harsh language or treatment.

Negro supremacy existed in his beloved country Aristile worked with ever-increasing enthusiasm toward his cherished dream. He had been unable, he told himself, to assist his brothers as a soldier because of the lineaments that Nature had imposed. But he would present them with a talisman like unto Aladdin's lamp that would work wonders for them in a world where to be blessed was to be white. But when the news reached him that Toussaint, the savior of his race, had been tricked and thrown into a French prison to die, he was plunged into the deepest sorrow and turned from his purpose in despair. Laying aside his implements, for a long time he could not be induced to take interest in anything. At length when his funds began to dwindle, it was bourne in upon him that men must work if they would live. Then he turned to the making of those limp figures in sweeping gowns that when Paupet saw them were no doubt of his own distorted mind, designed for standing in the farthest corner of the room—grotesque figures wearing hideous masks, the reflection, clowns and actors of the comic stage.

It was not very long before the place began to be frequented by patrons of the Quadroon Masques and of those open-air African dances and debaucheries knows as "Voodoo Carousels" held in the Congo Square. Later actors from the French Opera looked in upon him. Then he conceived the idea of having Clotile, his daughter, already an expert with the needle, prepare for his patrons of the masque and stage, to be rented at a nominal fee, those gowns and wraps that were now fading behind the glass doors of yonder cabinets. But though he worked continuously it had no power, apparently, to change his usual course of thought. His mind ever dwelt upon the disaster that had blighted his life.

And then came Julie in this atmosphere of depression to take up in time the work which fate decreed Clotile should lay down. As apt with the needle as her dead mother had been, she was able, when her grandfather through age and ill-health became enfeebled, to maintain them both. And those were formative years for the young Julie, obliged to listen to her grandfather's half-crazed tirade against nature's way of fixing a man to his clan through the color of his skin. Unaccustomed to thinking independently she, however, could see something of the disastrousness of it all because of the stringent laws confronting her in New Orleans. As much as she longed to do so, for instance, she dared not wear any of the head-gear of the times, although much of it was made by her own fingers, because of the law forbidding it; a bandanna handkerchief being decreed to all free women of color so that they might easily be distinguished from white ladies. And that was only one of the minor laws. There were others graver and more disastrous by far. So these conditions forced her to realize early that her grandfather had good reason for his lament. She too deplored the failure of his design—the making of a mask that would open the barred and bolted doors of privilege for those who knocked thereon. Without anything like bitterness for these conditions, she began to reason that color and not mental endowment or loftiness of character determined the caliber of a man. For did not color determine his destiny? He was rich or poor, happy or unhappy according to his complexion and not according to his efforts at all. And so the words superior and inferior were invariably dependent upon the color of his skin. She, a brunette-like quadroon, the counterpart of her grandfather, was far superior to the black slave-peddlers who sometimes came into the Quadroon Quarter begging a place to rest. And that was why the Quarter guarded the section so jealously from all black dwellers, however free they might be, because they wanted only superior people in their midst.

One morning some months after her grandfather's death she awoke trembling with a great discovery—for years, she reflected in wonderment, her revered relative had tried to make a mask that when fitted to a man's face would change his entire future and had failed. And lo! the secret had just been whispered to her. "To me," she whispered to herself ecstatically, "to po' lil' me. An' I know it ees tr-rue, yes. It got to be tr-rue. 'Cause madda Nature, she will help in de work, an' w'at else you want?" For the life-mate she would choose for herself would be an octoroon, as fair as a lily. With her complexion and his she knew that she would be able to give to her children the mask for which her grandfather had yearned. She saw now why he had failed. No doubt it was never meant for men to know anything about it at all. It must be in the keepings of mothers alone. "Now we will see," she told herself exultantly. "Ef my daughter got to wear a head handgcher lak me. Fo' me it ees notting. I cannot help. But jes' de same a son of mine goin' be king of some Carnival yet. You watch out fo' me."

And so when Paupet, the whitest octoroon that she had ever seen, came to the Quarter, she showed her preference for him at once. When, after their marriage, in the course of time their first born was expected she was like an experimentalist in the mating of cross-breeds, painfully nervous and full of the greatest anxiety over the outcome of a situation that she had been planning so long. What preparations she made! She fitted up a room especially for the event. She was extravagance itself in the selection of the garments, buying enough material to clothe half a dozen infants. She literally covered the fly leaves of the Bible with male and female names in preparation for the Christening; and made so many trips to town for all sorts of purchases that Paupet became full of anxiety for the outcome of it all.

To him she talked very freely now of her readiness in marrying him—it was really for the good of the child that was about to come to them. Her trials would not be her infant's. She had seen to that. He would look like Paupet, and could therefore choose his own way in life unhampered by custom or law.

To the midwife too she communicated her hopes and expectations, dwelling at great length upon the future of the child, the whiteness of whose face would be a charm against every prevailing ill. Such optimism augured ill to the midwife, who rarely vouchsafed her a word. When at length the child was born, the midwife tarried a long time before placing it into Julie's arms. It was sympathy upon her part that caused the delay. But Julie could not understand it. In the midst of her great sufferings she marvelled at it, until at length she caught a glimpse of her child's face. Then she screamed. With horror she saw that it was identical with the one in the locket about neck. It was the image of her chocolate-colored mother.

The Man Who Passed:
A Play in One Act

Characters:

Van (A Barber)

Kid (A Customer)

Fred Carrington (The Man Who Passed)

Joe and Tom (Friends)

Boy (A Newspaper Boy

Place: A side street in Harlem, about 1923

Time: About 10:30

(A basement barber shop. The furnishings are simple and rather old-fashioned, and indicate that the establishment has been doing a middle class trade for a number of years, and probably more so because the proprietor loves his work than because he wishes to accumulate wealth. The comfortable furnishings indicate that men might gather here at night to talk and play cards. The barber chair and mirrors, left corner, manicurist's table against left wall, real center, under low basement window center rear wall. Plain walls with one or two pictures or calendars. Open door leading to street, showing a few low steps going up to street, rear right. Through the iron grating

Source: Unpublished manuscript, Manuscripts, Archives and Rare Books Division, Schomburg Center for Research in Black Culture, The New York Public Library, Astor, Lenox and Tilden Foundations, n.d. Written under the pseudonym Henry Simons.

of basement window may be seen a small electrically lighted bar-ber's pole, or its reflection. Fairly large table front left with several Ne-gro newspapers and magazines. As curtain rises, Van the barber can be seen carefully inspecting and giving a few last touches to the head of a customer whose hair has just been "straightened" and waved. Van is a man of pleasing personality, rather corpulent, and probably in his late fifties.)

KID *(rising from chair and lovingly smoothing back his waved and glossy hair which he surveys in mirror as he struts around)*:   Yas sir! Dey sho' will call me de patent leather Kid now! H-m-m, smooth and glossy! Jes' what de good Lawd 'tended fo' folks lak me. Yas sir! *(Adjusts collar and tie.)*

VAN: Eh—satisfied, Kid?

KID: Satisfied! Ah sho is ma Pink Delala's patent leather chocolate baby now! *(Puts on top coat, flicks dust from his spotless shoes.)* Now, Mr. Van, Ah asks you, does dis vision resemble dat nappy headed shine what stepped in dat do a haf howah ago? Ah asks you dat?

VAN *(looking at watch, as he rearranges room)*:   No, Kid, you certainly don't! But I always aim to please. Come again.

KID *(shaping up his Stetson hat, smiling broadly)*:   Well Mr. Van, not too soon! If de good Lawd will jes' keep some of his raindrops up in Hebbon, so as not to 'sturb mah raven locks, so to speak, ah won't be back soon! Le's see: dere's de Gran' Ball given by the "Inspired Cousins of Georgia," at de Manhattan—a midnight show Tuesday at de Lafayette, to be followed by a breakfas' dance at Susie's to say nothing of a little private affair some of de boys is pullin' off for some high yaller visitin' ladies *(winking—goes to mirror as he carefully adjusts hat and takes up cane)*. Hum-m—de har you lubs to touch! Well—tootle-oo Mr. Van. *(Exits—street entrance.)*

VAN: Good night, sir! *(Hurriedly follows him out into areaway. Can be seen putting out street light, reenters and draws shade at center window. Picks up telegram from table and reads it.)* Hum-m, he said eleven o'clock! It's after eleven now. Hope—*(Stops abruptly as he hears tapping at window.)* Who's there?

VOICE *(outside)*: It's Fred, Van. *(The latter hurriedly opens door and a dapper and rather handsome man of about forty-five enters. He is fair and might "pass for white," but the removal of his hat shows kinky fair hair, and betrays his Negro blood.)*

VAN *(shaking his hand and giving him a resounding slap on the back)*: It's great to see you, "old timer."

FRED: It's good to see you! So this is where you moved to. *(Looking around.)* And I have to trail you all the way to Harlem to have the kinks taken out of this hair. I know you don't agree with what I'm doing, Van, but you've certainly been a pal to help me out all of these years.

VAN: It's alright, boy.

FRED: Well, here I am in Harlem, when I vowed never to set foot up here again. I was surprised when they told me you had left 59th Street. *(Removing coat.)* How's business?

VAN: Oh, fair, fair. Most of my old customers moved to Harlem six or eight years ago; there are a few like yourself you know, who think I'm the only one who can cut their hair, or even give them a shave. Guess I was the last of the old crowd to leave 59th Street, and I held on to the old place just as long as I could. I had no way to get word to you that I moved, but I know that they would tell you down there—well, well, take your things off, place is yours, you know. When did you get back in town? It's been six months or more since I seen you.

FRED: Last night, came in with the storm. That's why I'm up here so soon. *(Points sheepishly to hair.)* Can't take care of this stuff myself, when it gets too bad. Kept me busy figuring how I could get away from Fitzgerald though. *(Pulls off coat and collar and is about to unloosen tie.)* Boys coming, Van?

VAN: Sure thing. They'll be here in about a half hour now. They are anxious to see you. Let's get this little job over with. *(Turns to chair, arranges towels, straightening irons, grease, etc. Fred sits in chair with back to audience. Van stands and works with back to audience.)* How many years since you've been in Harlem, Fred?

FRED *(Slowly)*: Oh! Ten. Come up when I heard about the kid brother's death. Told my old man goodbye for good then. Well, Harlem's changing I guess. Why Fitzgerald's sister used to live in one of the Stanford White houses on 139th Street.

VAN: Yes—Well they call it "Strivers Row" now and most of those houses are owned by Negroes. *(Hesitatingly as he works.)* Of course you've heard—

FRED *(interrupting)*:   No. I haven't heard anything and don't want to hear anything about the colored brother.

VAN: But I mean—

FRED: No good, Van! I don't want to hear anything about it. I went on the other side fifteen years ago and I'm there to stay.

(Both quiet for a few minutes.)

FRED *(as if he is thinking aloud)*:   Gosh! Fitzgerald would have apoplexy if he came uptown and saw 125th Street black with darkies. *(Chuckles to himself.)*

VAN: Yes? Well he'd have to get over that first spell so that he could go up to Sugar Hill* and see them up as far as 155th Street and Edgecombe Ave.

FRED *(jumping around in chair)*:   What? Why old man Fitzgerald used to live right around that corner on St. Nicholas Ave. Big grey stone mansion! That's where I went to work for him, where I met Ella. Well, well, I'll have to drive up there and look the Brother over.

VAN: Better keep that big nosed car of Fitzgerald and your yellow face out of Harlem. *(Stops working for a moment.)* You know your own people have been pretty good to you, Fred! Ain' none of them spotted you out and hunted you down to tell your Boss Fitzgerald that one of the "Niggers" he hates is working for him, and living right in his own home. It ain't every yellow faced Negro who can pass for white for fifteen years, hold a white man's job, marry a white woman, and not get caught. Stay out of Harlem, boy, like you got some sense.

---

*Northwest sector of Harlem, near Washington Heights; site of apartment houses mostly occupied by professionals.

FRED: I guess you're right, and you've been pretty good to help me out all of these years. Say Van, is Joe coming tonight?

VAN: Surest thing you know. *(Looks at his watch.)* They'll be here any moment now.

FRED: Good old Black Joe. It's been years since—

VAN: Remember Walter Kindle? He's married and has five kids.

FRED: Five kids! Great Scott! What about Roy? Roy Wheeler.

VAN: Dead.

FRED: Dead? *(Expression indicates that he is recalling to mind some particular incident.)*

VAN: He was shot in an accident. What's the matter?

FRED: Oh, nothing. Does sort of make me feel cheap, you know. I met him on the street downtown, about two years ago—and well—I couldn't speak to him. I was with old man Fitzgerald and—well I've told you before, Fitz hates the sight of a "Nigger." Roy met us face to face as we were getting in the car. You know, Van, if I had so much as looked at him, it would have cost me my job. I've always known that he hated me for it though.

VAN: Oh maybe not—why should he care?

FRED: Well, we were buddies in school.

VAN: Have you ever wondered what Fitzgerald would do if he found out about you, Fred?

FRED *(with much confidence)*: There's not a chance.

VAN: Well—*(changing voice)* How's the wife, Fred?

FRED: Great!

VAN *(pointing to mirror as he finishes hair)*: Look at that wave! *(Stands back and observes his work, with great pride.)*

FRED *(surveying hair in mirror)*: Perfect! No one can do the job as you can. Well, you've been putting that same wave in there for almost fifteen years. *(Sound at window)* Who's that, Van?

VAN: One of the boys coming I guess—don't worry. *(Goes to window.)* The street light's out, so there won't be any one else here this late. Who's there?

VOICE: It's Tom, Van. *(Enters Tom—a middle-aged well dressed man, he has mixed grey hair.)*

TOM: Hello Fred. It's great to see you again after all of these years. I wanted to write you three weeks ago but—*(Van signals to him to stop.)*

FRED *(shaking hands)*:   Hello, Tom . . . Write me! *(Laughs)* You know I can't hear from you fellows. *(Knock at windows)*

VAN *(approaching window)*:   Who's there?

VOICE: Who's dere? Ha, ha! Open dat do' you big bozos.

FRED *(eyes shining)*:   That's Black Joe! (Opens door—Joe enters) Hello, you devil.

JOE *(entering. He is of dark complexion, fat and jovial in appearance, with wavy black curly hair)*:   Well, well, if it ain' our passin' frien' Fred Carrington. *(Laughter.)* Welcome home to Harlem son. You know when Van done tol' us dat you was comin hyah tonight, and wanted to see us, Ah done made up mah mine dat ah wouldn't miss dis chance to see an old shine friend of mine what's passin' fo' white all des yeah's for de world. *(Inspects Fred rather closely.)* Yo' ain' changed much—Does you feel white or black inside, Fred? *(Laughter.)* How's de missis?

FRED: Fine. This surely is a reunion, boys, for the four of us to get together again. I just felt that I wanted to see you once more.

TOM: Fifteen years! Any kids, Fred?

FRED: No!

JOE: Kids! ha, ha! Think Fred ain't got sense enough not to let dere be any babies? Why de fus' one would take back and look lak one of Aunt Hagah's chillun sho' as you' bohn. Ha, ha! See what Ah done bought Fred. *(Untying bundle.)* Smell dat! When has you had any fried chicken, boy?

FRED *(lifting up platter and smiling)*:   H-m-m—Smells good!

TOM *(going to overcoat)*:   Well I brought the drinks along.

JOE: Ah knows yo' hongry fo' some real food, boy! *(All sit around the table to eat and drink. Tom and Van fix food.)* Well, Ah see's Van's done fixed dat kinky head o' yourn. Bet you looked like any other frizzly haired tow-headed shine when yo' came in hyeah. Ain't it a shame yo' had to come in dis world wid kinks when yo' wants to be white so bad? Bet you'd give a thousand smackah's fo dis ebony locks o' mine . . . well, ah sho' wishes ah could give em to yo' pal—save you followin' Van around like he's you nurse maid all dese yeahs. Now he's moved up heah and you all has to come home to Harlem, so dat you can go down town and be mistah white man.

TOM: Cut it out, Joe. Have you seen your sistah, Fred?

FRED *(showing a quiet nervousness at the mention of his family)*: Not for ten years. Has she changed much?

JOE: Changed? Why man she's fine! Dere's a woman fo' yo' whose skin is lak de magnolia petals—but she thinks blacker'n black. Head of all de big organizations in Harlem. Miss Augustina Carrington, Lord! Dere ain't a man in Harlem who's ever heard her name, what don' admire huh. An' boy, when de King of—what's de name of dat place? *(Scratches his head.)* Well, any way when de King was heah and wanted to meet de Negroes of culture, you sistah was in de receiben line. Was you deah? *(Fred quietly shakes his head.)* Ah knowed it. You was in de crowds of cheap white trash on de curb, tryin' to catch a glimpse of his Majesty, while de King was on his way to meet de cultured colored folk includin' your sistah—Miss Augustina—

TOM: Cut it out Joe!

FRED: It's alright, Tom. I've always been the black sheep, so to speak. At least that's what they called me when I left Harlem.

JOE: He knows Ah's only kiddin'.

TOM *(sitting down in chair, smoking)*:   Fred, it certainly takes me back to old times to see you again. Say: Remember when we were kids together in old DeWitt Clinton? Remember the black eye you got when we were fighting that shanty Irish gang. When Peg-Top Jones opened his candy store on West 53rd St.

VAN: Gosh! That was a great fight! Why it lasted off an on for about a month until we convinced those micks that was our territory. Great days those—Why that's part of New York history if people but knew it. My dad was born just a block from where Macy's store stands today.

(Sounds of a small crowd gathering outside of window.)

JOE: Yes, even in school, Fred was allus sneakin' off, pretendin' he was white. You never did have any guts! Guess its a good thing you did turn white, where you'se only one in a million and nobody knows yo' on earth.

(They are interrupted by increasing noises outside. Shuffling sounds can be heard.)

FRED: What's that?

(Van puts out main light, leaving room in semi-darkness. A bright street light shows a crowd gathering outside of window showing what could be seen of the lower legs and feet of two small boys, clog dancing, urged on by an enthusiastic audience. Pennies are thrown to them. Sounds of hand clapping and humming of "Charleston, Charleston" can be heard as the feet of the boys are seen through the window, going faster and faster. Cries of "Shake 'em up, boy," "Faster kid," "Atta Baby," "Me for you, snowball," etc. Fred slowly goes to window, his eyes brighten and a smile breaks out over his face. He jumps up on a chair, and begins to hum and clap, keeping time with the music. He has forgotten his companions. Joe, Tom and Van watch him as his body begins to sway.)

FRED: Great stuff! H'mm, h'mmm. *(He strains to the window as the crowd slowly moves down the street, following the clog dancing youngsters. He is still up on the chair watching as Van pulls down the shade and puts the lights on.)*

FRED *(gaily, wiping his forehead)*:   God!—That was—

JOE (*eyeing him suspiciously*): You'll ain' quite froze all de Aunt Hagah out ob your bones yet, has you Fred?

FRED (*embarrassed, abruptly stops swayin' and sighs*): Gosh, that was great—I—

VAN: Guess this passin' is kind a lonesome business, ain't it boy?

FRED (*coming to himself with a jerk*): Lonesome, of course not! Why look at you fellows, shut up here in Harlem, why you don't know what half the world is like. You're not wanted anywhere you go, people look at you if you come in restaurants, or go to a theatre. You're just tolerated when it's necessary.

TOM: Oh, that's not quite true, Fred. As real estate dealers go, I think I've been pretty successful, and I have some good white friends who respect me as a black man.

VAN: That's true Tom. And you don't have to spend your nights worrying for fear they'll find out you colored. But Fred can do as he pleases.

FRED [*To Tom*]: Respect you as a *black* man. Hell! [*To Van*] Yes I can, and I am. Why should I go around with a placard on my back, saying, "please, mister white man, I'm just as white as you are, but I'm a Nigger." God! I hate it! I hate every drop of black blood that's in me, and I'd see every black man in Harlem dead before I'd be one again. (*The room is quiet.*) I *would* like to see my old man once again though. He kicked me out when I married Ella. Called me a white folk nigger and dared me to ever darken his door again. Well, I'm not, I'd see him in hell first.

JOE: Well, you done chose de way you wanted to go and yo' goin' aincha. I'se genuinely sorry dat de Lawd gave yo' conscious dat kinky remindah on yo' haid, ob what yo' really is.

(*A newsboy cries outside of window.*)

BOY: *Recorder! Recorder!* De world's greatest Negro weekly. All about de—

FRED (*listening*): Old Perry's paper. How is he doing now?

BOY: *Recorder, Recorder,* all about—

JOE: Doing! Why that man's worth billions boy! De world's richest Negro! Why he makes thousands a day from those red-head lines. Heah! Ah'll get you one. *(Goes to window.)* Heah, boy! boy!

BOY *(coming to window)*: Yes sah! All about de 'lection.

JOE *(takes paper through grating and starts to pay boy)*: Now! Ah shows you—why dis is las' week's papah, boy! Boy!! *(Boy comes back.)* What does you mean, kid? Dis is las' week's papah! *(Throws it back through window.)*

BOY: Awright, awright, mister. Ah thought mebber you ain' seen dat one yet. Ah gots to sell de lef ovahs too, ain' ah? Heah, take dis one den. *(Throws second paper through window.)*

JOE *(looking anxiously at date)*: Well, dat's battah. You may be black, son, but you sho' has got Jewish ways. Heah Fred! De world's greatest Negro weekly[.] *(Hands paper to Fred and turns to others.)* Well boys, les' mix a farewell drink for Fred, cause he sho ain' gonna wants see he collahed brethren again soon. *(All three begin to mix drinks, with their backs to Fred.)*

FRED *(rustling pages as he hurriedly glances at paper)*: Well, old Perry certainly has come up in the world. A real paper! Why I remember when he used to peddle a two sheet affair from door to door with only uppers on his feet. *(Reads.)* "Two Negroes burned at the stake in Texas." *(Comments arise.)* Guess the black fools were running after some white woman as usual. *(Reads.)* "New York's oldest Negro physician dies." *(Comments.)* Well, the old fool's probably butchered thousands of dumb devils in his life time. *(Reads.)* "Oscar Reid elected first Negro Judge in Chicago."

JOE *(interrupting)*: Read de' details boy, read de' details! Fifteen years of serbitude wid old man Fitzgerald has sho taught you how to properly nunciate de King Edward English! *(Shaking drinks.)* Now why was dose two darkies fried?

FRED *(reading)*: ————— God! That's all you hear from the day you're born—lynching, prejudice—segregation.

JOE: Dat's nough o' dat! What Negro physician of prominence is now deceased? In de meantime *(Fred is quietly turning pages, looking for article.)* we drinks to the happiest man—de man who passed! *(All raise glasses, laughing.)* To de black sheep what done turned white—to—*(Looks at Fred whose face is ashen, and expression changed.)* What's de mattah, boy, does yo' know de deceased?

FRED *(slowly dropping newspaper)*: I did! It's my father! He died two days ago. *(Quoting in a dull monotone.)* ["]. . . after twenty-five years of service among his people. While his death is supposed to have been due to old age and natural causes, his many friends know that he has grieved over the death of his wife, which occurred three weeks ago.["]

TOM *(picking up paper and finishing article)*: Loved and respected by black and white. *(Fred drops his head.)* Only his daughter was with him at the end. His son could not be located.

FRED: My mother dead too—why didn't you tell me?

VAN: We tried to Fred, but you wouldn't listen.

JOE: Going up to the house now, old timer?

TOM: We're—sorry, Fred.

FRED: Well—I—*(Rising to pick up coat.)* No, the black sheep could not be—located. I'll go downtown now. Thanks—old timers—so-long. *(Goes out street door—his footsteps sounding on the wooden stairs.)*

VAN: God!

JOE: Poor debbil.

Curtain

Why, How, When and Where
Black Becomes White

"It's just as easy as falling off a log." This is what our friend tells us when he wishes to show what little effort is required to bring a certain thing to pass. But falling off a log is really a difficult feat compared with the ease with which colored people in this country are sometimes transformed into white. At first blush it would seem that a camel with a hump could literally pass through a cambric needle's eye easier than an individual tainted with even a drop of the fatal African tincture could palm himself off as a bona fide white man in the United States. And yet colored people are doing this very thing in droves every year. It requires neither voluminous knowledge nor great profundity to comprehend why some colored people are tempted to pursue such a questionable course.

Let us take a colored man, for example, who is fairly well educated and is ambitious to make his way in the world. There are comparatively few trades open to colored people. These are generally overcrowded, which means poor pay. The officials of some labor organizations are not spending sleepless nights devising ways and means of adding negro workmen to their ranks. Our colored friend determines to be honorable. Several times he has been virtually employed, but he has stated frankly that he is colored. Then his services were quietly but quickly dispensed with. For a long time he knocks first at one door and then at another, which he finds can be opened only by a white man's hand. He becomes discouraged.

Source: Unpublished manuscript, Moorland-Spingarn Research Center, Howard University, n.d.

"What a curse it is to be a negro in this country," he mutters. Suddenly he looks into the mirror. He has done that before, perhaps. He has always been identified with the struggling race, but he has a fair skin and straight hair. Something asserts itself. There are those who say that it is his white blood. "What's the use of trying to row against the tide," he says. "Nobody but a giant can accomplish the impossible, and I am not a giant." There is bitterness in his tone, as he soliloquizes, and discouragement is written on his face. He quickly reaches a decision. He has thought of it before.

He has always put it behind him, however, as a last resort too contemptible and cowardly to be considered seriously. But—he is out of work now and he has been in that condition for a long time. Inability to get a good position has become chronic. The long, lingering look in the mirror occurred, let us say, Tuesday evening at eight o'clock. On Wednesday morning at precisely the same hour, he is a white man. Made so by virtue of last night's decision and nature's gifts. "Impossible," says one. That is only a dream or fairy tale. But what is done almost every day is not impossible. "Where does he go?" asks another. If the man happens to have no family in the city, and the city is large, he stays right there, in many instances.

How does he do it? Among other things he ceases to frequent his old resorts. He changes his lodging house, and betakes him to a portion of the city diametrically opposite to the one in which he formerly lived. His old friends see him no more, that is, they don't, if he can help it. When he sees them approaching, he makes it convenient to cross to the other side of the street. He isolates himself completely. He scrapes up acquaintances with some white people, who do not suspect that he has the fatal drop. Finally, he gets a job, which pays him well, and which it would be impossible for him either to have or to hold, if his employer knew the truth. Nonsense, you say. If an employer secures the services of a competent man, he is not going to stand in his own light by casting him adrift, simply because he is slightly connected with the negro race. But the facts are against such a supposition. If the employer discovers by hook or crook that he has employed a colored man by mistake, in ninety nine cases out of a hundred, he will discharge him immediately.

There are undoubtedly exceptions to this rule, though I myself have never heard of one. I am personally acquainted with three colored women, two of them young and one middle aged, who are competent and beautiful, and who were discharged from excellent positions, simply because the employer discovered that they were colored. It must be said to the credit of the women just mentioned that they did not secure their positions under false pretenses. They might have deserved their fate, if they had. No one of them labelled herself "colored" to be sure, when she went to seek a place. Self preservation is still the first law of nature. Each one went on her own merits and secured a fine position for the same reasons that a white girl would have obtained one and adopted the same methods that a white girl would use under similar circumstances. Each one was eminently successful in her special work according to the testimony of the employer. Curiously enough, two secured positions in department stores in the cities in which they were living at the time. In the meantime each one lived with her family and associated with her colored friends, though the latter did not make themselves especially conspicuous at the respective stores. The middle aged woman was at the head of the cloak department in a large store in New York City. She held this responsible position for a long time, before the awful secret leaked out. When it percolated to her employer, however, she was promptly discharged. The woman is as beautiful as a picture, and looks like a Madonna.

One of the young women went first to New York to win her spurs. Armed with a most complimentary recommendation from the large firm which employed her in New York, she came to her home in Washington to seek a position here. The proprietor of the Washington establishment was only too glad to secure the services of so competent a young woman, and she, too, was placed in the cloak department. She was suddenly discharged one day. At her request I went to intercede with the proprietor in her behalf, who happened, by the way, to be a Hebrew. It seemed especially unreasonable and cruel that a Hebrew should discharge anyone simply on account of race. He was perfectly honest and frank about the matter. He admitted without hesitation that she was one of the best saleswomen in the store. He regretted deeply that he had been obliged to discharge her. "But are you not master in your own store," I ventured to suggest. "There was no other course to pursue," he insisted. "For a long time," said he, "the salesgirls complained, because I had placed a nigger in the store. I denied that she was colored. They brought me indisputable proofs of the fact. Well, if you don't care to work in the store with Miss Jones," said I, "you may leave. After that they told my customers about it. Delegation after delegation of white women came down to protest against my employing a nigger saleswoman in the store. They threatened to boycott me, and made things so hot for me that I was forced to dismiss Miss Jones in self defense. Now if my business were in New York, I should keep her anyhow." But I thought of the fate of the colored forewoman, who had been discharged in the New York department store.

The last of the three cases which came under my observation was similar to the first two. A young colored woman in Washington, who did not show a trace of her African ancestry, was made forewoman in a fashionable tailor establishment for ladies. Her employer discharged her also, when he learned that the fatal drop was coursing through her veins somewhere. It is conceivable that no one of these colored women would have received their walking papers, if the employer had been unable to fill their places. It is difficult to find a trade, however, in which the workmen are so few that a place cannot be filled. These cases will show why some colored people are tempted to be white.

Even though there is absolute certainty that the chances of success are greater for a colored person who forswears his race than for the same individual, if he remains loyal to it, the vast majority do not yield to the temptation of passing for white. No better proof of this fact could be cited than the case of a young woman with whom I am personally acquainted. She is the daughter of one of the most courageous and prominent colored men that this country has ever produced. Though she is not very fair, she could easily pass for white, if she chose to do so. She has an exquisite complexion modelled after the Spanish or French. Her hair and eyes are black as midnight. She has a superb musical education. She married a young physician, who can also pass for white. They went to an eastern city, where the doctor had a large and growing practice. He suddenly decided that he would shake off the body of the dusky death, so to speak, and cast his lot with the dominant race. When he revealed his plans to his wife, she told him that she would rather live on a small income, if necessary, than have a large one, if she were obliged to forsake her family and friends. The husband could not be shaken from his purpose and the wife could not be persuaded to turn her back on her family. So they separated. She went South and he remained in the eastern city. When I see this accomplished young woman, as I often do, and her little daughter, who is as fair as a snow drop and pretty as a peach, I cannot help wondering how the husband and father could have summoned the strength and courage to bid them good bye.

It is very amusing to see some of the sons and daughters of Ham, after the metamorphosis has become un fait accompli. To some of us, who have grown up with them, it is disgusting perhaps. "Do you see that man over there," said one of my friends with whom I happened to be on a street car not long ago. "Well, that lady sitting beside him is his wife. She is white, but he is colored." "Are you sure he is colored?" said I, Doubting Thomas-like. "I ought to be," he answered, "He and I played together as children. At Grant's funeral in New York, we occupied the same room in the Grand Union Hotel. All of a sudden, he decided to be white. He cut himself loose from all his colored friends, acquired white ones, and now he is completely over on the other side." Just then the eyes of the two men met, and they bowed pleasantly to each other. "That man is an exception," said my friend. "When the average colored person passes for white, he cuts all his former colored friends dead, for fear of arousing the suspicion of the white ones, I presume." The man who had related the incident told me that at least one hundred of his own relatives from South Carolina had moved East, North and West and "gone over on the other side," as he expressed it.

There is both a humorous and a pathetic side to this metamorphosis of black into white. Several years ago a colored grandmother went to a large city in the southwest to visit her son, who had married a white woman. The grandmother was very fair, even in her old age. One day one of her grandsons, who was being prepared for college, came to her in great distress of mind. "See here, Grandma," said he, "what do you think? Jack won't consent to go to Harvard. I wouldn't give a rap to go anywhere else." "Where does Jack want to go?" asked the grandmother. "Jack wants to go to the University of Virginia. He says he wants to go somewhere niggers can't come." The feelings of the grandmother, who keeps a colored boarding house, can better be imagined than described.

A colored man, who had achieved considerable success dealing in real estate in an eastern city, and who found it more convenient and lucrative to pass over the dead line, was once confronted with the accusation that a dark drop of blood lurked somewhere in his anatomy. He was very indignant, of course. He quickly took the train for New York. When he returned, he bore with him a paper signed by a priest, who certified that the colored woman who reared him was his nurse and not his mother, as had generally been supposed. Unfortunately, however, there happened to live in the same city a woman, who had been present at the birth of the prosperous, colored real estate dealer. She did not molest him, and he went on his metamorphosed way rejoicing. Such instances might be multiplied almost indefinitely.

On account of the Jim Crow Car laws, the impossibility of securing accommodations at the hotels and because of other hardships, many fair colored leave the South every year and move North, where they lose their identity completely. Years ago during slavery white masters, who loved their colored children too dearly to shackle their limbs and dwarf their minds, introduced this fashion of making black white by sending them North or to Europe to be educated as white. Colored people do not deserve the credit of originating the scheme. They learn lessons quickly, however, and are famous for applying them. It might not create great surprise to learn that it is possible for colored people "who do not look their part," to palm themselves off as white on a northern community. It would astound some, however, to hear that the feat is sometimes performed in the South, where the whites are supposed to have a patent on detecting the "man and brother," no matter how he may rival the lily in fairness. I heard a very amusing story not long ago, which shows the ease with which the transformation is wrought even in the South.

An exposition was in progress in a certain city below the Mason and Dixon's line. A man, who is colored, but who is fair enough to be mistaken for something else, went to visit his sister. She was very enthusiastic about an East Indian with an unpronounceable name, who had astounded the natives by his wonderful feats. The most exclusive lady in that most exclusive white social circle had invited him to her home, where he transported the guests with wonder and joy by his adroitness and marvelous skill.

"Herbert," said the man's sister, to whom I have just referred, "I want you to meet this clever East Indian so much. Come with me and let me introduce you to him. He is at leisure just about this time." They wended their way to his office. "Mr. So and So," said the man's sister, "let me present my brother, Herbert Rutledge, to you." The eyes of the two men met in instant recognition. "Hello, Bert," said the great East Indian, reaching out his hand, "why we haven't seen each other for years." This case is all the more remarkable, because the East Indian had been born and brought up as colored in that very Southern city, and his relatives were still living there. He visited them almost every night after dark, but he grew so bold about it that his friends warned him to exercise more caution and discretion.

Perhaps one of the most remarkable cases in the history of American jurisprudence was caused by this vexed race problem. A well to do young white man of French extraction fell desperately in love with a beautiful, young colored girl in Tennessee. In spite of the threats and entreaties of his family and friends he married her. He was obliged to take her out of his own State to Arkansas, where there was no penalty attached on account of the intermarriage of the races. When the young couple returned home, a probable sentence to the penitentiary for seven years stared them both in the face. Without going into the full details of this case it was proved in a court of law that the young colored woman was white. The young lady had a creamy complexion but was far from fair. She had been reared all her life by a mulatto aunt with very curly hair. She had attended a college for colored youth only. But—as I have already said, the courts decided that she was white, and white she is to this day, in the same city in which she was reared as a colored girl and where she cannot possibly walk down town without meeting some of the colored friends with whom she associated in her youth. She herself attended the colored schools, but her children, who are rather swarthy, are in the white schools at the present time.

The Jim Crow Car law as applied to the street cars of New Orleans had been in operation just fifteen days, when the city criminal court decided it was unconstitutional, in that it "compelled conductors to decide which passengers were white and which colored, and this is not in their province or power." This very difficulty of distinguishing between white and colored people has recently caused several railroad companies to part with considerable hard earned cash. In one southern state several months ago a wealthy white woman with a rich olive complexion was forced to take a seat in the Jim Crow Car, because the conductor told her that he knew she was colored and he was hard to fool. Her husband sued the railway company for fifty thousand dollars, but compromised on twenty thousand. In Kentucky a short while ago a white man was forcibly ejected from a coach set aside for people of his own race and placed in a Jim Crow Car. The railroad company paid him ten thousand dollars for making such a terrible blunder. That the courts consider it a disgrace and a misfortune to be colored is shown by the large amounts cheerfully awarded, in order to heal the wounded feelings of white people who have been mistaken for colored.

I have often tried to imagine what must be the feelings of the colored grub during the chrysalis stage, before it develops into a butterfly, which the world shall henceforth call white. If he has a family or dear friends, how long does it take to make up his mind to forsake them for the rest of his natural life? The inducements to do so must weigh powerfully with him indeed. The mental process through which such a decision is reached would be interesting to a psychologist, I am sure. I shall not attempt to discuss how the character of the colored man or woman who pursues such a course is affected. An incident related by one of my friends may throw some light on the subject. Her grandfather, who was a white man, was forced against his will into the Confederate Army. All of his children were colored, though they showed no trace of belonging to their mother's race. When he entered the Army, this white father took his eldest son with him. The father was killed. After the war the colored son continued to play the role of white man which he had assumed when he entered the Army with his father. He married into one of the most aristocratic families of the southern State. In spite of forty years of exile from his colored mother's family, the desire to see his only living brother and his sister's children became so great that he journeyed East to gratify it. "The door bell rang one day," said my friend, "and the maid told me that an old gentleman who refused to give his name wanted to see me on important business. The moment I laid eyes on the stranger," said she, "I noticed a striking resemblance to my uncle Spencer, who has lived here for years, you know. 'Is this Sarah's child?' said the stranger rising and holding out his hand to me, 'Yes,' said I, 'Well, I am your uncle John. Surely your mother has told you about me." After we reviewed the history of the various members of the family, said my friend, "he wanted to see my children. Whatever you do, don't tell them who I am," said he. He refused flatly to see my husband for fear he might betray him in some way. 'My husband is a gentleman,' said I, 'and he would not harm you, if he could.' When he had seen my boy Julius, he lamented deeply that such a fine looking lad should be brought up as colored under the existing condition of things in this country. 'All of my children do not look like Julius,' said I. 'Three of them are quite dark. Surely you would not advise me to rear one half of my children as colored and the other half white.' As I looked at this old man," said she, "I could not help noticing the difference between my handsome, courageous, manly Uncle Spencer, who is just as fair as Uncle John, but who has never deserted his family, and this newly found uncle, who has lived a falsehood nearly all his life. His manner was nervous. He seemed uncertain of himself. About his eyes there was a hunted, haunted, fearsome look, which is said to be characteristic of men who have served a term in the penitentiary. As I noted these points of difference, if I had ever been tempted to rear any of my children as white, I should have been delivered from the temptation immediately."

The more one investigates the matter, the more certain does he become, that many whom the world accepts as white are in reality colored, according to established standards in this country. A colored man, whose career we all admire, likes to say, "The blood of the Negro is so powerful, that if a man has only one drop of it and ninety nine drops of pure Anglo Saxon, he is called a Negro just the same." "If I were white," said a young woman of my acquaintance, "and despised colored people, as the average white American seems to despise them, I should be perfectly miserable, I know. I should be constantly tormented by the fear that some day I might discover a trace of negro blood in my veins. I have always sympathized deeply with that young woman who committed suicide in a southern hotel, because, in settling her estate the lawyer made the startling discovery that her mother had been a slave."

A colored man who has traveled extensively and who has made a special study of this subject related some incidents in my hearing a short while ago which border on the sensational. According to him, and he offered proofs to verify his assertions, colored men who are supposed to be white have occupied and are occupying some of the highest offices and most desirable positions in the gift of the nation and the State.

I myself could give the names of at least forty families whom I have known as colored, with some of whom I have been intimately associated, who have crossed the Rubicon of prejudice and are going their way rejoicing "on the other side."

ZARA WRIGHT

From *Black and White Tangled Threads*

Chapter 1: The Three Cousins

It was late in the month of September and it had been raining hard since early morning. Now, at the close of day it seemed as if the clouds felt ashamed and disappeared from view, the sun shedding its last rays over the distant hilltops and the valley beneath, the mellow light causing the raindrops that linger on tree and bush to look like pearls. This beauteous aspect of nature makes one loath to leave the scene and enter where art alone is responsible for the beauty of the interior of a grand old mansion, situation on one of the largest plantations of the Sunny South.

Thus felt a beautiful young girl as she stood enchanted while the soft breeze gently blew her long black hair in confusion around her exquisite face.

After repeated calls from her cousins, she turned and entered the house, where they were soon discussing an important event. They were to start North in a few days to enter a select boarding school for young ladies.

Catherine Marceaux was the eldest, just sixteen, the daughter of a haughty, impoverished widow, who was a sister to Paul Andrews, the owner of the mansion.

Paul Andrews, tall and handsome, had married and lost his wife in just one year, leaving a little daughter whom he called Aline after her mother. She was a sweet child, possessed of a sunny disposition that won her the name of "Little Sunbeam," and was beloved by everyone.

Source: Excerpted from Zara Wright, *Black and White Tangled Threads* (Chicago: Barnard and Miller, 1920), pp. 9–22.

The father idolized his child and she in turn fairly worshipped her father and would often leave her play and be found in the library, sitting contentedly at his feet for hours, sometimes falling asleep while waiting for him to put aside his books and papers. Then she would feel rewarded by the welcome he gave her. He often wished that his dead wife could see their lovely daughter.

The third cousin, the heroine of this story, is the most beautiful of the three. Her face is oval and her features are perfect, yet some thought that the nose was inclined to tilt upward. But if you would observe more closely you would find that it was the upward poise of the head that was misleading. Her complexion was fair although of a richer hue than her cousins, and her wonderful jet black hair hanging in long natural curls reached far below her waist and made her look most fair indeed, and no one would suspect that there flowed in her veins blood of a despised race—the black slaves of the South. But such was the case. Zoleeta Andrews was a full cousin to Catherine Marceaux and Aline Andrews. The children of two brothers and one sister, Mrs. Marceaux bitterly resented it when her brother Paul brought home their orphan niece, making her one of the family, and as she expressed it, compelling them to come in contact with that negro child. She declared that Catherine should not recognize her as a relative.

To make matters worse, her brother was determined that Harold's child should have the same accomplishments and advantages as their children. It was in vain that his sister cried and pleaded to have Harold's child sent elsewhere, for Paul was inexorable, and she was compelled to abide by his decision.

Eighteen years preceding the events recorded, Paul Andrews and his sister Claretta, and a younger brother named Harold, lived with their parents, General and Mrs. Andrews, in the present homestead. At the age of eighteen Claretta married a man by the name of Leroy Marceaux, who was of French descent, as his name would imply.

It was some years later that their brother Harold ran away with and married Mildred Yates, a slave girl belonging on the plantation. His mother never recovered from the shock, shame and humiliation, but in the end forgave him and begged his father to forgive him also. Two years later, when General Andrews was laid beside his wife, Harold was still unforgiven.

Paul and his sister inherited all of the vast wealth. The homestead, a fine old mansion, fell to Paul. A few years later he had it remodeled and refurnished and no one was much surprised when he brought home a lovely bride. She was dearly beloved by all, but died a year later at the birth of their daughter Aline.

When Claretta married, her father gave her a liberal fortune, which she placed in the hands of her husband. Subsequently she placed in his hands the entire fortune that she inherited through the death of her father. A few years later when her husband passed away, it was found that there was nothing left of the large fortune that had once been hers. It was then that her brother Paul went after her and brought her and her little daughter to take charge of his handsome home, to rear his child and manage the servants. She gladly accompanied her brother and was once more installed in her girlhood home.

Mrs. Marceaux was very domineering to those whom she considered her inferiors and often took her brother to task for being too lenient with the servants. She was horrified to see his little daughter Aline walking hand in hand with the little colored children, but her brother only laughed and said there was no harm and that the children had but few pleasures and some of those consisted of being with his daughter and he had not the heart to separate them.

In a few years Aline would enter boarding school and all would be changed. But his sister could not forget how their brother Harold had disgraced them, and not having her brother's optimistic views, remained unconvinced of the wisdom of the association.

Mildred Yates, the slave girl whom Harold married, had more education than the average slave girl. Her mother, a trusted servant of old Mrs. Andrews, had [been] taught to read* and write and she had in turn taught her daughter Mildred all that she had learned, and with her limited opportunities and doubtful possibilities, succeeded in inspiring in her child a desire for knowledge. Her thirst for knowledge was so great that when her mother could teach her no more, she still tried to learn, but finding it difficult to proceed without help, went back to the beginning and went over all that she had previously learned.

Thus it was that her young master, Harold, found her one day when he was on a tour of inspection for his father. He was amazed at the sight of a beautiful slave girl, who had a piece of broken slate and a pencil trying to trace letters as her mother had taught her to do.

---

*Original text: "Her mother, a trusted servant of old Mrs. Andrews, had taught her to read. . . ."

She arose at the approach of her young master, but not from fear, as she had never been punished or scolded. She was afraid, however, that he would laugh at her; but he spoke so kindly, asking to let him see what she was doing, that she let him take the piece of slate. After looking at it for a moment, he returned it, complimenting her on her successful efforts. He asked her if she would like to learn and she answered very brightly that she would. He promised to teach her if she would not tell anyone. Needless to say, she gave the required promise.

Day after day they met in an obscure place, remote from all danger of discovery. She proved to be a very diligent pupil and learned quite rapidly. It was not long before she could do her sums in arithmetic. In fact, she made such rapid progress in all of her studies, and was thinking of taking up more difficult work, that when Harold's father decided to send him North to spend two years in college and another in travel, he at first rebelled, and declared that he would not go. He loved his mother dearly, however, and when she placed her arms around his neck and begged him to go for her sake, he consented.

He did not realize how dear Mildred had become to him until the hour of his departure. Besides being beautiful, her superior intellect gave promise of a glorious possibility in the future. He could no longer conceal from himself the fact that he was madly in love with his charming protege. Realizing that his heart was forever in the keeping of this beautiful slave girl, he resolved to have a talk with her before leaving for the North. Mildred had learned to love her young master as ardently as he loved her and unhesitatingly promised to follow his instructions in all things. Leaving her plenty of good books and admonishing her to be a good girl, he promised to return in three years and marry her.

Three years later when Harold returned to his home, he felt more than repaid for the love he had lavished on this slave girl. She had studied diligently and not only did she show mental improvement, but she had grown wondrously beautiful. Dressed in the garb worn by the southern slave, with no other adornment save those which nature had provided, a beautiful face, a graceful, willowy form that even her coarse garments failed to hide, she looked like some princess in disguise. In Mr. Harold, who treated her with that courtesy and consideration that he would [have], had she been his equal in birth and social standing, she had utmost faith, and he was never guilty of doing aught to betray the confidence of this poor, innocent, trusting girl.

Ere many weeks had gone by, he had severed the fetters that bound her and they were safely landed in England. They were married without delay. Although he knew his father would disinherit him, that was of small consequence. Having a comfortable fortune of his own—a legacy from his godmother, and being young and energetic, he felt that he would succeed—and he did.

He wrote to his parents after his marriage, assuring them that he and his wife would remain abroad, thus relieving them of any embarrassment that they might feel. He begged their forgiveness and in a manly way, without exaggeration, dwelt on his wife's many admirable qualities. Without defiance, but with that firmness of purpose which a deep and sincere love lends, he closed his letter by saying that he was very proud of his wife and had no regret for the step he had taken.

His father was furious. "Harold has acted in a senseless, idiotic way," said he. "What need to pluck one rose from the stem, when he could have inhaled the fragrance of many?" (Thus unconsciously paying a beautiful compliment to Harold's Afro-American wife.)

Paul felt the absence of his brother keenly, and greatly deplored the step he had taken. He often longed for his little brother, unmindful of the fact that his little brother had grown to be a handsome, broad-shouldered man.

Chapter 2: The Little Orphan

Some years later Paul received a letter from his brother, telling him that Harold's wife had died two years previous, leaving him a sweet little daughter. The letter also assured Paul that Harold's days were numbered according to the doctor's statement which said that he might possibly live six or eight weeks. He begged Paul to come and take his little daughter home, assuring him that she was well provided for.

"I came to India soon after my marriage," continued the letter, "and by careful investments and close application to business, have become a successful merchant, more than doubling my wealth."

When Paul received this letter, he was filled with consternation. He felt that he could not do the thing that his brother had not only asked him, but expected him to do.

"No. It is impossible to take that child into my home with a taint of slavery clinging to her ancestors," said he. "I could not let my daughter associate with her. It is not to be thought of."

His sister agreed with him and declared it was an outrageous imposition for Harold to shift his negro child on them. However, it was decided that Paul should hasten to his brother's bedside, take the child and place her in some institution until she became of age, making no other plans for her future, but trusting to time, circumstances and existing conditions to adjust matters satisfactorily to all concerned.

Paul left without delay and it was only by traveling night and day that he succeeded in reaching his brother's side before death claimed him. As he listened to his brother he was convinced that his marriage had been a supremely happy one. Although he seemed loath to leave his little daughter, he seemed anxious to meet his wife, who had preceded him to realms above. (Paul had not yet seen his brother's child, and therefore was much disturbed because he felt that he could not heed his brother's last request and asked himself how he could refuse to make his brother's last hours happy.) He was visibly agitated, knowing that his brothers eyes were scanning his face, perhaps reading perplexity and indecision there.

Presently there was a gentle, hesitating rap on the half open door. A sweet, childish voice said, "Papa, may I come in?" Feeling sure of her welcome and scarcely waiting for a reply, she softly entered the room. Upon beholding the beautiful child, Paul Andrews was speechless with surprise. She showed no trace of the blood of her mother's people, and was by far the prettiest child he had ever seen. He marveled at the beauty and grace of this little girl scarcely six years old.

The father, propped up in bed, looked on and felt that he could die in peace when he saw his brother open his arms and say: "Darling, come to your uncle." She unhesitatingly went to him, clasped her little arms around his neck and with her head pillowed on his breast, rested contentedly there. Ah! who knows by what instinct this little girl felt so content in the clasp of her uncle's arms, though she had never seen him before. Was it some unseen power that made it plain to this little innocent child that in her uncle's arms she would find a haven of rest, a shelter and protection from life's tempestuous storms in the trying days to come? Who knows?

Paul Andrews registered a vow as he stroked the long glossy curls of his niece, to stand by her through life. Little did he think at that time that he would be called upon to defend and protect her from the treachery of those who should have felt near and dear to her through ties of blood. When the time came he did not hesitate to do his duty by his dead brother's child.

Unclasping the little arms from around his neck, he glanced at his brother and realized that the Messenger had come—that Zoleeta was an orphan. Before she could realize that her father had gone to join her mother, her uncle had led her from the room. He told her that her father was now with her mother. At first, she was inconsolable, but after the first paroxysm of grief was over, she allowed her uncle to caress her while he explained that she would have two cousins to play with and they would love her dearly, for he had resolved to take Harold's child home and rear her in a befitting manner.

In looking over Harold's papers, he found two letters, one addressed to himself and one to Zoleeta to be given her when she became of age. Paul read his at once. His attention was called to a curiously carved ebony box that had been given his brother by an exiled prince, who lost most of his possessions and was forced into exile by existing conditions in his country. The death of the prince soon followed. This box was in an iron safe filled with precious stones, worth a king's ransom. Paul opened the casket containing the jewels and never had he in his life beheld such jewels representing a vast fortune. He hastily closed the box, resolving to say nothing of its contents until Zoleeta was old enough to understand and appreciate their value.

Paul worked hard to settle up his brother's affairs, but it was some weeks before he was ready to sail for home. He wrote his sister informing her of the death of their brother Harold. He also informed her that he would bring their orphaned niece home with him. When she read the letter she became very indignant because he had not placed the child in some institution as they had agreed to do.

Paul and Zoleeta finally arrived. Zoleeta's aunt was dismayed at the sight of the most beautiful child that she had ever seen. She was amazed at this lovely graceful child, who had no badge to proclaim to the world that she had descended from the degraded race of negroes of the South. She could not understand it, and hated her dead brother's child for her rare loveliness. She had no love in her heart for her little orphaned niece; no compassion for this helpless child, thrown on her care. [. . .]

"You will find out that you have made a mistake by bringing the child here," [said] Claretta, becoming more indignant as she [spoke], "and if after years, she develops traits and habits of her mother's people to the exclusion of the better blood flowing in her veins, causing us shame and humiliation, you must remember that I warned you and you will have no one to blame but yourself. In a few years, our daughters will make their bows to the world and a girl as beautiful as Zoleeta promises to be will prove detrimental to their prospects. Of course," continued she, "Catherine has enough beauty of her own and will not be disturbed by the beauty of Harold's child, but Aline is such a meek little creature that the chances are that she will be outshown by Zoleeta."

Paul was not disconcerted by this outburst of temper from his sister and was firm in his decision that each one should have an equal chance when they entered the social world.

Neither Zoleeta nor her cousins were aware of the secret of her parentage, and Paul impressed upon his sister that under no circumstances were they to be enlightened. There were old servants about the place who remembered their young master Harold, and that he had gone abroad and married, and who were not surprised when Mr. Andrews brought home the little orphan, telling them that his brother and wife had died abroad, leaving a little daughter who would henceforth remain in his home. No one, of course, had attached any importance to the disappearance of Mildred Yates, as it was not infrequent in those days for slaves to take advantage of every opportunity to escape. Paul felt that as no one except himself and sister knew the secret of Zoleeta's parentage, it was perfectly safe.

PART 2

DREAMING
IN COLOR

African-Americans who lived in the pre–World War I era found themselves bound by a multitude of restrictions often enshrined in law. (See introduction to Part 9.) Segregated schools, public facilities, and transportation were only the most obvious and tangible manifestations of their racial oppression; the women that concern us here also faced gender-based barriers that further narrowed their options and their ability to publish their writing.

Yet in their imagination they entertained a wide range of possibilities, as if black and white had exploded into all the hues of the rainbow. For a few, fantasy became a literary strategy that allowed them to press beyond "the narrow space" allotted to them as African-American women. Their writings tend to unmask the double standards implicit in racist and sexist exclusionary practices, and to give them a glimpse of a world without color lines. Whereas the title "Black and White Tangled Threads" suggests a harsh, two-tone reality, "Dreaming in Color" offers a myriad of prospects, just as in dreams all possibilities exist.

As might be expected, many of these dreams have to do with the quest for basic human rights. African-American women were painfully aware of the discrepancies between the ideology of American freedom ("liberty and justice for all") and its actual practice. At times they configured visions of home and hearth that seem oddly traditional or unfeminist by some standards. It is helpful to remember that the idea of managing one's own home looked good to many black women who had never had the option of not working outside the home.

Most of the writings in this section appear to deal only peripherally with race. Sometimes the characters are described as being people of color, and sometimes the reader is not sure what race the characters are. The absence of racial themes makes these works different from those in "Black and White Tangled Threads." When the stories do concern race, they often take the form of dreams about overcoming the rigid social limitations posed by race. Caroline Bond Day's "The Pink Hat" explores what life might be like if one could be magically transformed by an article of clothing. Day's main character puts on a "magic" hat and instantly has access to all that society denies her because of her race—libraries, boutiques, restrooms, art exhibits, plays, and lectures.

Other writings in this section divide themselves into two main categories: romances and nightmares. The tales of "true love" that these authors spin lift the characters into a world where "race is no object": two older men conspire to rescue a long-time friend from her "disgrace" of never marrying (Florence Harmon); a young couple perseveres in their union despite the bigots who deny the husband work on the basis of skin color (Alice Dunbar-Nelson); an old sailor returns to the woman who once loved him (Mae Cowdery); an unusual experience magically obliterates the color line (Effie Lee Newsome).

While romantic love is given free rein, sexuality and eroticism are often muted (Cowdery's story, "Lai-Li," is an exception), due to the constraints of the times on such expression. Black women in particular were obliged constantly to counter the numbing stereotype of themselves as oversexed beings.

Exploring the darker side of dreams—nightmares—some of the writers wrote stories of ghosts and messages from beyond the grave. In "The Noose," by Octavia Wynbush, a man is pursued by a vengeful spirit that leaves constant reminders of its existence. Finally, Edythe Mae Gordon exposes the bourgeois obsession with money through characters who scheme to realize their ambitions through devious means.

Belated Romance

Josiah Beede traced a series of intricate patterns on the tablecloth while he and his wife waited for the maid to bring in the dessert. Glancing up from his pattern-weaving:

"Mary, what can we do about Sabina Corning?" he questioned, anxiously. "Her account at the bank is dreadfully small, totally inadequate, if she should live a long time. We've tried to sell the Corning estate, but we don't get a bid. Fact is, nobody wants an ark like that nowadays. It's just a drug on the market, eaten up alive with taxes." He threw down the fork with an air of futility.

Mary Beede thought a moment before she answered. She always had a practical solution for every problem.

"Josiah, does it occur to you that the perfectly obvious way to settle Sabina's difficulty is to marry her off before she becomes more of a spinster than she is now? There's your brother Seth—and there's Henry Holcomb. I understand both of them have courted Sabina for the last thirty years. Why not prod Seth a little? We have made it so comfortable for him here that the idea of marrying never enters his head."

"Seth's a fool," retorted Josiah Beede.

"He that calleth his brother a fool," quoted Mary Beede, laughingly.

Josiah Beede joined in the laugh, and the entrance of the maid with the dessert put an end to the subject for a time.

Seth Beede had come in late and had stopped to hang up his hat in

Source: *Saturday Evening Quill* 1 (June 1928): 62–63.

the little hallway between the dining room and kitchen. Incidentally, he had heard every word of the conversation. It made him feel uncomfortable—as if he had defrauded somebody of something that was due him. He tried to appear casual as he came into the dining room, but he failed utterly.

His sister-in-law was quite sure that he had heard what she had said. She had intended for him to hear.

Josiah and Mary Beede did not remain long at the table. When they had gone Seth had a chance to think over what had been said. He tried to make excuses for himself . . . "When I was willing to marry Sabina she seemed to show a decided preference for Henry Holcomb, so I just naturally left the field to him." He blamed Sabina's father for being such a blundering idiot as to make bad investments and leave his daughter penniless. Sabina wasn't a woman that ever could work, for the Corning women had been ladies for generations. Perhaps she was in want. The thought struck Seth like a blow.

He decided something must be done about the situation, and done speedily. Having finished his supper, he took his hat and stick and went for his usual walk to the post office.

He knew where he could find Henry Holcomb and he would tell him a few things. He disliked going into Crane's general store, but he felt the case to be urgent. He never could understand why Henry Holcomb, coming from one of the best families of Hill's Village, chose to stand around in a grocery store like a common loafer[.] He went into the store, made a trifling purchase, then told Henry he would like to speak to him outside.

Seth found it more difficult to broach the subject than he fancied it would be. He made a plunge.

"Holcomb, didn't you pay Sabina Corning considerable attention once?

"Don't know but what I did, Seth . . . How about yourself?"

Seth Beede ignored the question completely and began to plead the cause of Sabina Corning eloquently. He pictured her in dire straits, and said, finally: "The only honorable thing for us to do is to propose to her and give her a chance to marry one of us."

Henry Holcomb didn't answer directly. He just elevated one eyebrow, which was slightly higher than the other, and agreed to propose to Sabina Corning. Accordingly, the next evening he lifted the brass knocker of the small house on the Corning estate.

Sabina greeted him cordially.

It was surprising how quickly, as we say in modern parlance, Henry Holcomb got that proposal "off his chest."

Sabina listened with the utmost deference, and hesitated the fraction of a minute. There was a hint of a smile in her eyes as she gently refused Henry Holcomb. She wondered why she was always reminded of a clown when Henry Holcomb elevated his eyebrow.

The next day, at the bank, he told Seth Beede of the success—or, rather, of the failure—of his mission.

Several nights later Seth Beede called on Sabina Corning—a thing he had been doing since he was twenty. Sabina looked charming as she sat before the open fireplace.

Seth noticed what fine, slender hands she had as she gracefully plied her tatting shuttle back and forth.

"How many times have you been around the globe with that shuttle?" queried Seth.

Sabina laughed—it was a musical laugh.

"In miles, or in fancy?" she asked.

There were several long pauses, broken once when Sabina snapped out a knot in her tatting thread.

Seth glanced toward the corner for the old grandfather clock.

Horrors, it was gone! There was only one explanation. Sabina had needed money, so it had gone the way of some of the other antiques.

Rather confusedly, she arose and stepped into the kitchen. She returned soon with some delicious-looking sponge cakes and a tall tumbler of mint and cider punch—a drink peculiar to the Cornings.

Seth sipped it with the air of a connoisseur.

It was now ten-thirty, the time Seth usually took his departure, but he made no move to go.

The cat meowed to be sent to the barn for the night.

The dog turned around several times, then settled himself to sleep.

Seth still sat.

The clock rebukingly struck eleven. Seth arose to go.

Sabina brought his hat and stick, but still he lingered. He felt like a boy who does not know how to swim, but takes a chance, plunging in deep water and hoping he will come to the surface again.

He took Sabina's hand and held it. "Sabina," he said huskily, "wasn't there a sort of understanding between us once?"

"I thought perhaps there was, Seth," she said softly.

"Did I ever do anything to mar that understanding, Sabina?"

"Not that I know of, Seth."

"And you never did, Sabina?"

"I think not, Seth."

"Sabina, is there any reason why we two should not marry?"

"Not that I know of, Seth."

Sabina remembered once before, about thirty years ago, that Seth Beede had bashfully kissed her at Henry Holcomb's birthday party.

Seth went out into the night with a look of exultation on his face— like a martyr who had offered himself for sacrifice, but found that the cause for which he had offered himself did not exist.

CAROLINE BOND DAY

The Pink Hat

This hat has become to me a symbol. It represents the respective advantages and disadvantages of my life here. It is at once my magic-carpet, my enchanted cloak, my Aladdin's lamp. Yet it is a plain, rough, straw hat, "pour le sport," as was [a] recently famous green one.

Before its purchase, life was wont to become periodically flat for me. Teaching is an exhausting profession unless there are wells to draw from, and the soil of my world seems hard and dry. One needs adventure and touch with the main current of human life, and contact with many of one's kind to keep from "going stale on the job." I had not had these things and heretofore had passed back and forth from the town a more or less drab figure eliciting no attention.

Then suddenly one day with the self-confidence bred of a becoming hat, careful grooming, and satisfactory clothes I stepped on to a street car, and lo! the world was reversed. A portly gentleman of obvious rank arose and offered me a seat. Shortly afterwards as I alighted a comely young lad jumped to rescue my gloves. Walking on into the store where I always shopped, I was startled to hear the salesgirl sweetly drawl, "Miss or Mrs.?" as I gave the customary initials. I heard myself answering reassuringly "Mrs." Was this myself? I, who was frequently addressed as "Sarah." For you see this is south of the Mason and Dixon line, and I am a Negro woman of mixed blood unaccustomed to these respectable prefixes.

I had been mistaken for other than a Negro, yet I look like hundreds

Source: Opportunity 4 (December 1926): 379–380.

of other colored women—yellow-skinned and slightly heavy featured, with frizzy brown hair. My maternal grand-parents were Scotch-Irish and English quadroons; paternal grand-parents Cherokee Indian and full blooded Negro; but the ruddy pigment of the Scotch-Irish ancestry is my inheritance, and it is this which shows through my yellow skin, and in the reflection of my pink hat glows pink. Loosely speaking, I should be called a mulatto—anthropologically speaking. I am a dominant of the white type of the F^3 generation of secondary crossings. There is a tendency known to the initiated persons of mixed Negro blood in this climate to "breed white" as we say, propagandists to the contrary notwithstanding. In this sense the Proud Race is, as it were, really dominant. The cause? I'll save that for another time.

Coming back to the hat—when I realized what had made me the recipient of those unlooked for, yet common courtesies, I decided to experiment further.

So I wore it to town again one day when visiting an art store looking for prints for my school room. Here, where formerly I had met with indifference and poor service, I encountered a new girl today who was the essence of courtesy. She pulled out drawer after drawer of prints as we talked and compared from Gritto to Sargent. Yet she agreed that Giorgione had a sweet, worldly taste, that he was not sufficiently appreciated, that Titian did over-shadow him. We went back to Velasquez as the master technician and had about decided on "The Forge of Vulcan" as appropriate for my needs, when suddenly she asked, "but where do you teach?" I answered, and she recognized the name of a Negro university. Well—I felt sorry for her. She had blundered. She had been chatting familiarly, almost intimately with a Negro woman. I spared her by leaving quickly, and murmured that I would send for the package.

My mood forced me to walk—and I walked on and on until I stood at the "curb-market." I do love markets, and at this one they sell flowers as well as vegetables. A feeble old man came up beside me. I noticed that he was near-sighted. "Lady," he began, "would you tell me—is them dahlias or pernies up there?" Then, "market smells so good—don't it?"

I recognized a kindred spirit. He sniffed about among the flowers, and was about to say more—a nice old man—I should have liked to stop and talk with him after the leisurely southern fashion, but he was a white old man—and I moved on hastily.

I walked home the long way and in doing so passed the city library.

I thought of my far away Boston—no Abby nor Puvis de Chauvannes here, no marble stairs, no spirit of studiousness of which I might become a part. Then I saw a notice of a lecture by Drinkwater at the women's club—I was starved for something good—and starvation of body or soul sometimes breeds criminals.

So then I deliberately set out to deceive. Now, I decided, I would enjoy all that had previously been impossible. When necessary I would add a bit of rouge and the frizzy hair (thanks to the marcel) could be crimped into smoothness. I supposed also that a well-modulated voice and assurance of manner would be assets.

So thus disguised, for a brief space of time, I enjoyed everything from the attentions of an expert Chiropodist, to grand opera, avoiding only the restaurants—I could not have borne the questioning eyes of the colored waiters.

I would press on my Aladdin's lamp and presto, I could be comforted with a hot drink at the same soda-fountain where ordinarily I should have been hissed at. I could pull my hat down a bit and buy a ticket to see my favorite movie star while the play was still anew.

I could wrap my enchanted cloak about me and have the decent comfort of ladies' rest-rooms. I could have my shoes fitted in the best shops, and be shown the best values in all of the stores—not the common styles "which all the darkies buy, you know." At one of these times a policeman helped me cross the street. A sales-girl in the most human way once said, "I wouldn't get that Sweetie, you and me is the same style and I know." How warming to be like the rest of the world, albeit a slangy and gum-chewing world!

But it was best of all of an afternoon when it was impossible to correct any more papers or to look longer at my own Lares and Penates, to sit upon my magic-carpet and be transported into the midst of a local art exhibit, to enjoy the freshness of George Inness and the vague charm of Brangwyn, and to see white-folk enjoying Tanner—really nice, likable, folk too, when they don't know one. Again it was good to be transported into the midst of a great expectant throng, awaiting the pealing of the Christmas carols at the Municipal Pageant. One could not enjoy this without compunction however, for there was not a dark face to be seen among all of those thousands of people, and my two hundred bright-eyed youngsters should have been there.

Finally—and the last time that I dared upon my carpet, was to answer the call of a Greek play to be given on the lawn of a State University. I drank it all in. Marvelous beauty! Perfection of speech and gesture on a velvet greensward, music, color, life!

Then a crash came. I suppose I was nervous—one does have "horrible imaginings and present fears" down here, subconscious pictures of hooded figures and burning crosses. Anyway in hurrying out to avoid the crowd, I fell and broke an ankle-bone.

Someone took me home. My doctor talked plaster-casts. "No," I said, "I'll try osteopathy," but there was no chance for magic now. I was home in bed with my family—a colored family—and in a colored section of the town. A friend interceded with the doctor whom I had named. "No," he said, "it is against the rules of the osteopathic association to serve Negroes."

I waited a day—perhaps my foot would be better—then they talked bone-surgery. I am afraid of doctors. Three operations have been enough for me. Then a friend said, "try Christian Science." Perhaps I had been taking matters too much in my own hands, I thought. Yes, that would be the thing. Would she find a practitioner for me?

Dear, loyal daughter of New England—as loyal to the Freedman's children as she had been to them. She tried to spare me. "They will give you absent treatments and when you are better we will go down." I regret now having said, "Where, to the back door?" What was the need of wounding my friend?

Besides, I have recovered some how—I am only a wee bit lame now. And mirabili dictu! My spirit has knit together as well as my bones. My hat has grown useless. I am so glad to be well again, and back at my desk. My brown boys and girls have become reservoirs of interest. One is attending Radcliffe this year. My neighborly friend needs me now to while away the hours for her. We've gone back to Chaucer and dug out forgotten romances to be read aloud. The little boy next door has a new family of Belgian hares with which we play wonderful games. And the man and I have ordered seed catalogues for spring.

Health, a job, young minds and souls to touch, a friend, some books, a child, a garden, Spring! Who'd want a hat?

ALICE DUNBAR-NELSON

Hope Deferred

The direct rays of the August sun smote on the pavements of the city and made the soda-water signs in front of the drug stores alluringly suggestive of relief. Women in scant garments, displaying a maximum of form and a minimum of taste, crept along the pavements, their mussy light frocks suggesting a futile disposition on the part of the wearers to keep cool. Traditional looking fat men mopped their faces, and dived frantically into screened doors to emerge redder and more perspiring. The presence of small boys, scantily clad and of dusky hue and languid steps marked the city, if not distinctively southern, at least one on the borderland between the North and the South.

Edwards joined the perspiring mob on the hot streets and mopped his face with the rest. His shoes were dusty, his collar wilted. As he caught a glimpse of himself in a mirror of a shop window, he smiled grimly. "Hardly a man to present himself before one of the Lords of Creation to ask a favor," he muttered to himself.

Edwards was young; so young that he had not outgrown his ideals. Rather than allow that to happen, he had chosen one to share them with him, and the man who can find a woman willing to face poverty for her husband's ideals has a treasure far above rubies, and more precious than one with a thorough understanding of domestic science. But ideals do not always supply the immediate wants of the body, and it was the need

Source: The Crisis 8 (September 1914): 238–244. Written under the name "Mrs. Paul Laurence Dunbar."

of the wholly material that drove Edwards wilted, warn and discouraged into the August sunshine.

The man in the office to which the elevator boy directed him looked up impatiently from his desk. The windows of the room were open on a court-yard where green tree tops waved in a humid breeze; an electric fan whirred, and sent forth flashes of coolness; cool looking leather chairs invited the dusty traveler to sink into their depths.

Edwards was not invited to rest, however. Cold gray eyes in an impassive pallid face fixed him with a sneering stare, and a thin icy voice cut in on his half spoken words with a curt dismissal in its tone.

"Sorry, Mr.—Er—, but I shan't be able to grant your request."

His "Good Morning" in response to Edward's reply as he turned out of the room was of the curtest, and left the impression of decided relief at an unpleasant duty discharged.

"Now where?" He had exhausted every avenue, and this last closed the door of hope with a finality that left no doubt in his mind. He dragged himself down the little side street, which led home, instinctively, as a child draws near to its mother in its trouble.

Margaret met him at the door, and their faces lighted up with the glow that always irradiated them in each other's presence. She drew him into the green shade of the little room, and her eyes asked, though her lips did not frame the question.

"No hope," he made reply to her unspoken words.

She sat down suddenly as one grown weak.

"If I could only just stick it out, little girl," he said, "but we need food, clothes, and only money buys them, you know."

"Perhaps it would have been better if we hadn't married—" she suggested timidly. That thought had been uppermost in her mind for some days lately.

"Because you are tired of poverty?" he queried, the smile on his lips belying his words.

She rose and put her arms about his neck. "You know better than that; but because if you did not have me, you could live on less, and thus have a better chance to hold out until they see your worth."

"I'm afraid they never will." He tried to keep his tones even, but in spite of himself a tremor shook his words. "The man I saw to-day is my last hope; he is the chief clerk, and what he says controls the opinions of others. If I could have influenced the senior member of the firm, but he is a man who leaves details to his subordinates, and Mr. Hanan was suspicious of me from the first. He isn't sure," he continued with a little laugh, which he tried to make sound spontaneous, "whether I am a stupendous fraud, or an escaped lunatic."

"We can wait; your chance will come," she soothed him with a rare smile.

"But in the meanwhile—" he finished for her and paused himself.

A sheaf of unpaid bills in the afternoon mail, with the curt and wholly unnecessary "Please Remit" in boldly impertinent characters across the bottom of every one drove Edwards out into the wilting sun. He knew the main street from end to end; he could tell how many trolley poles were on its corners; he felt that he almost knew the stones in the buildings, and that the pavements were worn with the constant passing of his feet, so often in the past four months had he walked, at first buoyantly, then hopefully, at last wearily up and down its length.

The usual idle crowd jostled around the baseball bulletins. Edwards joined them mechanically. "I can be a side-walk fan, even if I am impecunious." He smiled to himself as he said the words, and then listened idly to a voice at his side, "We are getting metropolitan, see that!"

The "That" was an item above the baseball score. Edwards looked and the letters burned themselves like white fire into his consciousness.

STRIKE SPREADS TO OUR CITY.
WAITERS AT ADAMS' WALK OUT AFTER BREAKFAST THIS MORNING.

"Good!" he said aloud. The man at his side smiled appreciatively at him; the home team had scored another run, but unheeding that Edwards walked down the street with a lighter step than he had known for days.

The proprietor of Adams' restaurant belied both his name and his vocation. He should have been rubicund, corpulent, American; instead he was wiry, lank, foreign in appearance. His teeth projected over a full lower lip, his eyes set far back in his head and were concealed by wrinkles that seemed to have been acquired by years of squinting into men's motives.

"Of course I want waiters," he replied to Edwards' question, "any fool knows that." He paused, drew in his lower lip within the safe confines of his long teeth, squinted his eye intently on Edwards. "But do I want colored waiters? Now, do I?"

"It seems to me there's no choice for you in the matter," said Edwards good-humoredly.

The reply seemed to amuse the restaurant keeper immensely; he slapped the younger man on the back with a familiarity that made him wince both physically and spiritually.

"I guess I'll take you for head waiter." He was inclined to be jocular, even in the face of the disaster which the morning's strike had brought him. "Peel off and go to work. Say, stop!" as Edwards looked around to take his bearings, "What's your name?"

"Louis Edwards."

"Uh huh, had any experience?"

"Yes, some years ago, when I was in school."

"Uh huh, then waiting ain't your general work."

"No."

"Uh huh, what do you do for a living?"

"I'm a civil engineer."

One eye-brow of the saturnine Adams shot up, and he withdrew his lower lip entirely under his teeth.

"Well, say man, if you're an engineer, what you want to be strike-breaking here in a waiter's coat for, eh?"

Edwards' face darkened, and he shrugged his shoulders. "They don't need me, I guess," he replied briefly. It was an effort, and the restaurant keeper saw it, but his wonder overcame his sympathy.

"Don't need you with all that going on at the Monarch works? Why, man, I'd a thought every engineer this side o' hell would be needed out there."

"So did I; that's why I came here, but—"

"Say, kid, I'm sorry for you, I surely am; you go on to work."

"And so," narrated Edwards to Margaret, after midnight, when he had gotten in from his first day's work, "I became at once head waiter, first assistant, all the other waiters, chief boss, steward, and high-muck-a-muck, with all the emoluments and perquisites thereof."

Margaret was silent; with her ready sympathy she knew that no words of hers were needed then, they would only add to the burdens he had to bear. Nothing could be more bitter than this apparent blasting of his lifelong hopes, this seeming lowering of his standard. She said nothing, but the pressure of her slim brown hand in his meant more than words to them both.

"It's hard to keep the vision true," he groaned.

If it was hard that night, it grew doubly so within the next few weeks.

Not lightly were the deposed waiters to take their own self-dismissal and supplanting. Daily they menaced the restaurant with their surly attentions, ugly and ominous. Adams shot out his lower lip from the confines of his long teeth and swore in a various language that he'd run his own place if he had to get every nigger in Africa to help him. The three of four men whom he was able to induce to stay with him in the face of missiles of every nature, threatened every day to give up the battle. Edwards was the force that held them together. He used every argument from the purely material one of holding on to the job now that they had it, through the negative one of loyalty to the man in his hour of need, to the altruistic one of keeping the place open for colored men for all time. There were none of them of such value as his own personality, and the fact that he stuck through all the turmoil. He wiped the mud from his face, picked up the putrid vegetables that often strewed the floor, barricaded the doors at night, replaced orders that were destroyed by well-aimed stones, and stood by Adams' side when the fight threatened to grow serious.

Adams was appreciative. "Say, kid, I don't know what I'd a done without you, now that's honest. Take it from me, when you need a friend anywhere on earth, and you can send me a wireless, I'm right there with the goods in answer to your S.O.S."

This was on the afternoon when the patrol, lined up in front of the restaurant, gathered in a few of the most disturbing ones, none of whom, by the way, had ever been employed in the place. "Sympathy" had pervaded the town.

The humid August days melted into the sultry ones of September. The self-dismissed waiters had quieted down, and save for an occasional missile, annoyed Adams and his corps of dark-skinned helpers no longer. Edwards had resigned himself to his temporary discomforts. He felt, with the optimism of the idealist, that it was only for a little while; the fact that he had sought work at his profession for nearly a year had not yet discouraged him. He would explain carefully to Margaret when the day's work was over, that it was only for a little while; he would earn enough at this to enable them to get away, and then in some other place he would be able to stand up with the proud consciousness that all his training had not been in vain.

He was revolving all these plans in his mind one Saturday night. It was at the hour when business was dull, and he leaned against the window and sought entertainment from the crowd on the street. Saturday night, with all the blare and glare and garishness dear to the heart of the middle-class provincial of the smaller cities, was holding court on the city streets. The hot September sun had left humidity and closeness in its wake, and the evening mists had scarce had time to cast coolness over the town. Shop windows glared wares through popular tunes from open store doors to attract unwary passersby. Half-grown boys and girls, happy in the license of Saturday night on the crowded streets, jostled one another and pushed in long lines, shouted familiar epithets at other pedestrians with all the abandon of the ill-breeding common to the class. One crowd, in particular, attracted Edwards' attention. The girls were brave in semi-decolleté waists, scant short skirts and exaggerated heads, built up in fanciful designs; the boys with flamboyant red neckties, striking hat-bands, and white trousers. They made a snake line, boys and girls, hands on each other's shoulders, and rushed shouting through the press of shoppers, scattering the inattentive right and left. Edwards' lip curled, "Now, if those were colored boys and girls—"

His reflections were never finished, for a patron moved towards his table, and the critic of human life became once more the deferential waiter.

He did not move a muscle of his face as he placed the glass of water on the table, handed the menu card, and stood at attention waiting for the order, although he had recognized at first glance the half-sneering face of his old hope—Hanan, of the great concern which had no need of him. To Hanan, the man who brought his order was but one of the horde of menials who satisfied his daily wants and soothed his vanity when the cares of the day had ceased pressing on his shoulders. He had not even looked at the man's face, and for this Edwards was grateful.

A new note had crept into the noise on the streets; there was in it now, not so much mirth and ribaldry as menace and anger. Edwards looked outside in slight alarm; he had grown used to that note in the clamor of the streets, particularly on Saturday nights; it meant that the whole restaurant must be prepared to quell a disturbance. The snake line had changed; there were only flamboyant hat-bands in it now, the decolleté shirt waists and scant skirts had taken refuge on another corner. Something in the shouting attracted Hanan's attention, and he looked up wonderingly.

"What are they saying?" he inquired. Edwards did not answer; he was so familiar with the old cry that he thought it unnecessary.

"Yah! Yah! Old Adams hires niggers! Hires niggers!"

"Why, that is so," Hanan looked up at Edwards' dark face for the first time. "This is quite an innovation for Adams' place. How did it happen?"

"We are strike-breakers," replied the waiter quietly, then he grew hot, for a gleam of recognition came into Hanan's eyes.

"Oh, yes, I see. Aren't you the young man who asked me for employment as an engineer at the Monarch works?"

Edwards bowed, he could not answer; hurt pride surged up within him and made his eyes hot and his hands clammy.

"Well, er—I'm glad you've found a place to work; very sensible of you, I'm sure. I should think, too, that it is work for which you would be more fitted than engineering."

Edwards started to reply, but the hot words were checked on his lips. The shouting had reached a shrillness which boded immediate results, and with the precision of a missile from a warship's gun, a stone hurtled through the glass of the long window. It struck Edwards' hand, glanced through the dishes on the tray which he was in the act of setting on the table, and tipped half its contents over Hanan's knee. He sprang to his feet angrily, striving to brush the debris of his dinner from his immaculate clothing, and turned angrily upon Edwards.

"That is criminally careless of you!" he flared, his eyes blazing in his pallid face. "You could have prevented that; you're not even a good waiter, much less an engineer."

And then something snapped in the darker man's head. The long strain of the fruitless summer; the struggle of keeping together the men who worked under him in the restaurant; the heat, and the task of enduring what was to him the humiliation of serving, and this last injustice, all culminated in a blinding flash in his brain. Reason, intelligence, all was obscured, save a man hatred, and a desire to wreak his wrongs on the man, who, for the time being, represented the author of them. He sprang at the white man's throat and bore him to the floor. They wrestled and fought together, struggling, biting, snarling, like brutes in the debris of food and the clutter of overturned chairs and tables.

The telephone rang insistently. Adams wiped his hands on a towel, and carefully moved a paint brush out of the way, as he picked up the receiver.

"Hello!" he called. "Yes, this is Adams, the restaurant keeper. Who? Uh huh. Wants to know if I'll go his bail? Say, that nigger's got softening of the brain. Course not, let him serve his time, making all that row in my place; never had no row here before. No, I don't never want to see him again."

He hung up the receiver with a bang, and went back to his painting. He had almost finished his sign, and he smiled as he ended it with a flourish:

WAITERS WANTED. NONE BUT WHITE MEN NEED APPLY.

Out in the county work-house, Edwards sat on his cot, his head buried in his hands. He wondered what Margaret was doing all this long hot Sunday, if the tears were blinding her sight as they did his; then he started to his feet, as the warden called his name. Margaret stood before him, her arms out-stretched, her mouth quivering with tenderness and sympathy, her whole form yearning towards him with a passion of maternal love.

"Margaret! You here, in this place?"

"Aren't you here?" she smiled bravely, and drew his head towards the refuge of her bosom. "Did you think I wouldn't come to see you?"

"To think I should have brought you to this," he moaned.

She stilled his reproaches and heard the story from his lips. Then she murmured with bloodless mouth, "How long will it be?"

"A long time, dearest—and you?"

"I can go home, and work," she answered briefly, "and wait for you, be it ten months or ten years—and then—?"

"And then—" they stared into each other's eyes like frightened children. Suddenly his form straightened up, and the vision of his ideal irradiated his face with hope and happiness.

"And then, Beloved," he cried, "then we will start all over again. Somewhere, I am needed; somewhere in this world there are wanted dark-skinned men like me to dig and blast and build bridges and make straight the roads of the world, and I am going to find that place—with you."

She smiled back trustfully at him. "Only keep true to your ideal, dearest," she whispered, "and you will find the place. Your window faces the south, Louis. Look up and out of it all the while you are here, for it is there, in our own southland, that you will find the realization of your dream."

MAE V. COWDERY

Lai-Li

Lai-li was dancing in the moonlight . . . Once more. Her brown body gleamed like gold in its path.

Fearfully he whispered her name. . . . . . . Once more.

"Lai-li. . . . . . . Lai-li. . . . . . ."

She did not answer . . . Ah! there was no need. . . . . . . She was coming nearer, nearer. Slowly she danced. There was no sound save for the pounding of his heart and the magic melody of the waves rolling slowly to shore. . . . . . . All was as on that night when first he saw her, Lai-li. . . . . . . "Moon Flower."

Many, many, years had passed since then. Time had dealt gently with her. She was even more beautiful.

He could feel her breath on his cheek, fragrant as the perfume imprisoned in the crimson petals of the flowers she wore in the ebon[y] coils of her hair. Closer she came, her tiny feet making no sound as she beat her love song on the silver sands.

Would she know him? Would she forgive?. . . . . . . Had her heart forgotten the wound he had dealt in the reckless days of his youth?. . . . . . . He surely had suffered.

And again he whispered her name.

"Lai-li. . . . . . . Lai-li. . . . . . ."

Her golden arms were twining around his neck. Her body yielded, as on that night—so long ago. Her lids drooped over eyes like midnight

Source: Black Opals 1 (June 1928): 6–8.

pools, hiding the fire within. . . . . . . Her lips were cool, like dew, on his feverish ones. . . . . As on that night. . . . . . . so long ago.

Once more they would dance the strange jungle dance she had taught him. . . . . . . once more they would dance. . . . . . . she had for-given. . . . .

God! He had forgotten he was no longer young[.] Time had dealt roughly with him . . . It was his punishment. His limbs could no longer bend and whirl. . . . . . . His arms could no longer hold close their precious burden, as he sought to lift her and dart to the shadows. . . . . . . once more.

"Lai-li! Lai-li! Do not go! Stay! Stay! I am coming! I. . . . . am. . . . . . . coming."

The moon passed behind a cloud: The waves paused an instant on their home-ward flight. Air hung silent.

Again two figures danced a jungle dance in the moon-light. . . . . . .Gold and ivory blending, caressed by the moon's silver breath. . . . . . . Two figures slept once more in the soft embrace of the sand, watched over by the cool shadows. . . . . . . Two loved once more. . . . . . .

In the pale grey light of morning the waves still crept to the shore. The sun was lazily peeping over the eastern hills. All was as it had been the day before. In the cove a fishing sloop of olden days lay, her decks deserted. As the sky turned to its usual topaz blue, two figures appeared on deck. One scanned the shore with searching eyes. Quickly they de-scended into a small row boat and rapidly made their way to the lonely beach.

"Wonder where the Capt's gone? Can't see a thing on this dump of sand. . . . . . . He sure must be a little off in the upper story to come to a place like this. He's a regular circus in all the sea ports with this ole sloop. I sure wouldn't have come on this trip if you hadn't been so blamed curious! Drat you. . . . . . . I'm just a soft hearted ole nut after all!"

"Well it ain't doing yaa a bit a good to grumble about it now. You oughta thought about that 'foe ya' come, perhaps we wus both a coupla nuts, but the Capt's been mighty good to us when we wus down and out. Any how he can't last much longer with that cough. . . . . . . Did you notice how he changed as we neared the blame island? He was blattin' to hisself about some Lily, or somethin'. . . . . . . Bet he had one of them native sweeties.

"Well I'll be jiggered! Here's the ole boy fast asleep!"

"Yeh? Well he won't be waking in this place. Poor old Capt. I'm glad he's happy! Lookit the smile on his face! There ain't a blooming wrinkle on it. I'm so glad he's happy. . . . . . ."

"S'awright Pat. We're just a pair of soft hearted blokes, but I'm blamed glad we brought him here. Let's bury him here. Seems like that wus what he wanted. . . . . He knew he wus'nt gonna last much longer. . . . . . ."

The two slowly made their way back to the sloop and as the sun finally beamed bright in the sky the sloop sailed around the bay and on into the open sea. The two on its deck failed to see. . . . . . . to hear. . . . . . .

Lai-li and the "Capt." walking arm in arm (as of yore) and singing to them a farewell song. . . . . . . could not see their figures blend in the spray of the waves as their lips met.

"Lai-li. . . . . . . Lai-li. . . . . . . Lai-li."

EFFIE LEE NEWSOME

Little Cornish, the "Blue Boy"

He didn't like the city much. He missed the flowers. Oh, he missed everything that the country has to make it a place of boundless delight, a great open garden wherein one may chase butterflies and rabbits in season and relish wild strawberries. The city was nothing like this.

And, moreover, since she had moved with him to town, Little Cornish's mother had remained ill. There was no one to support the two of them but an older son who had been working in Cleveland for some years before the mother and Cornish came there. With his brother gone all day and his mother propped up against pillows and dozing off from sheer weakness, Cornish was left to spend some lonely hours.

He would not have minded this in their home in the country. He could have had all sorts of fun trotting up the soft road for whatever he might find. And something was bound to be getting out of his way. Chipmunks proved especially interesting in this respect.

Cornish's mother kept dozing and waking up—sometimes to pat his head—dozing and waking up. Once when she had gone quite fast to sleep the boy of five crept downstairs and into the mysterious street. He stood on the dingy marble steps and stared in one direction a long time. When he turned his head to look the other way awhile he saw a wagon loaded with flowers halted near a corner church.

He thought they were flowers, at least, white flowers and purple and gold in hosts. Little Cornish gazed. At length the wagon was drawn round

Source: Opportunity 5 (April 1927): 117.

to what must be the front of the church and only the hind wheels remained visible to the child. He must find out what the men in the wagon were doing with those flowers.

Cornish started down the street, stopped a moment to look back guiltily, then trotted on. He got to the church and found a funny little door open. He had to climb some narrow steps to reach it. But up he toddled. He crept wonderingly through the door and into a cold, dark passage that opened upon a room of glass doors and a closet of white robes. He passed through all this to land in an immense room with pews and aisles, soft looking brown carpet, windows of every color one could imagine. There was a chancel and here were stacked lilies and proudly gracious hyacinths and palms. The sight of these made Cornish happy.

But his pleasure was brief. As he bent near the flowers to smell them, and perhaps to pluck one, he head loud voices very near. Some men had come into the room with great pots of lilies.

"Look at that little—" cried one of the men. I shall not tell you what he called the bewildered child with the pretty brown face. "How did he get in here?" the man wondered in tones that were not unkind.

"Sexton's kid left a side entry open when she went to tell her dad we were here," explained another flower bearer. "Here she's sneaked into the room behind us like a kitten," he had barely added when a child who had paused in the midst of the church to pick up a fallen floret of hyacinth cried with her eyes on Cornish:

"He isn't what you said at all. He's a blue boy. Blue all over. He's a *aw-ful* pretty boy."

The men placed their pots satisfactorily then looked again at Cornish to discover that he was wearing only a little night-shirt that cool April day. Light from a stained glass window had tinted the shirt pale blue and cast a blue glow upon the child's face.

"Blue boy, eh?" said one of the men. "Come along here, sonny. You'll die that way." He reached out an arm toward Cornish.

"Wait," cried the sexton's little girl, "I'm going to give him a flower. He came for a flower. Didn't you?"

She recklessly jerked at the stem of a lily and before the men could say anything had pushed it into Cornish's eager little hand.

He gave that lily to his mother.

Not many days after this she lay cold and they brought flowers into the house. Cornish, gazing at these and at her, thought of how she had kissed him when he took the lily to her. White flowers and the lily perfume!

If I were writing a book I would start another chapter here but as it is I must tell all within a few words. When Cornish grew to manhood he became a famous physician and practiced in a large city. Such joy he brought to hosts who lay weary and weak and wasting away! Not only did he take to their bedside his cheering smile, but he carried there flowers. He took the spring to them in his arms. He brought them the breath of nature and of God. For he never forgot the smile that had come like a golden light to his mother's face when he gave her an Easter lily.

OCTAVIA B. WYNBUSH

The Noose

The Louisiana moon, riding high in the sky, made a rippling path of light across the slow-moving waters of the Mississippi River. A boat rounding the bend in the river at this point, slid into the shadows cast by the high bank which sloped gently down to the water's edge. As the clumsy craft came silently and carefully to rest in the shadows, a man who had sat bunched at the oars leaped quickly ashore and dragged the boat to a sheltered spot. Without a backward glance he began climbing a narrow, shadowy path leading to the top of the high embankment.

At the top of the ascent the path lost itself between two lines of massive, wide-sweeping, live-oaks. The mighty moss-covered arms of these trees swept upward and met in an arch, which the light of sun and moon barely penetrated. Only an occasional ghost of a moonbeam shone now through the foliage, as the man, with the step of one long accustomed to treading this way, plunged into the path between these giants. He had not gone far, however, when a sudden rustle in the pathway turned him into a statue of attention.

"King?" A woman's voice breathed the word. "It's me, King, it's Leora."

"Leora? What you doin' here dis time o' night?"

In the dark a slim hand, young but coarsened by toil, touched him timidly, sliding down his shoulder, down his arm, and finally coming to rest in his own toil-roughened hand.

"I—I couldn't sleep, King. Nobody could sleep. Dey's all talkin' and speculatin' 'bout—'bout—"

Source: Opportunity 9 (December 1931): 369–371.

"'Bout him?"

"Yes. Is—is—it—"

"Yes, it's all over." There was an unmistakable satisfaction in his whispered response.

A sharp intake of breath from the girl. "O, King, he done daid?"

"Dat's it. Twelve o'clock sharp, de trap was sprung.—He died in [a] few minutes."

They were walking hand in hand through the tunnel of oaks. A few moments of slow, silent walking brought them to the end of the lane, and into a semi-circular clearing. They stood in silence, looking at the scene about them.

The black, indistinct silhouettes that formed the background of the cleared semi-circle were by day the oaks, pines, magnolias and pecan trees that with vines and ferns made up mysterious Devil's Swamp. Across the clearing, so close to the trees that the arms of some of them reached over and caressed its rotten roof, stood a cabin—King's cabin. The cleared space around it was what remained of a once-lovely flower garden—a garden that had been beautiful with jasmine, roses, and old-fashioned sweet William and honeysuckle when Nomia used to move among them.

King's face twitched suddenly at the picture that rose in his mind. Leora, womanlike, sensed his thoughts and squeezed his hand. A strangely contrasting pair they were, as they stood in the moonlight. Tall, magnificently proportioned, ebony black was the man. Strength, brute force rippled in the muscles of his body. His face, lined heavily had the sere* look of a leaf shrivelled not so much by the chill of winter, as withered prematurely by a drought, or the searing heat of a forest fire. His hair lay in a mat half tangled, half kink, over his head, suggesting some admixture of blood. His eyes were murky pools.

The girl, slender and yellow brown, her large dark eyes filling with tears that quivered down her hollow cheeks, squeezed King's hand once more.

"King?"

"What you want, chile?"

"Did he do it? Did he kill Jeems?"

"A judge and twelve jurymen said he done it."

"Yes, but dat don't mean nothin'. It could of been—"

---

*Withered, dry.

"It could of been who?" The question was shot at her with the force of a pistol report.

"Anybody. He don' say all time, he don' be guilty."

"He was guilty as hell! What did he do to you an' me, gal? Didn' he stole my wife and break yo' mammy's haht 'cause she done took so much pains to raise you gals so you kin hol' yo' haids up wid de best?"

"I—I know dat, too. But dat don' say he killed a man."

"Go home, gal! A man dat'll stole another man's wife will do anything else. Go home!" He gave her a little push toward an opening in the trees, an opening leading to her own home, where slept her father, unconscious of his daughter's nocturnal adventure.

Leora walked off a few paces, turned and looked around. King was striding toward his cabin. Leora stopped.

"King," she called softly.

"Huh?" Impatience had succeeded the anger in his last speech. He stopped in the shadow of the cabin, his hand on the latch.

"Do you know what he done tol' de preacher what seed him last?"

"What?"

"He done say he ain't guilty."

"You done tole me dat befo'."

"An' he say dat whoever be guilty—he comin' back an' tie dat same noose aroun' his neck."

King threw back his head and laughed a silent laugh, but hearty, and stepped into the moonlight.

"Git to bed, gal! Don' you know dere ain't no ghosts? Don' you know when a man goes to Hebben he don' wanna come back an' when he go to hell de debbil ain' let him come back? Stop fearin' de daid, gal, an' fear de livin'."

"I do." The penetrating glance from the girl's shrewd young eyes lingered a moment on the man's face, and she turned to run home.

King watched her out of sight, a startled, puzzled look on his face. There was something in Leora's tone which had started a question in his mind. What did she mean? What did she know? With a sudden shrug he turned toward his home again. Unlatching the door he entered the darkness. Taking a match from his pocket he made a light and applied it to the jagged wick of an oil lamp on a dirty, cluttered table. Through the cracked chimney a few straggles of yellow light made their way.

The unplaned planks in the flooring emerged from one shadowed end of the room, spread for a brief while in the dim light and vanished into the shadow at the other end before an open fireplace, cold and black now, in the heat of summer. On one side of the fireplace tilted a rickety cane bottomed chair. On the other side stretched a crude bunk nailed to the wall. A few rags of dirty bed-coverings were thrown across it. One or two boxes, a few traps piled in the corner, constituted the remaining furnishings of the room. Clothing in all states of use and disuse hung from nails driven into the walls. From the rafters of the cob-webby ceiling dangled bunches of red peppers, stuffed sausages and onions.

King fastened the door, made his way to the bunk and sat down. His head sank wearily into his hands, and his mind moved swiftly back into the past, bringing picture after picture into the dim cheerless room.

There was Nomia, first, Nomia, slender, undersized with her sharp, yellow features, brown eyes and abundant brown hair never tidily arranged, never becomingly dressed for her face. She had not the adeptness of her sister Leora in making her cheap clothes look becoming, yet he had loved her. The witchery of Nomia for him had been the witchery of youth, for she was twenty-one and he was forty. She danced before him now, singing in the liquid, untrained soprano that to him had seemed a miracle coming from a throat so slim. Tantalizing, laughing and deceiving, twisting him about her fingers with the lure of her youth, she stood before him.

The knuckles on King's huge fingers stood out sharply as he balled his hands into fists at another image. Jed—Jed who had been hanged that afternoon floated boldly, arrogantly into his vision. A rascal from the city whose summers spent in Chicago hotels had given him a patronizing, counterfeit "gentleman's air" as Nomia had called it. Jed's conquest of Nomia had been easy. His flattery, his oily compliments had sunk deep into her unstable, impressionable consciousness.

King groaned as he lived again through scenes which time had not erased for him. Jed's first long compliments to him on having a wife who could "sing like a mocking bird"; his long visits to the then cheerful cabin, ostensibly to see the husband; the chattering of the plantation women— chattering that, when King approached a group, gave place to meaningful signs, sly looks and nudges; the shock of coming home one day to an empty cabin, to a note from Nomia, stating she had gone away with Jed.

King felt again the days of black despair, the days when the opening magnolia blossoms and the scent of roses and jasmine Nomia's hands had planted, were to him as instruments of torture, squeezing closer and ever closer his soul, bursting his heart and draining it of life. He lived through the night of blackness his soul had touched and found to be an impregnable wall closing him from the light.

The great passion passed: the scene changed once more. Five years dragged across his life, five years of silence, hurt pride, withdrawal from his fellows except Nomia's sister and father. Then, one day, Jed returned to a neighboring plantation. Nomia had died during one of the cruel winters in the North. King recalled with a bitter smile the open, crude hints that had come to him from time to time, to "kill that rascal like a dog." But he had made no move. He preferred to suffer the scorn of those from whom he had practically withdrawn himself. He bided his time. Fate would devise a more subtle plan.

And fate did. King's smile became a sneer as there came before his mind the form of James Holloway. He heard again the searing slurring obscenity James had uttered at the general store one evening after the flight of Nomia and Jed. He remembered how, panting with rage, he had finally been dragged from the prostrate figure and shoved out of the store. Never again had King entered that store; not one word did he utter to anyone concerning his encounter with James, but a purpose was born in his mind.

Then, one night after Jed's return, Jed and James had come to blows over a card game. There had been threats and recriminations, with a threat on Jed's part to "settle later." A few nights after that Holloway was found dead, shot through the heart. No weapon was found, but the fact James was killed with a rifle of the same bore of one Jed owned, together with the fact that Jed's rifle had mysteriously disappeared, although he had been hunting with it the day before the killing, turned suspicion on him. Despite his frantic declarations of innocence, he had paid the debt.

"Dey ain't think I might know who killed Jeems, an' who hide Jed's gun," King chuckled. Then he thought of Leora's last remark and her strange, shrewd glance. Had she, in some uncanny fashion, guessed the truth?

With a yawn he rose from his bunk. It was high time to be in bed. Stretching in sheer weariness, he threw back his head. A sudden shiver ran through his body; his arms dropped sharply to his side. His shadow, huge, distorted, lay along the wall and partly across the ceiling. The head emerged from a noose, one end of which sprang upward as if attached to a beam out of sight. In a moment King recovered himself, and his agitation gave place to relief. The shadow of a coil of rope dangling from one of the rafters crossed his shadow so as to give the illusion of being around the neck of the huge, sprawling figure.

With shaking hands and a muttered oath he stepped to the table and blew out the light. What a fool he was getting to be! Leora's words about Jed's threat—had they taken such hold on him? Didn't he know that such talk was nonsense? What sensible man would take stock in such nonsense? Time for a man to be in bed when his nerves began jumping at his shadow. Leora had been brought up on tales.

Tales! A thousand plantation ghost stories of his boyhood rushed into his mind. Barred doors opening, and no hand seen opening them— wronged spirits coming back—the man murdered in his sleep by the ghost of a man he had murdered. He swore under his breath, as he kicked his boots across the room, and plunged into the tumbled bunk to sleep. It would not be long before daylight. Things always cleared up in the day.

Sleep came at last, fitful, broken with mutterings and dreams: Leora waiting at the end of the lane of trees; Nomia's face, mocking, smiling, teasing; James dropping like a log in the grass, dying without a sound; himself slinking down the path to the river, and dropping the gun into the swiftest part of the current; Jed's gray, agonized face, as he was half carried from the courtroom after pronouncement of sentence; the crowd outside the prison walls; noon whistles shrieking the last moments of the condemned man's life.

The night had given way to the blackness of early morning when King was suddenly shocked into wakefulness. Something sinuous, like a thread, was passing slowly across his throat. A cry of fear came from the awakened man's lips. What was it? What was this thing? He put up his hand to tear it away. He shrieked out again. It was a rope, a noosed rope tightening around his throat.

"Good God!" His hand crept fearfully to his throat again, striving desperately to summon strength to tear the thing away. Another cry. The cords were growing thicker and tighter.

"Help! God have mercy!" King made a lunge toward the floor. He was jerked to his knees on the edge of the bunk. Fearfully, he raised his eyes. A scream of agony broke through his burning lips.

"Jed! Jed! Don' do dat'! Don'! Have mercy! God have . . ." His voice broke in a gurgling sob. His body sagged limply on the bunk. Outside the early breeze of morning passed in a shuddering sigh through the lane of trees, in the first faint streaks of morning.

When, after a day, King failed to appear among his fellows, four men, under the guidance of Leora, broke into the cabin. On the bed they found him, his body rigid, his face set in mask of mortal terror. Over his face and around his neck were the broken filaments of a spider web.

EDYTHE MAE GORDON

If Wishes Were Horses

The boat churned its way up the harbor. Men, women and children filled the decks. Numbers of people sat on folding chairs. The wind blew fiercely. Women held down their skirts to keep their knees from showing.

In the shadows, near a corner, there sat a man holding the hand of a little girl. His brown felt hat flopped weakly over a sallow, hollow-cheeked face. He stroked his greying black hair with an impatient gesture. His harassed mind had been further disturbed. What had that gypsy fortune-teller meant, anyway? For the fun of it, he had gone into her tent on the beach. Now he could not dismiss from his mind this swarthy, dirty-looking woman in her outlandish costume of red, orange, and purple.

He got up and went below. He bought himself a magazine, and a bar of candy for the little girl. On their way up, they stopped to watch the greenish-white water dash angrily against the huge wheels.

The boat passed an island, and most of the passengers rose, went to the railing, and stretched their necks in an effort to see the prisoners the city kept there. Fred Pomeroy sat down. He was wretched in his dejection. His only interest lay in trying to fathom the meaning of the fortune-teller's prognostication. She had taken his hand and examined the lines of its palm. After several minutes, she had said:

"Things will be different. Your wife will be able to realize her desires. She'll do some of the things that she has long wished to do. You'll be the maker of her dreams."

Source: Saturday Evening Quill 2 (April 1929): 52–53.

Frowning, he glanced down at his trousers. Though neatly pressed, they were noticeably threadbare. They had been in service for three years. He had worked for five years in Shannon-Jones' Department Store, selling yards and yards of muslin to tired and irritable women. At night he wrote stories. He did not make much advancement at the department store. As to the stories, all he had been able to realize from them were pink, blue, and white rejection slips. Perhaps there was a check at home for the story "Love Will Find a Way," sent to "Love Art" magazine. Or perhaps, tomorrow morning, he'd get a promotion, with a ten-dollar raise, at Shannon-Jones'.

He gazed absently at Dorothea, who had slipped from his embrace. She was playing with a little boy on the deck. Pomeroy looked at her, but he was thinking, "What does it all mean?" He wondered why he had gone into the gypsy's tent at all. Why had he been attracted to "Madam Lenora," this woman who guaranteed to read one's entire life—the past, the present and the future—declaring that one would be wiser and happier after a visit with her?

"True," he reflected, "in a way." She did tell me something, but she read neither my past nor my present. She only told me of my future. I am not happier; certainly I am not wiser. I can't see how I can make Rachel's dreams come true, when I don't know what they are, even.

Pomeroy's magazine dangled between his slim, brittle fingers. He pondered, and his mood created these lines:

> Why are we always groping,—
> Why are we always hoping
> To obliterate the pain
> And happiness to attain?

When he walked from the boat down the gang-plank to the wharf, leading Dorothea by the hand, his eyes strayed to a poster:

EXCURSION DATES

CONSULT C. J. MANIX

Proprietor of the Beautiful Steamer

QUEEN MARY

SUNDAY EXCURSIONS

2:30 and 6:30 PM

Come early and make your reservations

Pomeroy made a grimace, grasped Dorothea's hand, and hurried away. He was tired of excursions. He never wanted to see a beach again.

Rachel's critical eyes noticed how listless her husband was at dinner. He ate but little, and complained as usual of feeling ill. She attributed his lackadaisical manner to fatigue. He seemed to be tired, exhausted, all the time.

They had been in bed for hours when Rachel awoke. She felt cold air blowing upon her, and she pulled the covers closer. Yet she shivered. She had dreamed that she was flying alone in an airplane. She had been sitting in the cockpit with perfect control, when, suddenly, something had gone wrong and the engine had died. The plane had plunged down into emptiness. It had struck an ice peak and had landed on a glaciated mountain. She had heard a roaring noise and had seen a huge block of ice split itself from the glacier. She had been unable to reach the wrecked plane because of the faceted spurs. No human being had been in sight . . . Her feet were freezing. She lay shivering.

She lay thus for several seconds. She felt colder all the time. It occurred to her that the room was as void of sound as the arctic wastes had been. She listened to hear her husband's breathing. There was no sound. Suddenly afraid, she reached out her hand and laid it on his face. He was icy cold. . . .

Some weeks later Rachel received a long blue envelope in the mail. When she opened it a check for $50,000 fell on her lap.

It was Pomeroy's insurance.

Nellie Niles, who had once lived across the street from the Pomeroys, sat reading the Sunday newspapers.

She idly turned to the society section. For the amusement it afforded her, she read column after column concerning marriages, bridge parties, weddings, club activities, church affairs, and the doings of the younger set. Her eyes came to rest on the headline:

SAILS FOR EUROPE

She read the accompanying story:

Mrs. Alfred Pomeroy, of 69 Academy Road, Boston, accompanied by her daughter, Dorothea, sailed Friday afternoon for Europe. After touring Italy, France, and Spain, Mrs. Pomeroy will be the guest of Mrs. Conklin Van Bruce, at her villa at Cap D'all, France.

Nellie Niles stared from protruding eyes, then she read the item over again, slowly. She laid the sheet on her knees, her heart beating painfully and her gaze straying off into space.

She sighed. In an acrimonious tone, she exclaimed aloud: "Gee, gosh!" Then she added mournfully: "Some people have all the luck!"

EDYTHE MAE GORDON

Subversion

The deepening twilight wrapped the world in a dusky veil of mystery. Like a tired runner, the wind sighed among the bare branches overhead. Houses and stores, people and automobiles, streets and sidewalks, all sank into indistinguishable shadow.

John Marley was a music teacher—a teacher of piano, and an unsuccessful one. His face was deeply furrowed, and the coat which he pulled protectingly about him was threadbare. In his tired, muddy eyes there lay a puzzled expression. Where was he to get the money to pay the note that was due? An immense self-pity gripped his throat.

He again ran over in his mind his most likely friends. Suddenly his muddy eyes grew clearer. How had he forgotten Charlie Delany?

Delany was a bachelor, and incidentally, a prosperous realtor.

"No luck this year," muttered John Marley.

He stumbled with an uncertain gait up Broad Street on his way to Delany's house.

"I've never asked him for anything," the music teacher thought. "And we've been good to him . . . No luck this year. No luck any year. The doctor said one lung's gone. Maybe I won't live long, anyway. I bet my wife will be glad. I'm a miserable failure . . . Then she'll have some money . . . my insurance . . ."

When he reached the intersection of Broad and Waverly streets he slipped and fell on the sidewalk. Automobiles whizzed by. A crowd gathered. John Marley looked foolish. He turned his head round to see who

Source: Saturday Evening Quill 1 (June 1928): 15–16.

had noticed him fall. He shuffled to his feet. A few yards away in the street lay his hat. He picked it up and smoothed out the folds made by the automobile. As he buttoned up his coat, he shivered and continued on his way.

"What's happened to you, Marley?" Charlie Delany asked, opening the door wide. He slapped Marley gently on the shoulder as he propelled his friend into the warm living room.

"Slipped on the icy sidewalk. Got all wet." John Marley looked ruefully at himself, then went over and stood in front of the sizzling radiator.

"Too bad! You can't go out in this condition . . . a wet coat. Take mine. I'll get it later." Charlie Delany's coat was of black broadcloth with collar, cuffs, and lining of soft beaver.

Finally, several bills of large denomination having been pressed into Marley's hand, he prepared to go. He said:

"Don't forget Lena and I expect you to dinner tomorrow, as usual." Being assured that Charlie would be present, he shut the door with vigor and departed.

Charlie Delany was an old friend. Since he was not married he always ate Thanksgiving dinner with the Marleys. They would not think of having him eat dinner in a restaurant on Thanksgiving Day.

On his way home Marley gradually began to see the things in a different light. Life seemed a bit more cheerful. His cough seemed less painful. Perhaps it was Charlie Delany's beaver-lined coat, with the beaver collar and cuffs, that made him feel different. One would feel different in a warm coat. Charlie Delany had given him a glass of gin—"to heat you up and keep you from catching more cold." It did more, for it enkindled in him the fire of renewed manhood.

Why didn't he get a good warm coat? Didn't clothes help determine what people thought of you? Didn't you have to be the master of your own fate? If he had a warm coat three years ago perhaps he'd have two strong lungs today. People didn't want him teaching their children when he was continually coughing. And he could not blame them. From one of the easy-payment stores he could get a fairly good coat. Ten dollars down and a dollar a week . . .

He straightened his shoulders and almost strutted up Broad street. When he reached a brilliantly-lighted store, whose window displayed a variety of merchandise, he turned the knob smartly and sauntered importantly through the door. He felt happy, and he must buy something for

Lena. He wanted to make her happy, too. From the variety of things in the store he finally decided upon a pretty but inexpensive scarf for Lena and a toy airplane for the boy.

He hoped the scarf would please his wife. Perhaps she would show him more affection. Perhaps she would not be quite so cold. He remembered how Lena had loved him before worries came, before the cough came, before slender times came. After all, who knew but that the doctor might be mistaken? He might live a long time. One could live quite a long while with one lung. He might even increase the number of his pupils, if he tried hard enough. He would then have more money . . . Lena would then love him as she had long ago.

He thought: "Lena used to quarrel every time I invited Charlie Delany to dinner. She'd make mean remarks. Gradually she changed her attitude toward him. Why shouldn't she change her attitude toward me, and love me again if I am more prosperous?"

John Marley went to one or two other places, among them the barber shop. He got a haircut and had his face massaged. It was eight when at last he reached home.

He was thinking, as he mounted the steps:

"What will Lena say when she sees me wearing this beautiful coat? She'll brighten up and run up to me and kiss me, I'll bet." He paused in the dark hall. He put his hand into the coat pocket for the key but it was in his own coat, and that was at Charlie Delany's. He rang the bell. In the dark hall Lena gave him a kiss and put her arms about his neck. She stood very close to him and stroked the beaver collar. She kissed him again and again and buried her head against the coat, now cooing softly:

"Marley isn't home, yet. The boy cried and called for you today."

Keen knife-thrust was Lena's voice. How weary he felt! How useless was life! How futile everything!

"Yes," answered John Marley, his voice striving treacherously to betray him. He kissed her tenderly. "Yes, he's home."

At dinner next day John Marley sat very quiet. At the table Lena tried hard to act as if everything was alright. One who noticed would have plainly seen that she was ill with fear. She wondered what her husband was thinking. She wished she had a chance to tell Charlie of last night.

While Charlie talked and laughed over his own stories, John sat staring at his son. He thought he saw Charlie's eyes and chin. Lena, Charlie, and the child ate. The husband hoped they did not notice him. He wondered what Lena thought, but could not look at her.

"You seem very quiet today, John." Charlie reached for the after-dinner mints. "Thinking about the accident of last night, I guess," he hazarded, sympathetically.

"Yes." John pushed back his chair, putting his hand to his mouth as if to hid the convulsive tremor of his lips.

"I'm thinking about my boy!" There was a pause, then he continued:

"I'm thinking of something else, too. I don't believe I'm going to live much longer. Life has given me all the joy it ever will."

As he spoke a vague incomprehensible solitude encompassed him.

"I want to thank you for your friendship Charlie. When I'm gone be kind to Lena and the boy. I can think of no more appropriate person to ask such a favor of."

Charlie Delany mumbled incoherently and was vividly red in the face. He looked away. Lena's eyes were twice their usual size. She acted as if she was going to cry.

PART 3

NATIVE DAUGHTER

The writings in this section explore ways of constructing personal identity amid contradictory definitions. Some writers focus specifically on the intertwining of African with European or Native American heritage. Instead of deploring hybridity, they embrace its uniqueness, going against the notion of racial purity promoted by social Darwinism.[1] A case in point is Florida Ruffin Ridley's "Preface: Other Bostonians," in which she presents the details of an interracial family tree in New England that includes Africans, Native Americans, and Europeans. These authors also write of the pride they feel in a heritage brought from Africa that survived despite slavery and its legacy in America. Partly in response to exclusionary concepts like that of "true womanhood" (reserved for white females), and to the idea that African-Americans are neither American nor African, they invented a more expansive discourse of their own.[2]

Some authors luxuriate in the images of a mythical Africa derived more from the richness of their own imagination than from maps. In Ottie B. Graham's "To a Wild Rose," a slave prizes her royal African descent. Similarly, Josephine Copeland's poem "The Zulu King: New Orleans (at Mardi Gras)" pictures a black man atop a Mardi Gras float in a New Orleans parade as if enthroned: "Surrounded by his brave warriors: /

---

1. The belief (derived from the principles of biological evolution proposed by Charles Darwin) that the system of "survival of the fittest" enables superior individuals—and racial groups—to gain wealth and power.

2. See Hazel Carby, *Reconstructing Womanhood: The Emergence of the Afro-American Woman Novelist* (New York: Oxford University Press, 1987).

a robust crew, with skin as glossy as / black satin." In Gladys Casely Hayford's "Nativity" there emerges a vision of an African Jesus, surrounded by black angels. All these authors idealize their African heritage to show readers its honor, beauty, and intrinsic worth. Sometimes, too, their Africanism takes on sad tones when Africa proves too remote, as when the character in Graham's "To a Wild Rose" discovers that her bloodline is not wholly African. These texts represent an attempt to redefine time and space between the African past and the American present.

Some of the authors in this section also stress the rootedness of their people in America. Through historical research and by recording oral accounts of their family histories in the United States, they subtly undermined the idea that blacks were interlopers in American society who could be treated like second-class citizens. More than simple attempts to document "untold history," these narratives—Lucy Mae Turner's "The Family of Nat Turner, 1831–1954," Era Bell Thompson's "Where the West Begins," Delilah Leontium Beasley's *The Negro Trailblazers of California,* and Ellen Tarry's "Native Daughter"—advance the project of incorporating the life and history of blacks into American history, both legitimizing the African-American presence as an agent in that history and fulfilling their self-imposed responsibility to educate and encourage future generations.

Regional diversity and nuance differentiate the women's stories, ranging from Tarry's stinging memories of the Ku Klux Klan's exploits in the South to the Thompson family's participation in the enterprise of settling the West. Despite this fact, however, there is a commonality found in the authors' belief that blacks share the values and life goals of other Americans. Ridley's tale of a prominent black Bostonian family; Thompson's history of her family, which could almost be that of any family living in the West; and Ida Rowland's refusal to believe that souls come in "different shades" all emphasize the commonality of the human experience in America. Instead of asserting the uniqueness of African-Americans, the aforementioned texts set out to demonstrate that there is no racial differentiation in human goals, and that therefore there should be no basis for different treatment.

In a wider sense, almost all of the writers in this section intend their writings to be weapons deployed against the advocates of racism: Tarry's essay describing the abuse of blacks sanctioned by white authorities, an abuse so extreme that it "demand[s] that those who call themselves . . .

friends [of blacks] take their stand and let the world know about it;" Beasley's biography of a black actress who succeeded *despite* the fact that she was black, implying that all the odds were stacked against her; Turner's history of her family, living in the shadow of their famous ancestor, Nat Turner; Ottie Graham's portrayal of the brutality of slavery; and Copeland's poem "Negro Folk Songs," describing the "fetid swamps of racial discrimination."

These women, daughters of Africa and America, native to both lands in spirit, root their writings in their personal and collective memory, thus serving two ends: establishing the authenticity of their presence and denouncing the unequal treatment accorded them.

OTTIE B. GRAHAM

To a Wild Rose

"Ol' man, ol' man, why you looking at me so?" Tha's what you sayin' son. Tha's what you sayin'. Then you start a-singin' that song agin, an' I reckon I'm starin' agin. I'm just a wonderin', son. I'm just a-wonderin'. How is it you can sing them words to a tune an' still be wantin' for material for a tale? "Georgia Rose." An' you jus' sing the words an' they don't say nothin' to you? Well listen to me, young un, an' write what you hear if you want to. Don't laugh none at all if I hum while I tell it, 'cause maybe I'll forget all about you; but write what you hear if you want to.

Thar's just me in my family, an' I never did know the rest. On one o' them slave plantations 'way down in the South I was a boy. Wan't no slave very long, but know all about it jus' a same. "Cause I was proud, they all pestered me with names. The white uns called me red nigger boy an' the black uns called me red pore white. I never 'membered no mother—just the mammies 'round the place, so I fought when I had to and kep' my head high without tryin' to explain what I didn't understan'."

Thar was a little girl 'round the house, a ladies' maid. Never was thar angel more heavenly. Flo they called her, an' they said she was a young demon. An' they called her witch, an' said she was too proud. Said she was lak her mother. They said her mother come down from Oroonoka an' Oroonoka was the prince captured out o' Africa. England took the prince in the early days o' slavery, but I reckon we got some o' his kin. That mean we got some o' his pride, young un, that mean we got some o' his pride. Beautiful as was that creature, Flo, she could 'ford bein' proud. She was lak a tree—lak a tall, young tree, an' her skin was lak bronze, an'

Source: The Crisis 26 (June 1923): 59–63.

her hair lak coal. If you look in her eyes they was dreamin', an' if you look another time they was spaklin' lak black diamonds. Just made it occur to you how wonderful it is when somethin' can be so wild an' still so fine lak. "My blood is royal! My blood is African!" Tha's how she used to say. Tha's how her mother taught her. Oroonoka! African pride! Wild blood and fine.

Thar was a fight one day, one day when things was goin' peaceful. They sent down from the big house a great tray of bones from the chicken dinner. Bones for me! Bones for an extra treat! An' the men an' the women an' the girls an' the boys all come round in a ring to get the treat. The Butler stood in the center, grinnin' an' makin' pretty speeches about the dinner an' the guests up at the big house. An' I cried to myself, "Fool—black fool! Fool—black fool! An' 'fore he could do anything atall, I kicked over his tray of gravy an' bones. Bones for me! Bones for an extra treat!"

The old fellah caught me an' started awackin', but I was young an' tough an' strong, an' I give him the beatin' of his life. Pretty soon come Flo to me. "Come here, Red-boy," she say, an' she soun' like the mistress talkin', only her voice had more music an' was softer. "Come here, Red-boy," she say, "we have to run away. *I* would not carry the tray out to the quarters, an' *you* kicked it over. We're big enough for floggin' now, an' they been talkin' about it at the big house. They scared to whip me, 'cause they know I'll kill the one that orders it done first chance I get. But they mean to do somethin', an' they mean to get you good, first thing."

We made little bundles and stole off at supper time when everybody was busy, an' we hid way down in the woods. 'Bout midnight they came almost on us. We knew they would come a-huntin'. The hounds gave 'em 'way with all their barkin', an' the horses gave 'em way steppin' on shrubbery. The river was near an' we just stepped in; an' when we see we couldn't move much farther 'less they spot us, we walked waist deep to the falls. Thar we sat hidin' on the rocks, Flo an' me, with the little falls a-tumblin' all over us, an' the search party walkin' up an' down the bank, cussin' an' swearin' that Flo was a witch. Thar we sat under the falls lak two water babies, me a-shiverin', an' that girl a-laughin'. Yes, such laughin'! Right then the song rose in my heart tha's been thar ever since. It's a song I could never sing, but tha's been thar all a same. Son, you never seen nothin' lak that. A wild thing lak a flower—lak a spirit—sittin' in the night on a rock, laughin' through the falls, with a laugh that trickled lak the water. Laughin' through the falls at the hunters.

After while they went away an' the night was still. We got back to the bank to dry, but how we gonna dry when we couldn't make a fire? Then my heart start a-singin' that song again as the light o' the moon come down in splashes on Flo. She begin to dance, Yes sah, dance. An' son, you never seen nothin' lak that. A wild thing lak a flower the wind was a chasin'—lak a spirit a-chasin' the wind. Dancin' in the woods in the light o' the moon.

"Come Red-boy, you gotta get dry." And we join hands an' whirled round together till we almost drop. Then we eat the food in our little wet bundles—wet bread an' wet meat an' fruit. An' we followed the river all night long, till we come to a little wharf about day break. A Negro overseer hid us away on a small boat. We sailed for two days, an' he kep' us fed in hidin'. When that boat stopped we got on a ferry, an' he give us to a man an' a woman. Free Negroes, he told us, an' left us right quick.

I ain't tellin' you, young un, where it all happen, cause that ain't so particlar for your material. We didn't have to hide on the ferry-boat, an everybody looked at us hard. The lady took Flo an' the man took me, an' we all sat on the deck lak human bein's. When we left the ferry we rode in a carriage, an' finally we stopped travellin' for good. Paradise never could a' been sweeter than our new home was for me. They said it was in Pennsylvania. A pretty white house with wild flowers everywhere. An' they went out an' brought back Flo to set 'em off. An' when I'd see her movin' round among 'em, an' I'd asked her if she wasn't happy, she'd throw back that throat o' bronze, an' smile lak all o' Glory. "I knew I'd be free, Red-boy. Tha's what my mother said I'd have to be. My blood is African! My blood is royal!" Then the song come a-singin' itself again in my heart, an' I hush up tight. Wild thing waterin' wild things—wild thing in a garden.

Thar come many things with the years; the passin' o' slavery an' the growin' up o' Flo. Thar wasn't nothin' else much that made any difference. I went to the city to work, but I went to visit Flo an' the people most every fortnight. One time I told her about my love; I told her I wanted her to be my wife. An' she threw back her curly head, but she didn't smile her bright smile. She closed her black eyes lak as though she was in pain, an' lak as though the pain come from pity. An' I hurried up an' said I knew I should a-gone to school when they tried to make me, but I could take care o' her all the same. But she said it wasn't that— wasn't that.

"Red-boy," she said, "I couldn't be your wife, 'cause you—you don't know what you are. It wouldn't matter, but *I* am *African,* and my blood is *royal!*"

She fell on my shoulder a-weepin', an' I understood. Her mother stamped it in her. Oroonoka! Wild blood and fine.

I went away as far as I could get. I went back to the South, an' I went around the world two years, a-workin' on a ship, an' I saw fine ladies everywhere. I saw fine ladies, son, but I ain't seen none no finer than her. An' the same little song kep' a-singin' itself in my heart. I went to Africa an' I saw a prince. Pride! Wild blood an' fine.

Thar was somethin' that made me go back where she was. Well, I went an' she was married, an' lived in the city. They told me her husband come from Morocco an' made translations for the gover'ment.

"Morocco," I thought to myself. "That's a man knows what he is. She's keepin' her faith with her mother."

I rented me a cottage. I wanted to wait till she come to visit. They said she'd come. I settled down to wait. Every night I listen to the March wind a-howlin' while I smoked my pipe by the fire. One night I caught sound o' somethin' that wasn't the wind. I went to my door an' I listen, an' I heard a voice 'way off, kind a-moanin' an' kind a-chantin'. I grabbed up my coat an' hat an' a lantern. Thar was a slow, drizzlin' rain, an' I couldn't see so well even with the lantern. I walked through the woods towards where I last heard the voice a-comin'. I walked for a good long time without hearin' anything a-tall. Then thar come all at once, straight ahead o' me, the catchin' o' breath an' sobs, an' I knew it was a woman. I raised my lantern high and thar was Flo. Her head was back, an' she open an' shut her eyes, an' open and shut her eyes, an' sobbed an' caught her breath.

An', spite o' my wonderin' an' bein' almost scaired, that little song started up in me harder than ever. Son, you never seen nothin' lak that. A wild, helpess thing lak a thistle blowed to pieces—a wild, helpless thing lak a spirit chained to earth. Trampin' along in the woods in the night, with the March wind a-blowin' her along. Trampin' along, a sobbin' out her grief to the night. Thar wasn't no words for me to say; I just carried her in my arms to the fire in my house. I took off her coat an' her shoes an' put her by the fire, an' I wipe the rain out o' her hair. She was a-clutchin' somethin' in her hand, but I ain't said nothin' yet. I knew she'd tell me. After while she give the thing to me. It was a piece o' silk, very old an' crumpled. A piece of paper was tacked on it. Flo told me to read it. That time when we run away from the plantation she took a little jacket all braided with silk in her bundle. 'Twas the finest jacket her mother used to wear. This dreary night, when Flo come to visit, she start a-ransackin' her old trunk. She come across the jacket and ripped it up; an' she found the paper sewed to the linin'. An' when I read what was on the paper, I knew right off why I found her in the woods, a-running lak mad in the March night wind.

Her mother had a secret, an' she put it down on paper 'cause she couldn't tell it, an' she had to get it out—had to get it out. Thar was tears in every word an' they made tears in my eyes. The blood o' Oroonoka was tainted—tainted by the blood of his captor. The father o' her little girl was not Negro, an' the pride in her bein' was wounded. She was a slave woman, an' she was a beauty, an' she couldn't 'scape her fate. Thar was tears, tears, tears, in every word.

I looked at Flo; her head was back. I never did see a time when her head wasn't back. It couldn't droop. She threw it back to laugh, an' she threw it back to sigh. Now she was a-starin' at the fire, an' the fire was a-flarin' at her. Wild thing lak a spirit—lak a scaired bird ready to fly. Oroonoka! Blood o' Oroonoka tainted.

"Red-boy," she said to me, an' she never look away from the fire. "Red-boy, I'm lookin for a baby in the winter. How am I gonna welcome my baby? Anthing else wouldn't matter so much—anything else but white. *That* blood in my—in my baby! Oh, Red-boy, I ain't royal no more!" I couldn't say much, but I took her hand an' I smoothed her hair, an' I led her back to the white house down the way.

Thar in the country she stayed on an' on, an' I stayed on too. Her husband come to see her every week, an' he look proud. He look proud an' happy, an' she look proud an' sad. She wandered in the woods an' she sang a low song. An' she stood at the gate an' she fed the birds. An' she sat on the grass an' she gazed at the sky. Wild thing, still an' proud—wild thing, still an' sad.

An' she stayed on an' on till the winter come. An' the baby come in the winter. She lie in the bed with the baby in her arm. Son, you never see anything lak that. A wild thing lak a flowerin' rose—lak a tired spirit. Flower goin', goin'; bud takin' its place. She said somethin' 'fore she died. She look at me an' said it.

"Red-boy, my blood is royal, but it's paled. Don't tell her—yes tell her. Tell her about the usurpers o' Oroonoka's blood."

But I never did tell her, I went away again an' I stay twenty years. I just find out not long ago where her father went to live. I went to see 'em an' I make myself known. I didn't do so much talkin', so the miss entertain me. She played on the piano and forgot that she was a-playin'. Right then she was her mother, yes suh, thar sat Flo. Wild thing. Royal blood! Paled, no doubt, but royal all a same.

Then she turned around, an' she wasn't Flo no longer. The brown skin was thar, an' the black, wild eyes, an' the curly dark hair. She spoke soft an' low, but she never did say, "*My* blood is royal! I am *African!*" An' she never did say "Red-boy." Her father had never told her about Oroonoka— that was it. An' I come back too late to tell her.

Well it don't matter no how, I thought, so long as she can hold her head lack that, an' long as she can look so beautiful, an' long as she make her mark in the world with that music. But the little song started a-singin' itself in my heart, an' I could see the flower agin.

Tha's your material boy. 'Member how I told it to you, a-fishin' on the river edge. 'Member how you was a-singin' "Georgia Rose." Thar's your material. Georgia Rose. Oroonoka. A wild, young thing, an' a little song in an old man's heart.

The Zulu King:
New Orleans (at Mardi Gras)

The Zulu King arrived at the new Basin
Canal in his royal barge,
Profusely decorated with palms and
Surrounded by his brave warriors:
A robust crew, with skin as glossy as
Black satin.
They were robed in tawny tiger skins
Armed with fantastic shields
And pointed menacing spears.
The barbaric floats passed in review,
A majestical parade.
Cheers rose from thousands of loyal
Subjects on Rampart Street.
On one float stood a huge ebony kettle
Containing a naked pot-bellied babe
Simmering over a mock bush fire.
Tom-toms beat a steady monotonous tune.
They stirred long buried savage impulses.
The blood quickened in my pagan heart;
Africa called to her own again.

Source: Arna Bontemps, ed., *Golden Slippers* (New York: Harper, 1941), p. 125.

123

Negro Folk Songs

Dark brooding, restless
Clouds of dreamy melody
Surging up from
Stark misery and dank despair

Oozing up from the fetid swamps
Of racial discrimination
Baptized by tears of
Racial frustration.

Rising like sweet incense
They stir the whole world
With the plaintive cry
Of a crucial race.

Source: The Crisis 47 (May 1940): 158.

Preface:
Other Bostonians

I have dragged the heavy old box from under the kitchenette shelf; it is one of those strongly built boxes which praise the honest workmanship of a former century and which, with other like furnishings, has accompanied those transitions from farm house to city house, from city house to city apartment.

Here, under the kitchenette shelf, it is wholly out of keeping with electric stove and refrigerator, being as large as one and much larger than the other. Besides, the unavoidable bruising of shins against its corners is becoming monotonously irritating, and the temptation to crowd into it all sorts of things that happen to be in the way has led to many unfortunate results—as when a bag of apples, stuffed hastily in a corner, was forgotten and left to decay, the stain almost obliterating the written words of a most charming love letter of the fifties.

So today the first step in the discard is being taken, a sorting of the treasures in the box preparatory to putting them into other and less clumsy containers.

What should be sacrificed and what preserved? It is impossible to deny the charm of things that connect with the past; and rifling old boxes for letters, documents, and pictures to meet the demand and interest, has become such a general pastime, one wonders if there be anything worthwhile that has not been already revealed. At least there would seem to be few phases of early American life that have not been wholly or partly disclosed through the contents of such boxes as these: we have been given more or less vivid pictures of life in old New England and of pioneer

Source: Saturday Evening Quill 1 (June 1928): 54–56.

life in the Middle West; we have been led to know the Dutch Master and the Puritan Preacher and to follow the Covered Wagon; but here is a Treasure Trove that is unique in its way, not especially because it represents the hundred-years' accumulation of an American family (in this it can be many times duplicated), but because its old deeds and Bibles, its letters and receipts, its pictures and pamphlets are the records of a Boston Negro family, a family justifiably but modestly making its claim as "Bostonian" because of three generations (through the maternal line) born in Boston and free in Massachusetts; a family which has its known beginning when a captured African escaped from a trading vessel in the port of New Bedford, fled to the woods around what is now known as Taunton, and took an Indian squaw as wife; a family one line of which was continued in that neighborhood through a venturing Negro from Martinique, and of which one descendant left the farming and basket-making of his forebears, settled in Boston, and married an English girl fresh from Cornwall; a family vividly representing the American "melting pot," that "melting pot" to which, in every section of this country, the Negro is largely contributing.

Through these varying phases of family life, the contents of this chest have travelled—phases and events which antedate the box itself—and now to meet the demands of the new generation and of the new times for more room, this sorting and filing is being done.

Old letters naturally comprise the bulk of the contents; some folded and sealed with postage to be paid at the door, all written on cheap and homely paper. Most of them are given over to family affairs, but many make astonishing yet unaffected references to persons whose names have place in American history.

Here, for instance, is a letter of comparatively recent date—November 28, 1862—which records the Thanksgiving Day when Governor Andrew came down Beacon Hill to dine with colored people in one of their homes on Phillips Street. An extract follows:

"We had a nice Thanksgiving dinner at home . . . turkey, oysters, plum pudding and Apple Jack . . . Mr. H—— came over in the afternoon to invite me to his home at five o'clock . . . I was seated next to Governor Andrew and was talking with him a good part of the time. The Governor was very affable and sat through all the courses from $5\frac{1}{2}$ to past 8 o'clock. The Secretary left about 7 o'clock to take his train."

Here is another letter in the neat, clear and fine handwriting of

Frederick Douglass, sent to a member of the family appointed as a Massachusetts Justice. Douglass's letter begins, "May It Please Your Honor. . . ." Here is another letter from Douglass sent from his office as Recorder of Deeds for the District of Columbia. To quote from it:

"Soon after entering upon the duties of his office, I was asked by Mr. Blaine, Secretary of State, to name certain colored men to be sent abroad. They were to be such as in my judgment would reflect credit upon themselves, the Country and the Republican Party. I asked him to give me time. The next day I sent him a letter with five names, and yours was first on the list."

Here is another, a family letter written the day after the assassination of President Lincoln, a simple letter, but significant as presenting a true picture of what Negroes in Boston were doing and thinking at that time.

Here are old Bibles with more than a century of family records; here are deeds and mortgage notes, and here is a memorandum of a grant of land to a collateral line; the grant made in 1786 by the Great and General Court of Massachusetts and recorded in the County Court of Taunton, near which city the land is located. This gift of the State was made in recognition of the services in the Revolutionary War of the receiver, who had been a Massachusetts slave and who was granted his freedom at the same time.

Here is a copy of the will of a forebear upon the paternal side, a document probated in the city of Richmond, Virginia, in 1839, and which lists and apportions to the family of the maker houses, money and furniture accumulated by a Virginia Negro at the end of the seventeenth century. Here are letters relating to the execution of this will and to the use of the money by one of the heirs, who was actively interested in the early Liberian Colonization Scheme. With these is a passport, issued in 1852, to one of the descendants of this old Virginian, a paper which gave him the privilege "as a free person of color," of moving about under certain restrictions, in his native city of Richmond.

In light relief to these documents of civic and legal bearing are those of social importance and significance. Here are bills and receipts for food, for furniture, for medical treatment, all indicating economic status; here are daguerreotypes and souvenirs, wedding invitations and calling cards. Among the souvenirs are dried and brittle relics of the old basket-work done years ago by the Taunton branch of the family, who were Yankee farmers during the summer and straw weavers during the winter; who used to send their cranberries into Boston for Thanksgiving and leave the planting of the June peas until after Anniversary-Week meetings in Boston.

The calling cards and invitations are combinations of the town branch of the family—glazed stationery seems to have been the mode in the Victorian Era, for this highly polished Silver Wedding Anniversary card was put out by "Loring" of high Boston repute. It carries the announcement of the twenty-fifth anniversary of the marriage of a Boston couple living on the then very desirable Shawmut Avenue, and the date of the affair is February 22, 1869. There are records that this Negro family further voiced its American prosperity by establishing in the fifties a small carrying trade between New Bedford and Liberia.

Branded with these evidences of striving for finer living, is an invitation of a difficult character. It is in the fine print which testifies to the fine eyesight of earlier Americans, and announces an Anti-Slavery Anniversary to be held in Music Hall, Boston, January 26, 1859. It is signed by women whose names are among the immortals: Helen Eliza Garrison, Maria Weston Chapman, Mary May, L[ydia] Maria Child, and many other women who had invited social ostracism and challenged physical and financial dangers by sponsoring the cause of the Negro.

This matter is of more or less extraneous character and belongs, if anywhere, here with the historical collection in the old chest: the early Negro newspapers which were beginning to be published in 1827; the reports of National Conventions of Colored Men held before and soon after the Civil War; copies of the old ballots which elected colored men to the Massachusetts Legislature in the sixties; speeches, state appointments certified by Governor Andrew, Governor Long, Governor Bullock; but, most interesting of all, the old portraits, either daguerreotypes or cards de visite.

How amazingly wide is the range they represent, when one considers the imposed limits and restrictions of Negro life.

Here are portraits of Negro ministers who had spoken not only from leading pulpits in Boston, but in Great Britain, also. Among them is the picture of Boston's first Negro minister, Thomas Paul, in his pulpit in the old Joy Street Church. Here are portraits of Negro Congressmen, only one of whom was born in Boston, but many of whom had close affiliation with the city, several having sent their children to be educated in the private schools of suburban Boston. These impressive-looking men were leading "Reconstructionists," "Monsters of Corruption," who allowed their ignorant and inexperienced followers to indulge in plush chairs and decorated cuspidors at the expense of the government; men who, for these laxities, are still being denounced by a high-minded electorate, but men, nevertheless, who were the first legislators to make laws establishing public schools in their states and laws against land monopolies; men who, according to Louis Post, "forestalled by forty years Lloyd George with his proposal for old-age pensions, and who, by nearly four, preceded Henry George in apprehending the deathly import of land monopoly."

Here are portraits of more Bostonians whose lives were more or less linked with the owners of the old chest: the first Negro graduate of Harvard College, a man of splendid presence, who became one of the terrible reconstructionists of South Carolina, and was later sent as a United States Consul to Russia; the first Negro graduate of Harvard Medical School; the first from Harvard Law School, who afterwards became a Massachusetts Judge; the picture of the colored girl who, in 1865, put the features of Colonel Shaw in enduring marble. Here the portrait of a one-time Lieutenant-Governor of a Southern State, and in the same cover the portrait of another family friend, a Negro who escaped with his wife from slavery and made his way by underground to Boston, where he established his home, an estate which, on the death of the widow, was bequeathed at Harvard College to form a scholarship for Negro boys.

Here, bearded at the age of twenty-three and in the Sergeant's uniform, is the portrait of the family hero who volunteered in '61.

I am stirred and thrilled as this drama of the past unrolls before me: a continuing drama, for herein is a record of a parlor gathering in 1890 of a half dozen Boston colored women, who met to consider some possible way to bring the millions of Negro women into touch with one another for common helpfulness and encouragement—a successful movement begun only thirty years after the Emancipation and Proclamation!

Musing in the gathering dusk over these mementoes and their associations, my mind by degrees drifts back into the present. It was only the day before that I had been present at one of those modern gatherings where members of the two races meet and, with painful earnestness, struggle, through planned and deliberate efforts, to establish "better race relations." In spite of efforts to approach the subject by new paths and from enlarged points of view, the old "bogey" has reared its head.

"Intermarriage? Socially impossible! The two cultures are not assimilable."

And then the ancient panacea—"Back to Africa!" Why, after all, is not that the reasonable solution?

Warmed and stirred by these records of men and women who had proved their essential Americanism, I could afford to be amused at the recollection of the cropping out of these usually irritating "perennials." Much of the failure to "adjust" comes, after all, not only from misunderstanding, but largely from lack of knowledge—lack of knowledge of the diversified phases of Negro life, for one thing. Doubtless my box and its contents may be duplicated in many a home, for all Negro life in America walks hand in hand with tragedy, and all phases are of the deepest significance. And those phases that are richest in suffering and heroism are not always recorded in collections.

It is surprising to find how definite a part of accepted technique has been the closing of eyes and ears and minds to phases of Negro life and character.

Negro life is always picturesque; viewing it, one is conscious of warmth and movement and color. Right here, from the worn contents of this old unconsidered box, there can be obtained a more telling, a more humanly appealing and, possibly, a more socially valuable picture of old Negro Boston, than can be gathered from any number of official records of diligently secured scientific findings.

GLADYS CASELY HAYFORD

Nativity

Within a Native hut, 'ere stirred the dawn,
Unto the pure one was an Infant born
Wrapped in blue lappah that His mother dyed.
Layed on his father's home-tanned deer-skin hide
The babe still slept—by all things glorified.
Spirits of black bards burst their bonds and sang,
"Peace upon earth" until the heavens rang.
All the black babies who from earth had fled,
Peeped through the clouds—then gathered round His head,
Telling of things a baby needs to do,
When first he opes* his eyes on wonders new;
Telling Him that to sleep was sweeter rest,
All comfort came from His black mother's breast.
Their gifts were of Love caught from the springing sod,
Whilst tears and laughter were the gifts of God.
Then all the wise men of the past stood forth
Filling the air East, West and South and North;
And told him of the joys that wisdom brings
To mortals in their earthly wanderings.
The children of the past shook down each bough,
Wreathed frangepani† blossoms for His brow;

*Opens.
†Frangipani: fragrant, flowering tropical tree or shrub (*Plumeria rubia*).

131

They put pink lilies in his mother's hand,
And heaped for both the first fruits of the land;
His father cut some palm fronds that the air
Be coaxed to sephyrs,* while He rested there.
Birds trilled their hallelujahs; and the dew
Trembled with laughter till the Babe laughed too.
All the black women brought their love so wise,
And kissed their motherhood into his mother's eyes.

Source: Opportunity 5 (January 1927): 13. Written under the pseudonym "Aquah Laluah."
   *Zephyrs: mild gentle breezes.

A Poem

Let my song burst forth on a major note,
Check the minor lilt in the Negro's throat.

But how can the Negroes play their harps,
With sorrow for intervals pain for sharps.

With a knife in the wound, and tears on the face
Should the song be quavered in treble or bass?

Though the tempo is kept by the shining stars,
Notation is writ on prejudice bars.

When God gives no sign when we reach the refrain
Have we the courage to start again?

With conflicting fugues and odd times to keep,
It's a wonder we laugh as well as weep.

It is a most marvelous wonderful thing
That in spite of all this, the Negro can sing.

Source: Opportunity 7 (July 1929): 220.

The Palm Wine Seller

Akosua selling palm wine,
In the broiling heat;
Akosua selling palm wine
Down our street.

Frothing calabashes
Filled unto the brim,
Boatmen quaffing palm wine
In toil's interim.

Tossing off their palm wine,
Boatmen deem her fair:
Through the haze of palm wine,
Note her jet black hair.

Roundness of her bosom,
Brilliance of her eyes
Lips that form a cupid's bow,
Whereon love's dew lies.

Velvet gleam of shoulder
Arch of bare black feet;
Soft caressing hands,
These her charms complete.

Thus illusioned boatmen
Dwell on 'Kosua's charms.
Blind to fallen bosom,
Knotted thin black arms.

Lips creased in by wrinkles,
Eyes dimmed with the years,
Feet whose arch was altered
Treading vales of tears.

Hair whose roots life's madness
Knotted and turned wild.
On her heart a load of care;
On her back, a child.

Akosua selling palm wine
In the broiling heat.
Akosua selling palm wine
Down our street.

Source: Opportunity 8 (February 1930): 41.

Rainy Season Love Song

Out of the tense awed darkness, my Frangepani comes;
Whilst the blades of Heaven flash round her, and the roll of
   thunder drums,
My young heart leaps and dances, with exquisite joy and pain,
As storms within and storms without I meet my love in the rain.

"The rain is in love with you, darling; it's kissing you everywhere,
Rain in the vale that your twin breasts make, as in delicate
   mounds they rise,
I hope there is rain in your heart, Frangepani, as rain half fills your
   eyes."

Into my hands she cometh, and the lightning of my desire
Flashes and leaps about her, more subtle than Heaven's fire;
"The lightning's in love with you darling; it is loving you so much,
That its warm electricity in you pulses wherever I may touch.
When I kiss your lips and your eyes, and your hands like twin
   flowers apart,
I know there is lightning Frangepani, deep in the depths of your
   heart."

The thunder rumbles about us, and I feel its triumphant note
As your warm arms steal around me; and I kiss your dusky throat;
"The thunder's in love with you darling. It hides its power in
   your breast.
And I feel it stealing o'er me as I lie in your arms at rest.
I sometimes wonder, beloved, when I drink from life's proferred
   bowl,
Whether there's thunder hidden in the innermost parts of your
   soul."

Out of my arms she stealeth; and I am left alone with the night,
Void of all sounds save peace, the first faint glimmer of light.
Into the quiet, hushed stillness my Frangepani goes.
Is there peace within like the peace without? Only the darkness
   knows.

Source: Opportunity 5 (September 1927): 275.

Is It Not Enough

Is it not enough,
That I should suffer poverty and disease,
Pay for crimes I do not commit,
Be burned at the stake for another's lust?

Is it not enough
That I should walk hand in hand
Each day with morbid fear,
Work for a pittance,
Laugh back the bitter tears
And live a life of make-believe?

No, it is not enough,
For I must have heaped upon
My already bowed head
The black prejudices of by-gone centuries.

Source: Ida Rowland, *Lisping Leaves* (Philadelphia: Dorrance and Co., 1939), p. 55.

Negroid Things

I cannot write of things negroid,
I cannot feel the things that are black,
I feel only life in its pulsing fullness:
The joys, the grief and troubled cares
That come with every life.

Are we a people set apart
To think with minds that are clouded with soot?
Do souls of men have different shades?
Must we always love with an ebony heart?

Then, I have defied the laws of God,
For I have dared to feel the wonder and beauty of life.
I lift my face to the wind and the rain and the sun
And feel a vibrant need for living.
I could not sift out the things that a black soul
Should not feel.

And on that last day,
When I must face a frowning Maker
I shall face him truthfully.
And in that fatal moment before I am plunged
To utter darkness,
I shall bow with humility and awe,
But with a voice that is firm with truth
I shall say to him:
"God, I could not feel the black."

Source: Ida Rowland, *Lisping Leaves* (Philadelphia: Dorrance and Co., 1939), p. 16.

Are We Different?

We love the wild unstinted ways of the west wind,
It is as music to our burdened souls.
We hate the fetters of prejudice
That keep pure minds from soaring to unlimited heights.
We are the sons of the soil,
Lithe muscles burned brown by Mother Sun.

We long for space and freedom,
For self-expression.
We are the open-handed, big hearted
Masters of our souls.

We need the shade and lazy solitude
For spontaneous expression,
Whether it be a jig or an immortal melody.

We want love and contentment,
And a life to live.

Source: Ida Rowland, *Lisping Leaves* (Philadelphia: Dorrance and Co., 1939), p. 12.

The Family of Nat Turner, 1831–1954

On a chilly, gloomy day in the fall of one of the years of the early 1830s, a little colored boy stood, barefooted, shivering and disheartened, by a country road in Southampton County, Virginia. The iron shackles of slavery were about his legs. An auction sale was going on,—an auction, not of land, not of furniture, and not of dumb beasts,—but an auction of God's humanity.

For, one slave, Nat Turner,* feeling the urge that God had put into him, had fought for and demanded his freedom, and the right to stand and walk upright, as befitted one made in the image of God. And now, as the result of his presumptuous thought and action, everyone with a drop of Nat Turner's blood must be shackled and sold into the far South, to be worked and whipped to death on the big plantations, as this way of reasoning among the slaves was the first real menace to the highly profitable institution of trafficking in human flesh. And, of course, this little boy, Gilbert, must be shackled and sold, for he was the son of Nat Turner.

Source: *The Negro History Bulletin* (March 1955): 127–132, 145–146; (April 1955): 155–158.

*Nat Turner (1800–1831) was an American black slave, a preacher, and the leader of a slave insurrection in August 1831. Turner believed he was divinely chosen to lead his people out of bondage. On August 21 he and five others killed his master, Joseph Travis; then, joined by approximately seventy other slaves, they killed fifty-seven whites—men, women, and children. Turner escaped, but he was captured, tried, and condemned to be hanged on November 11, 1831, in Jerusalem, Virginia. Afterward white mobs lynched approximately two hundred blacks, whether they had been involved in the revolt or not. The insurrection radically polarized debate over slavery throughout the United States.

The auctioneer, tall, gaunt, red-faced, cruel, had a rawhide whip in his hand. The whip came down with biting fury on the shoulders of a timid black woman, who stood cowering in a corner, trying to protect her baby, with a piece of gunny sacking, from the biting cold.

The little colored boy swallowed a smothered sob, as he saw the whip descend on the back of the humble black woman, and strike a glancing blow on the baby. For that woman was his mother, his beloved mother, and that baby was his sister, Melissa, now two years old. Gilbert knew that he must not cry out, and he hoped and prayed that Melissa would not sob, as he knew that the usual custom of slave auctioneers with colored babies, when they began to cry and become troublesome and thus interfere with the progress of the sale, was to grasp them by both heels, and to dash their brains out against the lintel of a door.

Little Gilbert Turner had seen nothing but despair and misery in his home since that memorable night in 1831, when his father, Nat Turner, known as a Baptist preacher and exhorter on the plantation, driven to desperation by the terrible beatings that were being given his people, when the fury of the master class was let loose on helpless Negro men, women and children alike,—when Nat Turner heard the voice of God telling him that he was the appointed of the Lord, to strike the first blow, to break this terrible institution, to rid both the white race and the Negro race of the scourge of slavery,—slavery that destroyed the body of the black man by its brutality, and that, furthermore, destroyed the soul of the white man by its inhumanity. Slavery was gilded and pictured to the outside world as a patriarchal institution where kindly, fatherly master looked zealously after the well-being of the slaves. This was true in a few cases where there were ties of blood between master and slaves. The slaves were sometimes brothers, cousins or children of the master. Sometimes, even these did not fare well. And slavery was a living Hades for those who had only Africa to look to for blood and ancestry.

"Fannie Turner, take the auction block!" came the raucous command of the slave auctioneer. As one who moves in a dream, so the black-haired, dark-faced Fannie moved, closely grasping the round-eyed frightened Melissa. Fannie moved, but she did not stand upright on the auction block, as was expected of her. Her heart was broken, and now she felt like the dead shell of a human creature.

Her husband, Nat Turner, was gone, executed, because he could not endure the injustices and cruelty of slavery. Her children were being taken away from her, sold into a torment worse than death. What fate awaited her, a young woman, still in her twenties, who could tell? She wished she could join Nat Turner in that great eternity, but life and breathing would go on.

So, contrary to all expectations, Fannie knelt upon the auction block, as though in prayer. She clasped the little Melissa in her arms. She fixed her eyes upon the little boy, Gilbert, her son, who stood about twenty feet away, and her lips formed some words. The auctioneer lifted his whip, as though to strike again,—but thought better of it. Why bruise up a N—— that could easily bring one hundred dollars? He saw the woman's quivering lips, and he thought she was praying. . . Well, all these N——s were superstitious, so why disturb her?

But the child, Gilbert, his senses quickened by the many sorrows that had beset his family, understood the message of those quivering lips. It was not the same message that his father, Nat Turner, and his faithful congregation of followers had sung in Turner's slave cabin, that last night, before the insurrection.

> Trust in the Lord,
> And you'll overcome
> Somehow,
> Somewhere,
> Someday.

"Hear ye, hear ye, hear ye! One healthy young N—— woman and baby for sale! Who'll give me fifty? Who'll give me seventy-five? Who'll give me one hundred? SOLD to Planter Yarborough of Alabama for one hundred and twenty-five dollars!"

With a great cry she could not repress, Fannie, as she was being led away by a fair-haired giant in hip boots, let loose to her pent up feelings. "Good-bye, Gilbert! GOOD-BYE, GOOD-BYE! GOOD-BYE!"

The vibrant echo of that cry stayed with Gilbert, even to his dying day. Little Gilbert stretched out his arms towards his mother and towards his baby sister as though his arms would encircle them for all eternity, but the small out-stretched arms of the little boy were futile. His arms could only reach through a foot or two of space, and the more powerful and inexorable arms of the law as then practiced were carrying away from the despairing child, Gilbert, the last remnant of his people,—

forever, and forever, and forever! No friend to turn to but the Lord. And, unheard by the auctioneer, and heard only by the child Gilbert, this tune of mingled supplication and praise rang through the air:

O LORD, O LORD, O LORD . . .

But, no time for silent sorrow and regret. The hand of the auctioneer was jerking Gilbert roughly.

"Get upon the auction block, Gilbert. We have cleared about a thousand dollars off your family this morning. Now, if we can get a couple of hundred for a healthy young black like you, we shall be fixed with money for the whole winter, besides sending all your family so far south into slavery that they will never again presume to think that they can be free like white people."

At that, the auctioneer gave the frightened little Gilbert a resounding crack with the whip, and caught him by one leg and one arm, in an attempt to lift him onto the auction block, which stood possibly two feet high. But, as the boy attempted to pull away from this rough bodily treatment, the auctioneer was suddenly stopped by a gentle but firm hand laid upon his arm. A gentle voice said: "Let go the boy, La Grone. The boy is my property. My father has allowed me to purchase him as my wedding present. Here is a check for five hundred dollars."

Gilbert turned, to see the tall, fair haired "Miss Mary," whom he had often seen sitting on the porch of the "big house," now acting as his rescuer. He had often seen her come down to the church meeting in Nat Turner's cabin. Gilbert knew that she had surreptitiously given his father the only Bible that he had ever possessed. Miss Mary had talked sympathetically to Nat Turner when he was being driven to desperation by the repeated whippings of his aged father, who was growing too weak to do the hard work expected of him on the plantation, and by the repeated insults to Nat Turner's aged and high spirited mother, who was reputed to be of royal African blood.

Miss Mary did not know of the plot preceding the Nat Turner insurrection, but she had always admired the tall, poetic, masterful, ambitious reddish-black young slave, with his noble character, his dreams, his faith in God, his love of his people,—his hopes, his aspirations, his talents,—all of which were dwarfed in this land of slavery and oppression. And she realized that Nat Turner, at the age of thirty-two, [. . .] had taken the only way out, and that was through the Doorway of Death. For, sometimes, there is a Victory in the Grave, which leads to a bright, eternal Heaven, where Faith, Hope, Charity, Love and Justice, shall last forever and forever, without ceasing.

Nat Turner was a slave who stood for a supreme, great brotherhood, Where men did not each other buy. And, missing this, he chose to die![. . .]

So, Mis' Mary, on her wedding day, took the little Gilbert to her new home, not far distant. Every day, he made her fires, and tidied her room. At night, he slept on a mat outside her door. The fact that Gilbert was the son of Nat Turner was a secret that Mis' Mary did not even tell her husband, who was a lawyer as well as a planter. Mis' Mary knew that no one owed loyalty to a slave any more than a dumb animal,—and it was an open season on slaves.

Once the master of the house was entertaining some of his lawyer friends at dinner. Gilbert, then a boy in his early 'teens, was waiting on the table.

"By George!" one of the lawyers exclaimed, "It is really remarkable how much that boy is like that Nat Turner that we tried and executed some years ago. His nose is just like Nat's, not flat like some slaves, and he has the same reddish-black color. Most slaves are grayish-lack, but those Turners were mostly reddish-black."

"Gilbert," Mis' Mary hastily interposed, "go out and cut that cord of wood behind the barn. If you don't get it done before night, we will have nothing with which to keep fires for our guests tonight." So what was nearly an explosive incident, passed off innocently. Nevertheless, Gilbert never again waited on the table for out-of-town guests from Petersburg or Richmond.

Gilbert Turner, as he grew up, thought many times of the struggles and sacrifices of his father, but he had no one with whom he could discuss the subject. Even Mis' Mary counseled him to silence, silence. The boy was not even known as Gilbert Turner. As was the slave custom, he took the name of the man to whom his young Mis' Mary was married.

Yet, Gilbert, in secret, thought many times of his early home, a happy home, in spite of slavery, for there was love and Christian fellowship in the home. He remembered the hours of daily family prayer in his father's cabin, the exhortations not to partake of strong drink, and thus defile the body, and not to take God's name in vain, and thus defile the soul.

Mis' Mary saw to it that he was privately fed by the cook, in the kitchen, and was not put down to eat out of the big trough, filled with pot liquor and scraps of corn pone, commonly provided for slave children.

Mis' Mary also early made it known that Gilbert was not to be subjected to the periodic lashings by the overseer, to which it was the custom to subject the young Negro boys, in order to break their will power.

Gilbert was grateful to Mis' Mary, but, in his inner mind, he could not be said to be happy. He knew from the teachings and example of his father that he was born to be a free man, and not a chattel. He plainly saw all the cruelty and inhumanity of slavery, though he was spared being subjected to some of it. He vaguely remembered stories his queenly-looking black grandmother had told of the happiness of the family in Africa, before they were captured, and before the dark days of slavery,—of their comfortable home along the beautiful river, of the flocks and herds, the fruits, the crops, the circle of loyal and contented friends.

According to slave customs, Gilbert was never allowed to have a book or paper in his hands, for fear he might, by some means, learn to read. He was permitted to attend only a white church, sitting in the gallery, for fear he might become a preacher, like his father, and thus a leader among his people, and might teach them that slavery was intolerable, and was an institution doomed for destruction.

After the Anglo-Saxon minister had gently led the aristocracy, that sat in comfortable pews on the first floor of the church, past streams of sparkling and living waters into a bright land of peace, flowing with milk and honey, he would lift his eyes and his voice, and address the gallery, dressed in blue-jeans and calico and, for the most part, barefooted. He had one perennial and perpetual text. It was, "Servants, obey your masters. That is your only hope for happiness on earth, and for entrance into Heaven."

The black servants dropped their eyes to the floor, in mute and apparent humble submission. Any skeptical looks would be akin to blasphemy, and would cause a number of floggings for unseemly decorum in the house of worship. But, as I later gathered [from] the reports from the ex-slaves, the gallery or balcony as it was called, was, in reality, filled with a congregation of Dissenters.

Gilbert often thought of running away to Ohio, the free state, that seemed so near to, and yet so far from, Virginia. But, a sense of honor held him back. Mis' Mary, who, as a young lady, had rescued and befriended him as a child, was having a struggle. If it had not been for her kindly act, Gilbert knew that he might not be alive today. Now that he had grown to be a young man, Mis' Mary was growing old. Her health was not good. Her children were growing up, young, rich, selfish,—and had little thought of their mother's comfort. Her husband, like many another cavalier of that day, had been poor, but of good family, and had married her, a rich young woman, caring more for what she possessed than he cared about Mis' Mary herself. According to the old custom brought over from England, a husband became absolute boss and possessor of all his bride possessed. Therefore, Mis' Mary saw her estate wasted, squandered on other women, and used for making a fine gentleman out of her husband, instead of being used for her own comfort. So, often, if the healthy young Gilbert had not gone deep into the woods to get fuel, and had not caught squirrels, rabbits and other game for her delicate appetite, and diligently looked after her own private vegetable garden, and sat up at nights to give her medicine at regular periods, when she was ill, Mis' Mary would have passed many miserable and neglected hours.

Gilbert had remarkable skill for working in iron. It seems to have been a talent he inherited from his African ancestors. He would fashion iron bowls and utensils of marvelous beauty and durability. Also, he could make them so small they could be used as mantel ornaments. These were the days before many imported articles had found their way into the South. So Gilbert's ornamental iron pieces became quite a fad in Southampton County, Virginia. Many fair-minded people were willing to pay the genial good-natured Gilbert a fair price for his wares, made at odd periods in the blacksmith shop on the plantation. Mis' Mary allowed no one to take this money from Gilbert. And, thus, he saved a few dollars for he feared that, if Mis' Mary should die, life might become so cruel and arduous for him that he might have to attempt to purchase his own freedom.

Gilbert was allowed no books, no newspapers, no periodicals, that his eyes could see. As far as possible, he was kept in ignorance. But there was one avenue of intelligence that even slavery could not close. That avenue consisted of Gilbert's ears. And, through his ears, Gilbert gained a fair degree of education.

Gilbert listened to the conversation of his masters as they sat at table. Through this means, he learned to speak perfectly correct English. He never used dialect. I never remember having heard him make a grammatical error. He, having good eyes and steady nerves, was used as carriage boy, to drive the masters to court, to political meetings, even to the Virginia Assembly, at Richmond. We must remember that the railroads were just getting well started in the days before the Civil War, and had not penetrated all sections of the country. Busses [*sic*] and automobiles were unheard of and, in most cases, undreamed of. The orthodox claimed that even to attempt to make a horseless carriage would be blasphemy against the Maker, who had created horses, donkeys and oxen as man's beasts of burden. So Gilbert, as carriage boy, sat quietly in the corner, hearing and digesting all things, while the masters acted the parts of lawyers, orators, judges.

Gilbert had his eyes open, even if his mouth was ordained by the law of the land to be closed. He knew that the South was fast getting at variance with the North. The walls of slavery's citadel were slowly but surely crumbling. His father, Nat Turner, with the prophetic eyes of Isaiah, had seen aright. "The ax was laid at the foot of the tree. The last should be first, and the first should be last."

Gilbert then thought of the words of his mother, whispered to him from the auction block:

> Trust in the Lord,
> And you'll overcome,
> Somehow,
> Somewhere,
> Someday!

Could it be possible that the government itself would get tired of slavery as a loathsome institution, without the slaves rebelling? He remembered what his father had told him about the Bible (Gilbert was not allowed to see or handle a Bible himself), about the freeing of the children of Israel, who wandered forty years in the wilderness. It had been nearly thirty years since Nat Turner's rebellion. Gilbert did not exactly know his age, but the slave overseers had him listed on their rolls as a man between thirty-five and forty years of age. Was it the will of God, that, after wandering for forty years in the wilderness of slavery, and misery, and toil, and family exile, that there ever was to shine on Gilbert the bright sunlight of human and blessed individual freedom? Was freedom ever to be a blessing bestowed on black people? [. . .]

John Brown rebelled, Lincoln was elected, and the Civil War was on in full swing. Like the rest of the Virginia slaves, Gilbert had to maintain a wooden face when any happenings, such as the defeat of a Confederate general, or the exploits of the Union soldiers, were mentioned. If a black person displayed, even by the flicker of an eyelid, that he was relishing the discomfiture of the Southern gentry and slaveholders, he was liable to be shot,—since it was impossible, because of war conditions, to sell him to the far south. Hence, the slave had to keep up the attitude that whatever was to the master's advantage and interest, was to the interest and for the well-being of the slave, also.

Then toward the heat of the Civil War struggle, Mis' Mary's irresponsible sons and husband were called to war. They were a pleasure-loving set, not used to hardships and deprivation, but given to a life of riotous living and selfish ease. Being past middle age, Mis' Mary's husband might have stayed at home, but, being a slave holder, he went forth, to protect his "property interest." Mis' Mary, fearful for their safety, asked that they take along the sober, strong willed Gilbert, in name to be their cook and body servant, but in reality, to be their protector.

Gilbert was not loath to go. Prophetically, he knew very well how the struggle would turn out. Slavery would soon be over, and the bondmen would be free. Had not his father, Nat Turner, seen it thirty years before, in the eclipse of the sun, in the stars, and in the leaves? Nat Turner had told all his men the epic story of slavery, and that the slaves could be free, if they would purchase their freedom with their own blood, and have the manhood and the courage to themselves strike the first blow. A few black men believed, and went forward to sacrifice themselves upon the altar of freedom. But the white men turned a deaf ear, and would not believe him. They would not let his people go. They had to have these truths borne in upon their minds and engraved upon their hearts, by blood and sweat and tears, and by the slaughter of their first born sons during the dark days of the Civil War.

So Gilbert went cheerfully along with the army of his masters. It mattered not with which army he went. The results of the conflict had already been decided in Heaven. But Gilbert, by going, could fulfill his trust to Mis' Mary, by protecting her family, just as she had sought to protect his family.

This going to war with the Confederate army had its compensations also. While Gilbert had been taken to many places in Southampton

County and other parts of Virginia, always calling Farmsville his home, he had not had much contact outside of the state. Now he traveled far and widely. He had first hand views of the great men of the Southland in action: General Lee and President Jeff Davis and other great and near-great. He went with the conflict from Virginia to the Carolinas, and back again.

Then, when the great and decisive day came, and Lee surrendered the Confederate army at Appomattox Court House, Gilbert saw all the celebrities from both sides of the conflict as he stood on the sidelines, holding the army mules in check. His thankfulness knew no bounds, that the long awaited day of deliverance had at last arrived, and his heart sang so loudly that Gilbert thought it was the voices of the angels, singing in the air.

Well, the Confederate army returned home, the Caucasian part, tired, dismantled, disgruntled that their "Property" had, in the twinkling of an eye, been transformed from "Property" to free men,—the colored part, secretly jubilant, treading on air, but scared to show it, for to laugh or even smile at the defeat and discomfiture of the proud Southland was utter blasphemy, and a sin for which there was no forgiveness.

Mis' Mary was very ill when her husband and sons returned, with the servant, Gilbert. The war, with its heartaches and privations, had been too much for her. Her eldest, most thoughtful and most highly talented son, had been killed near the close of the conflict.

She called Gilbert to her bedside. "My dark son, Gilbert," she said, "for thirty years I have sought to protect you from this terrible scourge of slavery. Now that it is over, I beg of you to go, and go at once. For who knows that slavery is really dead? It may be only stunned and sleeping. It may awake in a few short months to be a more deadly monster than it had ever been in the past. I am an old woman now. I have only a few more months to live. But I could not die in peace, if I thought I was leaving you to be sold far South, to toil and sweat and die, under the overseer's lash, and the blazing sun of a southern plantation."

So Gilbert took her advice and headed for the North with nothing but a strong constitution to show for nearly forty years of slave labor. His master, who controlled all the property, offered him not a penny to help him on his journey, but graciously told him if he could not make it up North, and ever wanted to return "home," to get some one to write for him, and the master would send him a ticket.

Gilbert smiled graciously as he bade goodby[e] to his master. But his inward comment was, "I have been in Hell once. Now that God is leading me out, *I don't ever mean to go back into Hell again!*"

A Union army was boarding the train for Ohio, and the soldiers offered free passage to any ex-slave who wanted to go along. So Gilbert went along, trusting God, in his heart, his sole possession being a clean suit of work clothes, and having not a cent in his pocket, to buy either food or shelter.

Gilbert well understood the gracious offer of his master to send him a ticket home if he could not make it to the North. The master thought that no friendless, penniless, untutored slave, at the age of forty, had it in him to make a living and forge his way, in a land of white men, who had social, educational and money opportunities for countless generations. But Gilbert vowed within himself that he would either succeed or hide his failure in the grave. Had not the Divine Master said, "Come unto me, all ye that are weary and heavy laden, and I will give you *Rest!*"

When Gilbert, who had now taken the surname of Turner, which rightfully belonged to him, left the train at its first stop in Ohio, safely across the Mason and Dixon line, he found himself in the city of Marietta. He was welcomed to the city by a little band of colored Christian free people, who had banded themselves together to assist members of the race just let loose from slavery. They found temporary lodging for him by providing a cot in the hallway of the Baptist Church. They fed him in the church kitchen. They held night school for him in the church auditorium, where he soon learned to read and write under the tutelage of some members of the church, who had themselves received a fair common school education. Gilbert Turner was glad to receive, as a text book, not only a McGuffey Reader, but also a Bible. In slavery, he had been forbidden to even look at or handle a Bible, for he might be inspired with a desire to read it. The only text considered needful by the masters for the slaves to know, was: "Servants, obey your masters!" And this text was preached every Sunday by the white clergymen to the silent and submissive slaves in the church galleries.

All these books, food and services were paid for by the band of free people themselves, out of their meagre earnings, usually fifty or seventy-five cents per day. After setting the Negroes free, and thus doing their Christian duty, the majority class seemed to give little thought to the economic condition of the ex-slaves. They could sink or swim, survive or perish, each according to his ability, good luck, or whatever you might call it. And, in fact, many did perish, in the first years of freedom. They received such meagre food, that many of them starved to death. Many were turned loose, well past fifty, penniless, their bodies warped by lashings and hard labor, their kindred sold away from them, and if they ventured North, there was nothing for them but starvation or the poor house.

So, many of them remained with their masters after the Emancipation Proclamation, and worked for their board and keep, in a condition of semi-slavery. The people of this year, 1955, must remember that in the seventies, the eighties and even in the nineties, there were no such funds even dreamed of as Relief, Unemployment Compensation, Child Aid and Old Age Pensions. The most soul-stirring song of the day was: "Over the Hill to the Poor-House!" Most of the poor people had either sung it, or were fearful that they might have to sing it soon. And to many a weary ex-slave, who had spent the strength of his youth in toiling for his master, without thanks or compensation, the county poor house was a bare but restful haven. It, at least, protected him from the rigors of the weather when he lay down to die.

Because of his skill in iron, Gilbert Turner soon got a job in a small iron foundry. Now that he had found a job, it was up to him to prove to the world that he was able to handle his freedom, even though he had never had a free day until he was nearly forty years old. He knew that all the master class were property owners. So Gilbert wasted little time in boarding and rooming.

Being a sober, frugal man, he saved his wages, and in about a year, bought several hundred feet of land in the heart of the city of Marietta. There he built a small comfortable house, largely constructed by his own labor, and there he lived alone, under his own vine and fig tree.

He cooked, washed, ironed and scrubbed for himself. The steady work habits learned in slavery stood him in good stead. He was quite popular among the young Christian people of Marietta, for, at forty, he still had the strength and youthful appearance of a man in his early twenties.

Gilbert Turner probably would have made Marietta his lifetime home, had not a destructive flood visited Marietta early in the 1870s, and washed away his home and other accumulations of nearly ten years of hard labor. Then Gilbert learned that Marietta was so near the Ohio River that it was often visited by such floods. But Gilbert took his loss cheerfully, echoing with Job: "Though He slay me, yet will I trust Him!"

Gilbert decided not to build again upon the Marietta land. He had gotten too far along the road to old age to risk the loss of ten more years of back-breaking labor. So he decided to still hold title to his Marietta land, but to move on up into Ohio, and seek higher ground. From some fellow workmen he had heard of a town, Zanesville, Ohio, in the valleys of the Muskingun and Licking Rivers, but skirted on all sides by high hills, almost of mountainous heights. Here a man named Blandy, of the historic and wealthy Blandy family of that day, had a foundry, employing only white workmen, probably because no colored men of the town knew the iron trade.

So Gilbert Turner journeyed to Zanesville, about the year 1873, and was there given shelter by Dr. McSimpson, a wealthy colored herb doctor.

Mr. Blandy, although from a wealthy family, sympathized with this ambitious ex-slave, nearing middle-age, who was trying so hard to make his way in the world. When Gilbert showed Blandy some of the iron ornaments he had made Blandy was much pleased.

"Why, Gilbert!" he exclaimed, "You know more about iron manufacture than even my head foreman!" He bade Gilbert go into the foundry and start work at once. And Gilbert went.

When the fairer skinned workmen saw a dark skinned workman among them, they were incensed. There were no labor unions in those days, but there was the age-old sentiment against Negro skilled labor. The white men went to Blandy in a body. "Turn him off," they cried. "Turn him off. We want only white men in our foundry!"

Blandy's answer was so short, so true, so just and so forceful, that it should go down in history as an epic epigram.

"You don't have to eat with that N——, and you don't have to sleep with that N——, and if you can't work with that N——, go down to the office and get your pay!"

So a truce was called, and everybody went back to work, and Gilbert was soon the most valued and popular man about the place. Gilbert worked at the foundry for over seven years, until it was dismantled on the death of Blandy.

Gilbert received good money for his work, and true to his motto of showing that he had as much business sense as his southern masters, he bought, with his savings, a palatial brick house, at 99 Eighth Street, in Zanesville, Ohio.

This brick residence, bought by Gilbert Turner, had once been the mansion of a rich family. It had eight large rooms, light and airy, vestibules, broad halls, carved banisters, winding staircases, a stone porch, and a roomy lot, well shaded by trees. This house was in the principal part of town, known as the Third Ward, not far from the Court House and the business section. The place was high and dry, where no floods could come.

Gilbert Turner worked long and faithful 'til 1880, affiliated with the Union Baptist Church, paid entirely for his home, furnished it with Brussels carpets and carved and cushioned furniture, such as he had seen in the homes of his Virginia masters, and in the home of his patron saint, Mis' Mary.

Then he felt like, at last, he was in the position to ask some one to share his fortunes. So he took himself a wife. She was Sarah Ellen Jones, a very modest woman, the thirty year old daughter of the Rev. Isaac Jones, pastor of the Baptist Church in Putnam, a suburb of Zanesville, and at the present time annexed to the larger city. [. . .]

So Sarah Ellen Turner, being sincerely in love with Gilbert, whom she admired and respected for his long and hard fight against stupendous odds, did her best to make his home a happy one. She also worked long and hard that her children might have the best in education. When Gilbert was out of work, Sarah, though a frail woman of little over one hundred pounds, would go out to do the washings, every day of the year, sometimes through snow waist deep, getting less than one dollar per day. She knew that food, clothing and school books were needed by her children. For when the children were going to school in the 1890s, Gilbert was fast approaching seventy years of age, and even with his iron constitution, his strength was beginning to fail. Then, too, the pressure against colored men in industry was beginning to be felt, and colored men found it impossible, in some cases, to find employment.

Then Gilbert Turner used the talent that to this day has made him remembered and famous in the history of Zanesville, Ohio. He had a voice of remarkable beauty and carrying power. It had the clearness of a clarion and the ring of a bell. Once lifted, his voice could set the echoes reverberating from hill to hill, and his cry could be heard for ten or more miles, among the hills. It is said the Africans signal with drums and voice, and Gilbert, as a child, may have learned how to do it from some old African he met in slavery.

Foundry work having failed, Gilbert Turner took up the trade of putting iron hoops on the wooden washing tubs of that day. In fact, years ago, it had been a part of Gilbert's duty to thus keep in repair the washing tubs used on the plantation of Mis' Mary. Very few of the slaves could measure well enough to fit these hoops accurately, neatly and water-tight. So Gilbert often earned, in slavery, a few pennies by hooping tubs on neighboring plantations.

"Any washing tubs to hoop?" was his cry, and it could be heard reverberating all over the hilly town of Zanesville, Ohio and echoing far into the country. [. . .]

Gilbert Turner named his first child, born in 1882, Fannie, after that dearly beloved but long lost mother of his, who was sold away from him, so cruelly, on the auction block, when he was but a little boy. The next child, born in 1884, was named Lucy, after her maternal grandmother, the wife of Rev. Isaac Jones. Two twin children were born a few years later, Gilbert Jr. and Gracie, but both of these twins died within a few weeks of their birth. It was a great sorrow to both parents to lose these two children, particularly little Gilbert, the only son in the family. But they bowed in humble submission to God's will. [. . .]

The family moved to [a] farm on Coopermill Road in April 1892. The place was very beautiful, level and fertile in the front, with orchards and vineyards, and even a hot house or green house, covered with a roof of glass, and filled with all kinds of small fruit and flowering shrubs. At the back of the level land there was a rippling brook, and then arose a hill, rounded and forest-covered. To be found in the hill were coal, building stone and other minerals. The house was a comfortable dwelling of a Colonial type of architecture. [. . .]

But, one cold night in November, 1892, a few months after moving to the farm, the country home and all the treasured family possessions were destroyed by fire. The family was left homeless and penniless in the street.

We will remember that, in those days, there was no such thing as public aid,—at least, the poor colored people received none. If one got out of work or out of doors, he just wandered around until he mercifully froze to death or starved to death. If he survived long enough for his misery to become a shame, a rebuke and a reproach to his more prosperous neighbors, then such poor outcast was sent to the county poor farm, deep in the heart of the country, so as not to constantly remind the rich of their religious duty to practice the Golden Rule.

But Gilbert Turner was like Job. His faith in God was so great that he showed to the world the truth of the verse: "Though He slay me, yet will I trust Him." Gilbert found a large dwelling house, abandoned, in town, and was able to buy it for the sake of the lumber in it. Though nearly seventy years old, he tore it down, single-handed, although the house was nearly two and one-half stories high. I, Lucy, as a child of seven or eight, used to sit in the yard of the house, as a protector, to summon aid, in case he should fall. But he never fell, being protected by God.

Soon, the Turner family was back on the Coopermill Road farm in a comfortable one-story cottage, not as large as the first house but more practical. The day of bungalows and smaller homes was coming in to replace the large luxurious mansions of Civil War days. They were cheaper to purchase, easier to heat, and easier to be managed without the help of slaves or servants.

My sister Fannie and I were well pleased. We enjoyed the healthful atmosphere of the country. We had learned much. We now knew that there were really snakes, and that the crawling creatures which were called snakes when we lived in town on English Street were, in reality, only fishing worms.

Our farm neighbors were mostly Dutch and German, and very friendly. But, since we went to town to attend integrated grade school and high school and the Union Baptist colored church, we kept in close touch and formed enduring friendships with both the colored adults and the children.

We will understand that this was just a little over twenty years after the slaves were freed, and both the white and colored people still retained some warped ideals. All the adult population had lived in the days of slavery. Many of the whites were disgruntled because they had been reduced to poverty by the freeing of their slaves. Such would openly tell the freedmen that they wished they had the money that the slaves used to bring them in the open market. To them, it would be the signal for a verbal outburst to even mention the name Nat Turner.

Many of the Northern born colored people whose ancestors had, through various means, obtained their freedom and moved away from the South before the Emancipation Proclamation, openly snubbed the recently freed slaves, as being of a much lower social stratum, and vastly inferior to themselves. They had not the hard common sense and reasoning power to check their prejudices and to disclose to them, that, in those troublous [sic] times, it was but a trick of fate whether one obtained his freedom in 1843, 1853, or not until 1863. The only means for the advancement of the whole colored race was in their working harmoniously together. [. . .]

I, Lucy, was a favorite child with all the adult ex-slaves, my father's friends and associates. My father, who had succeeded just a little better financially than some of the other ex-slaves, opened his home to any newly arrived ex-slave who found himself penniless and stranded in the town. My father felt it his Christian duty to give them free board and lodging until they were able to get along independently. He was prayerful and grateful, and never forgot the day when he himself needed the assistance of his fellowmen.

These ex-slaves would sit by the open fireplace of evenings, and go through the story of slavery from Nat Turner's insurrection to the assassination of President Abraham Lincoln. They would fight the Civil War from Tom Brown at Harper's Ferry to Lee's surrender. Some of the older ones had lived on George Washington's plantation, and could remember faintly back to his times. Most of these slaves had been house servants, and were full of quaint anecdotes about Lee, Clay, Calhoun, Jeff Davis and others,—which anecdotes, though true, never found their way into polite United States history.

Negro History, in those days, was a profane subject, only to be whispered in the chimney corners and never discussed in the open or in polite society.

My father, Gilbert Turner, has now been dead for forty years, having died in November, 1914, and, had I known how interesting those old folk tales would be today, I would have endeavored to write them out in long hand, the purchase of a typewriter having been for me a financial impossibility at that time. Still, after forty years, his voice still echoes in my ears, telling the story of slavery.

Where the West Begins,
from *American Daughter*

Mandan marks the beginning of the real West. It is here Mountain Time begins, here the Indians come from the reservation to greet the tourist trains and dance at the big rodeo; here, on this side of the river, live the rattlers; and farther to the west, in the Bad Lands, is the town of Medora, once the ranch home of Teddy Roosevelt and his fabulous friend, the French nobleman, the Marquis de Mores.

The town was proud of its historical significance, worked hard to maintain it. Few Negroes had ever lived in Mandan—never more than two or three at a time. Most of its seven thousand people were Russian-German, living in Dutch and Russian hollows, bits of the Old Country, complete in their quaintness, transplanted deep between the sharp hills at the north end of town. Scrubbed wooden benches leaned against light blue and pale green houses, earthenware jugs stood by the doors. English was seldom spoken.

Here Pop opened his secondhand store in a little four-room house on Main Street between Wagner's Hotel and the Morton Construction Company. For a long time the store smelled. Its former tenant made and sold moonshine, and the tenants before him had babies—so many babies they were said to have slept sideways in the bed. Pop scrubbed the store, drenched it with creosote, and burned sulphur, but it retained the sour odor of bad liquor and something else—customers. All night long men tapped on the back doors and windows calling softly for a boot-legger named Joe. They thought Deacon Thompson was running a speakeasy.

Source: Excerpted from Era Bell Thompson, *American Daughter* (Chicago: University of Chicago Press, 1946), pp. 145–152.

When I joined Pop in Mandan, our neighbors were already our friends. I was a godsend to Elsie Wagner, living in the rear of the hotel with her parents and brothers—and the old men who sat around in the lobby like gray vultures, their eyes following every female figure, their mouths drooling tobacco. Elsie and I became inseparable. Pop said that every time he looked up there was Elsie, and that when he looked again we were both gone. The elder Wagners said it was the same with me. "She's a gute girl, that Era Bell," Mrs. Wagner would say, and Pop would tell her, "I'm glad she's with your girl. Let 'em have fun while they're young, laugh while they can. What you s'pose they always laughin' at?"

"Oh, God, I don't know!" Mrs. Wagner would smile her tired smile. "They laugh alla the time, always laughing. They don't need not'ings to make them laugh."

We didn't know, either. Sometimes we would just stand before a mirror and giggle, and when we'd catch Pop watching us we'd giggle all the harder. He'd laugh, too. He'd shake his head and say to himself, "Lord, Lord! I wonder is they crazy sure 'nuff?"

In all Mandan there was not one Baptist church, so with many apologies to his past faith, Pop succumbed and went to Mass. "They all right," he commented dryly when we got home, "but I'm too old for that religion." He rubbed his knees. "Them prayer-benches and all that gettin' up and gettin' down—and with my rheumatism, too—Lord, today, I wouldn't last out the week!" He looked at me. "You join if you want to, one religion just as good as another with you 'cause you ain't goin' to do no different no way."

"They wear hats to church," I replied. "I hate hats."

So Pop and I went over to the pretty Methodist church, where they stayed put in their pews and sang doleful hymns and took Deacon Thompson on probation and accepted me and my sins in full.

As rodeo time drew near, Pop's excitement grew with that of the town, and the call of the kitchen was strong upon him. "Lots of money to be made out there at that thing," he reasoned. "Now, I could sell some chicken sandwiches an' make a killin'." So, when the rodeo opened, Pop, like the Indians, pitched his tent at the fairgrounds and began to hawk his wares. Afternoons and evenings I sold sandwiches over the oilcloth counter, while Pop mysteriously converted each wizened, over-aged hen into sixteen golden-brown, highly inflated morsels at a quarter a sandwich. Business got so good I went to Bismark and got Gwyn to help us. Carnival people, fed up on the traditional American hot dog and hamburger, flocked to our stand, and even the Indians deserted their tents and tepees—after I found Priscilla. She was living with the other Indians at the far end of the racetrack, where spotted ponies grazed on wild grass, dried meat hung in long strips on ropes between the trees, and dogs snapped at the flies and scratched their mangy sides. When Priscilla came to visit me, she asked for a hot dog.

"Try chicken," I urged. "You've got dogs at home."

"How much?" she asked.

"Ten cents to you." I looked at the old woman beside her. "Is that your mother?"

"Yes." She said something in Sioux. The woman pulled her shawl around her thin shoulders and smiled at me. She said nothing. "My mother don't speak American," said the girl.

Old Country, I thought. Only it wasn't Old Country: it was this country. Nearly all my friends were second generation; their parents spoke the mother tongue, wore the native clothes, had the ways of the fatherland, even the Indians. In a sense I was second generation, too, only Pop had no other language, but in the ways of the world he was far ahead of me. My Latin and geometry didn't make any more sense to my father than they did to my friends' fathers. They didn't make too much sense to me.

"Both of you try chicken," I offered, giving them the biggest pieces I could find.

The next morning the old lady returned. Gwyn and Pop tried to wait on her, but she stood at the counter, silent and unmoved. When I came at noon, she was still there. "Chick-on," she said, holding out a dime.

"So that's why she waited for you. Tell her chicken's a quarter, and we don't pick out no more big pieces," Pop said peevishly.

"More," I said, picking up a quarter from the cash box. "Like this."

She shook her head and smiled. "Chick-on."

"Pop," I pleaded. "You know I can't talk Indian. This is Priscilla's mother. Priscilla is my friend from the School. Can't we let her have it this time? She likes your cooking; she'll tell her friends, and you'll get lots of trade."

Pop had visions of the whole tribe descending upon him with dimes. "Give her somethin' an' git her away from here. She been takin' up cash-customer room all day. Then you go find that friend of yours an' stop them folks, hear? I got no time to interrupt my cookin' to go fightin' Indians." [. . .]

I loved the Indian war dances. Every evening they gathered in front of the grandstand in the twilight, dressed in all their fine feathers and elk's teeth and beaded moccasins, the chiefs and warriors wearing long headdresses and carrying hatchets in their fringed buffalo pants. Beneath the war paint were gentleness and quiet joy in their make-believe. The dance was a picturesque thing, weird and exotic. A tall brave would step out into the center of the chanting circle, head bent low, knees pumping high, dancing to the throb of the tom-tom; a strenuous dance it was, punctuated by bloodcurdling yells, a dance that raised beads of sweat on his naked, brown back, made his makeup run down his high cheeks. While the bucks danced, I often joined the squaws in a smooth little sidestep around the edge of the circle until some brash individual asked what tribe I belonged to: the Crows or the Blackfeet. [. . .]

Hardly a morning passed that some hobo or tramp didn't cross over the tracks and come to our store. They were like Slim, the I.W.W.* who helped us thresh: happy-go-lucky, philosophical, radical, religious; all ages, all nationalities, come to buy or barter for clothing, shaving equipment, pocketknives, pans—yes, even Bibles. One old man came and went with the birds. He had a gold chain—a beautiful chain, with a large cross at the end. The first time we saw him, he talked with Pop about God, about brotherly love. Pop asked him where he was going.

"Nowhere," he said. "Can't stay long in one place. I like to feel free, to not be beholdin' to any man, so I follow the birds and talk with God, and I am happy."

"You hungry, too?" Pop looked at him closely.

"No, no," he said pleasantly. "God feeds me."

"He feeds me, too," Pop countered. "We'll have a bite together. I was just goin' to make some coffee anyhow."

After they had eaten, the old man pulled out his chain and broke off a few links. "I have no money." He held the links out to my father.

"No, no. I don't want your chain. You don't owe me nothin'."

"Take them, brother, they are for you."

"I'm a Christian, too. I can't do that," Pop protested.

"Then keep them, brother, till I need them."

Pop kept the chain in the Bible where it said, "Inasmuch as ye have

*Industrial Workers of the World (IWW) was a radical international industrial labor union organized in Chicago; it disintegrated after 1920.

done it unto one of the least of these." Each time the old man came, his chain was shorter and shorter. He would take no money, so Pop fed him, gave him shoes and coats, and they talked about God, took up where they left off as if it were only yesterday. The last time we saw him, only the big cross remained. Pop took his links from the Bible and slipped them into his bundle.

"I got a feelin'," Pop said when he was gone, "that he won't come back no more. He's come to the cross, and his journey's most nigh over." But every spring when the birds flew North and every fall when the tumbling tumbleweeds began to roll, Pop stood at the door and watched the tracks. He did not come again.

When Elsie and her brothers started to school in the fall, I wanted to attend the local business college, but there was no money except the thousand-dollar note the elevator man still owned us for the farm. Crops failed miserably after we left Sterling, and land values decreased until the note was worthless.

"Maybe I could get something out of it," I told Father.

"How you goin' to collect when the lawyers couldn't?"

"If I get anything, can I have it?"

"Yes, Lord, if you get it."

I sat down and wrote the elevator man a letter about the business college, and he sent me a check for seventy-five dollars. Pop never quite got over it, but he let me keep the money. In October I went up to the high school and talked to the principal. It was a little irregular, he said, but if I thought I could make up the work, why, yes, I could take a postgraduate commercial course; so I went back to school and kept the seventy-five dollars.

My first day wasn't too happy. As the principal and I started down the hall for the commercial room, classes began to pass down the long, dark corridor, and the students were upon us before they noticed me. Some stopped stock-still and stared the way people did on Main Street, some shied away, and one big, husky boy even screamed. I hurried along, trying to keep up with the long strides of the principal, ignoring the confusion that followed in my wake.

The blonde shorthand teacher was wholly unprepared for my coming. As she talked her big, gray eyes never moved from my face. She was seeing her first colored girl.

"She'll work hard and catch up," the principal was saying; "I'm sure she will."

"Catch up! Why, we're a month ahead of her now. A whole month, and I already have one backward class."

"I know, I know," he soothed. "She'll take her work home, she'll practice hard. Won't you?" He stopped short with sudden apprehension; but I was so busy returning the stare I nearly missed my cue.

"Well," she said peevishly, "I'll try it. But if she can't keep up, she can't stay."

I stayed, and had a wonderful time. The first few days the little class was divided between those bent upon being nice to me and the others. By the end of the second week they were all bent on being nice to me, vying to walk home with me. Teacher changed, too. With nothing else to do except shorthand, I caught up so rapidly she urged me to join her bookkeeping class and she let me practice typing when there was an extra machine. And when there wasn't I used the principal's portable. Soon I was writing for the school paper, taking part in all their activities, and creating a few of my own. [. . .]

That winter I found another interest—the *Chicago Defender.* By enlarging upon and fictionalizing the commonplace events of the [Evans] and Thompson households, I created enough news to become a correspondent. My first feature, an attack upon Marcus Garvey's "Back to Africa" movement for Negroes, brought my first fan mail, a letter from one of his followers who even scorched the outside of the letter; so I gave up social reform, assumed the pseudonym of "Dakota Dick," and became a contributor to the "Lights and Shadows" column as a bad, bad cowboy from the wild and wooly West. The Mandan Chamber of Commerce could not have done better. Came friendly letters from colored pen pals beyond the hills. When an article to *Physical Culture* magazine netted me three dollars, I [. . .] hooked my wagon to a literary star.

DELILAH LEONTIUM BEASLEY

From *The Negro Trailblazers* *of California*

The writer on giving this history of the Negro in California has, by careful research, endeavored to secure the name of every "Trail Blazer," from the first Negro guide with an exploring party, to the having of Spanish documents translated for the truthfulness of statements made by other writers concerning the Negro in California. At great expense she has solicited and entreated persons of the race who have blazed a trail in any particular line to allow this history to give their experience for the encouragement of the race. Often the desired information has been withheld through a false pride as to the struggle and hardships encountered in their upward climbs. They seem to forget that they owe it to the future generation of Negroes to tell of this struggle that it might aid them to not lose heart. This has not been the policy of "Madam Sul-Te-Wan," who has secured her place in the motion picture world.

The motion picture, which we have all learned to appreciate as a mode of advanced entertainment, has but few Negro players who serve with white companies. In California it is a great industry. Many of our women made good wages serving motion picture actresses. There is one and only one Negress motion picture actress in "stock" on the Pacific Coast. She is employed at a good salary by Mr. D. W. Griffith, the producer of the film "The Clansman." This little lady, Madam Sul-Te-Wan, is a legitimate actress and her upward climb into the motion picture world is most interesting and worthy of the pen of a great writer. Nevertheless the

Source: Excerpted from Delilah Leontium Beasley, *The Negro Trailblazers of California* (reprint, New York: Negro Universities Press, 1969), pp. 239–241.

author will attempt to give the reader some of the facts in her upward climb to this high position, for she is glad of the fact that she is a true representative of the race and her sketch will show that she has reached this position on merit alone.

There are some persons in the race who do not like to speak of their lowly birth because of the poverty of their parents, forgetting that honest poverty is no disgrace. Madam Sul-Te-Wan is proud of the fact that her mother was a washerwoman and, as a widow, washed for actresses that she might secure good prices and ready pay. This little lady, as a girl, would deliver the washing to the actresses at the stage door, and thereby was often permitted to remain and see the show. This was in Louisville, Kentucky. The next day she would rehearse the act at school and tell her classmates that some day she, too, would be an actress.

The mother was too poor to have her daughter trained either to sing or dance. But all the time she was delivering the washings to such well-known actresses as Mary Anderson and Fanny Davenport, two of the best teachers possible and who could not have been employed for any sum as a teacher. These renowned actresses and singers became very much interested in this nut-brown daughter of their washerwoman. So convinced were they that she had talent that they enlisted the assistance of the then Mayor of Louisville, a Mr. James Whalen, who had charge of the Buckingham Theater. He gave this little colored girl a trial, and used, as an attraction at his theater, twenty-five little colored girls who did singing and dancing. He offered a prize for the best "buck and wing dancer." The first prize was a granite dishpan and granite spoon. It was won by the subject of this sketch. This gave her confidence in herself. Her mother was very proud of the granite dishpan and spoon, and decided to allow her daughter to fill other engagements. After she was fully convinced that she did have talent she moved with her to Cincinnati, Ohio.

The move to Cincinnati was a good venture for this widow washerwoman, for it gave her daughter a broader field in which to develop her talent among strangers. This little dancing protege of Mary Anderson and Fanny Davenport readily found work for weeks at a time at the Dime Museum, located on Vine Street, Cincinnati, Ohio. Afterward in the family theaters "Over the Rhine," as a section of that city is known. This led to her finally joining a company called the "Three Black Cloaks." She played under the title "Creole Nell" while in Cincinnati and won recognition. By assuming this title she soon again came in communication with Miss Fanny Davenport, who sent her a telegram to secure for her some colored players to take some minor part in a play she was playing, as she was coming to Cincinnati.

Her experience in Cincinnati, and the aid given to Miss Davenport, gave this little actress supreme confidence in her own ability, and she, too, decided that she could and did organize a company which was known as "The Black Four Hundred," which employed sixteen performers and twelve musicians. She traveled throughout the eastern States with this company, meeting with great success. The next season she organized and staged another company which she called "The Rair Back Minstrels." The success attending this adventure was so very great that she was besieged to marry and did marry.

But alas, the marriage of an actress or singer does not always spell success and happiness! The subject of our sketch came to the Pacific Coast and, after a residence in California of about two years, her husband deserted her with three little boys, the youngest being three weeks old. She became so reduced in finances that she was compelled to go before the Forum Club and beg for assistance, which they gave her three different times. She was presented to the Forum by Mr. J. W. Coleman, the employment agent. She was accompanied by her three children. When the time came for her to address the grand body of gentlemen, she began to cry, whereupon her oldest son, who was not yet seven years, looking up into his mother's face said: "Mother, you are not begging. We are going to sing and earn what they give you." He and his little brother sang as they had never sung before and greatly impressed the Forum Club.

Madam Sul-Te-Wan was living in Arcadia, and her husband not only deserted her with these three children, but he failed to pay the rent with the money she had sent home from her singing and dancing. She was left with ten months' back rent to pay. The Associated Charities of Los Angeles brought her into town and rented a place for her and her children. It is pitiful to hear how she then struggled to obtain work. Madame Sul-Te-Wan had never done anything else from a little girl but sing and dance. She knew nothing about housework, for she hired someone to stay with her children while she danced in the East and for a while in California. The first time in her life she was confronted with a mighty problem, how to become an immediate bread-winner for herself and three children. The white theatrical booking companies did not give her any engagements, claiming that they did not make independent bookings, and other excuses. She did not wish to become a charge on the charity of the neighbors and her children must have bread. She finally secured an engagement at the Pier Theater of Venice, California. This short engagement did not pay very much and it did not require long for her to use the money up. There was a long, long spell of idleness and tramping the streets to try and find something to do. Finally, as a last resort, she decided to go to Mr. D. W. Griffith, who at the time was producing "The Clansman." She had heard that he was employing a great number of colored people. She personally went to Mr. Griffith and presented her card. He immediately hired her at three dollars per day, which seemed like a fortune to her at the time. After the first day's work he immediately gave her five dollars per day. He was so impressed with her acting that he immediately had written a separate sketch for "The Clansman," in which she appeared as a rich colored lady, finely gowned and owner of a Negro colony of educated colored citizens, who not only owned their own land, but she drove her own coach and four-in-hand. This scene was to show the advancement of the Negro from ante-bellum days to this present period. After the picture was made (and Madam was so proud of the money she had earned), the censor cut the part out in which she appeared as a rich colored lady, and other parts, leaving only the bitter-gall portions for the insults of the Negro race throughout the nation. Madam also appeared in the mob scene in the "The Clansman," and carried a fan given her by Mary Anderson when she was a school child carrying the washing to the stage door. During her acting in the mob scene she lost the fan and stopped her action, whereupon Mr. Griffith called through the speaking trumpet, "Go on; I will buy you another fan. Your acting is good; go on." After "The Clansman" was finished there was nothing else for her to do, and the three little children must have bread and rent must be paid. So one day she decided that she wanted the money that Mr. Griffith would give for the purchase of a new fan, as he had said on that particular day. She went out to the studio and asked him if he would not give her the money that he would give to purchase her another fan, as he had said on that particular day, as she needed the money worse than the fan, even if it was a keepsake gift from Mary Anderson, whereupon Mr. Griffith gave her a check for twenty-five dollars and placed her on the pay-roll at five dollars per day, work or play. He then went to New York with the picture, "The Clansman."

"The Clansman" at the same time began to play in Los Angeles and the Negro people proceeded to have the censor cut out some objectionable features of the film. The next week's pay envelope contained a notice, "You are no longer needed." She inquired of the manager in charge why she was being discharged, and at first he would not give her a hearing. Then he told her some white actress had lost a Christian Science book and thought that she had stolen it and that she was responsible for the colored people fighting the film, "The Clansman." Madam Sul-Te-Wan was very angry and replied that her struggle for bread for her three children had prevented her from coming in contact with the educated members of the race who had time to read and study as to whether the film was detrimental to the race. She came seeking an opportunity to honestly earn bread for her three little children, and the work in "The Clansman" was the only door open for her to earn it. Madam further replied to the manager in charge that she would immediately get in touch with some of the educated and influential Negro people of Los Angeles and ask them to defend her from the accusation of being a thief and the arousing of unpopular sentiment against "The Clansman" after it had given her bread. She knew that they would deal justly with her as they were able to do with the film "The Clansman."

She left the studio and decided to go to that great humanitarian and lawyer, Edward Burton Ceruti, who, without cost to her, defended her, sending a letter to Mr. Griffith in New York and the manager in Hollywood at the studio. This resulted in Madam being reinstated on the pay-roll and later was featured in "The Marriage Market," in the film "Intolerance." She was also featured in "Happy Valley's Oldest Boy" and "Up from the Depths."

Last Spring [1917] the thought occurred to her that it would not be a bad idea to ask for a letter of recommendation, which Mr. Griffith readily consented that she was entitled to and instructed his manager to write the same. Afterward he relieved Madam Sul-Te Wan's fears that she might not secure work with other companies by introducing her to some of the leading motion picture film producers on the Pacific Coast, who have given her work in some of the best and most popular pictures made in the State. He also introduced her to Theda Bara and was the means of her employing Madam Sul-Te-Wan's middle son, John, to feature in "Madam DuBarry."

ELLEN TARRY

Native Daughter:
An Indictment of White America
by a Colored Woman

As a Negro, I have been greatly pleased to note the haste with which the literary world has acclaimed Richard Wright, author of the book "Native Son," as the greatest writer of his race. I rejoice not only because, like Richard Wright, I am a Negro, but because I am also familiar with the obstacles that confront young Negro writers. Even in the literary world, there are those who find it hard to visualize a black Bernard Shaw or a Louisa Alcott with kinky hair. For us, therefore, Richard Wright's triumph is signal.

However it is not Richard Wright's laurels that concern me so greatly. It is rather that in Catholic circles many have lamented the fact that the Negro writer who has arisen as the spokesman for his race should be a communist.

When Mr. Wright addressed a group of book lovers at the 135th Street branch of the New York Public Library on Thursday, March 7, I have been told that the young writer said he was a God-fearing communist. Be that as it may—if the young man said it, it only stresses his *conversion* to communism. I confess, by the way, that this is my first inkling that the communists included God in their ideology. I had also believed that these people *feared* Stalin only.

Yet as an American Mr. Wright is entitled to his own political and religious beliefs. And we must accept, even if regretfully, the fact that Richard Wright, acclaimed America's most powerful Negro writer, is a communist.

Source: Commonweal 31 (April 12, 1940): 524–526.

But Richard Wright was not born a communist. Existing social, economic and political conditions have made him so. I also doubt, very much, that Mr. Wright was taught to fear God by his communist mentors. We learned about *Him* long before the communists *discovered* us. And it is this inherent belief in God—only—that has kept all of us from turning to the *isms* that accept us as men and women, despite our black skins.

There may be Catholics who will not read "Native Son" because its author is a communist. But, did you ever stop to think that Catholics may be among those who are responsible for some of the conditions that have led Richard Wright and scores of others into the ranks of the reds?

The time has come for Christian America to shed its coat of hypocrisy and admit its sin. Even today, years later, I sicken as I remember the manner in which the Negro's lack of human rights was etched upon my memory. It was soon after I had returned to Alabama from a school conducted by the Sisters of the Blessed Sacrament. While well aware of the fact that I was a Negro, being colored did not seem strange, for so were my friends. True, I knew white people, but they were the nice white people whom my parents served. From them we received nickels, toys and many useful gifts. The atmosphere in our home was such that it gave no hint of the bitterness that corrodes so many black breasts.

There was the time, I'll admit, when I heard talk of a race riot. But being a dramatic child who welcomed any new excitement, I was intrigued by the hushed whispers and drawn shades. Being too young to understand the consequences, I was really disappointed when the scheduled riot failed to take place.

A Ku Klux Klan parade had been another one of the highlights of my childhood. How well I remember my mother taking me from bed in the middle of the night and carrying me in to the parlor. Father, in an old-fashioned nightshirt, with his fists clenched, was standing at a front window. On a couch sat the old woman who nursed my little sister, praying as she clutched the tiny baby to her breast. Outside there was the clatter of horses' hoofs. As the light from a fiery cross, held high by white-robed men on horseback, flashed its warning of destruction to all Catholics, Jews and Negroes, I saw my father open the drawer of a nearby table. The reflection of the light glistened on the steel of a pearl handled revolver. My mother tightened her hold upon my arm. But, childlike, I broke away and pressed my nose against the window pane—the better to see the men in white robes who rode fine horses and carried fiery crosses.

As the last clop-clop died in the distance, there was a dreadful silence. My mother shook the old nurse. "Davie," she said, "you can stop praying now. They've passed us by."

My Education

Time passed and there followed years under the watchful eyes of white Sisters. I returned to my parents a young lady. Ready to take my place in the world, the Sisters had said. And on that memorable night, when the plight of my race was so clearly explained, one of the neighborhood boys had borrowed a car and called to take me to my first party.

Now the business section of our town had spread until it fringed our neighborhood. This had caused most of our friends to move to other sections of the city. The people who had moved into the houses they left vacant were unknown to us and, on the whole, a pretty motley lot. Even Aunt Lizzie, who had lived in the next house as long as I could remember, had moved to "the hill." And not only did we have a new next-door neighbor, but my mother said she feared they were "a wild bunch."

So on this particular night as I prepared to sally forth to my first party, I was not wholly surprised to see a car, occupied by two white officers of the law, drive alongside an automobile that was parked in front of the next house. But I was anxious to be on my way and called to my escort to come along.

"Wait!" my mother fairly hissed.

And having the sort of mother who meant what she said, I waited.

"Get out of that car!" I heard one of the police call to the two young Negroes who were sitting in the parked auto.

"And get out with your hands in the air!" the other officer instructed, as he leaped from his car with drawn gun.

"You boys got corn (whiskey) in this car and we're gonna find it tonight!" said Officer No. 1.

"Well," asked the second officer, "what you standing there like two dummies for? You have got whiskey, haven't you?"

"No, Sir!" the Negroes cried in unison, their arms stretched heaven-ward.

"Well, we'll see!" and the policemen began searching the car.

As we watched from the porch, it seemed to me that they were making that car into a swell job for some junk dealer. Cushions were thrown in the street. Tools were scattered about and boards ripped from the floor. But this was all in vain, for the zealous officers found nothing that bore evidence of any violation of the law.

"Well," one of them admitted, as he pulled out a handkerchief and wiped the sweat from his brow, "we didn't get you tonight, but we'll catch you yet!"

The sight of the white men working so hard—and in vain—must have amused the smaller of the two Negroes (they called him "Shorty"), for he giggled.

"So it tickles you, eh?" said one of the officers. "Well, laugh this off!"

There was a succession of thuds, as the butt of the officer's service revolver cracked against the little Negro's skull again and again. Finally, his form lay crumpled on the asphalt street, as his friend stood helplessly by—his black hands high above his head.

"I reckon this'll teach you not to be so smart next time," laughed the other fiend who wore a policeman's badge, as he walked over to the Negro's prostrate form and began kicking him. His laughter only increased as the Negro feebly groaned.

To me, it had all seemed like a page from some terrible story book. But that Negro's groan struck a note of reality.

"Why you dirty dog!" I screamed, "you're kicking a man who's flat on his back!"

Quickly a hand was clasped over my mouth. "You little simpleton!" my mother muttered, "don't you know that they can do the same thing to you and I can't do a thing about it?"

In that moment, I fell heir to my heritage. I understood the whispers about the race riot. Again I saw white robed figures and heard the clatter of horses' hoofs, as an old Negro woman prayed and clutched a tiny baby to her breast. I understood why my father could not look me in the eye after the Ku Klux had passed by.

And, if that Negro who was kicked, at the point of a gun, as he lay flat on his back, is today a member of any organization pledged to over-throw the brand of order that allows such atrocities—who is to blame? [. . .]

Most of us are familiar with the National Association for the Advancement of Colored People and the wonderful and constructive work it has done. We black folk enjoy many privileges that might not be ours if there had not been such an organization as the NAACP. Right now, however, I am thinking of one of the cases in which the NAACP was helpless; there is no organization under the sun that has the power to breathe life into the dead. And that is the only solution that would have satisfied those of us who loved Edna D——.

Edna came to our home from a nearby school. The City Federation of Colored Women's Clubs had been contributing to the support and educational expenses of Edna and her sister, Nobie. Neither of these girls were particularly interested in an education. As they were orphans, Edna felt she had been dependent upon others too long and left the institution. Nobie, who had lost both arms during early childhood, realized her handicap and remained at the school.

In those days there was a weekly deadline against which I had to write, and before long, Edna became the "head-lady" around our house. Two years went by with this happy arrangement. Then one day we were discussing the idea of my going to New York.

"If I go away, what will you do?" I asked Edna. "Oh," she replied, "you go ahead. If you go to New York and study, maybe you'll get to be a real good writer. But be sure and send for me just as soon as you get a place for us to stay."

Though the girl was usually slow of comprehension, she had found out that we needed each other. Little did she realize, though, that she was slated for martyrdom.

Like most literary moths, I came on to New York. But life in the big city was not as easy as it had been pictured in the books I had read. Months passed and once in a great while there was a letter from Edna. Each one contained the same question: "Don't you think you'd better hurry and send for me?"

But the winds of winter were cold and there were times when my daily crust of bread was not enough for me, let alone another. So I didn't send for Edna.

Then one day a newspaper clipping fell out of a letter that my mother had sent on by airmail. The clipping was an account of the fatal shooting of Edna D——, a Negro woman (she was barely 18) by Detective —— for resisting an officer of the law. Once more I had been forced to swallow the bitter brew of America's farcical justice!

Edna, as the story goes, had attended a party. In the course of the evening one of the young women present had drunk a little more than [was] wise. Then someone lost a pocketbook and, after several heated discussions, the majority of the merrymakers decided that the lady who had tilted her cup so often had also taken the pocketbook. It seems that

Edna had, for some reason, decided that someone else took the pocket-book. When the crowd began beating the silly woman, Edna became furious. And a furious Edna was something to reckon with.

Lacking about three inches of being six feet tall, with a frame well covered with flesh, Edna looked much like some African princess who had never been contaminated by the various bloods that race through the veins of most of us.

Though slow to comprehend, right and wrong dictated the course of Edna's actions. When she saw the crowd beating a woman she believed to be innocent, she went to the aid of the unfortunate woman and, single handed, subdued the rest of the crowd. Innately kind, with more than her share of maternal instinct, Edna then went home taking the woman with her.

Of course the people at the party were very angry with Edna. And they decided to play a trick on her that they knew would give the girl a good scare. They called police headquarters and told the officers to go to "913 North 16 Street. There's a bad Negro woman there."

In a few moments the police walked into Edna's room. She had put the intoxicated woman to bed and was changing her shoes. You see Edna persisted in wearing shoes that were smaller than her generously propor-tioned feet. Her first act upon entering the house was naturally to seek comfort for her feet.

And so when the officers said, "Put up your hands!" Edna, intent upon changing her shoes and always slow to comprehend, simply looked up to see what was happening. That was the resistance that caused an officer of the law to shoot Edna.

There was an investigation, all the findings of which I do not know. I do know, however, that Edna's slayer kept his job and received no legal punishment.

Meanwhile, I prayed and waited. If this man escaped all punishment, I reasoned, surely I was following the wrong path.

Still I prayed and waited. Time passed. Then last year another clipping came in a letter I received. It was an account of the death of the man who had slain Edna D——. He met his death at the hand of another culprit who had resisted arrest. "Vengeance is mine!" saith the Lord. *He* had charted my course.

These unfortunate and inappropriate experiences have been re-corded here not to spread hatred, stir up sectional strife or arouse ill feeling. Neither have they been easy to share with you. But the cause for which I have written about these experiences is the salvation of millions of souls, and any suffering these memories might have recalled is only a small part of the contribution hundreds of us are ready to pay so that our more handicapped and less articulate brothers may enjoy the inherited rights of every man created to the image and likeness of God.

I would not have you believe that I have sought to paint a picture of a barbarous South. Indeed not! For I love my home and some of my most highly esteemed friends are white. But my nice white friends, who are thoroughly familiar with these conditions, allow public officers to brutalize and murder helpless and inarticulate Negroes. It is this silence of kindly intentioned America that is causing Negroes everywhere to demand that those who call themselves our friends take their stand and let the world know about it.

Without a doubt Mr. Wright is recording the harvest of hate that White America has, perhaps unwittingly, sown. Can you honestly blame him?

PART 4

LONGINGS

During the early decades of the twentieth century, African-American women writers witnessed many social transformations. Among them were the Great Migration, which carried many thousands from the pre-dominantly rural South to northern industrial cities, and the First World War, which drew many black men into combat on foreign soil. The ever-expanding horizons of their experience only heightened the women's awareness of their disenfranchised state, and of the complicated duality of being both black and female. As African-Americans, they were aware of how quickly the doors of opportunity could shut, as they had at the turn of the century during the post-Reconstruction period; as women, they had particular concerns about their place in society and their responsibility to a new generation of black children.

Georgia Douglas Johnson's life and poems speak to the unresolved duality of being both black and female. When she published her first volume of poetry, *Heart of a Woman* (1918), she was criticized for having no feeling for her race. Although her next book of poems, *Bronze* (1922), does focus on the African-American's plight, much of her work expresses a longing to resolve the gender-color duality by speaking about women within the context of race.

"Love's Way: A Christmas Story," by Carrie Williams Clifford, gives voice to the longing for a traditional home and hearth, a luxury often denied to black women because of both the need to work and the legacy of slavery.

For other African-American women writers, longing encompasses the full scope of human life. While Nellie Bright longs for release from daily turmoil into a "black opal" landscape of her imagination, Anita Scott Coleman's "The Eternal Quest" is the story of one man's search for peace and meaning in a world where it seems nonexistent. Ethel Caution Davis bridges a gap by writing of both the longing for racial and gender equality and the more abstract longings for peace of mind. Poems such as "In '61" obviously speak to race, while "Long Remembering" and "Longing" reveal her overall restlessness and her desire to be a part of the peace that she finds only in the pristine natural world.

Though she cannot name what it is she actually feels, Clarissa Scott Delany writes during her college years of a "vague and baffling discontent" and "yearning." Her verses, charged with a melancholy that attempts to embrace healing for her troubled spirit, are a vehicle to escape the turmoil and desolation of her environment in an institution in which educated white women partake of privileges not meant for black women.

Similarly, Jessie Fauset's poems speak of her longing for freedom from her troubles: in "Oblivion" she writes of her desire to be buried anonymously, where a "note of jealousy and hate" cannot be heard, where she will truly rest "in peace." Her poems also speak of the troubled course of romantic love: the short-lived passion ("Dead Fires"), unrequited love ("La Vie C'est la Vie"), and lovers' quarrels ("Words! Words!"). In these poems, her voice is that of the universal lover, subject to the same emotions as any human who loves or longs for love.

If by dreaming in color African-American women writers could grasp without hindrance all that they could imagine, through their writings they dared to add tangibility to those dreams, moving closer to the longed-for fulfillment of their promise.

Calling Dreams

The right to make my dreams come true
I ask, nay, I demand of life,
Nor shall fate's deadly contraband
Impede my steps, nor countermand.

Too long my heart against the ground
Has beat the dusty years around,
And now, at length, I rise, I wake!
And stride into the morning-break!

Source: Georgia Douglas Johnson, *Bronze* (Boston: B. J. Brimmer, 1922), p. 23.

Question

Where are the brave men, where are the strong men?
Pygmies rise
And spawn the earth.
Weak-kneed, weak-hearted, and afraid,
Afraid to face the counsel of their timid hearts,
Afraid to look men squarely,

Down they gaze
With fatal fascination
Down, down
Into the whirling maggot sands
Of prejudice.

Source: Georgia Douglas Johnson, *Bronze* (Boston: B. J. Brimmer, 1922), p. 75.

My Son

Stronger than man-made bars, the chain,
That rounds your life's arena,
Deeper than hell the anchor sweeps
That stills your young desires;
Darker than night the inward look
That meditation offers,
Redder than blood the future years
Roll down the hills of torture!

But ah! you were not made for this,
And life is but preluding—
The major theme shall hold its sway
When full awake, not dreaming,
Your ebon foot shall press the sod
Where immortelles are blooming;
Beyond the glaze of fevered years
I see—THE DAY IS COMING!

Source: The Crisis 29 (November 1924): 28.

Armageddon

In the silence and the dark
I fought with dragons:
I was battered, beaten, sore,
But rose again.
On my knees I fought still rising,
Dull with pain!
In the dark I fought with dragons—
Foolish tears! Cease your flowing!
Can't you see the dawn appears?

Source: The Crisis 29 (March 1925): 231.

Interim

The days lie dark between our jeweled meetings
Like wintry burials.

My heart bows low before the cheerless hearth
Until your voice rings through the gloom
And bids me
Wake!
And live!

Source: Georgia Douglas Johnson, *An Autumn Love Cycle* (reprint, Freeport, N.Y.: Books for Libraries Press, 1971), p. 11.

Ivy

I am a woman
Which means
I am insufficient
I need—
Something to hold me
or perhaps uphold.
I am a woman.

Source: Georgia Douglas Johnson, *An Autumn Love Cycle* (reprint, Freeport, New York: Books for Libraries Press, 1971), p. 25.

I Wonder

I wonder—
   as I see them pass unheeded down the
way,
(The women who were once beloved,
imperious and gay)
Holding with frail, pale hands the cup
Of Life's discarded wine
If memories
Are bliss enough
To make the dregs—divine!

Source: Georgia Douglas Johnson, *An Autumn Love Cycle* (reprint, Freeport, New York: Books for Libraries Press, 1971), p. 30.

Afterglow

Through you I entered heaven and hell,
Knew rapture and despair,
I flitted o'er the plains of earth
And scaled each shining stair:
Drank deep the waters of content,
And drained the cup of gall,
Was regal and was impotent,
Was suzerain and thrall.

Now, by Reflection's placid pool
On evening's mellowed brow,
I smile across the backward way
And pledge anew my vow;
For every glancing, golden gleam,
I offer gladly—pain!
And I would give a thousand world[s]
To live it all again!

Source: Georgia Douglas Johnson, *An Autumn Love Cycle* (reprint, Freeport, New York: Books for Libraries Press, 1971), p. 70.

CARRIE W. CLIFFORD

Love's Way: A Christmas Story

Where is now the merry party—
I remember long ago,
Laughing round the chimney-fire,
Brightened by its ruddy glow;
Or, in summer's balmy evening
In the field upon the hay?
They have all dispersed and wandered
    Far away, far away.

Oh, the pathos in the tones, the world of sorrow, regret, despair in the thin, quavering voice of Miss Milly as she sang! Christmas eve had come again, and with it the sad memories of another Christmas eve, 30 years before when she had been so young, so pretty, so gay and happy. And she had sung the same song; only then it had been for the pure joy of singing. For surrounded as she was with her merry party of Christmas guests (boys and girls who were her girlhood friends) and better than all else, her heart's idol among them—he to whom she had plighted her troth— what power could have foreseen this lonely desperate ending to all her dreams of bliss!

Then she had been Millicent Clarke, the belle of the village, and her voice was full, sweet and clear as a lark's, and when Tom Wentworth joined her

Source: Alexander's Magazine 1 (January 1906): 55–58.

in singing, with his deep rich bass, one was constrained to stop and listen to the ravishing melody.

Thirty long, lonely, weary years had passed since that happy Christmas eve, and she had now long been known as "Miss Milly," the village old maid.

For she and her lover had quarreled, as lovers will; she had been firm and unyielding; he, proud and stubborn.

On Christmas, the day after the memorable party, Tom Wentworth had called alone upon his beautiful sweetheart. Her face beaming with love and joy, she ran to meet him; and with all the eagerness of a young lover he stretched out his arms to draw her to his breast. Tenderly he bent and kissed her; but quick as a flash she wrenched herself free, and with horror in her face and eyes asked whether he had not been drinking.

"Certainly," he said; he had had a glass or two with the boys, but surely this was no great sin, and on Christmas day, too, when every one was making merry.

But this little maiden had serious objections to "making merry" after this fashion, at any time or season, and said so plainly. Further, she exacted a pledge that he would abstain thenceforth from all intoxicating liquors.

He could see no reason in such a demand; he was no drunkard; he seldom tasted wine; it was only on occasions like this, that he drank with his fellows simply to be sociable. He would take no such pledge; she would accept nothing less; neither would yield, and so they parted in anger.

After Tom had stamped through the hall and closed the door with some vehemence behind him, Millicent's heart began to misgive her. Had she not been a little too hasty? And yet, would he not have promised her anything if he had truly loved her? So, she cried herself sick, and went to bed firmly believing that he would see things in a different light by morning, and be anxious to be restored to her favor.

As he strode down the street, his heart was hot within him. Surely she did not love him, or she would not be so unreasonable! What had he done to merit such treatment at her hands? A single glass with his comrade, who had toasted "the prettiest girl in N——; Millicent Clarke."

He was very, very angry with Millicent; and to show how little he cared that she had cast him off, he went back to the club where he drank again and again in a spirit of pure bravado.

* * *

The next morning when Millicent was anxiously awaiting a penitent letter or perhaps a call, the gentleman in question was nursing a very bad head, and feeling like a low-down, contemptible fellow. By nature very impetuous, and being angry with Millicent and angrier with himself, he determined to throw over all his bright prospects and enlist in the navy. He got up and out into the street. Once there, he felt a mighty yearning to go to his darling and heal the breach. But with that thought came the remembrance of how he had acted upon leaving her. Were not the effects of his night's debauch still plain upon him? How could he see her thus?

In sheer desperation, he turned and hurried in the opposite direction toward the wharf.

Like wild fire spread the news that Tom and Millicent had quarreled and Tom had gone to sea! The effect of this news upon Millicent was terrible. When she learned that he had gone without one line, one word, and that he could not if he would, return for five long years, she uttered one heartbreaking moan and fell like a broken lily.

A long and serious illness followed; then she began to return slowly to health, but the old Millicent was gone forever. This wan, sad-eyed, serious woman was not the round, rosy, hoydenish* creature whose high spirits and wild pranks had been the pride of N——.

Thirty years had passed since then, and Miss Milly, as she was now called, was left alone in the great house in the park. Old friends had passed away; those near of kin were sleeping in the dust. For many years now, Miss Milly had been the good angel of the village. Her hand was ever ready to help, her purse ready to succor the poor, the miserable, the destitute.

The children whose fathers were the victims of the drink-habit were her special wards. For these despairing ones, there was in her heart a bottomless well of sympathy.

On this Christmas eve of which we write, she had again invited a little party to her home; but, oh, how different from that first one!

The other party had been composed of bright, joyous young men and women, rich in wealth, in happiness, and worldly store; this was a com-

*Boisterous.

pany of that most pathetic thing in life—careworn, burdened children, old in want, misery and woe.

When Miss Milly finished her singing, her mind travelled back into the past. In the first years of her sorrow, she had waited and watched for some word from her erring lover; she thought he must return, at the end of the those five, cruel, silent years. But five, ten, and twenty had passed, and still no word, no sign!

But Miss Milly's faithfulness to the absent one never wavered. She took all the blame upon herself.

She had been hasty, stubborn, unjust, and she had earned her punishment, so she told herself.

Thirty years went by, and tonight as she sat alone she thought of the stream of years that had rolled into eternity since that night when she had been so deliciously happy.

During all this time, Miss Milly had never missed sitting alone in the parlor on Christmas eve, singing that never-to-be-forgotten song, and calling up visions of the past.

Long since she had ceased to expect the return of the wanderer; her cry was now ever, "If I could but know his fate, I would be satisfied!"

A ring at the door bell recalled Miss Milly with a start! She hurried into the hall, and with a face glowing with love and good fellowship, admitted her quaint little guests.

The first thing Miss Milly did was to sit them down to such a feast as never was before. "All the delicacies of the season," failed to express the abundance of the good things to eat. And how the children enjoyed it!

Miss Milly had never before seen victuals vanish, as did turkey, oysters, sweet potatoes, cranberry sauce, pickles, mince pies, pumpkin pies, custard pies and plum pudding, on this occasion. When they could eat no more, games of all kinds were indulged in; ending in a big romp of blind man's bluff and hide and seek. After this came the nuts and fruit, and then each was given a well-filled basket to carry home. At last the wraps were all on, the baskets distributed, and the thoroughly tired youngsters starting for home.

As Miss Milly stood in the hall door with the light streaming upon her angelic face, she called after the retreating forms, "A Merry Christmas to you, children, and God bless you every one!" and the happy children shouted back, "The same to you, Miss Milly."

With a patient little sigh, and her hand pressed to her heart, which was never quite free from the old aching pain, she stood for a moment in the doorway.

Suddenly she became aware of the figure of a man approaching. Laboriously he mounted the steps and with a muttered "At last," fell senseless at her feet.

Oh, the unspeakable chord of love! Old, changed, broken as he was, on glance was all-sufficient to assure Millicent Clarke that this was her old lover—Tom Wentworth.

"Thank God," was all she said. She rang for the butler, and together they lifted him into the sitting room, and laid him upon the couch. Everything that could be done was resorted to, until the doctor, who had been telephoned, should arrive.

The years had given him back—changed, but a shadow of his former self, almost dead; yet Miss Milly was as happy as a queen. How she hovered over him, kissing his brow, chafing his hands, bathing his forehead, moaning in those plaintive dove-like accents.

God had heard her prayer. He had ended the suspense. He had granted that she should know his fate, whatever it was to be, and she dared ask no more!

When Tom Wentworth returned to consciousness, he was lying in a massive bed in an elegant chamber, and Millicent Clarke was bending over him. As though the intervening years had been a dream, he whispered "Millicent," and drawing her head upon his bosom he kissed her.

When he was strong enough he related a tale of a wasted life, of wanderings, of carousings, of a stubborn pride, then of longing and regret and shame.

For many years pride had kept him from returning; then shame had stepped in to torture and harass him. But at last he swore that nothing should keep him from her longer. Like the prodigal, he would return.

With all his sin, his heart had ever remained true to her. Even in the wildest excesses he had ever borne good will to his fellow man. Whatever else he was, he was no coward, and many were the lives he had saved at risk of his own. Many letters testifying to his bravery and many medals for gallant seamanship were his.

"But the temper in the wine cup has ever been my undoing," he confessed at last when all was told. "Each returning Christmas night has seen a wilder debauch. At first only on Christmas did the fiend have power over me; but as the years rolled by, the outbreak grew more frequent, so that each succeeding year rendered it more impossible for me to return to you. But I have come at last. You will not cast me off, oh, say you will not cast me off!"

"If you knew, if you could but realize the desperate battle I've fought with the fiend to reach your side untainted! But, thank God, I've won! Old, scarred, dying, yet blessed to come into your presence without the taint of liquor. Will you receive me again? Milly, can you forgive me?"

More than once during the recital she had vainly striven to check him. Now, all her loving, tender woman's heart was overflowing. She baptized him with her tears, she covered him with kisses, she called him by every endearing name under [the] heavens.

Forgive him! When she had done so 30 years ago. In fact, the fault had all been hers; her hasty temper, her imperiousness had been the cause of all.

And so mutually forgiving and forgetting the past, under the influence of her caressing hand he fell asleep.

The full light of the glad Christmas day was shining into the room, when he again opened his eyes. He was very weak; he knew the sands of life were running low. "Milly," he called softly. Instantly she was beside him.

"Did you call, dearest one?" A pause, then he answered, "I have a strange fancy, the fancy of a dying man. Can you—will you marry me, Milly? It will not be for long and I can die happier."

"I have been betrothed to you for 30 years," was her low fervid reply.

"Then send for the minister; there is no time to be lost."

The intervening hour was spent in that blessed communion known only to lovers. It was a bit of Paradise here below.

When the minister came, the woman knelt by the bedside, and took upon herself the vows, "for richer, for poorer, for better, for worse, in sickness, in health until death us do part"; and so they were married.

To one unacquainted with their story, the wedding would have seemed a sad one; but to them it was one of unspeakable joy, for it was so much more than they had believed it possible to be granted to them!

The day was dying in the west when Tom, his head pillowed on Millicent's arm and a smile of infinite sweetness on his lips, entered into rest.

And Milly, though with streaming eyes, was looking longingly into the future; satisfied that she would follow soon, and that the glimpse of Paradise vouchsafed them here, would be continued there, into infinity.

CLARISSA SCOTT DELANY

Joy

Joy shakes me like the wind that lifts a sail,
Like the roistering* wind
That laughs through stalwart pines.
It floods me like the sun
On rain-drenched trees
That flash with silver and green.

I abandon myself to joy—
I laugh—I sing.
Too long have I walked a desolate way,
Too long stumbled down a maze
Bewildered.

Source: Countee Cullen, ed., *Caroling Dusk: An Anthology of Verse by Negro Poets* (New York: Harper, 1927), p. 140.
    *Carousing.

The Mask

So detached and cool she is
No motion e'er betrays
The secret life within her soul,
The anguish of her days.

She seems to look upon the world
With cold ironic eyes,
To spurn emotion's fevered sway,
To scoff at tears and sighs.

But once a woman with a child
Passed by her on the street,
And once she heard from casual lips
A man's name, bitter-sweet.

Such baffled yearning in her eyes,
Such pain upon her face!
I turned aside until the mask
Was slipped once more in place.

Source: Countee Cullen, ed., *Caroling Dusk: An Anthology of Poems by Negro Poets* (New York: Harper, 1927), p. 143.

Interim

The night was made for rest and sleep,
For winds that softly sigh;
It was not made for grief and tears;
So then why do I cry?

The wind that blows through leafy trees
Is soft and warm and sweet;
For me the night is a gracious cloak
To hide my soul's defeat.

Just one dark hour of shaken depths,
Of bitter black despair—
Another day will find me brave,
And not afraid to dare.

Source: Countee Cullen, ed., *Caroling Dusk: An Anthology of Poems by Negro Poets* (New York: Harper, 1927), pp. 142–143.

Solace

My window opens out into the trees
And in that small space
Of branches and of sky
I see the seasons pass
Behold the tender green
Give way to darker heavier leaves.
The glory of the autumn comes
When steeped in mellow sunlight
The fragile, golden leaves
Against a clear blue sky

Linger in the magic of the afternoon
And then reluctantly break off
And filter down to pave
A street with gold.
Then bare, gray branches
Lift themselves against the
Cold December sky
Sometimes weaving a web
Across the rose and dusk of late sunset
Sometimes against a frail new moon
And one bright star riding
A sky of that dark, living blue
Which comes before the heaviness
Of night descends, or the stars
Have powdered the heavens.
Winds beat against these trees;
The cold, but gentle rain of spring
Touches them lightly
The summer torrents strive
To lash them into a fury
And seek to break them—
But they stand.
My life is fevered
And a restlessness at times
An agony—again a vague
And baffling discontent
Possesses me.
I am thankful for my bit of sky
And trees, and for the shifting
Pageant of the seasons.
Such beauty lays upon the heart
A quiet.
Such eternal change and permanence
Take meaning from all turmoil
And leave serenity
Which knows no pain.

Source: Countee Cullen, ed., *Caroling Dusk: An Anthology of Poems by Negro Poets* (New York: Harper, 1927), pp. 141-142.

Noblesse Oblige

Lolotte, who attires my hair,
Lost her lover. Lolotte weeps;
Trails her hand before her eyes;
Hangs her head and mopes and sighs,
Mutters of the pangs of hell.
Fills the circumambient air
With her plaints and her despair.
Looks at me:
"May you never know, Mam'selle,
Love's harsh cruelty."

Love's dart lurks in my heart too,—
None may know the smart
Throbbing underneath my smile.
Burning, pricking all the while
That I dance and sing and spar,
Juggling words and making quips
To hide the trembling of my lips.
I must laugh
What time I moan to moon and star
To help me stand the gaff.

What a silly thing is pride!
Lolotte bares her heart.

Heedless that each runner reads
All her thoughts and all her needs.
What I hide with my soul's life
Lolotte tells with tear and cry.
Blurs her pain with sob and sigh
Happy Lolotte, she!
I must jest while sorrow's knife
Stabs in ecstasy.

"If I live, I shall outlive."
Meanwhile I am barred
From expression of my pain.
Let my heart be torn in twain,
Only I may know the truth.
Happy Lolotte, blessed she
Who may tell her agony!
On me a seal is set.
Love is lost, and—bitter ruth—
Pride is with me yet!

Source: Countee Cullen, ed. *Caroling Dusk: An Anthology of Verse by Negro Poets* (New York: Harper, 1927), p. 67.

Dead Fires

If this is peace, this dead and leaden thing,
   Then better far the hateful fret, the sting.
Better the wound forever seeking balm
   Than this gray calm!
Is this pain's surcease? Better far the ache,
   The long-drawn dreary day the night's white wake,
Better the choking sigh, the sobbing breath
   Than passion's death!

Source: Palms 4 (October 1926): 17–18.

Oblivion

(From the French of Massillon Coicou —Haiti)

I hope when I am dead that I shall lie
  In some deserted grave—I cannot tell you why,
But I should like to sleep in some neglected spot,
  Unknown to every one, by every one forgot.

There lying I should taste with my dead breath
  The utter lack of life, the fullest sense of death;
And I should never hear the note of jealousy or hate,
  The tribute paid by passers-by to tombs of state.

To me would never penetrate the prayers and tears
  That futilely bring torture to dead and dying ears;
There I should lie annihilated and my dead heart would bless
  Oblivion—the shroud and envelope of happiness.

Source: Arna Bontemps and Langston Hughes, eds., *The Poetry of the Negro, 1746–1949* (Garden City, N.Y.: Doubleday, 1949), p. 69.

La Vie C'est la Vie

On summer afternoons I sit
Quiescent by you in the park,
And idly watch the sunbeams gild
And tint the ash-trees' bark.

Or else I watch the squirrels frisk
And chatter in the grassy lane;
And all the while I mark your voice
Breaking with love and pain.

I know a woman who would give
Her chance of heaven to take my place;
To see the love-light in your eyes,
The love-glow on your face!

And there's a man whose lightest word
Can set my chilly blood afire;
Fulfillment of his least behest
Defines my life's desire.

But he will none of me, nor I
Of you. Nor you of her. 'Tis said
The world is full jests like these—
I wish that I were dead.

Source: The Crisis 24 (July 1922): 124.

Words! Words!

How did it happen that we quarreled?
We two who loved each other so!
Only the moment before we were one,
Using the language that lovers know.
And then of a sudden, a word, a phrase
That struck at the heart like a poignard's blow.
And you went berserk, and I saw red,
And love lay between us, bleeding and dead!
Dead! When we'd loved each other so!

How could it happen that we quarreled!
Think of the things we used to say!
"What does it matter, dear, what you do?
Love such as ours has to last for aye!"
—"Try me! I long to endure your test!"
—"Love, we shall always love, come what may!"
What are the words the apostle saith?
"In the power of the tongue are Life and Death!"
Think of the things we used to say!

Source: *Palms* 4 (October 1926): 17–18.

The Eternal Quest

When Evan Given gave up his wife to that grim reaper who holds a mortgage on every man's house and forecloses with or without notice, he turned with a stolid, white-hot passion to his baby, a year-old daughter, for what little comfort he could squeeze from life. The love that he severed with such visible effort from the mother to bestow upon the offspring doubled and trebled in the years during which Polly Given grew up.

At eighteen, she was a sweet flower of a girl. Then, as stealthily as comes the dew at eventide, the Reaper struck again, deftly, swiftly, and Polly sped forth into the unknown whither Evan dared not follow. And the reason that he dared not was because of a tiny spark that glowed in the very depth of his being—his faith. He believed in life after death, and that the self-destroyer forfeited much if not all of the future existence.

Because Evan Given was one of the foremost surgeons of his day, and dabbled in science as a side-line, it was not altogether incredible, after his burdensome grief, that he elected to give up the one in which he had won fame and fortune for the other, the lesser as a buffer for his sorrow. Quietly, and with no more ado than is usual for a man changing his barber, he dropped all else, and took up the study of science—the science of faith. He closed his house, the palatial dwelling he had erected for his daughter; cut his London connections, and set himself adrift, as much as was possible for a man of his standing to do.

Source: *Opportunity* 9 (August 1931): 242-243.

What is this thing faith . . . Why does it suffice for some . . . Why is it insufficient for others . . . Why believing as I do that God is the giver, and therefore has a Divine right to take when and as He wills, am I rebellious because he has bereft me of mine? These were the questions Evan Given sought to solve.

No. 60 in ward 400 was one of the strangest cases ever admitted to the county hospital. His was an unique malady and of a far-reaching scope. Plainly it came under the category of cases wherein the great Evan Given had labored so magnificently. It was known that the famous English surgeon was sojourning in the American city. If he could be prevailed upon to grant but an hour of his time, if for no more than a consultation, if only for an observation, anything he might choose to do would be a priceless gift to the medical profession.

At last, when all arguments had failed, someone mentioned that, which seemed to him, the strangest phase of the case in question, that this great hulking giant of a fellow—No. 60 was well over forty—should lay day after day, calling for his mother.

"That," said Evan Given, instantly, "is faith. Wait. I will come."

The span of No. 60's shoulders came near to over-taxing the width of the white iron cot. His massive head pressed against the headpost. His feet protruded through the foot rails. He was easily six foot ten, and he was delirious when Evan Given saw him first. He was strapped, but yet the strong thongs were proving inadequate, the motions of the man lifted the cot until it tossed about like a frail craft on a windy sea. And always, he screeched the one word, "mom-mer."

"Too late . . . Nothing can be done!" proclaimed the great man. "At least, he can be made comfortable. Send for his mother!"

"There can be no visitors." Head Nurse of ward 400 voiced a protest that was curbed at a glance from the Surgeon.

No. 60's mother arrived when he was at his worst. It was the crucial hour. He was seeking with maniacal strength to break his bonds, and screaming fiendishly. The mother, after a brief period with the great London physician, hurried to her son's bedside.

She was a small woman, a tightly shriveled hard little person, not unlike a black walnut . . . Her timidity fell from her, as she drew near the bed. She became no longer an uneasy visitor among countless strangers, but a mother with her only son, and it was he and she against the world.

The great Evan Given was a close observer of all that passed. This was a pregnant moment to him, in his study of faith.

The mother said quickly and a little shrilly, "Lie down 'dar." Then in firmer tones, and quieter: "Be still. Didn't ah tells you!"

Magically, the huge form upon the bed grew clam.

"What's you a-laying here fo', disturbin' these yere folks, ain't yo' mammy done taught yo' better'n 'at . . ." Her voice was crooning. "Ain't yo' shame yo'self. Here's yo' mammy done come this long ways to see yo', and yo' is lying here yellin' like yo' is possessed."

"Mommer. . . ."

To the amazement of those watching, the man on the bed was muttering in his turn to the old woman. The mother down on her knees bent her head to hear. Quickly, she stood erect, and called loudly.

"Nurse . . . Doctor . . . somebody come quick and take off dese bindings. My boy wants to die free . . . Come quick, somebody quick."

Evan Given came—interns and nurses together removed the straps. No. 60 heaved a great sigh of relief. His head jerked back convulsively, and his eyes rolled wildly towards his mother. "De Lord's done come," he intoned majestically, and fell into his final sleep, peacefully as a babe.

"Faith," jotted Given, mentally.

The old woman sat beside the cot with folded hands. Evan cleared his throat. Surely this was a strange manner in which to meet death, not a tear, in no wise did she betray regret.

"Why-er—why-er," began Evan.

"Blessed lamb . . . Sweet Jesus, done come and set my po' suff'ring boy free," chanted the old woman, almost gaily.

"Faith," tabulated Given in his scientific mind.

"What will you do?" he inquired curiously, and not unkindly.

"Do heah this man," exclaimed No. 60's mother, "I'se goin'er do my wo'k." As an after-thought, "I'se got 'er wo'k for sho' now, 'cause dis boy a-lying heah is my sole suppo't. But de Lord will provide."

"Faith," said Evan Given audibly in the voice of a man who talks often to himself. "I must find it."

In '61

Early in '61 the Fifty-fourth Massachusetts* disembarked at Charleston. Rumors of their approach had reached the city before them, so that their progress up the main street to the Citadel Green was not unwatched. The door of an imposing residence opened slowly to let an aged black form, resplendent in white apron and red bandanna, out on to the piazza. She tottered down the walk, every now and then casting a half-frightened glance back at the house. The gate slammed after her decrepit figure. This called forth a final glance to the house. Then into the road she went, right into the path of the approaching soldiers, and took her stand. Trembling with age and emotion, she showed no fear of the approaching horse, whom the rider reined in with difficulty.

"Is yo' Mas' Yankee?"

"Yes," somewhat irritated at this delay.

"Is yo' Mas' Yankee?"

Then remembering that he had come to fight for the Union and for such of his race as this old woman, he answered with a break in his voice: "Yes, we're the colored Yankees."

And with tears streaming down her face, the old woman replied: "Tanky Jesus! Tanky Jesus!"

Source: The Wellesley College News (October 1911), p. 9. The author published under several names, including Ethel M. Caution, Ethel M. Davis, Ethel Caution, Ethel Caution Davis, and Ethel Caution-Davis.

*The first regiment of African-American soldiers, which fought during the Civil War (previously, blacks were prohibited from bearing arms). The film *Glory* (TriStar Pictures, 1989) is based on the experience of this regiment.

Longing

To-day my heart is all a-quiver with longings—for the ocean, but white capped and restless it must be; for the song of the whippoorwill, solitary in the midnight stillness as I heard it last; for the exquisite song of the humming-bird; for any and all things that are restless, solitary, inexplicable, for such is my mood to-day.

Source: Wellesley magazine (April 1911): 300.

Sunset

The sun goes slowly
Down the golden ladder
That swings from heaven
To where a fringe of pines
Tops the distant hill.
Step by step he goes
Till near the end
He takes a sudden leap
And disappears.
So you went slowly
Down the ladder of the years
Smilingly step by step
Till one late afternoon
You took the sudden leap
And passed beyond my ken.

Source: Otelia Cromwell et al., *Readings from Negro Authors* (New York: Harcourt, Brace, 1931), p. 52.

Long Remembering

If I should go to sleep to-night
Knowing I ne'er should waken,
I would not be dismayed.
My soul, glad for release,
Would wing its way unto a long remembering

Of mornings spent upon the Siasconsett* strand
Watching the sun rise
Dripping red spray from ocean's eastern rim.
Of hours on Narragansett's craggy coast
When, perched in solitude upon a rock,
Feet dipping in the spray,
I listened to the waves
Beat their high sounding paean on the shore.

Of evenings in mid-ocean when the moon
Laddered its path of gold
From sky down o'er the waves
To where I stood ship-bound
Trying to quench undying thirst
With wonder of the night.

Of dusk in distant balsam wood
When nature poured her evensong
From thrushes' throat.

Of moments with a cardinal—
He perched upon a swaying pine,
I tip-toe on the sod—
Talking to each other of happiness and God.

*On the island of Nantucket, Massachusetts.

Of blue flags by a Carolina stream.
Of dogwood tracing petals pink
Against a silver sky.
Of flowers peeping through June snow at Scheideg*;
Of Spietz reflected in the Thunersee;†
Of English gardens
and purple heather hemming in the Scottish lochs.

Of Capri's grotto blue
And cedars silhouetted against the Carmel sea.
Of lacy spires etched against the sky
Of Chartres and Senlis, St. Patrick's and Milan.

Of music in a child's unstudied laughter;
Of unexpected handclasps by the way.

If I should go to sleep to-night
Knowing I ne'er should waken
I would not be dismayed.
My pagan soul, if thus it be,
Clothed only in such robes as these
Would wing its way into Eternity
Asking that afterlife long enough
For such remembering.

Source: The Crisis 11 (October 1928): 292.
    *The name of a town and a mountain in Switzerland.
    †A town and a lake south of Bern, Switzerland.

NELLIE R. BRIGHT

Longings

I want to slay all the things just things
That they tell me I must do.
I would drown them all in the tears I weep
When each breathless day is through.
I want to flee to a cool sand dune
On a wind-swept beach where the humming tune
Of the wind, and the waves, and the heart of me
Drums in my ears, and my lips are wet with the tang of the sea.
I want to feel the rain on my cheek,
The thrill that comes from a lark's long note,
I want to see the sky at dawn through that lacy green of a
    willow tree.
I want to look deep in a pool at night, and see the stars
Flash flame like the fire in black opals.

Source: Black Opals 1 (Spring 1927): 1.

PART 5

SPUNK

African-American women of the early twentieth century developed strong spirits and survival strategies—bulwarks against the multiple obstacles of race, gender, and class. Their strength was manifested in several ways: through political and social organizing, through humor, and in the articulation of a black female discourse of activism. For these women, longing turned into a resolve to cultivate a voice of their own. By establishing an African-American women's "club movement" and other women's affiliations (literary salons, professional organizations, and the like), they created support networks that would become incubators of activism. In this section, activism and writing go hand in hand, to inform, to persuade, to denounce, and to make common cause.

In "Early Days in Cleveland," Jane Edna Hunter traces her own steps from plantation to profession, and tells of her efforts to create social services for displaced women. Recounting her life's story, she lays bare the conflicts that accompanied her efforts to help rural black women arriving in the big city. The autobiography of Ida B. Wells-Barnett, who mounted a formidable campaign against lynching, offers insight into the political lives of activist writers. Details that Wells-Barnett gives of her own varied political experiences, including a meeting with President Woodrow Wilson about segregation in government offices, help to document the leading role she played in both the women's movement and the civil rights movement. Pauli Murray's writings give further evidence of a fighting black female spirit, modeling the strength to think critically and successfully resist attempts to deter the advancement of the race. And Marion Vera Cuthbert, in her article "The Negro Today," exposes and refutes sterotypes while documenting African-American demographics and contributions to American life.

Black women writers of the period also registered protest through the use of satire. Mercedes Gilbert's dramatic monologues in dialect, written for live performance and radio broadcast, question the Darwinian theory of evolution often deployed to devalue black people. Gilbert subtly challenges the racist idea (built on Darwinism and the pseudo-scientific theory of eugenics) that blacks are part human, part monkey. Her use of dialect and black folk wisdom constitutes an attempt to place black experience at the center of interpretation.

Hallie Quinn Brown celebrates her family's record of civil rights activism through stories patterned on nineteenth-century abolitionist literature. Building on oral sources and personal testimony, she weaves accounts of slaves whose freedom was won through the Underground Railroad. Her characters are "spunk" come to life, as they buck the formidable system of slavery.

In her story of romantic entanglement, Zora Neale Hurston draws from popular oral tradition to portray her female characters' courageous fight against sexual exploitation.

Overall, these writings point to the sources of black female consciousness, creativity, and resilience. Whether in analytical commentaries, personal reminiscences, or humorous criticism and portrayals of the society in which they lived, the writers in this section demonstrate the spirit called "spunk." The response of these writers to a society ready to counter their every advance was sustained and undaunted.

JANE EDNA HUNTER

Early Days in Cleveland,
from *A Nickel and a Prayer*

The train which bore me to Cleveland on May 10, in the year 1905, was forced to wait near Delaware, Ohio, until a severe storm—rain, hail, and high wind—had subsided. The storm, while it did not frighten me, to my imaginative spirit, standing on the threshold of a new adventure, suggested the turbulence and inclemency which I might encounter there. When the storm ceased, it was good to find a hopeful sign in the blue skies ahead. [. . .]

Faith in God and hope for the future were the only assets I had when we arrived in Cleveland. My first quest found me knocking unknowingly at the door of a house of prostitution. The owner saw that my appearance was different from that of the usual applicant; and, besides, [my friends] the Colemans were with me. Had I been alone, I might have walked into a dangerous situation. The accommodations which we finally found on Central Avenue certainly were not to my liking; but, tired of walking, we accepted them. After I had paid one dollar and twenty-five cents for a week's lodging in a rooming house and twenty-five cents for a stewed beef dinner, there was only a quarter left in my purse. I must find work soon. My self-respect would not let me depend upon the generous Colemans whose resources were almost as meager as my own.

Meanwhile, my search for lodgings gave me a keen insight into the conditions which confront the Negro girl who, friendless and alone, looks for a decent place to live in Cleveland.

Source: Excerpted from Jane Edna Hunter, *A Nickel and a Prayer* (Cleveland: Elli Kani Publishing Company, 1940), pp. 66–77.

I remained on Central Avenue for only a few months. Answers which were received to my advertisements by which I hoped to secure patients and build up a practice in hydrotherapy and massage opened my eyes to the dubious and unsavory implications of my address in this district. A strong intimation of the evil influence of this rooming house came when I observed the pink silk undergarments of the landlady's daughter, who went out regularly every afternoon and returned home quite late at night, and more often, in the early morning.

"Where does Velma go every afternoon, dressed so beautifully?" I asked. "Oh," explained her mother, "she shops for wealthy women. They give her those lovely silk hose she wears when she goes away." It was not long until I discovered that Velma's "shopping" took her to the dives of Hamilton Avenue, a district from which, in a few years, the stream of vice would pour into other parts of Cleveland.

Soon enough I found that it was necessary to be on guard against the friendliness of Velma and her family. Sometimes, coming into the kitchen suddenly, I was aware of the hasty pushing of bottles under a table or into a cupboard. Constantly I was urged to drink beer because, being thin, I was thought to be in need of a tonic. However, the few months on Central Avenue made me sharply aware of the great temptations that beset a young woman in a large city. At home on the plantation, I knew that some girls had been seduced. Their families had felt the disgrace keenly—the fallen ones had been wept and prayed over. In Charleston I was sent by the hospital to give emergency treatments to prostitutes, but they were white women. Until my arrival in Cleveland I was ignorant of the wholesale organized traffic in black flesh.

One evening loneliness and desire for a little fun—I had no recreation since coming to Cleveland—led me to accept an invitation to go to Woodluff Hall. There would be dancing and good music, I was told.

True enough, the music was good. But there was not a little in the conduct and appearance of the guests to cause me uneasiness—women with heavily painted faces and indecently short skirts; men slightly intoxicated and somewhat noisy. I learned later that there was a saloon on the first floor, but full enlightenment came only by a happy chance. A neatly dressed young man introduced himself and asked me to dance. After the dance he tarried for a few minutes' conversation. I gave him my name, my profession, and told him how I was earning and hoped to continue to earn a living in Cleveland. "Little girl," he said, looking seriously at me and speaking somewhat severely, "you're in the wrong church and the wrong pew. This is not the place for nice girls like you. I want you to meet my mother and sister." [. . .]

Woodluff Hall, I discovered, was the resort of bad women, coming largely from the Hamilton Avenue district. It was also a recruiting station for the notorious "Starlight"—procurer for wild, wealthy men; later, master of the underworld; and, finally, manipulator of the Negro vote for unprincipled politicians. "Starlight" at that time was scarcely more to me than the ogre of the fairy tale. The time would come when he would be a real monster, standing in the path of my life's greatest endeavor. Annoyed and somewhat alarmed, although I regretted to leave the Colemans, I moved to Arthur Avenue, located in a quieter and safer neighborhood, and took up abode with another family far superior in character to my first contacts in a rooming house.

Only less serious than the moral aspect of the lodging problem for the homeless girl, I decided, was the economic aspect. Indeed it was a strong contributing factor to the situation which too often ended in the moral degradation of the girl. In the average rooming house of that period—and the same conditions prevail today—the Negro girl had to pay one dollar and a quarter a week for a small, low-roofed, poorly furnished room. She was charged extra for the use of the laundry gas. If she wished to invite a caller, she was frequently required to clean the whole house in payment for the privilege. The use of the bath tub, when there was one, was discouraged. I remember one landlady in whose home there was an enamel tub; she permitted the use of a single tea kettle of hot water for a bath.

These observations gave me a first-hand knowledge of the dangers and hardships that beset the Negro woman who is a stranger in a large city, together with an overwhelming sympathy for her defenseless condition. I did not at that time realize that, when the moment of my inspiration should come, the reaction between my sympathy and this knowledge would produce the interesting work of my life.

But these things were stored up in my heart as I tramped the streets and looked for work. How often I met rebuffs which seemed much more severe than those encountered in my upward struggle in Charleston. One physician, who was approached by me for work, told me to go back South—that white doctors did not employ "nigger" nurses. These words I had not heard before, for in the South Negro nurses were favored by white people. My indignation was stronger than my wounded feelings. "I am not a 'nigger'" was my reply, "and if there are other nurses practicing in Cleveland, I have enough faith to believe that I, too, can succeed."

The physicians to whom I applied in those first days, with one exception, offered me no encouragement. Dr. Christian LaTrobe Mottley, a West Indian of good standing in his profession, brought me employment through introductions to many of his white colleagues.

But even unprejudiced physicians were not immediately responsive. Meanwhile a cousin who had learned that I was in Cleveland looked me up, offered a loan of ten dollars, and arranged several cleaning jobs for me in the building in which he worked on Prospect Avenue and East Twenty-Second Street.

His assistance tided me over until it was my good luck to wander into the office of Dr. L. E. Sieglestein, who gave me my first professional engagement in Cleveland. When I presented my diploma, he said, "That piece of paper cannot do my work. If you can deliver the goods, I will employ you."

Upon Dr. Sieglestein's recommendation, Mrs. John T. Kepke, the wife of his assistant, employed me to give her a course of massage treatments; other engagements followed. Now I could enjoy two good meals a day, pay my room rent in advance, and return the loan [from] my cousin. While employment lasted I earned fifteen dollars a week; but there were slack times when I was glad to go to my cousin for cleaning jobs or to take odd laundry jobs for women who had more laundering than they could do.

Living in the east end of Cleveland, I was near Bolton Presbyterian Church. On my appearance there I was welcomed and soon invited to the Young Women's Bible Class. Mrs. Cornelia F. Nickens and her son were the only colored members of the church. Although they and many of the white members were kind and helpful in many ways, I was homesick and longed to be in a church of my own people. Accordingly, I became a member of St. John's A.M.E. Church where I met the office secretary of Dr. H. F. Biggar, Sr., a physician to the late John D. Rockefeller. Through this contact Dr. Biggar placed me in the best nursing position I had yet received. I spent five months as a nurse in a home on Euclid Avenue in the exclusive millionaire row. This employment saved me from starvation, and the prestige and favor won through working for Dr. Biggar sent my stock in the profession bouncing upward. To Mrs. Marie Taylor Gates, whose influence made this possible, I owe a debt of affectionate gratitude.

Later I nursed in the home of Mrs. W. S. Gilkey on Amesberry Avenue, another exclusive residential section, with beautiful lawns and flowers. This was only the first of many periods of employment in this home. As long as I was active in the profession, Mrs. Gilkey would have no other nurse. In her home it was my good fortune to meet Dr. Harlan Pomeroy, at one time dean of the nurses' training school of Huron Road Hospital, and his son, Dr. Lawrence A. Pomeroy, fresh from the Yale Medical School. With admiration I watched the skill of the young surgeon whose methods and technique, so lately learned, were new and marvelous to me. My meeting with the Doctors Pomeroy was the beginning of my success as a nurse. These physicians were free of prejudice. They not only recommended me frequently, but were prompt to defend me against the discourtesy and prejudice of others.

Dr. Lawrence A. Pomeroy invited me to Huron Road Hospital to sit through an operation on a Negro girl in whom I was interested. Upon my appearance at the door the sterilizing room, I was made to feel the resentment of one of the nurses who treated me as an interloper. Dr. Pomeroy politely asked her to place an apron and cap on me. When she pretended not to hear, he repeated the request again with politeness, but with a peremptory note that brought compliance. Never again was I embarrassed at Huron Road Hospital. I was always on the alert to do my best and appear well groomed in my profession, as I was keenly aware of the prejudices which were hurled against a Negro nurse. In trials such as the one encountered here it was helpful to remember the good advice given me by the late Dr. James H. Dillard, who on many occasions related the difficulties he had experienced in trying to win to the cause of education for the Negro men whose minds were prejudiced because of a lack of knowledge and proper understanding on their part. [. . .]

Slowly winning my way to success, the problem of daily bread was becoming less insistent. There were days, however, before success came, when my daily diet was one raw egg, a plate of hot rice, and a glass of milk. Often I walked five miles from Arthur Avenue to the old Sheriff Street Market to buy seventy-five cents worth of food. Car fare, of course, did not come within the budget. I did not mind the hardships—all I desired was a chance to serve.

Once, when asked by a patient if I saved my money, my reply was,

"Yes, I save every dollar that I can." "Save the pennies, and the dollars will take care of themselves," she advised. Her smugness both nettled and amused me; but I wisely forbore to tell her the story of my self-denial and careful scrimping to keep body and soul together. I knew that the less I cried, "poor," the more respect my friends would have for me. [. . .]

In these experiences I am again and again reminded of the sustaining influence of the song I used to sing as I traveled alone on the plantation in Pendleton—the comforting words in the hymn:

I need Thee every hour; stay Thou near by,
Temptations lose their power, when Thou art nigh.

A girl alone in a large city must needs know the dangers and pitfalls awaiting her. She must have abiding faith in God's love and care for His own. I was glad to have had a real Christian faith taught me; for in hours of distress and hunger He, like a shepherd, has led me on my way.

MARION VERA CUTHBERT

The Negro Today

It will be necessary at the outset to insist upon the actuality of the problem of the Negro in this country. For those who doubt such insistence it is only necessary to call to their attention the number of times the whole matter is dismissed as being irrelevant or overemphasized or presented in an unnatural setting. The facts are these:

The Negro constitutes one-tenth of the total population of the United States. All hope that he would die out as a group is gone, the 1930 census reporting that he has a birth rate in the excess of the whites. Even with health conditions among the worst in the country he seems able to resist sufficiently those encroachments of disease that will ultimately wipe him out, and with increasing knowledge of sanitation, hygiene and a better economic foundation upon which to build he will probably hold his own for the immediate years. While the percentage of mixed bloods is high, varying in estimates from 40 to 80 per cent, there is no possibility that he will lose his physical identity and merge with the present population in the near future, although amalgamation of some sort is doubtless inevitable for the coming centuries. Gone also is any hope that he can be transplanted to another country; Africa is divided as spoils among the European powers who find far too many blacks left on their hands to entertain the idea of taking on any more, while possibilities of isolation in this country would wreck everything from individual property rights to state sovereignty itself. The Negro landed on these shores at the same

Source: Church and Society (January 1932): 1–2.

time as the whites, whether by coercion or not, and has plenty of historical evidence for considering this his permanent home. And no longer can
he confine himself to the South even if he would. The perilous state of
agriculture in this country makes the hope of obtaining a living as a small
farmer a more and more doubtful one, and coupled with this is the
closing of foreign markets to one of our big crops, cotton. Moreover,
industry in various sections of the country has made and continues to
make a bid for cheap labor and the Negro will be drawn to the newly
developing activities along with other groups. The closer union of all
sections of the country by improved means of transportation must not
be left out of the picture. The resultant lure of "there" as contrasted to
"here" operates just as surely in the case of the Negro, to cause him to
move from place to place, as it does with other groups.

And lastly as a very real part of the problem is the feeling of the Negro
that he is, above everything else, absolutely American, an intensity of
feeling so great that he identifies himself with the majority in the country
which considers itself essentially right, even virtuously right, in most of
its acts, even when such identification works the rankest injustice to his
own group.

In all that we call American civilization, the Negro has shared. In the
Old South he was not only the unskilled but the skilled laborer; today
he performs the same function in a much more competitive field, and
has found new lines of occupation even though the numbers in those
new fields are as yet few. It is staggering to think what the sudden wiping
out of one-tenth of the American population, both as producer and con-
sumer, would be if the Negro were suddenly to be effaced from the
picture.

But while the Negro has filtered into much of American life, the
process has been slow and painful, hampered by traditional concepts of
himself which it seems almost impossible to eradicate from the popular
mind. One of the oldest of the concepts was that the Negro is an in-be-
tween man, not rightly beast or man, but inclining, if anything, more
toward the bestial side. The early days were filled with debates as to
whether he had a soul, and even today vestiges of this early concept linger
in the singular brutality with which any of his acts against society are
treated. They meet with such summary vengeance as if indeed he were
a wild beast of the jungle. The appalling maintenance of both whites and

blacks at a low level of social control because of this belief is one of the saddest spectacles of the contemporary American scene.

Another concept relegates him to a position of inferiority imposed, according to those who hold the relationship with an iron hand, because of his inherent mental disabilities. Such arbiters of his destiny either do not see or do not care to see that their control is an economic one and that what they fear is not a havoc wreaked in their midst because of his inability to comprehend so intellectual and complex a civilization, but that he will become a real contender for some of the honors and spoils of the world. Closely identified with these is a naive group who imagine that the differences in appearance which they find so striking are but the outward signs of inward differences even more striking, and that whether the Negro has mental abilities or not, those abilities would not operate like a white man's, but would produce an odd, and African culture.

But by far the greater portion of our population view the Negro as a delightful entertainer, something that must be amusing and furnish amusement because here is a creature as nearly the opposite of the prevailing type of the country as the world affords. Black vs. white in complexion; straight vs. kinky hair; broad vs. aquiline features—therefore grotesque, therefore a mistake, therefore some sort of practical joke. A genial nature had been taken for one incapable of knowing or retaining any depth of thought or feeling; dramatic ability in him is only buffoonery; his music delightful but jungle-like—in fact, he is the dark playboy of the Western World, with all the exuberance of the New World at its best but in caricature.

However he may be held by contemporary white American society, there is a stern necessity to include him in any planning for the future of the United States. If he is considered as a worker he represents an unwieldy mass of labor to be exploited, to be used to thwart organized labor in this country by being used as strike breakers, or to keep wages low; or as material with a high rate of grievances that make him a fertile field for revolutionary propaganda.

If he is considered as a citizen it must be as a voter. [. . .] One gap in our existing state is the total disregard for constitutional amendments, and in the long run it is likely that the total disregard by the southern states for the provisions of the 14th and 15th as they affect the Negro as a voter, may do as much if not more to undermine our set-up as the immediate hysteria about the non-enforcement of the 18th.*

The Negro has shown himself capable of the highest training our educational systems afford. Undoubtedly the coming years will add to his creative thinking in the lines of art and science, which [is] already recognized and promising.

And finally the Negro will have to be reckoned with as a spiritual force. In these people are massed some of the most burning hopes and yearnings of any group of people in the country. What a people believes, what a people hopes for, what a people projects in powerful desires, will play a tremendous part in their own destiny and in the destinies of all people with whom they come in contact.

Considering the necessity for including the Negro in any plans for the country from another angle, these considerations must obtain: those who produce American civilization earn the right to share the fruits of their labors, and if white workers in their struggle for freedom against the tyrannies of the present capitalist system do not include the Negro worker in a united front, they leave a weapon to be used against them in the struggle, and a considerable one to be true. Secondly, the whole structure of democracy may fail unless its basic tenets are adhered to and serfdom abolished in a country designed for freemen. No one who has the good of the country at heart can fail to be apprehensive upon this point, for the position of the black men may be that rift in the dike through which waters of dissolution seep to boom some day into flood. Thirdly, all narrowness is incompatible with the scholars' world, and the attempt to hold down the mental achievements of one group will consume the energies of the group so concerned and leave them impotent in the end. And lastly, if spiritual force is to be considered in terms of Christian concepts, there simply is no Christianity without the inclusion of the black man in all proposals for right living, for the measurement of man by a God-ideal.

*The Fourteenth Amendment (1869) states that all persons born or naturalized in the United States are citizens of the United States. No state can abridge the rights of its citizens, "nor shall any State deprive any person of life, liberty, or property, without due process of law; nor deny to any person . . . the equal protection of the laws." The Fifteenth Amendment (1869) states that "the right of citizens of the United States to vote shall not be denied or abridged by the United States or any State on account of race, color, or previous condition of servitude." The Eighteenth Amendment (ratified 1919; repealed 1933) prohibits the manufacture, sale, or transportation of alcohol within the United States.

MERCEDES GILBERT

A Talk on Evolution

Who was dat fust monkey's ma?

As we all know, dis is de greatest subject of de day. I don't know who started it, but I can say dis, whoever it was dey ain't give us no real proof, dat dey know any more 'bout it den we does.

But, we do know, dat dis world is all upset, an' gettin' worser every day.

Folks done all gone crazy, an' dey don't care what dey say.

Dey starts 'er trying to dispute, 'bout old man Adam being de fust man on de earth.

An' den dey goes on sayin' things dat is worse.

Dat we all jes' comes from monkeys. Did you ever hear dey lak's of dat?

'Course tis true when folks gits old, dey surely do look queer wid dere face all full of wrinkles, an' dere heads all scarce of hair.

A baby sure is cute with its imitatin' ways, and it acts jes' like a monkey, whin it hips 'round and plays.

Though man don't swing from limb to limb, away up in de trees. You must admit dat he's mighty quick, when he puts his head to learnin' dem high flyin' trapezes tricks.

I'se seen some folks' faces, and I declare dey looked so bad, to say dey looked lak' monkeys, sure would make dem monkeys mad.

Source: Mercedes Gilbert, *Selected Gems of Poetry and Drama* (Boston: Christopher Publishing House, 1931), pp. 40-41.

But, all dat don't stand for nothin', 'cause dere had to be a startin' place.

Someone had to be de fust, so whar did de fust monkey come from, when he come on dis earth?

Folks is sure smart dese days, dat we'll admit, but dey's got this thing all mulled up in places it sure don't fit.

You can't finish nothin', if you never do begin. You can't go out de door, if you never ain't comed in. Dere must be a start made, to do any kind of thing.

Now, what dey got to prove to me, where did dis monkey business begin.

Can't nobody make themselves, of such I ain't never heard, de shell as got to be cracked, 'for we sees de little bird.

No matter how smart you is you'se had a pa and ma tho' you may be smarter den dey ever was.

No matter how dey twist it, dar ain't nobody dumb, so what's I'se waitin' for dem to prove to me is, "Where did dat fust monkey come from."

Dis old thing dat dey calls science, will jes' git you in a whirl.

Wid dem high fluttin' words, dat jes' gets your tongue all in a curl.

But folks wants facts dese days, and jes' lak dey know dat a monkey was our pa. I'd lak for dem prove dey know who was dat fust monkey's ma!

'Til dey does dat, I'm goin' keep on b'lievin' 'bout Adam an' Eve, an' in dat garden way back dere.

'Cause none of us had got her den, but ain't it jes' as easy to b'lieve, as b'lievin' 'bout des monkey men?

Dey at least had a beginnin' an' it ain't half as queer, as dis here havin' monkeys sprin'in' right out de air.

Let dem have dere new fangle ideas, havin' tadpoles evolutin' into hummin' birds and such.

'Cause of dat kind of business, I ain't thinkin' much.

But let dem go right on talkin', I ain't gonna b'lieve what dey say nohow.

Til dey prove to me, dat dey know, who was dat very fust monkey's ma.

IDA B. WELLS-BARNETT

The Equal Rights League, from
Crusade for Justice

In the fall of 1915 a committee appointed to wait upon President Wilson in Washington, D.C., called his attention to the segregation enforced in the departments of the government, and asked him to use his influence as president of the United States in abolishing discrimination based on the color line. I was a member of the committee, which was led by Mr. William Monroe Trotter of Boston, executive secretary of the National Equal Rights League.

President Wilson received us standing, and seemingly gave careful attention to the appeal delivered by Mr. Trotter. At its conclusion he said he was unaware of such discrimination, although Mr. Trotter left with him an order emanating from one of his heads of the department, which forbade colored and white clerks to use the same restaurants or toilet rooms. The president promised to look into the matter and again expressed doubt as to the situation.

As the only woman on the committee I was asked to make some comment, but I contented myself with saying to the president that there were more things going on in the government than he had dreamed of in his philosophy, and we thought it our duty to bring to his attention that phase of it which directly concerned us.

The year went by and no word was received from the president, nor was any action taken by him on the matter. Again I was asked to be one of the committee to visit him, but it was not convenient for me to do so.

Source: Excerpted from Alfreda M. Duster, ed., *Crusade for Justice: The Autobiography of Ida B. Wells* (Chicago: University of Chicago Press, 1970), pp. 375–382.

However, Mr. Trotter and his committee made their visit. It seems that the president became annoyed over Mr. Trotter's persistent assertion that these discriminations still were practiced and that it was his duty as president of the United States to abolish them. President Wilson became very angry and he told the committee that if they wanted to call on him in the future they would have to leave Mr. Trotter out.

The Associated Press sent the incident throughout the country, and many papers heralded the assertion that "Mr. Trotter had insulted President Wilson." I knew very well that there had been no breach of courtesy, but that President Wilson had simply become annoyed at Mr. Trotter's persistence. Many of our colored newspapers followed the lead of the white ones and condemned Mr. Trotter's action. The Negro Fellowship League extended him an invitation to visit Chicago and deliver our emancipation address.

We thought that the race should back up the man who had the bravery to contend for the rights of his race, instead of condemning him. Mr. Trotter had never been West; and I thought that he needed to get out in this part of the country and see that the world didn't revolve around Boston as a hub, and we were very glad to give him an opportunity to do this.

We engaged Orchestra Hall and were forced to charge an admission fee to pay that three-hundred-dollar rental. Again I believed that the loyalty of our people would assert itself and that the encouragement we would give to this young leader would be of great service to him and to the race. We did this all the more readily because the city of New York, which had already engaged him to appear, had recalled its invitation. It so happened that our celebration fell on Saturday night, the first of January being Sunday.

It also happened to be one night in the year in which all our churches have watch night meetings. Some of the ministers urged their congregations not to attend the Orchestra Hall meeting because they were having services in their churches. One of the leading ministers had announced that he too had a national speaker and they would not have to pay anything to hear him.

Still others announced that Mr. Trotter was a Democrat and that they owed him no support. Suffice it to say that the meeting was a failure in attendance. Had I not been able to have a white friend stand for the rent I would have been unable to open the doors of the hall. We held our meeting, however, and both Mr. William Thompson and Chief Justice Olsen, tentative candidates for mayor, also made short addresses.

Mr. Trotter was my guest for ten days. Through the efforts of friends he was invited to other meetings, and thus we succeeded in giving him the one hundred dollars I had promised. Not only this, but we made engagements for him as far north as Saint Paul, Minnesota; as far west as Omaha, Nebraska; as far south as Saint Louis, Missouri. When Mr. Trotter returned East it was with the assurance that the West had approved his course and upheld his hands.

The National Equal Rights League met in New York City, 20 September 1917, and I was the guest of Madam C. J. Walker when I went on as a delegate. Nothing startling took place in this session except that Madam Walker entertained the entire delegation royally. She was a woman who by hard work and persistent effort had succeeded in establishing herself and her business in New York City. She already had a town house, beautifully furnished, and had established beauty parlors and agents in and around New York City, thus giving demonstration of what a black woman who has vision and ambition can really do.

Madam Walker was even then building herself a home on the Hudson at a cost of many thousands of dollars. We drove out there almost every day, and I asked her on one occasion what on earth she would do with a thirty-room house. She said, "I want plenty of room in which to entertain my friends. I have worked so hard all of my life that I would like to rest."

I was very proud of her success, because I had met Madam Walker when she first started out eleven years before. I was one of the skeptics that paid little heed to her predictions as to what she was going to do. She had little or no education, and was never ashamed of having been a washerwoman earning a dollar and a half a day. To see her phenomenal rise made me take pride anew in Negro womanhood.

She maintained a wonderful home on 136th Street, and she had learned already how to bear herself as if to the manner born. She gave a dinner to the officers of the Equal Rights League and left the meeting a short time before it adjourned, in order to oversee dinner arrangements. When we were ushered into the dining room, Madam sat at the head of her table in her décolleté gown, with her butler serving dinner under her directions.

I was indeed proud to see what a few short years of success had done for a woman who had been without education and training. Her beautiful home on the Hudson was completed the next year, when Madam took possession, surrounded by prominent people from all over the country. It is a great pity to have to remember that she was permitted to enjoy its splendors less than a year after she moved in. Seven months from the day in which its doors were opened, they laid her away in her grave. The life had been too strenuous and the burden had become too heavy.

The next year the Equal Rights League came to Chicago for its annual meeting at my invitation. The trend of events seemed to show that the world war would not last much longer, and a motion prevailed that we call a national meeting to be held in Washington in December to arrange to send delegates to France to attend the Peace Conference which must follow the close of the war.

The idea met with great favor among the people of the country. And delegates were sent to Washington, at which time delegates and alternates were elected to go to Versailles, for the Armistice had already been signed between the close of the National Equal Rights League meeting in Chicago and the meeting of the Democracy Congress in Washington in December. Madam Walker and myself were the two women elected to go, and there were seven other persons. But none of us got to go because President Wilson forbade it.

The committee which was chosen to bring in nominations at first left out Mr. Trotter, on the ground that his presence would be objectionable to President Wilson. I asked the committee if they were going to allow President Wilson to select our delegates, and whom did they think deserved the right to go if not the man whose brain had conceived the idea. When the committee's report was brought in Mr. Trotter's name was included among those whose expenses were to be paid. Madam Walker and myself had been chosen as alternates with the distinct understanding that we would have to pay our own expenses.

I got the floor on a question of personal privilege and thanked the congress for the honor it had done me, but I regretted that the years I had spent in fighting the race's battles had made me financially unable to accept the honor which they had offered me. I therefore declined with thanks. Immediately a clamor arose; the committee's report was halted and an amendment was made by which both of the women named were included on the list of regular delegates.

Only Mr. Trotter got across after all, and he did so by subterfuge. He disguised himself as a cook and went across on a ship after he as well as the rest of us had been refused a passport.

Not only had I been elected by the Democracy Congress as a delegate, but Marcus Garvey's Universal Negro Improvement Association had already elected me in New York nearly a month before the convening of our congress. Mr. Garvey had visited Chicago a few years before, when he had recently come from Jamaica to accept an invitation that had been extended him by Booker T. Washington to visit Tuskeegee.

Mr. Washington had passed away before he came; so Mr. Garvey was traveling from place to place to arouse the interest of other West Indians who were living in the United States to assist him in establishing an industrial school in Jamaica. He visited my husband's law office, and Mr. Barnett brought him home to dinner.

In the course of his conversation he said that ninety thousand of the people on the island of Jamaica were colored, and only fifteen thousand of them were white; yet the fifteen thousand white people possessed all the land, ruled the island, and kept the Negroes in subjection. I asked him what those ninety thousand Negroes were thinking about to be dominated in this way, and he said it was because they had no educational facilities outside of grammar-school work. He wanted to return to his native home to see if he could not help to change the situation there.

Instead he went to New York, began to hold street meetings, and got many of his fellow countrymen as well as American Negroes interested in his program of worldwide Negro unity. For a time it seemed as if his program would go through. Undoubtedly Mr. Garvey made an impression on this country as no Negro before him had ever done. He has been able to solidify the masses of our people and endow them with racial consciousness and racial solidarity.

Had Garvey had the support which his wonderful movement deserved, had he not become drunk with power too soon, there is no telling what the result would have been. Already the countries of the world were beginning to worry very much about the influence of his propaganda in Africa, in the West Indies, and in the United States. His month-long conference in New York City every August, bringing the dusky sons and daughters of Ham from all corners of the earth, attracted a great deal of attention.

It was during this time that he sent me an invitation to come to New

York to deliver an address. I accepted the invitation and was met by him at the train on the afternoon of the evening on which I was to appear. The Universal Negro Improvement Association no longer met on the streets. It was housed in the Manhattan Casino, and I talked to an audience of nearly three thousand persons that evening.

Before this Mr. Garvey had spent a couple of hours acquainting me with his idea of establishing what he called the Black Star Line. He wanted me to present the matter that night, but I told him that it was too big an idea and would require more thought and preparation before it should be launched. He had shown me the restaurant that had been established, the newspaper which was circulating regularly each week, and own or two smaller ventures. He had complained that none of them were self-sustaining because they had not been able to obtain efficient help.

I knew that the work involved in a shipping business called for a much more complicated program than he had helpers to carry out, and I advised him to defer the matter. This he did not do, but presented himself after I had finished my talk, with that eloquence for which he was so famous, and it took among that people like wildfire.

Perhaps if Mr. Garvey had listened to my advice he need not have undergone the humiliations which afterward became his. Perhaps all that was necessary in order to broaden and deepen his own outlook on life. It may be that even though he has been banished to Jamaica the seed planted here will yet spring up and bring forth fruit which will mean the deliverance of the black race—that cause which was so dear to his heart.

PAULI MURRAY

To the Oppressors

Now you are strong
And we are but grapes aching with
ripeness.
Crush us!
Squeeze from us all the brave life
Contained in these full skins.
But ours is a subtle strength
Potent with centuries of yearning,
Of being kegged and shut away
In dark forgotten places.

We shall endure
To steal your senses
In that lonely twilight
Of your winter's grief.

Source: The Crisis 46 (January 1939): 18.

Mr. Roosevelt Regrets

What'd you get, black boy,
When they knocked you down in the gutter,
And they kicked your teeth out,
And they broke your skull with clubs
And they bashed your stomach in?
What'd you get when the police shot you in the back,
And they chained you to the beds
While they wiped the blood off?
What'd you get when you cried out to the Top Man?
When you called on the man next to God, so you
thought,
And you asked him to speak out to save you?
What'd the Top Man say, black boy?"
"Mr. Roosevelt regrets . . . ."

Source: The Crisis 50 (August 1943): 252.

HALLIE QUINN BROWN

From *Tales My Father Told and Other Stories*

Foreword

Very recently the Monongahela House of Pittsburgh, Pennsylvania, was torn down to make room, in the onward march of Time, for more modern and commodious structures. This hostelry stood the storm and stress for nearly a century, a silent witness to many thrilling incidents of historic interest as the old city of antebellum days developed into the Pittsburgh of today of greater enterprize and wider activities.

As I read the account of the passing of the old building a troop of memories took possession of my mind. For years my father followed the river for a livelihood. My earliest and most vivid recollection is of our Canadian farm home. When the broad meadows and streams were shrouded in snow, the bitter cold weather was heralded with joy, because we knew the great Mississippi River was sure to be frozen and father would soon be coming home. Then came the time when the jingling of bells announced his coming—the shaking of snow from his great fur coat and fur cap—the stamping of feet and the glad welcome. Our childish glee broke forth afresh at the gifts and trinkets brought from the states, even from the warm waters of the far Southland. The long winter evenings were spent in the living-room where a great log fire roared up the chimney and radiated warmth and cheer to the farthest corner of the room. A large lamp glowed on the center table with its bright chintz cover.

In fancy I see our dear Mother seated in her rocking chair, making the

Source: Excerpted from Hallie Quinn Brown, *Tales My Father Told and Other Stories* (Wilberforce, Ohio: Homewood Cottage, 1925), pp. 3-7.

knitting needles fly, her sweet serene face wreathed in smiles. Once more I hear her soft sweet voice in loving kindness or gentle admonition. On the other side of the table sat Father in his arm-chair. As we ate the rosy-cheeked apples or cracked the nuts brought from the big baskets on the hearth, Father told us stories from his wonderful store of information and experience. Many of these stories, like our loved ones themselves, have vanished and gone. Some few remain and have become household property.

The tearing away of the Monongahela House recalled the stories and is the only excuse I have for reviving "The Tales My Father Told."

"Lizette—The Beautiful": A True Story of Slavery

One blustery March evening in 18— a carriage rolled up and halted at the front entrance of the Old Monongahela House in Pittsburgh, Pennsylvania. I was acting as night porter. The entire force of employees was composed of colored men and women of intelligence and considerable native ability. They deserved better places in life, but this was before the Civil War, in the dark days of slavery when persons of color were mainly employed as menials. The city of Pittsburgh boasted of stalwart characters in those days. Lewis Woodson, Augustus Green, and William Wells, powerful pulpit orators; John Peck, the first Negro to own and control a fine Hair Goods Establishment; Joseph Miller, leader of the famous choir of Old Wylie Street Church; George B. Vashon, Samuel Neal, and Martin H. Freeman, noted professors of Avery College, and other city schools. Martin R. Delany, distinguished physician and scholar; George Knox, Jesse Wells, William Austin, Barney Mahoney, Matthew and Charles Jones, and a host of others I could mention. Ah! these were giants in their day! Given a fair chance in the race of life they would have measured arms with the greatest of earth's noblemen. They served their day and generation; noblemen they were in point of splendid service. But to return to my story—The big Hotel was managed by Mr. and Mrs. Crossan, the proprietor and his wife. They were strong abolitionists and reposed the utmost confidence in their employees who assisted in providing for the comforts of an exacting public.

As I said at the beginning a carriage halted at the main entrance. Two travelers, a man and a woman, alighted and walked rapidly to the door, which I opened to admit them, then hastily closed it against the swirling snow and the biting blast which swept the street.

The arrivals were without baggage except a small leather bag, carried by the man. I directed him to the desk. As he removed his gloves and unbuttoned his overcoat, diamonds flashed from his fingers and bosom. He was below medium height, slender and dark, straight hair fell over his collar. A heavy drooping mustache could not hide the sneering curl of his lip. A wide brimmed black hat shaded small ferret-like eyes which were deep-set and restless. His appearance and manner proclaimed him a southern planter before he uttered a word. He spoke in an undertone to the clerk who turned to me and said, "Show the gentleman to room 18 second floor. Take the girl to room 40 third floor back. The gentleman will give you further orders." At the word *girl* I looked keenly at the woman who, until now, stood in the shadow of a pillar. The bright light fell upon her fair face. Never shall I forget that lovely young girl! Her tall slender form was enveloped in a long cloak of some dark stuff. The hood which had partly concealed her face was thrown back revealing her wondrous beauty. Her finely chiseled features and clear olive complexion were enhanced by large dark eyes which glowed, but held within their depths both fear and sorrow. Glossy black hair waved from a smooth broad brow and was hidden beneath her cloak which she drew closely about her.

At a glance I comprehended the situation. This girl was a slave: the man her master. That moment I was fired with determination to rescue her from his clutches, no matter what the cost might be. The man snapped his fingers in her direction, signifying she was to follow him. For an instant she recoiled, her face paled, then flushed. With downcast eyes she walked gracefully to the corridor followed by admiring glances from loungers in the lobby. At No. 18 the man bade me halt while he entered the room and deposited his bag; then followed the girl and myself to No. 40, third floor back. I unlocked and opened the door and turned on the light, the man following closely behind. He carefully scrutinized the room; tested the walls; opened and examined the closets; raised the window sash, looked out and down as if measuring the distance to the pavement below; shut and locked the windows. Apparently satisfied with his findings he turned on his heel, walked out of the room without so much as a glance at the girl. He shut and locked the door, and pocketed the key. Although I towered head and shoulders above him and felt myself infinitely his superior as a man, he said, "Boy, are you on watch all night?" [I replied] in the affirmative [and] he continued, "Bring this girl some bread and butter and tea. How soon will dinner be served?" "In half an hour, Sir." "Bring the girl's supper at once," he said, consulting his watch. "Yes Sir," I replied, hastening away. In less than twenty minutes every sympathizer in that Old Monongahela House knew there was a slave girl locked in No. 40 third floor back and indignation ran high. On my return with the tea, I found the planter impatiently pacing the hall. He unlocked the door and we entered. I placed the tray upon a small table which stood in the center of the room. The girl had thrown off her wrap and was seated on a stool at the foot of the bed. Her hands, tensely locked, lay in her lap. Her wavy black hair was unconfined and literally swept the floor, falling like a cloud about her girlish form. She raised a tear-stained face in mute appeal. I dared not look at her again for fear I should say an imprudent word or commit a rash act, so I stepped into the hall where I could observe all without being seen. The girl arose, stood erect with the palms of her shapely hands pressed to her temples. The sight of that stricken girl exasperated the master beyond expression. He advanced toward her with menacing finger, stamped his foot and cried angrily but with suppressed wrath—"Lizette stop this nonsense, eat your supper, then lie down until you are called. Come now, stop that snuffling. Mind what I say and be quick about it, too." From the hall I heard the angry words and saw the look of utter despair on Lizette's face but not a murmur escaped her trembling lips. Again the master locked the door and kept the key. Almost immediately the light in the girl's room went out.

With a muttered imprecation, he commanded me to call the girl at 11 P.M., to order a cab to take them to meet the midnight express South, then strode haughtily downstairs and into the dining room.

Shortly afterward a half dozen determined men held a brief but decisive consultation. Mrs. Crossan and the chamber-maid on the third floor were taken into our confidence. Watches were stationed in the several halls and on stairways; a special one was placed to observe the movements of the planter. The headwaiter was instructed to delay serving the courses at dinner. With all speed messages were dispatched to friends in the city. The word soon came that a closed carriage would be at the door at 9 P.M. The planter had met some boon companions and everything favored our daring scheme. I was given the task of getting the girl out of the room. How was it to be done? The clerk, whom we did not trust, held the pass key, the planter had the other one safe in his pocket. Keys were brought from every part of the house, but the lock [to] No. 40 would not yield. All plans and suggestions failed. Time was flying! We were getting desperate! Finally I called in a low tone through the key hole. "Lizette, Lizette, we are your friends, come nearer. Are you a slave?" "Yes," came the faint answer. "Do you wish to be free?" "Yes, God knows I do." "Will you trust us and do as we tell you?" "Yes, I will," came the prompt response. How were we to get her out? Like a flash the idea came to me. There was but one way, draw her through the transom over the door! "Quick," I cried, "bring a strong rope and ladder!" Then the thought: would she consent? Had she courage for such an ordeal? It was a trying moment! We worked nervously, almost breathlessly. The rope and the ladder were secured. We made a noose, threw it through the transom. The girl put it around her waist as we directed. With great daring and heroism she suffered herself to be drawn through the transom into the hall. We could have shouted for joy, but the battle was yet to be won.

Lizette was hurried into the chamber-maid's room and dressed in male attire. Her shapely head was quickly shorn of its beautiful tresses; green goggles concealed her bright eyes; a wide brimmed hat shaded her face. I threw a gentleman's cape about her shoulders. Leaning on my arm, as an invalid, we passed within a few feet of the master, puffing his after-dinner pipe in great contentment; passed the loungers in the lobby, the clerk at his desk—out into the street and the wintry gale. The poor girl trembled so violently I feared she would fall. I actually carried her from the door to the carriage. A Quaker lady gathered Lizette in her arms as I quickly closed the door. The whip was given to the horses and the vehicle was soon lost in the blinding snow storm. I returned to the lobby just as the clock chimed the hour of *nine.* Our work was accomplished! As we passed, confederates in a holy cause, we silently grasped each other's hands and tears welled to our eyes.

At the home of the Quakeress Lizette told her simple story. She had gone from Virginia to Baltimore, Md., as maid to her mistress. Longing for freedom she ran away, but was apprehended. At her third attempt to escape, her master, who was her half brother, decided to sell her to a Georgia Soul Driver, who was to claim her the next day. With the master she was on her way to the place where she was to be turned over to her purchaser when they had halted at Pittsburgh and her rescue had occurred. Kind friends dressed her in a dark travelling suit, gave her a well filled purse and by 10 P.M., she was on the north bound train speeding to Canada and Freedom.

Not waiting for "Watch" to call the girl, ten minutes to 11 o'clock the master went to No. 40, rapping loudly and saying it was time to be up. Getting no response he unlocked the door and turned on the light, only to find the room empty. *The bird had flown!* He screamed in rage and called, "Lizette, Lizette, where are you, Lizette?" The cry was so loud and insistent that doors were hastily thrown open, while guests and servants alike ran into the corridors, thinking the cry an alarm of fire. It was with great difficulty that he was quieted and only on the promise that a thorough search would be made in the morning. As no one had seen her escape, he was led to believe that she must be in the house.

The planter refused to retire, but sat, the remainder of the night, in the office near the main entrance to watch, and stationed watches at all other exits. By daylight the house was in an uproar. The planter ran here and there calling excitedly and incriminating *everybody.* Detectives searched the premises but without avail. The house watchmen were arraigned. The planter demanded their arrest. They were about to be taken into custody. At that moment all the employees in the house stepped forward and asked for their wages, signifying their intention to quit the service.

With uplifted hands, Mrs. Crossan exclaimed, "For my sake, Brown, don't leave. The guests are at the table and there is no one to serve breakfast." "We are men, madame, and must be treated as such," I replied. Mr. Crossan turned to us and said, "You may resume your work without threat or fear." Then addressing the planter he added with emphasis—"Sir, I have a set of men whom I can trust. If you lay your pocket book down you will get it again, *but I will not vouch for your nigger.*" The planter left immediately, swearing eternal vengeance against the Old Mononga-hela House and everybody in it, all Pittsburgh and the North generally— *but beautiful Lizette he never saw again.*

ZORA NEALE HURSTON

Spunk

I

A Giant of a brown-skinned man sauntered up the one street of the village and out into the palmetto thickets with a small pretty woman clinging lovingly to his arm.

"Looka theah, folkses!" cried Elijah Mosley, slapping his leg gleefully, "Theah they go, big as life an' brassy as tacks."

All the loungers in the store tried to walk to the door with an air of nonchalance but with small success.

"Now pee-eople!" Walter Thomas gasped. "Will you look at 'em!"

"But that's one thing Ah likes about Spunk Banks—he ain't skeered of nothin' on God's green footstool—*nothin'*! He rides that log down at saw-mill jus' like he struts 'round wid another man's wife—jus' don't give a kitty. When Tes' Miller got cut to giblets on that circle-saw, Spunk steps right up and starts ridin'. The rest of us was skeered to go near it."

A round-shouldered figure in overalls much too large came nervously in the door and the talking ceased. The men looked at each other and winked.

"Gimme some soda-water. Sass'prilla Ah reckon," the newcomer ordered, and stood far down the counter near the open pickled pig-feet tub to drink it.

Elijah nudged Walter and turned with mock gravity to the new-comer.

"Say, Joe, how's everything up yo' way? How's yo' wife?"

Joe started and all but dropped the bottle he held in his hands. He swallowed several times painfully and his lips trembled.

Source: Opportunity 3 (June 1925): 171–173.

"Aw 'Lige, you oughtn't to do nothin' like that," Walter grumbled. Elijah ignored him.

"She jus' passed heah a few minutes ago goin' thata way," with a wave of his hand in the direction of the woods.

Now Joe knew his wife had passed that way. He knew that the men lounging in the general store had seen her, moreover, he knew that the men knew *he* knew. He stood there silent for a long moment staring blankly, with his Adam's apple twitching nervously up and down his throat. One could actually *see* the pain he was suffering, his eyes, his face, his hands and even the dejected slump of his shoulders. He set the bottle down upon the counter. He didn't bang it, just eased it out of his hand silently and fiddled with his suspender buckle.

"Well, Ah'm goin' after her to-day. Ah'm goin' an fetch her back. Spunk's done gone too fur."

He reached deep down into his trouser pocket and drew out a hollow ground razor, large and shiny, and passed his moistened thumb back and forth over the edge.

"Talkin' like a man, Joe. 'Course that's *yo'* fambly affairs, but Ah like to see grit in anybody."

Joe Kanty laid down a nickel and stumbled out into the street.

Dusk crept in from the woods. Ike Clarke lit the swinging oil lamp that was almost immediately surrounded by candleflies. The men laughed boisterously behind Joe's back as they watched him shamble woodward.

"You oughtn't to said whut you did to him, Lige—look how it worked him up," Walter chided.

"And Ah hope it did work him up. Tain't even decent for a man to take and take like he do."

"Spunk will sho' kill him."

"Aw, Ah doan' know. You never kin tell. He might turn him up an' spank him fur gettin' in the way, but Spunk wouldn't shoot no unarmed man. Dat razor he carried outa heah ain't gonna run Spunk down an'cut him, an' Joe ain't got the nerve to go up to Spunk with it knowing he totes that Army .45. He makes that break outa heah to bluff us. He's gonna hide that razor behind the first palmetto root an' sneak back home to bed. Don't tell me nothin' 'bout that rabbit-foot colored man. Didn't he meet Spunk an' Lena face to face one day las' week an' mumble sumthin' to Spunk 'bout lettin' his wife alone?"

"What did Spunk say?" Walter broke in—"Ah like him fine but tain't right the way he carries on wid Lena Kanty, jus' cause Joe's timid 'bout fightin'."

"You wrong theah, Walter. Tain't 'cause Joe's timid at all, it's 'cause Spunk wants Lena. If Joe was a passle of wile cats Spunk would tackle the job just the same. He'd go after anything he wanted the same way. As Ah wuz sayin' a minute ago, he tole Joe right to his face that Lena was his. 'Call her and see if she'll come. A woman knows her boss an' she answers when he calls.' 'Lena, ain't I yo' husband?' Joe sorter whines out. Lena looked at him real disgusted but she don't answer and she don't move outa her tracks. Then Spunk reaches out an' takes hold of her arm an' says: 'Lena, youse mine. From now on ah works for you an' fights for you an' Ah never wants you to look to nobody for a crumb of bread, a stitch of close or a shingle to go over yo' head, but *me* long as Ah live. Ah'll git the lumber foh owah house to-morrow. Go home an' git yo' things together!' 'Thass mah house,' Lena speaks up. 'Papa gimme that.' 'Well,' says Spunk, 'doan give up whut's yours, but when youse inside doan forgit youse mine, an' let no other man git outa his place wid you!'"

"Lena looked up at him with her eyes so full of love that they wuz runnin' over, an' Spunk seen it an' Joe seen it too, and his lip started to tremblin' and his Adam's apple was galloping up and down his neck like a race horse. Ah bet he's wore out half a dozen Adam's apples since Spunk's been on the job with Lena. That's all he'll do. He'll be back heah after while swallowin' an' workin' his lips like he wants to say somethin' an' can't."

"But didn't he do nothin' to stop 'em?"

"Nope, not a frazzlin' thing—jus' stood there. Spunk took Lena's arm and walked off jus' like nothin' ain't happened and he stood there gazin' after them till they was outa sight. Now you know a woman don't want no man like that. I'm jus' waitin' to see whut he's goin to say when he gits back."

II

But Joe Kanty never came back, never. The men in the store heard the sharp report of a pistol somewhere distant in the palmetto thicket and soon Spunk came walking leisurely, with his big black Stetson set at the same rakish angle and Lena clinging to his arm, came walking right into the general store. Lena wept in a frightened manner.

"Well," Spunk announced calmly, "Joe come out there wid a meat axe an' made me kill him."

He sent Lena home and led the men back to Joe—crumpled and limp with his right hand still clutching his razor.

"See mah back? Mah close cut clear through. He sneaked up an' tried to kill me from the back, but Ah got him, an' got him good, first shot," Spunk said.

The men glared at Elijah, accusingly.

"Take him up an' plant him in Stony Lonesome," Spunk said in a careless voice. "Ah didn't wanna shoot him but he made me do it. He's a dirty coward, jumpin' on a man from behind."

Spunk turned on his heel and sauntered away to where he knew his love wept in fear for him and no man stopped him. At the general store later on, they all talked of locking him up until the sheriff should come from Orlando, but no one did anything but talk.

A clear case of self-defense, the trial was a short one, and Spunk walked out of the court house to freedom again. He could work again, ride the dangerous log-carriage that fed the singing, snarling, biting circle-saw; he could stroll the soft dark lanes with his guitar. He was free to roam the woods again; he was free to return to Lena. He did all of these things.

III

"Whut you reckon, Walt?" Elijah asked one night later. "Spunk's gittin' ready to marry Lena!"

"Naw! Why, Joe ain't had time to git cold yit. Nohow Ah didn't figger Spunk was the marryin' kind."

"Well, he is," rejoined Elijah. "He done moved most of Lena's things— and her along wid'em—over to the Bradley house. He's buying it. Jus' like Ah told yo' all right in heah the night Joe wuz kilt. Spunk's crazy 'bout Lena. He don't want folks to keep on takin' 'bout her—thass reason he's rushin' so. Funny thing 'bout that bob-cat, wasn't it?"

"What bob-cat, 'Lige? ah ain't heered 'bout none."

"Ain't cher? Well, night befo' las' was the fust night Spunk an' Lena moved together an' just then as they was goin' to bed, a big black bob-cat, black all over, you hear me, black, walked round and round that house and howled like forty, an' when Spunk got his gun an' went to the winder to shoot it, he says it stood right still an' and looked him in the eye, an' howled right at him. The thing got Spunk so nervoused up he couldn't shoot. But Spunk says twan't no bob-cat nohow. He says it was Joe done sneaked back from Hell!"

"Humph!" sniffed Walter, "he oughter be nervous after what he done. Ah reckon Joe come back to dare him to marry Lena, or to come out an' fight. Ah bet he'll be back time and again, too. Know what Ah think? Joe wuz a braver man than Spunk."

There was a general shout of derision from the group.

"Thass a fact," went on Walter. "Lookit whut he done; took a razor an' went out to fight a man he knowed toted a gun an' wuz a crack shot, too; 'nother thing Joe wuz skeered of Spunk, skeered plumb stiff! But he went jes' the same. It took him a long time to get his nerve up. Tain't nothin' for Spunk to fight when he ain't skeered of nothin'. Now, Joe's done come back to have it out wid the man that's got all he ever had. Y'all know Joe ain't never had nothin' or wanted nothin' besides Lena. It musta been a h'ant* cause ain't nobody never seen no black bob-cat."

"'Nother thing," cut in one of the men, "Spunk wuz cussin' a blue streak to-day 'cause he 'lowed dat saw wuz wobblin'—almos' got 'im once. The machinist come, looked it over an' said it wuz alright. Spunk musta been leanin' t'wards it some. Den he claimed somebody pushed 'im but twan't nobody close to 'im. Ah wuz glad when knockin' off time come. I'm skeered of dat man when he gits hot. He'd beat you full of button holes as quick as he's look atcher."

IV

The men gathered the next evening in a different mood, no laughter. No badinage this time.

"Look, 'Lige, you goin' to set up wid Spunk?"

"Naw, Ah reckon not, Walter. Tell yuh the truth, Ah'm a li'l bit skittish, Spunk died too wicket—died cussin' he did. You know he thought he was done outa life."

"Good Lawd, who'd he think done it?"

"Joe."

"Joe Kanty? How come?"

*Ghost.

"Walter, Ah b'leeve Ah will walk up thata way an' set. Lena would like it Ah reckon."

"But whut did he say, 'Lige?"

Elijah did not answer until they had left the lighted store and were strolling down the dark street.

"Ah wuz loadin' a wagon wid scantlin' right near the saw when Spunk fell on the carriage but 'fore Ah could git to him the saw got him in the body—awful sight. Me an' Skint Miller got him off but it was too late. Anybody could see that. The fust thing he said wuz: 'He pushed me, 'Lige—the dirty hound pushed me in the back!'—he was spittin' blood at ev'ry breath. We laid him on the sawdust pile with his face to the east so's he could die easy. He helt mah han' till the last, Walter, and said: 'It was Joe, 'Lige . . . the dirty sneak shoved me . . . he didn't dare to come to mah face . . . but Ah'll git the son-of-a-wood louse soon's Ah get there an' make Hell too hot for him. . . . Ah felt him shove me. . .!' Thass how he died."

"If spirits kin fight, there's a powerful tussle goin' on somewhere ovah Jordan 'cause Ah b'leeve Joe's ready for Spunk an' ain't skeered any more—yas, Ah b'leeve Joe pushed 'im mahself."

They had arrived at the house. Lena's lamentations were deep and loud. She had filled the room with magnolia blossoms that gave off a heavy sweet odor. The keepers of the wake tipped about whispering in frightened tones. Everyone in the Village was there, even old Jeff Kanty, Joe's father, who a few hours before would have been afraid to come with ten feet of him, stood leering triumphantly down upon the fallen giant as if his fingers had been the teeth of steel that laid him low.

The cooling board consisted of three sixteen-inch boards on saw horses, a dingy sheet was his shroud.

The women ate heartily of the funeral baked meats and wondered who would be Lena's next. The men whispered coarse conjectures between guzzles of whiskey.

PART 6

MY GREAT, WIDE, BEAUTIFUL WORLD

For those few black women who could do it, traveling abroad opened an avenue of opportunity that was closed to most women of color in America. Once away from the United States, they found themselves beyond the reach of racial intolerance and positioned to gain new perspectives on their lives and on race relations. While they discovered that biases existed in other countries, these were not as firmly institutionalized, nor even remotely as constraining, as those in the United States. Having grown in their knowledge of other societies and social arrangements, these women acquired the tools to further their own creativity.

For some, the destination was Western Europe: primarily England, Spain, and Germany; a number traveled there upon graduating from college. Others went to Africa (Idabelle Yeiser, Eslanda Goode Robeson) or the Caribbean (Zora Neale Hurston, Katherine Dunham) as part of field projects related to their professions. One woman, Juanita Harrison, went all over the world on the wages she earned as a domestic.

Traveling abroad was not something these women could take for granted. Finances were always a concern, and often scholarships from churches, sororities, or foundations provided the support critical for their overseas voyages. It was also difficult for a black person to obtain passage, as Nellie Bright describes in her story, "Black." Often passports were denied or withheld, especially if officials suspected that the individual would expose unpleasant truths about America's racial problems; in addition, commercial steamship companies were reluctant to sell tickets to black passengers.

Once overseas, African-Americans found release from the ever present

239

restrictions and from their worries about the color line. They became simply human beings moving in the general stream of life, free to explore and to meet new people in ways unimaginable to them at home.

Gwendolyn Bennett's stories afford a glimpse of the lives of American blacks—mostly musicians—who moved to Paris permanently, where they encountered racial conflict only occasionally, and then only among white American tourists and expatriates. "Wedding Day" tells the story of an African-American who lives in Paris precisely because it delivers him from racist practices ingrained in America.

Turning to the African continent, Idabelle Yeiser recounts an incident in her trip to North Africa with a group of Europeans. There, the only mention of Yeiser's dark skin is made when a group of native Africans ask about her and are told—in a surprisingly true though not factual explanation—that she was taken from Africa as a child and is now returning home. Eslanda Robeson's trip to Africa was more than a sightseeing adventure: she aimed to gain direct knowledge with which to challenge European academic perceptions of African culture, as well as to accomplish a field study of a society based on raising dairy cattle. Katherine Dunham's experiences in Jamaica were likewise part of a quest to find hidden sources of black creativity.

NELLIE R. BRIGHT

Black

Have you ever longed to go to Hankow, or Nice, or Scheveningen,* but you never went because your shekels† were too few? That often happens to me, but last summer I went to Scheveningen on the North Sea.

Getting passage is quite an adventure.

As I wanted to get accommodations in the tourist third cabin, I went to the steamship office six months before sailing. The clerks looked at me in great amazement over the shining black counter. Then, they looked at each other. As I continued to stand, one arose and came to me. "What can I do for you?" he asked doubtfully.

"I should like to get passage on one of your steamers carrying tourist third accommodations."

"They're all booked," he said, eyeing me in a strange way.

"But this is February and I don't want to sail until July. Are you sure there's nothing left?"

At this unexpected sally, another clerk came to his assistance. "You see," he began suavely, "this is one of the oldest and most popular lines and we book early. We really have nothing left."

"Thank you," I breathed, and headed for an office on the opposite corner. The force must have seen me enter the rival office, for as I went in every clerk was on his feet. One stood expectantly looking in my

Source: Opportunity 5 (November 1927): 331-334.
    *Hankow, China; Nice, France; Scheveningen, Netherlands.
    †Monetary unit of ancient Israel (paper bill or silver coin), also an ancient, originally Babylonian, unit of weight.

direction. In my handbag was an advertisement that I had cut from the morning paper. "Now you are permitted more than a dream of the old fame of Europe." Go the "new way," by "tourist third." "In the first place, of course, it is really intended for students and teachers, writers, artists, and people of this class on both East-bound and West-bound sailings."

This was just what I wanted. As I turned from closing the door, a clerk said, "Well—?"

I repeated my query as to accommodations on their tourist third to Europe. "We haven't any tourist third. I suppose that we're the only line that doesn't have it."

"But," I began, taking the ad from my bag, "here is your announcement giving dates for these accommodations."

"Some mistake. We don't—." I waited to hear no more.

That morning I went to five steamship offices, making the same request, and was looked at in great consternation, answered glibly or curtly, but always with the flat denial that there were any bookings left. I had no idea what a tremendous business steamship offices carried on six months before sailings!

Perhaps the ——— Line had a berth left. When I entered, all of the clerks became so suddenly entranced with their typing or 'phoning that none saw me. I waited, the blood pounding at my temples, my heart beating at such a pace that when a little boy was sent to ask me what I wanted, I could only gasp.

"The manager wants to know why you're waiting in here."

"I'm waiting here to get information concerning your bookings to France," I answered loudly enough to be heard by the office force and the clerk at the rear behind a screen.

No one lifted his eyes from his work. There was a stillness as if fingers had suddenly forgotten the keys of the typewriters. After a brief conference, during which I heard the rasping voice of the manager, and saw the screen move, then return to its former position, the boy came to me and said, "We don't sell tourist third to Negroes."

"Sacre bleu!"

Then, that was it. It wasn't that it was a curse to be poor, but in my case it was a curse to be a Negro. My skin was brown. In my excitement in planning for the adventure, I had committed a new crime. I had forgotten that I was a brown girl. Now, I saw clearly how foolish I had appeared to those Nordic clerks. I was too eager to be "permitted more than a dream of the old fame of Europe." I was a "student," but brown. A brown "student," a brown "teacher" should not "wish to make a trip to Europe at moderate cost, in comfort, and with a minimum expenditure for the ocean passage." God!

I had always wanted to go to Europe. When a few years old I had gone with my father and mother. As I grew, I never wearied of retraversing the scenes dear to my father, as he described our first service in Westminster, or a sail down the Thames, as he told of the ivy-covered walls of Christ Church, or a jaunt to the island of Marken. I must go to the "Cheshire Cheese," to Anne Hathaway's cottage, to the Louvre.

Then, in those years I had become a student. I was even now engaged in writing a thesis and I must go to Bodley and to the British Museum to search out old manuscripts for myself. I, a brown girl, would reveal to the world of literature knowledge that has lain secret for centuries. But, since they did not want to give me passage, I wondered if, after all, the trip would be worth the effort. Wouldn't I be meeting Nordics everywhere? I was going to the north of Europe. Wouldn't the American students tell the librarians what a despicable creature I was because my skin was brown, and would they, because of this, say, "We can't register any more students to search records. You see this is one of the oldest and most popular libraries, and we register early."

And, when I went to Bodley, would the keeper of the manuscripts look at me queerly when I asked to see the original "Roland," which I had translated the year before from photostats, and say, "You are permitted no more than a dream of the old fame of the 'Roland.' We don't expose it to the gaze of Negroes"? And, when I stood at the end of that long corridor in the Louvre with the vision of the Venus de Milo luring me from the velvety shadows, would an attendant come silently to me and say, "You must go no nearer; you see the Venus is dazzling white, and her beauty would be marred by the blackness of your visage. We must protect our masterpieces for the white men of the earth." And, being so near, would I withdraw in confusion without steeping my soul in the loveliness of that statue, because I was black?

Thus debating the question, I threaded my way through the traffic like one bearing a life apart, and entered another steamship office. How alert they were in that last output, and how busy. They must be too busy to see me, I thought. But, after waiting five minutes, a woman came forward and asked, "What do you want?"

"I should like to book passage on your tourist third for Liverpool," I ventured. Without a word, she turned and called to Mr. Johns, who evidently did the booking. I told him my errand and he proceeded to take out a huge book. As he turned the leaves, he shook his head. Before he could say, "We're full," I asked him for two dates and told him that I could make the first payment immediately. "Have a seat and I'll tell you in a few minutes."

Mr. Johns consulted three other clerks [and] then, "Here's something that will suit you," he said. We settled the dates and the first payment. He took my name and address. This surely looked as if I were going to Europe. But I was weary with their subterfuges and thought as soon as I was out of the office, "That's only a bluff, too. I suppose he took my address so as to be able to identify that audacious person who wanted to go on a holiday with the 'best youth of America.'"

I had seen enough of American youth in the schools and at the University. I knew only too well how the "best" would smile with their faces and draw their skirts aside at my coming. What I wanted was the cleanliness, the wholesome food, deck space, comforts that I would not get in the steerage. While the American youths smirked and smoked and babbled of Freud and Ford, I should be wrapped in my blanket, my thoughts racing with the waves.

Sailing day came! I was rushed down, down, down into the hold of the ship. My father, who knows ships would not look at me. He did not want me to see the hurt in his eyes. I didn't have tourist accommodations after all. This ship didn't carry student tours. Black! What did it matter?

That night I sat upon a coil of hawsers. There were no chairs for steerage passengers. At my back, the winches black with shining grease. The soft night wind caressed my cheek and my breath came quickly as I watched for the first star. I had eaten no supper. When I emerged from my stateroom in the hold of the ship, I felt that I would never eat again, so choked was I with the echoes of the voices of lily-white liars in steamship offices.

Gradually, my fellow passengers came up from the dining saloon. There was the ruddy-checked black-haired woman who had embarked so stylishly dressed with her husband and two boys. She now wore a loose sweater over an ill-fitting blue dress. She sat moodily, her family near her. The red-lipped girl whom I had fancied a Paquin model came on deck, her raven locks hidden beneath a somber scarf. The Welsh woman who had put her babies to bed chatted with the old Spaniard. He had come aboard in a dapper blue suit and yellow shoes but now had a red kerchief knitted at his throat and his feet encased in knitted bedroom slippers.

An elderly man, graying hair at his temples, sat beside me. I kept my gaze fixed upon the deepening sky, for should he see even in the dusk the black of my face he might leap away. And I was too lonely to have a fellow creature shun me just then.

Voices babbled incessantly. Everybody talked but me. They were talking about themselves. Two English boys, having made a fortune, were returning to care for their mother. I heard the Irish girl say that she was being deported because she had no wealth save her fur coat.

Presently, a voice beside me asked, "And what of you lass? Are you going home too?"

"No," I answered, "America is my home." The muscles of my throat tightened. "I'm off on a holiday." At the mention of holiday, several forms loitered nearer. Some had never had a holiday. What a joyful thing it must be to go just where one wanted and to do the things one liked best. The Englishman became eloquent. "You must go to the cheese market at Shrewsbury Shop in 'petticoat alley' on a Sunday morning. Don't miss the changing of the horse guard at Whitehall. Go to Kew and to the Tower. I'll make a list of the places that you must visit."

"You're very kind," I murmured, skeptical at his enthusiasm. He surely hadn't seen my face. How could he know that the word "holiday" had made my voice husky, that my holidays were honey drained from crystal cups with jagged edges?

As we talked, the lights came on. They looked full upon my face. I looked straight at them, a challenge in my eye. None even winced. Then, they knew—and didn't care? I pondered this while they chatted.

The Spaniard, his face gashed with wrinkles, wondered if his family in Madrid would recognize him after forty years. He was darker than I. Perhaps they talked to me because they thought me a Spaniard, too. Odd! Anything but a Negro.

One day, the social worker (she knew) came to me, her eyes wet. "Do go over and talk to that poor boy by the railing. He's a Nigerian and was brought to America by missionaries. But he seems so depressed and he won't tell me what troubles him. Perhaps he'll tell you."

"I didn't know that such a person was on board," I replied. "Where has he been all this time?"

"They've had him locked in his cabin for fear that he would injure himself," she explained. "But go to him, now."

The boy, a youth of eighteen, stood gazing fixedly at the horizon, much as I had done that first night at sea. Already, I knew his sorrow, I thought. He is suffering as I did. I stood near him for a moment, then made a casual remark about the speed of the vessel as is the way with fellow passengers.

"It can't fly too swiftly for me," replied Oojoula, looking at me almost fiercely.

"Where are you going?" I asked.

"To my home, five hundred miles from the Gold Coast, where my father is chief and where the white man has never set foot."

"How long were you in America?"

"Four long years."

"Were you in school?"

"Yes, civilized, educated, Christianized. They made me a Christian. Think of it—a Christian! I was but a child then. I even believed in their Christ until I felt their hatred for us. My people are more loyal to their gods than Christ's followers to Him. I would have killed myself, but I must go back to the jungle. I go to my people. I shall warn them against the white man. I would record their history. It is necessary. The world must know how noble black men are."

Oojoula turned his eyes from mine. I was forgotten.

How could I help him? This poor, disillusioned boy? He hadn't grown up with them as I had. He didn't know that equal opportunity for us meant denial of opportunity, or a struggle for opportunity that is so bitter that, when the end is realized, our strength and enthusiasm are spent. How was he to know that these people whom he hated with an intensity greater than the blackness of his skin, felt it their duty to prevent a Negro from enjoying the simplest of pleasures, from having the barest comforts. I could never make him understand.

We were too different. He had lost faith in man suddenly. I had been losing mine all through my childhood, all through my time of dreams, all through my college days. It was simply this: I had been born in a country where a man was good or evil according to the color of his skin. Oojoula had not.

When the ship's orchestra dropped down the ladders from the second class deck to entertain us that afternoon, the first and second class passengers crowded the rail. To look down upon the steerage passengers was quite a diversion. Oojoula, unable to bear the amused stare of the "superior" group, pointed out to me the priest and his wife who were taking him back to Africa. Then he locked himself in his cabin.

That night, while the ship's orchestra played in the first class saloon, a fiddler from Lisconnel perched himself upon a capstan and drew his bow across the strings. Forms rose from the shadows, swaying. There was the click of heels, the clap of hands. They were "stacking the barley." A rollicking dance. One of the English lads held out his hands to mine. "Come, jig with me," he urged, his feet beating a tatoo to the rhythm. The blood tingled in my veins. I drew away. How could I, a brown girl, dance with him? I loved to dance—but—with an English lad! He must be joking. I was a Negro. I had only danced with boys of my own race. All the inhibitions that had grown up with me forbade me to put my hand into his and swing with him in the sheer enjoyment of the dance.

"No," I said, my heart contracted with fear—the fear that he had chosen me to play the fool because I was black.

"No?" he repeated; "I don't take 'no' for an answer. I just know that you dance. You're like a willow. Won't you try it? Look, it goes like this." He showed me the steps. He was in earnest. I mustn't be rude. He was simply being kind. But, why? Wasn't he white and I—? Queer!

He insisted. What could I say? I was confused. "I do dance," I stammered, "but not the Irish folk dances, so you'll have to get another partner."

"No, I don't," he persisted. "I'll teach you to 'stack the barley' in a trice. Come!" He seized both my hands in a firm grip, drawing me to my feet. My body, singing with the music, danced one round. As the fiddler laid by his bow, I fled to my cabin.

What had I done? I had danced, a joyful thing in itself, but I had degraded myself by dancing with a Nordic.

As I lay in my berth, I marveled at many things. I thought of what I had done, of Oojoula, of my fellow passengers. They were Nordics, to be sure, but they had seemed kind. They had treated me as a human being. But, perhaps, that was only the camaraderie of the traveler. We would soon land in old England. Would they perchance know me if they spied me on the pier? If we should pass each other in Piccadilly, would they see me?

At times as I sat silent in black isolation for fear of inviting insult, they had come to me and chatted of the merits of farming in Poland, or of Yeats' poetry, or of their families. Sometimes, I found myself holding the Portuguese baby while its mother took her turn about the deck. Again, I was the center of a group swapping yarns. They hadn't seemed to notice.

Perhaps, after all, these people were different from Americans in that they did not despise my color. My doubts would soon be quelled for we were nearing Queenstown, our first stop; then England, Belgium, France.

The next day there was a perceptible restlessness among the passengers and crew. Gulls began to follow the ship. As sailors walked the deck they would stop, lean far over the port rail and peer toward the horizon. Toward sunset, I discerned an opalescent mist low in the sky. Knots of passengers began to watch the cloud. Field glasses were eagerly borrowed. The mist remained, began to take definitive shape against the sky. This was no cloud. Land! The wild, rocky coast of Ireland. There was a cry of joy that thrilled from every deck. There came a shout, and a song of Erin floated across the waves to Killarney.

The people with whom I had lived for eleven days embraced each other and some wept for joy. They rushed below and returned, dressed in their stylish American clothes. Once more they saw their beloved Ireland. They were going home. I rejoiced with them. Oojoula looked on from his cabin. He, too, was going home. He was thinking of the kindly black faces that would greet him.

At eleven o'clock that night, we set off two flares. In the wavering ribbon of light picking out a path of quicksilver from Queenstown to our steamer, glided the pilot's tiny boat. I drew my coat close against the cold. There was the roar of the propeller as we swung round toward the city. There was the tang of green hills in the air. Shrill cries and deep laughter mingled with the clanking of chairs and the bustle of passengers. Two tenders chugged along side. My fellow passengers beamed upon me. As soon as the mail had been taken off, they would go. As they went across the bridge to the second class deck, I went with them. Irish women who had just come on board with huge baskets were selling lace and shawls of soft silk. I stooped to look, then fled down the deck as the order came, "Steerage passengers not debarking, go below."

I must bid my friends goodbye as they went down the gangplank to the waiting tender. It began to rain, a sharp, drenching shower. Lights flowed from the city across the harbor to us. Those that were leaving wrung my hands, smiled wistfully, and were gone. I followed with my eyes and smiled as the steamer was lost in the thick night. I was weeping.

Was it because I should never see those kindly faces again, or because I had thought them kind when they only thought of me as black?

ESLANDA GOODE ROBESON

From *African Journey*

I wanted to go to Africa.

It began when I was quite small. Africa was the place we Negroes came from originally. Lots of Americans, when they could afford it, went back to see their "old country." I remember wanting very much to see my "old country," and wondering what it would be like.

In America one heard little or nothing about Africa. I hadn't realized that, consciously, until we went to live in England. [. . .]

In England, on the other hand, there is news of Africa everywhere: in the press, in the schools, in the films, in conversation. English people are actively interested in Africa economically and politically. Members of families are out in Africa in the civil service, in the military, in business; everywhere you go, someone's uncle, brother, or cousin is working, teaching, administering, or "serving" in Africa. Women go out to Africa with their men, or go out to visit them. There are courses on Africa in every good university in England; African languages are taught, missionaries are trained, and administrators are prepared for work "in the field." Everywhere there is information about Africa. [. . .]

I began reading everything about Africa I could lay hands on. This proved to be considerable, what with the libraries of the British Museum, the House of Commons, London University, and the London School of Economics. I began asking questions everywhere of everybody. The reading and the questions landed me right in the middle of anthropology

Source: Excerpted from Eslanda Goode Robeson, *African Journey* (New York: The John Day Company, 1945), pp. 13–17, 83–126.

(a subject I had only vaguely known existed) at the London School of Economics under Malinowski and Firth, and at London University under Perry and Hocart. It was all very interesting and exciting and challenging. At last I began to find out something about my "old country," my background, my people, and thus about myself.

After more than a year of very wide reading and intensive study I began to get my intellectual feet wet. I am afraid I began to be obstreperous in seminars. I soon became fed up with white students and teachers "interpreting" the Negro mind and character to me. Especially when I felt, as I did very often, that their interpretation was wrong.

It went something like this: Me, I *am* Negro, I *know* what we think, how we feel. I know this means that, and that means so-and-so.

"Ah, no, my dear, you're wrong. You see, you are European.* You can't possibly know how the primitive mind works until you study it, as we have done."

"What do you mean I'm European? I'm *Negro.* I'm African myself. I'm what you call primitive. I have studied my mind, our minds. How dare you call me European!"

"No, you're not primitive, my dear," they told me patiently, tolerantly, "you're educated and cultured, like us."

"I'm educated because I went to school, because I was taught. You're educated because you went to school, were taught. I'm cultured because my people had the education and the means to achieve a good standard of living; that's the reason you're cultured. 'Poor whites' have neither education nor culture. Africans would have both if they had the schools and the money. Going to school and having money doesn't make me European. Having no schools and no money doesn't make the African primitive," I protested furiously.

"No, no," they explained; "the primitive mind cannot grasp the kind of ideas we can; they have schools, but their schools have only simple subjects, and crafts; it's all very different. You see, we've been out there for years and years (some ten, some twenty, some thirty years); we've studied them, taught them, administered them, worked with them, and we know. You've never been out there, you've never seen them and talked with them on their home ground; you can't possibly know." [. . .]

---

*"European," a term which is very widely and somewhat loosely used among anthropologists, usually means white, not only in color but also in culture: a white person with a Western (rather than an "Oriental" or a "primitive") education, background, and set of values. (*Author's note*)

I asked Africans I met at universities, taking honors in medicine, in law, in philosophy, in education, in other subjects: "What is all this about primitive minds and abstruse subjects, about only simple subjects and crafts in your schools?"

"Oh, *that*," they said with a twinkle, "there's nothing primitive about our minds in these universities, is there? And how can we cope with any but simple subjects and crafts in our schools, when that is all they will allow us to have? Actually, they rarely give us any schools at all, but they sometimes 'aid' the schools the Missions have set up for us, and those we have set up for ourselves with our own money and labor. But they definitely limit our curricula."

I began to see light. It was the old army game every Negro in America will recognize: The white American South says the Negro is ignorant, and has a low standard of living; the Negro says the South won't give him adequate schools or decent wages. [. . .]

This pattern was familiar to me also. In America Negroes get the same reaction. White America generalizes in its mind about the primitiveness, ignorance, laziness, and smell of Negroes. When we protest that these descriptions are just not true of us, nor of millions of our fellow Negroes, they answer: "But you are different; you are the exceptions." No matter how many facts we marshal to prove their statements untrue, they close their minds against these facts. It is more convenient for them to believe their own generalizations than to face the facts. So the facts become the "exceptions." But we "special" Negroes look closely and thoughtfully at the facts. We know we aren't essentially different from our fellow Negroes. We know also that others' merely saying we are different does not make us so.

So far, so good. But I had no answer to the constant "You have never been out there." [. . .]

Paul couldn't go to Africa with me. He had contracts ahead for two years and couldn't risk not being able to fulfill them. We knew nothing, firsthand, about climate and conditions in Africa. Paul doesn't stand the heat well, changes of climate are hard on him, changes of diet and water put him off. Perhaps it was best for me to go first, find out as much as I could about everything, and next time we could go together.

And so we began to plan: While I was away, Mother could go to Russia to visit my two brothers who live and work there. Paul would go to Russia later on and spend some time with Sergei Eisenstein, who was making a film in the country outside Moscow. The idea of Paul making a Russian film had been discussed; this would give him a chance to perfect his Russian and observe Soviet methods of film making.

That disposed of everybody but Pauli, our beloved only child. He was eight—a fairly tender age; he was sturdy, but Mamma had always most carefully supervised his diet and general regime, which was rather strict. But he was adventurous, like me.

What was more important, Paul and I remembered vividly the time when, on the set of the *Sanders of the River* film, Pauli had been astonished and delighted to see all the Africans. "Why, there are lots of brown people," this then six-year-old had said happily, "lots of black people too; we're not the only ones." We had been profoundly disturbed by the realization that he had been living in an entirely white world since we had brought him and my mother to live with us in England, when he was ten months old. The only Negroes he had seen besides ourselves and Larry (Lawrence Brown, our colleague and accompanist) were the occasional ones who visited at our home. His young mind had thought we were the only brown people in a totally white world. [. . .] So it was decided that Pauli would go with me.

We made our plans: We would go by sea from England to Capetown and Port Elizabeth, right at the bottom of South Africa. [. . .] Then we would go on to Johannesburg and maybe see the mines; and perhaps work in a trip to Swaziland; and maybe I could manage to run up to see Tshekedi Khama, the African regent we had all been so thrilled about. Then we would go down to Mozambique in Portuguese East Africa, pick up a ship and sail up the east coast to Mombasa. [. . .]

July 16. In the train. I have been thinking back over our trip up the east coast. Leaving South Africa we saw fewer and fewer Europeans. In Beira everyone we saw was African except the storekeeper. In Dar-Es-Salaam there were a number of Europeans, but many more Indians and Arabs, as well as Africans. Zanzibar was quite different, almost oriental, with many Indians, Arabs, and Moslem Africans. Mombasa was rather cosmopolitan, with European tourists and settlers, Indians, and Arabs, and a great variety of Africans—Moslem, Christian, and traditional.

We woke at dawn in the train, hoping to get a view of Kilimanjaro, the famous mountain peak 19,320 feet above sea level on the Kenya-Tanganyika border. We were lucky. At first the peak seemed to merge with the clouds which surrounded it. Gradually we made out the snow-covered plateau-like top. Then the sun came out and the mists cleared, and Kilimanjaro stood revealed, towering majestically in the distance.

All this part of Kenya is very high. We have been climbing steadily since we left Mombasa and the heat of the coast, for the cool green of the highlands. The great baobab trees are everywhere; there are mango trees, coconut palms, and great seas of green hills. There are occasional small villages, and people on the roads and in the fields. Climbing still higher, we passed mountain range after mountain range, all covered with a wealth of green. [. . .]

When we stopped at a village called Athi-River, I noticed three separate retiring rooms in the little station, all clearly marked: Europeans, Asiatics, Africans. It always strikes me as amusing, pathetic, and a bit silly when I see Europeans taking so much trouble to segregate themselves in public places, when I know these same Europeans fill their homes with all kinds of Native servants, who come into the most intimate contact with their food, clothing, and especially with their children.

July 17. Arrived in Kampala after two hot, tiring but interesting days on the train. We were met by Archdeacon and Mrs. Bowers, who brought a telegram from Nyabongo, the African friend whom we had come to visit. It seems Nyabongo was delayed in the cross-country trip, and had asked the Bowers' to meet us and keep us overnight. They are typically pleasant, comfortable English people, kindly, intelligent, and very hospitable.

The Bowers' live in a very attractive comfortable house next door to an African girls' school, where there are usually four to five hundred students. The whole staff is African, except the headmistress, who is European. Mr. Bowers says his church (Anglican) uses as many Africans on its staffs as possible; that in some areas there are as many as two hundred staff members to only one European. He tells me that all the education in Uganda is in the hands of the church. [. . .]

Mr. Bowers and I got on very well together until we came to the question of salaries for teachers. Here in Uganda, as everywhere else in Africa, the salaries for Europeans—officials, teachers, clerks, and all workers—are royal when compared to the infinitesimal wages paid to Africans for exactly the same work, even though, as often happens, the African is better trained and more efficient at the job. Mr. Bowers, who until then had seemed to me quite reasonable, took this great difference in salaries as a matter of course, quite normal and right, and seemed surprised when I questioned and pressed the matter.

"Why, surely you realize the European has a higher standard of living than the Native, and therefore needs more salary?" he asked. I said no, I didn't see that at all. I said I thought he was putting the cart before the horse. The European pays himself higher salaries, and therefore is able to maintain a higher standard of living. The European pays the African much lower salaries, and therefore the African must inevitably have a lower standard of living.

So far I have come across many Europeans here in Africa who I am sure are living at a much higher standard than they were accustomed to in the home country. Africans tell me they themselves—the vast majority of them—are living at a much lower standard now than before the coming of the European.

It looks to me as though the African has been forced to lower his own normal standard in order to make possible the often unjustifiably high standard which the European arbitrarily insists upon maintaining for himself. [. . .]

July 18. Nyabongo fetched us early from the Bowers'. He is a cousin of the Mukama (King) of Toro, and we met him in England when he was studying anthropology at Oxford. He is taking us to Kabarole, his home in Toro, where I will do my anthropological field work on cattle culture in Uganda.

I am particularly lucky to have Akiki Nyabongo for host in Toro, because he knows nearly everyone there, knows the history and general background of the people, and is of course entirely familiar with custom and tradition. He is actually part of custom and tradition. He is young, intelligent, friendly, and efficient.

Before we left Kampala he took us to pay our respects to the Mulamuzi (the African chief justice of Buganda). The Mulamuzi was cordial, and explained that he had been prepared for us to spend the night with him in his home, but when he saw "the Europeans had us" he decided to remain in the background. He is a big handsome intelligent man, youngish, with a wonderful sense of humor, and speaks English fluently. We had a good talk, and I liked him very much indeed.

His home was very attractive. While we were there, the Kabaka's (King's) son was sent over to play with Pauli. He proved to be a delightful boy of about nine—just about Pauli's age—and speaks English well. The Mulamuzi's son is fourteen, too old for Pauli really, though they all played together.

The hospitality of these Africans is something special. Imagine the thoughtfulness behind sending a child Pauli's own age to play with him! The boys hit it off together at once, and seemed to enjoy each other's strangeness. In between play and games, which after a few words of explanation on either side they understood immediately, they plied each other with questions, the Kabaka's son always courteous and considerate.

After this happy visit, we stopped for a few minutes at the hospital in Kampala to see Nyabongo's sister who is a nurse there. [. . .]

The house [of our host] is a typical average one, they tell me; that's why Nyabongo chose it rather than a chief's house. It is small, with a sitting-eating room, a bedroom, and one other room. There is very little furniture. The bicycle leaning against the outside wall immediately caught Pauli's eye. They tell me everyone in Africa who can afford it owns a bicycle. It is like owning a small car in England. In the courtyard at the back of the house are several enclosures surrounded by high fences. The larger enclosure is the bathing place, the smaller one near by is the lavatory. They took Pauli out to the bath enclosure, undressed him, gave him a full bath African fashion, and re-dressed him. When he came back he said he felt like a new boy, rested and refreshed. Nyabongo also had a bath. They offered me one, but seeing no women about, I settled for washing my face and hands. Afterward Nyabongo told me laughingly that the women would have appeared and taken me to their own bathing place and washed me. Well, now I know. [. . .]

When we collected again in the sitting room, clean and cool, our hosts offered us coffee beans from a charming little woven basket. This is the customary gesture of welcome and hospitality, comparable perhaps to the offering of appetizers in Europe and America. We each took a bean, tentatively, and Nyabongo showed us how to break off the outside shell with our teeth, then chew the real bean inside. I ended by sucking mine soft, then chewing it. It was good. As we left, they gave me the little basket, complete with coffee beans inside. (I *must* remember not to admire things.)

We had lunch. At table, we all first had our hands washed—formally. No Batoro (Ba-Toro, meaning people of Toro) will eat before washing his hands. A man comes around the table with a basin and pitcher of water.

He holds the basin near you, you hold your hands over the basin, and he pours water over them; you shake them dry while he passes on to the next person.

Plates were put before us, but no silver. No "weapons," as Pauli says. From a big wooden dish set in the center of the table we were helped to plantains which had been steamed to a solid mush, sweet potatoes cooked whole, and meat (which was roast goat). The goat had been especially killed in our honor, and we saw its skin pegged out on the ground in the courtyard, drying in the sun. Nyabongo sliced off small pieces of meat for us, and we ate entirely with our fingers, African fashion. It was quite a feat, and Pauli and I had to watch carefully and experiment for a while before we could even begin to manage it. The trick is to knead some of the solid plantain mush into a little ball, bringing the ball to a sort of point between the forefinger and thumb, then make a cup-like depression in the ball with the thumb, dip the ball into gravy, which fills the little depression, then eat the ball. It takes a bit of doing, but both Pauli and I were greatly interested in the procedure and did our best. I enjoyed eating with my fingers, legitimately, as much as Pauli did.

There was no dessert, as Africans do not have dessert. We finished by washing our hands and mouths—which by then certainly needed washing—again over the basin which was brought around.

After lunch people came in to see us from all the surrounding villages. They first bowed to Nyabongo, then sat on the floor just looking and listening. Still no women. Finally I asked about them, and our host took me to another courtyard and introduced me to his wife. She was very attractive and modest, spoke some English, and explained that it is quite incorrect in their society for the women to eat with the men, that they always remain well in the background and usually out of sight, but that they have definitely important, responsible, and respected places in their homes, families, and society in general. [. . .]

July 25. Today is Saturday. It seems strange, but it makes no difference what day it is. The only important or especially significant day in the week is market day. That is the day everyone looks forward to, the day when you see and chat with everybody, exchange what news there is, and do your shopping.

Today was pretty important for me, however, because I did my first actual field work. We spent the day in Kahungere, a cattle village about five miles from here, right at the foot of Rwenzoli, where I studied the details and customs of the care of the cattle—the milking, watering, etc. Kahungere is in what is known as the "west grazing ground" of Toro.

We got up early, dressed in long trousers and mosquito boots as protection against flies. We took "the path," which is so narrow we had to walk single file through the countryside. On either side of the path the elephant grass was more than three times our height, and in many places it was so high as to make the path nearly dark, as though in a forest. The moment you step off the road you are practically invisible.

At first Pauli and I were nervous, thinking of the possibility of lions, snakes, etc.; but Nyabongo and the three men who were with us were so gay and unconcerned we decided all must be well. Soon we realized that the path was hard and well traveled. It wound over the hills, crossing many other paths, often crossing the open road. [. . .]

In the village we rested in a kraal, the home of Kymuhangire, Nyabongo's former nurse. It was a typical herdsman's house—small, dark, but beautifully clean, with a fresh dried-grass floor on the porch, fresh grass mats in the yard and on the floor of the sitting room where chairs had been placed for us, and in which we rested.

People came to greet us from all the surrounding villages—all herdspeople. Nyabongo held council for a short time, sitting in state under the roof of an open hut in the enclosure, with everyone sitting on the ground in front of him.

In the center of the cattle kraal was a large open area stamped clear of grass and burned black by fire. The cattle were brought here from the grazing grounds and made to circle around a smoking fire to drive away the flies. [. . .]

Near the open area is the milking kraal, a fenced-in space with a gateway in the center of which is the herdsman's fire—*komi*—a sacred fire which is never allowed to go out, except when the king dies. The cows are driven into the milking kraal two or three at a time, are stood over the smoking fire, brushed with long grass for flies, and their hides cleaned. Then they are walked over to the milking space. The calves are brought in, are allowed to suck each nipple clean and to start the flow of the milk, then are led away. The herdsman then washes his hands with water from a horn, a clean fumigated milk bowl is placed between his knees by the herdgirl, and he squats almost to the ground (does not sit) holding the bowl between his knees. He milks directly into the bowl, making foam as he does so. This is expert work. Milking without foam is called *buhule,* and is ordinary. Milking with foam is called *ifuro,* and is elegant. No good herdsman will milk without foam. The milker, called *mata,* is usually elderly, with great experience. Women never milk.

The cows circling the smoking fire in the open space lowed and called, and made what sounded like intimate conversation with the cows inside being milked. The cows answered back in kind. The herdsmen seemed to understand these noises, and laughed and made jokes about them.

After the cows had been milked their teats were smeared with soot from the fire to make them too bitter for the calves to drain. Then they were driven out and other cows brought in.

After a while we went back to the house, and Nyabongo again held council. Then we had lunch; millet cooked to a thick mush and very starchy, goat meat, and our first taste of *sim-sim* prepared with mushrooms—which was very good indeed. After lunch Nyabongo put Pauli to bed, then went out and held further council with the men, while I talked with the women through an interpreter. They first welcomed me and thanked me for coming to their obscure village. They wanted to know what kind of work women did "outside," how they brought up their children, how their men treated them, how they dressed, whether they went to school with the men. They wanted to know if I thought our black children will have a place in the world, a real place, or will "they only be told what to do?" "We are tired of being told what to do. Our children will be more tired of it." [. . .]

July 29. Both Pauli and I have been very ill. The wild indigestion developed into something quite serious. The bananas formed into hard lumps which very nearly gave him intestinal obstruction.

Nyabongo's sister, who is the nurse in the Kampala Hospital, and Queen Sister came over to help Nyabongo nurse us.

Then I went down with a terrific fever and was in bed three days— very faint, couldn't even sit up. I was too low to worry about our being such a nuisance to our hosts. I must say it gives one a feeling of confidence to see how the people mobilize for illness, take it in their stride as part of the ordinary business of living, and know just what to do and how to make you comfortable.

Medicine plants and medical knowledge are almost entirely women's work. The young ones get information from their mothers and grandmothers (from "the old ones") and learn the roots, plants, leaves, medicinal clays, and their uses. A man doctor is never called except for extreme or very serious illness. All the minor general ailments are women's work. You call in another woman if you don't know yourself. Royal women especially know a great deal about these things. It is considered one of their accomplishments to know medicine. Queen Sister knows far more than her contemporaries. [. . .]

The schoolteachers came in from the surrounding districts to see me this evening, to talk and listen and to ask questions. How I longed for Paul to help me. There were about fifty of them, most of them young, eager, and intelligent. They wanted to know all about schools in England and in America: Do black and white people go to the same schools, or do governments waste money by maintaining separate schools? May black people study medicine, economics, law, and the classics, as well as agriculture and crafts? Is education expensive, or do one's taxes cover it? Are there black teachers? How do black people earn money? Are they allowed to do every kind of work, skilled as well as unskilled—do they work side by side with white workers? Do they get the same pay? Will I please tell them about the so-called "backward peoples" of Russia, and what are they doing now? (Africans have been disposed of so long as "backward" that they are eager to hear what is happening to other "backward" peoples.) They were heartily encouraged by what I could tell them about the successful integration of nomads like the Yakuts into the highly industrialized modern Soviet society.

"How long did it take, this integration?" they asked anxiously.

"Ten to twenty years," I said.

A long sigh went through the crowd: "Not the thousand years they say it will take us! Though we are not 'backward' in any sense of the word. What do they mean by this 'backward'?"

Before I could answer, or try to answer, a fellow teacher said: "They mean people they have kept back, and continue to keep back."

I told them that some of the more primitive tribes of Russia had had no written language, and the government had brought people from such tribes to Leningrad, to the Institute of Minorities, where they had themselves worked out a written form for their own languages, with the help of the great scholars and teachers of the country, and that now the history and folklore of all these tribes have been recorded by their own people, in their own languages.

This impressed my listeners enormously. They wanted to hear everything about this country which looked after its "children" so well. I told them every scrap I could.

After a satisfying evening, I walked with them to the outer gate of the enclosure. The moon was up, half full, and was as clear as could be. It was quite light and a bit chilly, but the night was very pleasant and peaceful. [. . .]

August 1. I have been working with the herdswomen in the dairy, learning a lot about custom and tradition. Everything connected with the handling of the milk after it is collected from the cattle is called *bisahi* (dairy) and is women's business. *Bisahi* is considered elegant work for ladies, and they take great pride in their knowledge and expertness. Experience in any branch of *bisahi* is definitely an accomplishment.

The ladies are delightful, intelligent, companionable, and have a great sense of fun. They think it a bit silly for me to learn all about *bisahi,* when I have no cattle and no hopes of getting any. But they like me, and I like them. They feel there must be some good reason for my learning, so they have settled down to doing their utmost to teach me. They are also pleased with my interest in and respect for their customs. Some of them speak a little English, I have been accumulating a few words of Rotoro, and we all understand gestures and inflection of voice, and so we are able to manage.

We often went off into gales of laughter over misunderstandings, and we all agreed after the second day that one of the most important words in any language is "why?" We enjoyed a lot of gossip while we worked, became very good friends, examined each other's hair, skin, clothes. We each found out how the other managed her husband, home, and children.

It was a wonderful experience for me. I learned a great deal about the very important business of living, and as a result have rearranged my sense of values to some considerable extent. The leisurely approach, the calm facing of circumstances and making the most of them, is very different from the European hustle and hurry and drive, and worry and frustration when things don't go well. The African gets things done, gets a great deal done, but gets it done without the furious wear and tear on the nervous system. Because the European doesn't see his own hustle and bustle he says the African is lazy, in spite of the fact that the African gets the work done. [. . .]

The women deplored the fact that the herds of cattle are fast dwindling. They say that as recently as 1933 Nyabongo had a herd of 2,000 cattle, and that even the ordinary person had 20 to 50 head.

"Then the government began to inject all cattle with needles, and the cattle died. We understand that needles are helpful for some diseases. One must study and understand needles on the one hand, but one must also study and understand cattle on the other. Our cattle were healthy. We had no milk or cattle disease. Yet all our cattle were given the needle, and many of them died. This civilization business," they sighed, "can be very destructive. Now we have little or no cattle, and must return to the soil."

This return to the soil is acutely felt by the herdspeople because their wealth and prestige, traditions and customs are associated with the possession of cattle. The herdspeople were the high caste, the aristocrats, and the agriculturists the lower class, the common men. [. . .]

August 5. At the hotel [in the Congo], which was a very sad affair, we sat in the lounge while a great deal of conversation went on between the Belgian hotel owner and our D.C. There was a lot of "*noir, noir*" in very rapid French and we tried to look blank as though we did not understand the language. (I believe every Negro would understand and recognize the word "black" in any language. He would certainly recognize the tone of voice which goes with the word!) After considerable pressure from our D.C., and a lot of "*distingué*" and "important" on his part against the "*noir, noir,*" the owner finally gave in and showed us to our rooms. When we saw them we wondered what all the discussion had been about. They were scarcely fit for animals.

Wedding Day

His name was Paul Watson and as he shambled down rue Pigalle he might have been any other Negro of enormous height and size. But as I have said, his name was Paul Watson. Passing him on the street, you might not have known or cared who he was, but any one of the residents about the great Montmartre district of Paris could have told you who he was as well as many interesting bits of his personal history.

He had come to Paris in the days before colored jazz bands were the style. Back home he had been a prize fighter. In the days when Joe Gans was in his glory Paul was following the ring, too. He didn't have that fine way about him that Gans had and for that reason luck seemed to go against him. When he was in the ring he was like a mad bull, especially if his opponent was a white man. In those days there wasn't any sympathy or nicety about the ring and so pretty soon all the ringmasters got down on Paul and he found it pretty hard to get a bout with anyone. Then it was that he worked his way across the Atlantic Ocean on a big liner—in the days before colored jazz bands were the style in Paris.

Things flowed along smoothly for the first few years with Paul working here and there in the unfrequented places of Paris. On the side he used to give boxing lessons to aspiring youths or gymnastic young women. At that time he was working so steadily that he had little chance to find out what was going on around Paris. Pretty soon, however, he grew to be known among the trainers and managers began to fix up bouts for him. After one or two successful bouts a little fame began to come into being for him. So it was that after one of the prize-fights, a colored fellow

Source: Fire!! (November 1926): 25–28.

came to his dressing room to congratulate him on his success as well as invite him to go to Montmartre to meet "the boys."

Paul had a way about him and seemed to get on with the colored fellows who lived in Montmartre and when the first Negro jazz band played in a tiny Parisian cafe Paul was among them playing the banjo. Those first years were without event so far as Paul was concerned. The members of that first band often say now that they wonder how it was that nothing happened during those first seven years, for it was generally known how great was Paul's hatred for American white people. I suppose the tranquility in the light of what happened afterwards was due to the fact that the cafe in which they worked was one in which mostly French people drank and danced, and then too, that was before there were so many Americans visiting Paris. However, everyone had heard Paul speak of his intense hatred of American white folks. It only took two Benedict-ines* to make him start talking about what he would do to the first "Yank" that called him "nigger." But the seven years came to an end and Paul Watson went to work in a larger cafe with a larger band, patronized almost solely by Americans.

I've heard almost every Negro in Montmartre tell about the night that a drunken Kentuckian came into the cafe where Paul was playing and said:

"Look heah, Bruther, what you all doin' ovah heah?"

"None ya bizness. And looka here, I ain't your brother, see?"

"Jack, do you heah that nigger talkin' lak that tah me?"

As he said this, he turned to speak to his companion. I have often wished that I had been there to have seen the thing happen myself. Every tale I have heard about it was different and yet there was something of truth in each of them. Perhaps the nearest one can come to the truth is by saying that Paul beat up about four full-sized white men that night besides doing a great deal of damage to the furniture about the cafe. I couldn't tell you just what did happen. Some of the fellows say that Paul seized the nearest table and mowed down men right and left, others say he took a bottle, then again the story runs that a chair was the instrument of his fury. At any rate, that started Paul Watson on his siege against the American white person who brings his native prejudices into the life of Paris.

It is a verity that Paul was the "black terror." The last syllable of the

*A liqueur.

word, nigger, never passed the lips of a white man without the quick reflex action of Paul's arm and fist to the speaker's jaw. He paid for more glassware and cafe furnishings in the course of the next few years than is easily imaginable. And yet, there was something likable about Paul. Perhaps that's the reason that he stood in so well with the policemen of the neighborhood. Always some divine power seemed to intervene in his behalf and he was excused after the payment of a small fine with advice about his future conduct. Finally, there came the night when in a frenzy he shot the two American sailors.

They had not died from the wounds he had given them, hence his sentence had not been one of death but rather a long term of imprisonment. It was a pitiable sight to see Paul sitting in the corner of his cell with his great body hunched almost double. He seldom talked and when he did his words were interspersed with oaths about the lowness of "crackers." Then the World War came.

It seems strange that anything so horrible as that wholesale slaughter could bring about any good and yet there was something of a smoothing quality about even its baseness. There has never been such equality before or since such as that which the World War brought. Rich men fought by the side of paupers; poets swapped yarns with dry-goods salesmen, while Jews and Christians ate corned beef out of the same tin. Along with the general leveling influence came France's pardon of her prisoners in order that they might enter the army. Paul Watson became free and a French soldier. Because he was strong and had innate daring in his heart he was placed in the aerial squad and cited many times for bravery. The close of the war gave him his place in French society as a hero. With only a memory of the war and an ugly scar on his left cheek he took up his old life.

His firm resolutions about American white people still remained intact and many chance encounters that followed the war are told from lip to lip proving that the war and his previous imprisonment had changed him little. He was the same Paul Watson to Montmartre as he shambled up rue Pigalle.

Rue Pigalle in the early evening has a sombre beauty—gray as are most Paris streets and other-worldish. To those who know the district it is the Harlem of Paris and rue Pigalle is its dusky Seventh Avenue. Most of the colored musicians that furnish Parisians and their visitors with entertainment live somewhere in the neighborhood of rue Pigalle. Some time during every day each of these musicians makes a point of passing through rue Pigalle. Little wonder that almost any day will find Paul Watson going his shuffling way up the same street.

He reached the corner of rue de la Bruyere and with sure instinct his feet stopped. Without half thinking he turned into "the Pit." Its full name is The Flea Pit. If you should ask one of the musicians why it was so called, he would answer you to the effect that it was called "the Pit" because all the "fleas" hang out there. If you did not get the full import of this explanation, he would go further and say that there were always "spades" in the pit and they were as thick as fleas. Unless you could understand this latter attempt at clarity you could not fully grasp what The Flea Pit means to the Negro musicians in Montmartre. It is a tiny cafe of the genus that is called *bistro* in France. Here the fiddle players, saxophone blowers, drumbeaters and ivory ticklers gather at four in the afternoon for a [glass of] Porto or a game of billiards. Here the cabaret entertainers and supper musicians meet at one o'clock at night or thereafter for a whiskey and soda, or more billiards. Occasional sandwiches and a "quiet game" also play their parts in the popularity of the place. After a season or two it becomes a settled fact just what time you may catch so-and-so at the famous "Pit."

The musicians were very fond of Paul and took particular delight in teasing him. He was one of the chosen few that all of the musicians conceded as being "regular." It was the pet joke of the habitues of the cafe that Paul never bothered with girls. They always said that he could beat up ten men but was scared to death of one woman.

"Say fellow, when ya goin' a get hooked up?"

"Can't say, Bo. Ain't so much on skirts."

"Man alive, ya don't know what you're missin'—somebody little and cute telling ya sweet things in your ear. Paris is full of women folks."

"I ain't much on 'em all the same. Then too, they're all white."

"What's it to ya? This ain't America."

"Can't help that. Get this—I'm collud, see? I ain't got nothing for no white meat to do. If a woman eva called me nigger I'd have to kill her, that's all!"

"You for it, son. I can't give you a thing on this Mr. Jefferson Lawd way of lookin' at women."

"Oh, tain't that. I guess they're all right for those that wants 'em. Not me!"

"Oh you ain't so forty. You'll fall like all the other spades I've ever seen. Your kind falls hardest."

And so Paul went his way—alone. He smoked and drank with the fellows and sat for hours in the Montmartre cafes and never knew the companionship of a woman. Then one night after his work he was walking along the street in his queer shuffling way when a woman stepped up to his side.

"Voulez vous."

"Naw, gowan away from here."

"Oh, you speak English, don't you?"

"You an 'merican woman?"

"Used to be 'fore I went on the stage and got stranded over here."

"Well, get away from here. I don't like your kind!"

"Aw, Buddy, don't say that. I ain't prejudiced like some fool women."

"You don't know who I am, do you? I'm Paul Watson and I hate American white folks, see?"

He pushed her aside and went on walking alone. He hadn't gone far when she caught up to him and said with sobs in her voice:—

"Oh, Lordy, please don't hate me 'cause I was born white and an American. I ain't got a sou to my name and all the men pass me by cause I ain't spruced up. Now you come along and won't look at me cause I'm white."

Paul strode along with her clinging to his arm. He tried to shake her off several times but there was no use. She clung all the more desperately to him. He looked down at her frail body shaken with sobs, and something caught at his heart. Before he knew what he was doing he had said:—

"Naw, I ain't that mean. I'll get you some grub. Quit your cryin'. Don't like seein' women folks cry."

It was the talk of Montmartre. Paul Watson takes a woman to Gavarnni's every night for dinner. He comes to the Flea Pit less frequently, thus giving the other musicians plenty of opportunity to discuss him.

"How times do change. Paul, the woman-hater, has a Jane now."

"You ain't said nothing, fella. That ain't all. She's white and an 'merican, too."

"That's the way with these spades. They beat up all the white men they can lay their hands on but as soon as a gang of golden hair with blue eyes rubs up close to them they forget all they ever said about hatin' white folks."

"Guess he thinks that skirt's gone on him. Dumb fool!"

"Don' be no chineeman. This old gag don' fit for Paul. He cain't understand it no more'n we can. Says he jess can't help himself, every time she looks up into his eyes and asks him does he love her. They sure are happy together. Paul's goin' to marry her, too. At first she kept saying that she didn't want to get married cause she wasn't the marrying kind and all that talk. Paul jus' laid down the law to her and told her he never would live with no woman without being married to her. Then she began to tell him all about her past life. He told her he didn't care nothing about what she used to be jus' so long as they loved each other now. Guess they'll make it."

"Yeah, Paul told me the same tale last night. He's sure gone on her all right."

"They're getting tied up next Sunday. So glad it's not me. Don't trust these American dames. Me for the Frenchies."

"She ain't so worse for looks, Bud. Now that he's been furnishing the green for the rags."

"Yeah, but I don't see no reason for the wedding bells. She was right—she ain't the marrying kind."

. . . and so Montmartre talked. In every cafe where the Negro musicians congregated Paul Watson was the topic for conversation. He had suddenly fallen from his place as bronze God to almost less than the dust.

The morning sun made queer patterns on Paul's sleeping face. He grimaced several times in his slumber, then finally half-opened his eyes. After a succession of dream-laden blinks he gave a great yawn, and rubbing his eyes, looked at the open window through which the sun shone brightly. His first conscious thought was that this was the bride's day and that bright sunshine prophesied happiness for the bride throughout her married life. His first impulse was to settle back into the covers and think drowsily about Mary and the queer twists life brings about, as is the wont of most bridge-grooms on their last morning of bachelorhood. He put this impulse aside in favor of dressing quickly and rushing downstairs to telephone to Mary to say "happy wedding day" to her.

One huge foot slipped into a worn bedroom slipper and then the other dragged painfully out of the warm bed [—these] were the courageous beginnings of his bridal toilette. With a look of triumph he put on his new gray suit that he had ordered from an English tailor. He carefully pulled a taffeta tie into place beneath his chin, noting as he looked at his face in the mirror that the scar he had received in the army was very ugly—funny, marrying an ugly man like him.

French telephones are such human faults. After trying for about fifteen minutes to get Central 32.01 he decided that he might as well walk around to Mary's hotel to give his greeting as to stand there in the lobby of his own, wasting his time. He debated this in his mind a great deal. They were to be married at four o'clock. It was eleven now and it did seem a shame not to let her have a minute or two by herself. As he went walking down the street towards her hotel he laughed to think of how one always cogitates over doing something and finally does the thing he wanted to in the beginning anyway.

Mud on his nice gray suit that the English tailor had made for him. Damn—gray suit—what did he have a gray suit on for, anyway. Folks with black faces shouldn't wear gray suits. Gawd, but it was funny that time when he beat up that cracker at the Periquet. Fool couldn't shut his mouth he was so surprised. Crackers—damn'em—he was one nigger that wasn't 'fraid of 'em. Wouldn't he have a hell of a time if he went back to America where black was black. Wasn't white nowhere, black wasn't. What was that thought he was trying to get ahold of—bumping around in his head—something he started to think about but couldn't remember it somehow.

The shrill whistle that is typical of the French subway pierced its way into his thoughts. Subway—why was he in the subway—he didn't want to go any place. He heard doors slamming and saw the blue uniforms of the conductors swinging on to the cars as the trains began to pull out of the station. With one or two strides he reached the last coach as it began to move up the platform. A bit out of breath he stood inside the train and looking down at what he had in his hand he saw that it was a tiny pink ticket. A first class ticket in a second class coach. The idea set him to laughing. Everyone in the car turned and eyed him, but that did not bother him. Wonder what stop he'd get off—funny how these French said descend when they meant get off—funny he couldn't pick up French— been here so long. First class ticket in a second class coach!—that was one on him. Wedding day today, and that damn letter from Mary. How'd she say it now, "just couldn't go through with it," white women just don't marry colored men, and she was a street woman, too. Why couldn't she had told him flat that she was just getting back on her feet at his expense. Funny that first class ticket he bought, wish he could see Mary—him a-going there to wish her "happy wedding day," too. Wonder what that French woman was looking at him so hard for? Guess it was the mud.

IDABELLE YEISER

Letters

Letter One

Algiers.

Dear Chum:

I know you will be astonished when you notice this postmark, but miracles never cease to happen. Truly I scarcely know how it all came about, except that being asked to come, I accepted the invitation before taking time for reflection. Our party is an odd one. There are three of us:—an Italian girl, a Norwegian fellow, and myself. We sailed from Port Vendres, a place you have doubtlessly never heard of, and probably won't even find on the map. It is on the French coast, very near the Spanish border. From the station at Port Vendres we were driven to the hotel in a queer rickety old coach, drawn by two half-fed, overworked horses. But a bit of beauty awaited us. Behind the hotel rose the mountains, before it stretched the sea,—and there, just within a three minute walk from the hotel was the boat—our boat. Sleep that night was almost impossible.

Our enthusiasm continued during the entire journey. The sea was calm and blue, the bluest blue possible. We drifted along peacefully for about twenty-four hours. The morning we landed, I was up about five o'clock, expecting to see land, but none was in sight. However, to compensate, there was a sunrise. Picture the deep blue sea; then picture the sun, a huge red ball, rising above the horizon, casting its reflections in the water, and sending a golden path from the horizon to our boat. Wasn't that worth getting up for?

Source: Opportunity 5 (July 1927): 206–207.

On entering the harbor a few hours later we were both impressed and a bit afraid. Impressed by the glaring whiteness of the city and chilled with fear at the sight that confronted us. There was every type of human being imaginable. And such shades. Every degree from the blackest black to the whitest white. Arabs, Africans that belonged in the jungles, and Europeans! Beggars, laborers, merchants! We welcomed the sight of our hotel where the cleanliness was in stark contrast to the filth at the dock.

After resting a bit and securing a guide we began our sight- seeing expedition. Being but little interested in the buildings of the European quarter, we took a tram to the Casbah in order to start there and walk back down through the Arabic quarter. The real meaning of Casbah is "a fortified place." In ancient times that section served as a fortification. The building, where some of the former rulers used to have their harem, is like a prison. The guide explained that the rulers' wives used to peer from each tiny grated window that adorned the third story. Now the place is used for soldiers.

Outside the walls of the Casbah were seated a group of Arabs intently listening to a native story-teller. This made me think of Arabian Nights and wonder if it was in this manner that some of the tales originated. From that elevation we had a good view of the native quarters. Noticing that some of the houses, monotonous in their whiteness, were painted here and there with blue, I asked why. The ones with the blue, I learned, are the houses of the Jews. Being forbidden by religion to occupy the same houses as the others, they must designate their homes with a blue mark-ing around the doors or windows. Upon closer inspection of the quarter, we found conditions abominable. The streets, no more than a series of steps, are very narrow—in fact so narrow that the tops of the houses almost touch, thus shutting out the sun and sky. Men in their white robes and turbans either lounged in the doorways or strolled through the streets. The veiled, white-robed women added a quaintness to it all.

In fact these natives in their costumes, mingled with the Turks and the Europeans, made Algiers quaint and picturesque. Some of the natives are beautiful, while others are so poverty-stricken and dirty that they give one the creeps.

We descended step after step, through these narrow streets, passed the Arabian University and continued until we came to a pretty park—Park Morengo. There was one path that was bordered on both sides with orange trees laden with fruit. How beautiful and fresh it seemed after the native quarter. Though there were many other places to visit, there was nothing of unusual interest.

À bientôt,
Pal

Letter Two

Biskra.

Chum, dear:—

When we left France, we didn't plan to come as far south as Biskra but this city is the best starting-point for a trip to the Sahara Desert. Surely it would be a pity to be in Africa and not glimpse the desert. On the way here, however, we stopped through Constantine. Its chief interest is in its natural beauty—its ravine.

We visited a large Mosque there. An Arabian church or mosque is of special interest, perhaps because of its sharp contrasts to our places of worship. There are no seats; the altar always faces Mecca; there is always a row of shoes at the door—for worshippers and even visitors must leave their shoes on the threshold before stepping on the sacred rug. There is another odd religious observance which we noted while en route from Constantine to Biskra. We stopped at one station about five o'clock and all the Arabs descended, faced Mecca and prayed. You might also be interested in knowing that the Arabian religion permits the men to have more than one wife. They may have as many as four, provided they are able to support them all. Often we encounter one with his several women. I don't believe I would like to belong to a harem, for I fear I should always be jealous of the other wives. I'm convinced, though, that any religion is acceptable as long as one follows it reverently.

But you must be impatient to hear about Biskra. Never visit Algiers without coming here. The city itself is a small, rather unattractive place but it contains a Treasure Island—the Garden of Allah. I am certain you have read Hutchinson's book, *The Garden of Allah*. Read his description of the garden again and try to form a mental picture of this bit of paradise. Never have I seen [such] beauty: we walked through avenues of palms, then wandered through smaller lanes, too impressed to speak. The garden, with its tropical beauty, seems to have been made for lovers and dreamers.

As I said, Biskra is a good starting-place for a trip to the desert.

Civilization has taken such strides as to permit travellers to see the desert in an automobile, but that method didn't appeal to us. Instead we secured a guide and camels and took a day's jaunt to the beginning of this immense sea of sand. We had to pass through "Vieux Biskra" with its old sun-baked houses and its curious old inhabitants. Once, we saw a group of women approach the guide, and point toward me while jabbering something in their Arabic dialect. I grew alarmed, and asked the cause. The guide said, smilingly, "They think you are one of them, so I told them you were taken away when a baby and had now come back to visit your native land." This story had evidently satisfied them for they hurried away to pass it on.

We jogged along and passed a nomad village. Here we stopped to snap a picture only to have curses heaped upon us for not paying for the privilege of taking the picture. Farther on we encountered a band of gypsies who tried to persuade us to have our fortunes told. Soon, however, we had left all signs of life behind us and there, stretched before us, was the Great Sahara. We lingered till sunset and were well repaid for so doing. A sunset on the desert! Would that I were an artist to paint it, but even words fail me in trying to describe the beauty that clothed this barren expanse. Not even a rainbow can vie with such colorings. I shall let you form your own glorious images.

Pal

KATHERINE DUNHAM

Twenty-Seventh Day, from
Journey to Accompong

This afternoon I was very despondent. Mai was away on private business of her own, Ba' Teddy and Ba' Weeyums were at work in the fields, Rachel and Hannah and Sweetie were in Maggotty, and all of my old friends seemed to have deserted me. I would even have welcomed the Colonel, but he was in Balaclava visiting his sick daughter. Any other afternoon I would have been much relieved to have a few moments to myself, but today I must begin to think about leaving this country, and being alone, the thing that had been secretly troubling me for some days again confronted me. What a failure to come so far to see the dances of the Koromantee, and to have them always elude me! To find the quadrille and the shay-shay the sole expressions of the dance among these isolated people. Where, then, my theory on the survival of this particular art form which is among all primitive peoples so closely bound up with their superstitions and joys and sorrows and religion and cosmology? The one fleeting moment at Mis' Ma'y Cross's gravediggin' when Ba' Weeyums and his friends, well under the influence of rum, had entered the hut was the only indication that it existed here, aside from the Colonel's promises. And if I met with such failure on this first stop, would further wanderings through the islands of the West Indies be more fruitful?

For long I had doubted my own ability to gain the confidence of the people. Then I began to feel the hypocrisy of the Colonel and his promises. Then I was certain that such dances did not exist here, had been long

Source: Excerpted from Katherine Dunham, *Journey to Accompong* (New York: Henry Holt, 1946), pp. 125–137.

ago forgotten, and were buried in the dust of the old goombay. Then a little *demon* would hop up and ask me what dances the Colonel would have taken to Kingston, whether he could or not; how could he have planned on and promised these dances if they really were forgotten, as some said, or if he forbade them, as others said, or if there was no goombay and no one to play it if there were one? It all seemed very complicated, and the more I thought about it the more depressed I became; so I decided to begin to pack, because early tomorrow I would have to go to Maggotty on business, and the remaining days would be crowded with last-minute preparations for departure. But first I read a little from my notes on these dances, more to torment myself than for consolation.

[. . .] Apparently, at one time, the Maroons danced something quite differently from the set dances at the parade. And that was not so long ago that they should profess this state of amnesia.

I began to gather odds and ends which I must pack: the woven hammock and the rice sifter and the tambourine and the flute and my bowl of cedarwood and the table scarf Hannah had embroidered and presented as a gift to me and the river reed basket Mis' Holiday had sent me and numerous other trinkets. Suddenly I remembered that I must leave room for the goombay. And after all, why wasn't the goombay here by now? Ba' Foster had promised it for yesterday. It was growing dusk, and glad for an excuse to leave the house, which seemed a little dreary in the half-light, I decided to walk down the mountain to Ba' Foster's yard and find out what was delaying it.

The two weird little mouse-bats whirled past my head as I stepped out into the yard, and settled under the rustling straw roof with a great flapping of wings and a contented squeaking. I had never liked them, and tonight they were especially repulsive with their flash of sharp white mouse teeth and webbed furry wings.

Nearing Ba' Foster's house, I began to feel an excitement in the air, and almost involuntarily my step quickened and I was breathing faster without knowing why. Then I became aware of a *drum*. Not the deep booming of the revivalist Salvation Army drum, but the sharp staccato of a goatskin drawn tightly over a small hollowed trunk and beaten expertly by gnarled black palms. [. . .]

I skidded down the last rocky decline and directly into Ba' Foster's yard. This was deserted. But farther down in the hollow, well hidden from the road behind a tangle of pimiento and breadfruit and coconut trees, I could see the smoky glow of kerosene torches and a circle of tense eager bodies, faces ecstatic in the flickering half-light; and in the middle of the circle, Mis' Mary and an old man whom I did not know performing a strange ritual, more pantomime than dance. And to one side Ba' Weeyums, squatted over the goombay, *my* goombay, his face streaked with perspiration, his eyes brilliant, and his hard palms beating the goatskin, the tone changing from sharp to sullen, from a command to a coaxing by a deft sliding of the side of the palm along the face of the drum.

Ba' Teddy saw me first. Yes, even he was there. I felt suddenly in the midst of traitors to find here these, my bosom friends.

"Evenin', evenin', Missus," said Ba' Teddy softly.

"Evenin'," I replied, winking back a tear. Ba' Foster stepped quickly forward with the goombay under one arm.

"Me jus' gwi bring eem you, Missus!" he said, with too much emphasis. "Me on de way now we'n we meet up wid' Ba' Weeyums en eem ax er play eem jus' dis' once."

I looked at Ba' Weeyums. He was first on one foot and then on the other, twisting his little felt hat around his forefinger and looking anxiously at me the while. Then suddenly I realized that this was the long hoped-for opportunity—that here were the dances I had waited so many weeks to see, and that it was not for a fieldworker to bear personal grudges and carry personal grievances, but to get what the field has to offer in as graceful a manner as possible. Now it was my turn to look anxiously at Ba' Weeyums.

"But everyone's going!" I said. And to be sure, of the score of old and young who had circled the dancers when I arrived there were now less than half.

"De' goombay eem good 'nuf," said Ba' Weeyums slowly, "but eem need *rum*. Don't no goombay talk like eem should talk eef eem no had de *rum*."

The rum! The rum! Of course. I loudly asked Ral if he would go up to my cottage and bring down the jug of rum from under Mai's bunk in the kitchen. He was off with unusual alacrity, whether because of the rum or because of the chance that Mai might by this hour have retired to the bunk, I do not know.

While we waited Ba' Weeyums explained that of course he could have beat the drum for me any day, but that there had been no drum to beat.

Ba' Teddy explained further that all this was strictly forbidden by the Colonel, that he had cautioned them against doing these dances while I was there (my suspicions of hypocrisy were well founded), that Ba' Foster's story was true that nothing had been planned but only by the accident of Ba' Weeyums' drum beating had these passers-by gathered, and that were the Colonel not at Balaclava even this would have been out of the question. Of course I must not mention these dances to anyone, and tomorrow it would be best if I would have forgotten all about them. Further, we must be very brief tonight, because while the thicket and the seclusion of the spot and the direction of the wind prevented the sound of the drum from traveling far, it wouldn't be long before all Accompong would be aroused by these almost-forgotten drum rhythms which stripped them of the veneer of the Scotch minister and cricket games at the parade and set dances, and the sleeping Koromantee and Eboe and Nago would come to the fore and things would happen that the Colonel would be certain to hear about, even at Balaclava. Just a little while, I pleaded, to break in the goombay and so that I might partake once of the things that belonged to the Maroons in the old days.

Ral returned, and Ba' Weeyums took drum and bottle off to one side. There he poured rum on the goatskin head, rubbed it in, took a long drink himself, then spat a mouthful at the drum again. Between times he mumbled in a tongue which I gathered was Koromantee. Then he poured a few drops of rum on the ground, and the baptism was over. This was for the spirit of the drum, he explained. Then he squatted over the drum again, and indeed it seemed to me that it was suddenly alive. Though the body of the drum was shallow, and it more resembled a square stool than any drum I had previously seen, the tone was full and less staccato than before, and I was almost inclined to believe that it was alive, and that it *was* the spirit of some Gold Coast god come to life to grumble a protest against the long silence.

Gradually they returned, slipping from behind the coconut palms and up from the ravines and down from the mountains. I don't know how many, because I was in the midst, and there was now only one kerosene torch, and the rum was going the rounds and it all became unreal, though it all happened because the dances are still very clear to me.

I might not have come at all, for the difference that it has made. I was accepted and one of them.

The dance I had interrupted was a myal dance. Ba' Teddy explained it, as, fascinated, I watched Mis' Mary and the old man. They were facing each other. The old man took the part of the myal "doctor" and the dance was to entice into his power an evil spirit, the "duppy"* of some dead worker of black magic. Ba' Weeyums led a chant in Koromantee, and the women answered. The dance interested me too much for me to try and remember the sound of the words. The evil spirit circled around the doctor hesitant, advancing and retreating, her eyes fixed, mouth clamped shut tightly, body rigid. The doctor squatted in front of her, arms wide as though to embrace her, fingers wide open and hands trembling violently. As he advanced slowly toward her, his pelvis began to move with an unmistakable sexual purpose, and the duppy responded in like manner. They hesitated in front of each other, swaying. Then she eluded his embrace with a sharp convulsive bend, and was on the other side of the circle, taunting, enticing features still hard and set but body liquid and so full of desire that I could scarcely believe that it was old Mis' Mary, grandmother of goodness knows how many.

The doctor reached out for her, gesticulating, grimacing, insinuating. Then she came to life suddenly and the pursuit was reversed. The doctor was afraid of this thing which he had done, of this woman whom he had raised from the dead with these fleshly promises. They were face to face, bodies touching, both of them squatting now with arms pressed close to their sides, elbows bent, and widespread fingers quivering violently. Ba' Teddy had stopped explaining and among the onlookers there was no sound except heavy breathing, but the chant continued and the drum, and it seemed that the air was heavy with some other heat and sound. The duppy leaned over the man, who cowered in fear from her, though their bodies were pressed tightly together. As I decided that I must close my eyes for a moment, Ba' Teddy raised his hand, and the drum and chant stopped on a single note: there was a blank silence that left both dancers and spectators dangling helplessly in mid-air.

"Dat dance bad dance," Ba' Teddy muttered, trying to calm his voice and appear merely annoyed in spite of his quick breathing. I opened my mouth to speak, but he anticipated my question and answered sharply. "Bes don' ax no furder questions, missus. Me don' see dat fer long time, en hit bad. Dat mix up wid bad biznuss. Better fer missus ef she fergit."

I was almost relieved to be thus reprimanded. But the mood of the

*Ghost.

dance had already changed, and to a far livelier rhythm. Two men were hopping about in the circle mimicking two cocks in the thick of a fight. They switched their middles, bobbed their heads, wrinkled their faces, and stuck their necks far out crowing a challenge. The audience, tense a moment before, was now in a hysteria of laughter. One of the dancers picked up his foot high and hopped around in a circle, the other following at a gallop, hand thrust in coat pocket and flapping widely for wings. Finally one was vanquished and with a feeble squawk rolled over sadly, feet in the air. The other strutted over to him, looked disdainfully around, and flapped his wings in victory as he trotted around the circle.

I plead with Ba' Weeyums for a Koromantee war dance, and find that it is no other than the wild dance which I saw only a suggestion of at Ol' Mis' Cross' gravedigging. In this I join, along with Simon Rowe and others who have only watched so far. The few young people who are here, however, do not join in these traditional dances. They are ashamed, and I am sure that I shock them greatly; on the other hand, I feel that they watch us rather wistfully, wishing that they had the courage to give themselves up for a moment to their traditions and forget that there is a market at Maggotty and cricket games on the outside, and store-bought shoes.

The war dances are danced by both men and women. The introduction seemed to be a disjointed walking around in a loose circle, much like the warming up of an athlete. Then Henry Rowe* and I are facing each other doing a step which could easily be compared to an Irish reel. Hands on hips, we hop from one foot to the other, feet turned out at right angles to the body or well "turned out," in ballet vernacular. This hopping brought us closer together, and I had to watch the others closely to keep up with Henry. We turned our backs and walked away, then turned suddenly again and hopped together. The songs are in lusty Koromantee, and from somewhere a woman procured a rattle and is shaking it in accompaniment to Ba' Weeyums. Some of the men wave sticks in the air, and the women tear off their handkerchiefs and wave them on high as they dance. Henry and I grabbed each other around the waist and ran circles around each other, first one way, then the other. A few of these turns and we separate in a melee of leaping, shouting warriors; a moment later we are "bush fightin'," crouching down and advancing in line to

*This name is inconsistent in the original.

attack an imaginary enemy with many feints, swerves, and much panto-mime. At one stage of the dance Mis' Mary and I are face to face, she no longer a duppy but a Maroon woman of the old days working the men up to a pitch where they will descend into the Cockpit and exterminate one of his Majesty's red-coated platoons. She grabbed me by the shoulders and shook me violently, then we were again hopping around each other with knees high in the air, handkerchiefs and skirts flying.

When this was over we were all exhausted. The Maroons have not been accustomed to this sort of thing for a long time; nor am I who until now have known only the conventional techniques, and the far less strenuous set dances. We dispersed and I was in possession of the goom-bay. Ba' Teddy and Ba' Weeyums and I labored up the mountainside, and behind us shutters closed and candles were extinguished and I knew that they were all talking about the escapade of the evening, and how angry the Colonel would be if he knew, and that the "missus" must have known things that she hadn't so far divulged, about myal and obi and the old Koromantee traditions, maybe even the language. [. . .]

At my cottage door, I could hear Mai snoring peacefully within, and this was very comforting after the orgy in the ravine. I remembered vaguely that Ral had left the dancing soon after he returned with the rum, and was certain that he was responsible for Mai's not having come to the dance, and perhaps for her peaceful snoring.

I pulled off my muddy shoes and crawled on top of the marosh, ignoring the bowl of rice and gourd of fresh coconut water that Mai had thoughtfully left on the kitchen table for me. I felt extremely tired and extremely comfortable. My notebook still lay open on the table. Earlier in the day I had harbored a strong resentment against the Maroons and a strong disappointment in myself. Now I had the delicious thrill of accom-plishment, of having conquered an unseen enemy (the Colonel, no doubt), and of belonging completely. I only regretted as I pulled the sheet up around my chin that it had all happened so late. Well, if I ever return—and I sincerely hope that I shall—at least I shall know where to begin.

BRENDA RAY MORYCK

Why

Janey and Alphonse were playing with their "political" dolls on the second balcony. In the midst of the viceroy's important speech to his council, Janey jumped up and rushed to the balcony rail, to the astonishment of the august politicians, and to Alphonse's intense disgust. Jancy had heard the carriage stopping before the front door. Lovely Mother was going to drive, and Janey formed a sudden determination to accompany her.

She rushed across the balcony, giving no heed to the authoritative Alphonse, slid down the ballisters and arrived at the entry just as Lovely-Mother seated herself in the carriage. Janey felt very moist and warm as she regarded Lovely-Mother, cool, immaculate and beautiful in her white hat and dress,—one finger pressed against her lips, her grey eyes far away.

Finally Lovely-Mother noticed Janey and asked rather absently,

"Well, Janey-baby, what is it?"

Janey smiled shyly.

"I thought,—I—I just remembered,—I mean I was just wondering where you are going,—'cause, 'cause I just thought I might like to go with you." Then seeing the troubled look in Lovely-Mother's eyes, and remembering her manners, she hastened to add,

"That is, if you'd like to have me, Lovely-Mother."

Lovely-Mother sighed before speaking. Something was evidently troubling her greatly, for she never before seemed so far away and quiet.

"Janey-dear, I remember I promised to take you to drive with me this

Source: Wellesley College Magazine (supplement to the *Wellesley College News*) 23 (June 1915): 6–14.

afternoon, but I want you to excuse me this time, dear. I've just had a message from the 'Spanish Lady' and one of her children is very ill and I'm going there to see what I can do. I can't take you with me to-day. I'm sorry, pet, but you understand don't you?"

Janey's smile vanished. She was disappointed, terribly so, but then that "you understand, don't you?" consoled her somewhat. She swallowed the rising lumps in her throat, and summoned back the smile. Tears never brought the desired things, Janey well knew.

"Well, I fancy, if you don't mind, Lovely-Mother, that I'd like to drive just a little way with you, just maybe only to the gates, or—or—down the Boulevard a little ways,—just a little ways, Lovely-Mother," she pleaded.

Lovely-Mother considered her thoughtfully, biting her under lip and frowning slightly.

"Well, I can't think what it is that I have forgotten, and I can't wait any longer. I'll drive by the 'Hill' and leave you at Aunt Consuelo's if you are so very disappointed, Janey. Put her in, Casian," to the coachman.

But even this turn of events did not please Janey. She wanted to go, of course, for she just loved Aunt Consuelo, and the little cousins over on the "Hill," but what could Lovely-Mother possibly be thinking of to want to take her with her when she was not dressed—and to call on her cousins! Lovely-Mother must be indeed upset about the poor little Span-ish boy, for in Janey's home, His Majesty's lovely island down in the sea, one observed the same formal etiquette with one's nearest relatives as one did with one's most distant acquaintances. A little girl could not possibly go to call on her cousins in a brown linen dress, and tan slippers and socks. One always went calling in white, and carried one's best white parasol. Lovely-Mother must have forgotten.

"I'll tell Lala to dress me in such a hurry an' I'll help her too an' I won't be a minute," Janey suggested, anxiously eyeing Lovely-Mother.

But Lovely-Mother was in a hurry, and commanded Casian to put her in the carriage immediately. When Lala appeared to warn Lovely-Mother about yellow fever, the carriage was already rolling away and so Lovely-Mother did not answer, but after awhile turned to Janey and said:

"You must not drink or eat anything outside of Aunt Consuelo's house, Janey dear. You won't forget, will you, pet?"

"Yes, Lovely-Mother," Janey answered. She was too miserable to ask questions. Brown linen was hot enough on such a June afternoon, but to have a Lovely-Mother sitting beside one in cool and dainty white was quite too much.

Finally Lovely-Mother noticed Janey's unwanted silence and said pleasantly, "Perhaps Hubert will be there, Janey. He must have arrived last night or this morning," and then lapsed into silence again.

Janey did not mind that silence now. What cool balm to a very warm soul was this delightful news. Oh if Hubert only would be there, what an added joy it would be to the afternoon's pleasure. For Janey always anticipated pleasure when she went to Aunt Consuelo's. She just loved Aunt Consuelo,—dear, gay, beautiful Aunt Consuelo. Best of everybody in the world, excepting Lovely-Mother, of course, she loved Aunt Consuelo. Aunt Consuelo was always sweet and kind to her. People said that Aunt Consuelo did not love children, that she shamefully neglected her six (she had only six then), but Janey didn't believe it. It was true that when the doctor had wanted to give Aunt Consuelo another baby, she had cried at first, and said she didn't want another,—she had too many anyway, and she had made a great fuss. Janey had been in the next room when he was there (for she had a most inconvenient habit of being where she was not supposed to be) and she had heard all about it, but months afterward when the doctor had brought little Donjon, Aunt Consuelo had loved him just as much as she did the other children. Not quite as much as Hubert, of course. At the thought of that adored cousin, Janey's heart quickened. All personal discomfort was forgotten in the hope that Hubert might have come home, for he had been gone away almost a year—away across the ocean to school. Janey remembered him as a very handsome, vivacious boy of ten, when he went away,—slender, black-eyed and black-haired, just like Aunt Consuelo. And he knew so many wonderful things,—all kinds of new games, and how to catch fish, and field mice, and scorpions. And he was always teasing the cook and the yardboy and the gardener, but no one was ever angry with Hubert. He was too nice to be angry with, and he had the loveliest smile. He was quite like the princess in her English History, only he didn't have yellow hair. Maybe he was the Black Prince,—but then the Black Prince was wicked.

Anyway, he could not only play the piano better than they all could, even counting Alphonse, but he could play a great, big pipe-organ, and he could sing beautifully.

Janey sighed as the carriage rolled into "Hill House" grounds. She did hope that Hubert had not changed. Maybe he wouldn't even notice her now, especially in the brown dress.

As Janey and Lovely-Mother approached the house, they saw the three babies and Mimi in the palm arbor. Donjon, the youngest, sat silently and serenely in his airing-basket, while Peter and Lamar, Junior, distant, black-eyed, little boys, aged three and four, amused themselves quietly, by rolling a ball along a bench. They did not even deign to look up as the carriage passed them. Ordinarily, the sight of plump, stolid Donjon would have lured Janey from even Lovely-Mother's side, but today the possibility of seeing Hubert drew her past her pet without a regret.

Lovely-Mother had not time to leave the carriage, but Aunt Consuelo allowed her siesta to be broken, and came out on the piazza.

"Why, here is little Lovedom," she cried gaily, greeting Janey. "I'm so glad you've come over to spend the afternoon with us. Your little cousins are still in Patty's care. Ah! here is Hubert. Hubert, here is your Aunt Rosalys and Janey!"

Janey dimpled and beamed. Aunt Consuelo was always sweet to her, and yes, there was Hubert—the same Hubert of old, somewhat taller, and a trifle slenderer, but with the same dear, happy smile, and the same easy, gracious ways.

He climbed into the carriage, bowed and shook hands with Lovely-Mother, and then kissed her on both cheeks. Then he got out and hugged Janey.

"Hello! Janey old pal? How are you? Grown a good bit since I last saw you, haven't you? Been catching any worms lately? I'm glad you've come over this afternoon. We'll have a jolly time. I'm so glad you aren't all rigged out so you can't play. How is Alphonse?"

Janey was tongue-tied with delight. She struggled to say something equally polite, but before the words came, Hubert was flying up the steps again at his mother's request.

"Hubert, run in and tell Margaret and Ursula and Joan to come down to greet their Aunt Rosalys and Janey, and tell Patty to come take Janey's things," called Aunt Consuelo.

"Yes, madam," he answered.

While he was gone, Lovely-Mother explained her errand.

"That's too bad," said Aunt Consuelo lightly. "You are always doing good to others. Well, remember the Governor-General's ball tonight, and don't overtire yourself. Why not let me send after your clothes. It will save time if you stop and dress here on your way back. I'll write a note to Channing,—Oh, nonsense! Your precious Janey will be well taken care of. Ah, here are 'my jewels!'"

The three immaculate little cousins appeared in their spotless afternoon white, and simultaneously dropped their curtsies to Lovely-Mother. They were very lovely little girls, aged seven, nine and ten,—with mops of thick, bushy, black hair, hanging unberibboned to their shoulders, and large, serious dark eyes.

"How do you do, Aunt Rosalys, how do you do, Janey," they said politely. Janey eyed them pleasantly. She was not at all miserable now because they were in white and she was not. Hubert had on a blue linen suit.

"What perfect children," said Lovely-Mother softly to Aunt Consuelo.

Aunt Consuelo eyed the little girls amusedly for a few moments. "Yes," she answered still more softly, "Too perfect. They're little prigs." But Janey heard. She did not know what prigs were, but she knew that somehow the little girls did not quite satisfy their wonderful mother.

"Hubert, my son," she said, and her eyes shone like stars when she looked at him, "take Janey and your little sisters down to the playhouse, and give them a good time."

"Remember, Janey, pet," Lovely-Mother said as she drove away, "what I told you about drinking and eating." Then to Aunt Consuelo, "You know the yellow fever has been discovered in the poor quarters."

Aunt Consuelo did not seem impressed.

"Yes? Well, the children never leave the grounds, and Mimi and Patty watch them carefully."

Lovely-Mother departed, and the children ran down to the playhouse.

"I tell you what, let's have a fine good game of hide and seek," suggested Hubert. "We'll have partners. Margaret, you'll have to go with Joan and Ursula, 'cause you see Janey and I aren't all rigged out in white, and we can go hide in places where you'd get all dirty. Now you three go and hide, while Janey and I count a hundred, and then we'll come and find you."

The little girls obediently sped away and hid. Of course they were found immediately, perched daintily on the boughs of a magnolia tree. Their dazzling white shoes gave them away. Then Janey and Hubert rushed off to hide. Oh the wonder of that mad flight, when hand and hand, with lovely Cousin Hubert she ran on, and on, over the smooth, green lawn, down through the weedy fields, climbed the plantation fence and went skulking through the sugar gardens—that forbidden but enchanting region. Oh the comfort of that brown dress! and those easy, unsoilable brown slippers!

At last Hubert flung himself down and Janey tumbled down beside him, worn and happy.

"Janey, they'll never find us now! You'll never tell, will you, where we've been? Cross your heart: you'll never tell where we've been. Honor bright!"

Janey crossed. "Honor bright!" she answered.

"Ssh!" cautioned Hubert, suddenly sitting up, on the alert. "There're some workers near here. Listen, they're talking."

"Let's get away quick an' hide somewhere else, 'fore they see us," cautioned Janey.

"All right. Wait! Let's hear what they're saying. I heard 'yellow fever.' I wonder if it's on the island." He drew Janey down beside him again, and they wriggled partially under some old, cut-down stalks, and further in among the growing plants. The voices drew nearer.

"W'ite man he go'an agin. Go' ansure an fars' dis' time. Yellow fever, she cartch him quick," one voice droned pleasantly.

"De Wes' Indiman, he sure are de fav'rit' of de Lord. Wes' Indiman he no get cartch by de fever. Yellow fever she no cartch no all-Wes' Indiman" answered the other, with the happy assurance of being one of the "favored of the Lord."

"They're coming here," whispered Hubert. "Let's run."

The voices receded a little, and Janey and Hubert wriggled out of their hiding place, crawled cautiously to a path, and then ran headlong, climbed the fence again, and tore through the fields until they reached the guava orchard. Weary and breathless, they flung themselves down under a tree.

"By Jove, but I'm thirsty," exclaimed Hubert. "When we've rested a bit, let's go over to the Swamp brook and get a drink, hey, Janey?"

Janey's heart beat with anxiety. What was she to do? Lovely-Mother had particularly cautioned her against drinking, and now Hubert was inviting her to do so. She was thirsty, and it would be babyish to refuse.

"I—I fancy I'm not so very thirsty, Hubert," she stammered. "That is, I think I better,—I mean I fancy I'll wait 'til I get back to the house."

"Oh, all right," Hubert assented graciously. "But come on with me while I get one."

Then Janey's heart smote her. If it was not good for her to drink the water, it surely could not be good for Hubert either. Oh it was hard to seem so like a little girl, but rather than have Hubert made sick, she would brave his displeasure.

"Oh, you mustn't drink the water either, Hubert. You see Lovely-

Mother told me not to 'cause it's something to do with yellow fever. Maybe your mother didn't tell you 'cause, 'cause she's so busy an' everything, but you mustn't Hubert," Janey eyed him with big, anxious eyes.

"Don't you worry, little Janey. I know what you mean. You mean yellow fever germs are in the water maybe. But not in this water, Janey. Just look how nice, and cool, and clear this is. But didn't you hear what those men said over in the sugar garden! West Indians are immune from the yellow fever: They can't ever get it. I guess your mother forgot that. You and I are West Indians, Janey. We couldn't get the yellow fever even if the germs were here, and I'm sure they're not."

Still Janey held back.

"Hubert, what is yellow fever?" she said.

"Why, yellow fever is a disease, Janey, something that makes you very sick, and you most always die with it, but only Caucasian people have it, never West Indians. You see, Janey, God made this island for West Indian people and when too many Caucasians, especially Americans, begin to crowd onto it, He sends the yellow fever, and kills them all off. So you see we're safe, Janey. Come on, if you want a drink."

"But,—but Hubert, you aren't so very West Indian. I am. 'cause, 'cause I'm brown, but you are very fair Hubert, an', an', an' maybe you aren't so West Indian," Janey persisted, vaguely feeling that somehow she must prevent him from drinking.

Hubert laughed gaily. "Oh Janey, you're too funny. Of course I'm West Indian." He stood up and tossed back his thick, black hair, and squared his straight little shoulders. "Why I'm a thoroughbred West Indian, I am. My mother is West Indian, and my father is West Indian and I'm West Indian," he said proudly. "The only reason you're brown an' I'm not is because you 'harked back.' Father said so."

That settled it. Janey decided to drink. Hubert made a cup of his hands, and allowed Janey to drink the clear, cool water. Janey drank three scoops, and when she had finished, Hubert drank five. Then he took her hand, and together they ran back, not minding the heat in their high spirits. When they arrived at the piazza steps, Hubert gave Janey's hand a squeeze.

"Janey, old pal, you're a good sport," he said merrily, and Janey felt amply repaid for all that she had endured.

Aunt Consuelo and Lovely-Mother were rocking on the piazza as they came up together, tired, flushed, moist and weary.

"Hubert!" said Aunt Consuelo, "Where did you take Janey, you naughty boy? Aren't you ashamed to run away from little sisters like that?" But when Hubert regarded her with his mischievous bright eyes, she relented, and took his warm face between her soft, white hands, and said lovingly:

"My dear, dear little man! Run in now and dress, and send Patty to get Janey. Little sisters have had their supper, and are going to bed. Aunt Rosalys wants to hear you sing, too, Hubert, my son."

Janey tumbled wearily into Lovely-Mother's arms, regardless of her own soiled condition, and Lovely-Mother's spotless one.

"Oh Rosalys, I forgot to ask you about the child. I've been so busy speaking of the ball," said Aunt Consuelo, when Hubert was gone, and Janey was apparently sleeping.

"He died," answered Lovely-Mother quietly.

"Poor little wretch," commented Aunt Consuelo. "Ah well; it's just as well. What does one poor little miserable being matter more or less. What jewels are you going to wear tonight?"

Lovely-Mother did not answer for some time, and then as though she had not heard Aunt Consuelo's question she said,

"It was very tragic. The poor mother's whole cry was if it had not been so sudden, if the little boy had only died naturally. If he could only have spoken to her a few moments. Oh, it was most pathetic."

Aunt Consuelo considered the distant shrubbery.

"What caused his death?" she asked uninterestedly.

"Ptomaine poisoning. The mother's grief was heartrending."

"Pshaw, why do you burden yourself with other people's griefs? You'll go long-faced and sad-eyed to the ball now," said Aunt Consuelo lightly, and rather impatiently.

Lovely-Mother replied, "Oh it was all for the best. There are three other children whom the woman can scarcely support. I've promised to do what I can. Look here, the precious pet has gone to sleep."

Janey thought it best to keep on feigning sleep, and let Patty carry her into the music room, where Lovely-Mother and Aunt Consuelo soon followed, and where Hubert appeared, washed, brushed, powdered, and arrayed in white from head to toe, ready to sing.

Janey never forgot the figure that he made, standing at the piano beside his mother, while she played for him,—a straight, slender, erect little boy, with his finely formed head thrown back, his eyes starry and happy. He sang several of Lovely-Mother's favorites, alone in his clear, sweet treble, and then several duets with his mother, and ended up with

"My Ain Countree," Janey's favorite hymn. Nor did Janey ever forget the look in Aunt Consuelo's eyes as she sang to Hubert, "Thou shalt be a man!—Son of Mine," as she played that old pirate song. Then Lala arrived in the carriage to take Janey home.

Janey kissed Lovely-Mother sleepily, and murmured thanks and what a good time she'd had to Hubert, and was borne out to the carriage.

"Good-bye, old sport," called Hubert gaily. "Come again soon, and we'll have some more good fun. We certainly had a jolly time, didn't we, Janey? Good-bye."

The next morning Janey was so dreamy and inattentive at her lessons that the kind governess took pity on her unwonted lethargy, and excused her to go lie in the hammock. Janey thanked her politely and wandered off listlessly among the scuppernong vines. She was not ill. She just wanted to talk with Lovely-Mother. Finally she went back to the north balcony, slipped through a French window, approached Lovely-Mother's desk. Lovely-Mother, her head bound with a wet cloth, was writing furiously, surrounded by a multitude of books. She did not look up until Janey sighed deeply and audibly. Then she was struck by the tragedy in Janey's face.

"Why Janey-baby, whatever is the matter?" she said, gathering her into her lap, and removing the wet head cloth.

Janey gulped. "Maybe the Spanish Lady loved her little boy, Lovely-Mother," she answered slowly and miserably.

Lovely-Mother looked bewildered, then as light seemed to break upon her comprehension she replied anxiously:

"Why of course the Spanish Lady loved her little boy, Janey. What made you think she didn't?"

"Why,—why you and Aunt Consuelo s-said she oughtn't to have cried, 'cause he died,—an', an', an' she had enough children anyway an' didn't need him. Maybe she loved him too, an' wanted him. Maybe she didn't think she had too many children, Lovely-Mother," Janey pleaded pitifully.

"Oh my little baby," cried Lovely-Mother. "Janey, my precious, you don't understand. Your Aunt Consuelo and I never meant anything of the kind." Then with a sudden afterthought, "When did Aunt Consuelo say that to you?"

"She didn't say it to me, she said it to you last night. You, you,—all two of you didn't care 'cause the poor little boy died an' an' you didn't think his mother ought to care. Maybe she didn't mind having too many children, Lovely-Mother. Maybe she loved him,—maybe as much as you love Alphonse."

There were tears in Lovely-Mother's grey eyes as she answered, hugging Janey close to her.

"Oh my precious pet, I'm so glad you came to mother about this. Come, let's go out on the balcony, and mother will tell you all about it."

When they were settled cozily in the willow swinging couch, Janey, doubled up opposite Lovely-Mother, her troubled eyes fixed on Lovely-Mother's face, Lovely-Mother began.

"You see, it's this way, Janey. God makes all the little children in the world, and sometimes He sends more children to some people than He does to others. Well, sometimes He looks down from heaven, and He sees some one little boy or girl that He wants very much back in heaven, so that after awhile He can send the little boy or girl to someone else as a new baby. And then He takes the little child away to heaven where it is very, very happy."

"Is it an angel, then?" asked Janey, in awe.

"Yes, Janey. God makes the little boy or girl a lovely little angel. Well, God is very good, and very, very kind, as you know, dear; so He tries as often as He can to take little boys or girls from families where they have other children so that the mother and father won't be so lonesome. You see the Spanish Lady has three children left to make her happy. That is why mother and Aunt Consuelo don't feel badly about it. God knew best, you see."

"Umm," Janey nodded. For a while she looked into space.

"God wouldn't take Alphonse, would He, cause there aren't enough of us," Janey said serenely, but all the same she was wishing God would make her a little angel.

"Does God sometimes take little children who have lots of nice things and everything?"

"Oh yes, Janey, very often, but He always does what is right and best Janey-pet," Lovely-Mother was rising, "and He makes the little child very happy—and it is very nice." The last words were uttered vaguely and Lovely-Mother stepped through the window.

Janey went skipping down the steps. It was all right about the little boy dying,—God wanted to make him an angel, and make everybody happy. Because, of course, his mother would be so happy to have one of her children an angel, and she had three left. How nice God was to make angels, and distribute the children evenly. That is why Lovely-Mother and Aunt Consuelo had so soon forgotten about the little boy dying, and his mother who cried. That is why they had laughed, and gone to a ball, and danced all night, and had a gay time. It was quite right that they should,—dying made everybody happy. Oh how glad she was that it was so!

All that week Janey and Alphonse played "making angels." Alphonse was God, of course, who took away Janey's many children and made them angels one by one, leaving her at last, a supremely happy widow with just three children! "Making angels" was such a delightful game. Even Alphonse was enthusiastic, and it was he who suggested that when the little cousins from the "Hill" came over, they should use Lamar and Peter and Margaret for angels. The game promised to hold good for all summer, but then something happened.

One afternoon Janey was seated on the lower hall steps, quietly playing with her dolls, and trying to keep cool, when she heard the carriage drive up to the front steps, at a fearful rate, quite unusual with the careful Casian. In a second, Lovely-Mother rushed up the steps, and into the hall, her face white and drawn. Janey sprang to meet her, but Lovely-Mother pushed her away.

"Oh, don't,—where—where is your father?" she cried in desperation.

Before Janey could answer, the Secretary hurried into the hall, and Lovely-Mother fell into his arms.

"Oh Channing,—Channing," she sobbed. "The most awful, awful thing has happened. Hubert,—Hubert," (she fairly screamed his name), "is dead,—dead, Channing,—do you understand me? Little Hubert died this afternoon of—of—of—yellow fever!"

"My God!" ejaculated the Secretary. "Hubert! Dead! Yellow fever! My God!" He seemed unable to comprehend the words. Then he added compassionately, "Poor Consuelo!"

"Channing,—w-will you go over there now? Consuelo is raving. They can't do anything with her. Oh Channing, it was so sudden and so awful." Lovely-Mother leaned against the Secretary, and gave herself up to uncontrolled grief.

Janey stood dumbly on the steps and watched.

The Secretary led Lovely-Mother to a chair, and there she poured out the story of the tragedy.

"He was only taken ill this morning. Yesterday Consuelo said he seemed rather listless, but she thought it was only the heat. This morning he complained of severe headache, this noon he became unconscious, and at 4 o'clock he died, died without ever saying one word. Consuelo has almost lost her mind. She says she could stand it better if he could only have spoken to her. Where he ever got the yellow fever from we none of us know."

Janey knew. Hubert had gone to be an angel, and now she would go too. Why did Lovely-Mother cry? It was nice to be an angel, it made everybody happy. If it was the suddenness with which God decided to make little angels, she could spare them that.

She stepped up to the Secretary very bravely, and took his hand.

"Don't mind, Father,—don't you cry Lovely-Mother, Hubert is gone to be an angel and I'm going too,—most prob'bly tonight or tomorrow, 'cause I drank the water too."

"Janey!" screamed Lovely-Mother,—"drank the water,—what water? Oh my baby, what have you done now!" Lovely-Mother searched Janey's face with terror and anxiety. "Tell mother, quick, Janey, what water did you drink?"

"I can't tell you what water," Janey answered evenly, "'cause I crossed my heart honor bright to Hubert that I'd not tell, but it was in a brook, an' Hubert an' I all two drank it, only Hubert said it didn't have yellow fever in it an' anyway West Indian people never could get yellow fever; so we all two drank it an' it was nice, an' clear, an' good, an' now I'm going to be an angel."

The Secretary's face blanched with horror. Lovely-Mother raised her arms above her head and screamed. The servants came rushing in from everywhere. Even Janey began to feel a little frightened.

"Get a doctor, quick!" commanded the Secretary, and snatching up Janey carried her up to bed.

In five minutes she was undressed, and lying in her little white bed. The doctor came and jabbed a needle in her arm, and did various other unkind things and announced that Janey would not have yellow fever,— that she could not have it. Vaguely she understood that it had something to do with "pigment." Evidently "pigment" was something which she had, and which Hubert had not. Now she was not going to be an angel.

Janey cried.

One evening, a few days later, Janey heard her father say to Lovely-Mother: "Poor, poor Consuelo. If something doesn't happen, she'll either die or go insane. She hadn't eaten or slept since Hubert—Oh! God, why couldn't it have been one of the babies or one of the girls."

Why indeed? Janey had been tempted to step out and tell her father right then that God knew best, and probably some lady on the island wanted a beautiful boy like Hubert. They always did, that was why God took Hubert.

"It is tragic, tragic," Lovely-Mother had answered, "but we must not grieve so, on Janey's account. I have taught her that death is very beautiful."

The next day Janey resolved to visit Aunt Consuelo and explain to her the beauty and happiness of Hubert's going away. Perhaps Aunt Consuelo didn't understand. In the morning she asked permission to take her dolls, and the puppy, and some lunch, and spend the day in the palm groves. Then she set out bravely on her journey. It was a long, long walk across the fields to the "Hill" by the shortest cut, but Janey was undaunted. Within an hour, she had reached the house garden, but it was long, long, before she could get near the house. First, she spied Patty airing the imperturbable Donjon in his carriage, on the walk before the house; then she saw Margaret and Ursula sewing in the playhouse; later Peter and Lamar wandered about with their little watering cans, trying to assist the gardener, and the yard boy and the laundress were always in evidence in the rear of the house. Janey stayed in the palm grove, played with the one doll which she had brought, and ate her little lunch serenely.

Then at four o'clock her chance came. Patty took the babies to walk on the Boulevard. Ursula, Margaret, and Joan, she knew, were confined on the upper galleries for their supposed siestas,—the servants had all retired to the cookhouse, for their afternoon chat. She stole up to the piazza, slipped across it and entered the house. Softly she crept upstairs. She knew just where Aunt Consuelo would be—out on the little canopied gallery adjoining her room.

But when she arrived in Aunt Consuelo's room another halt was enforced. Mimi was with Aunt Consuelo. She would have to wait until she left. She must see Aunt Consuelo all alone.

"Madame she take jus' lil' bit o' this?" coaxed Mimi's soothing voice. "Jus' lil' Madame take?"

No answer for some time.

Then, "Oh Mimi," suddenly a petulant voice broke out strangely like Aunt Consuelo's, and yet so different. "Please go away, and let me alone."

Mimi left the gallery. For a few moments Janey's purpose wavered.

Aunt Consuelo might command her to leave her just as she did Mimi. No, it was only because she did not understand about Hubert being an angel, that made her cross with Mimi.

Janey advanced to the doorway and looked out. Then she stood stock still. Her face grew rigid with astonishment and fear. The lady in the hammock was not Aunt Consuelo at all—it must be somebody else. She had on Aunt Consuelo's beautiful pink negligee, and Aunt Consuelo's wonderful signet ring, and she had Aunt Consuelo's lovely black hair, but oh how thin and white her hands were, and how pale and drawn her face, so different from beautiful, gay Aunt Consuelo. Just then the lady turned her head and looked at Janey. Yes, it was Aunt Consuelo, but how different her eyes were. They used to sparkle like stars with life, and fun, and now—now they made Janey feel as though she wanted to cry.

"Janey!" cried Aunt Consuelo in sharp and angry surprise. She sat up, shaking, and her breath came in short, quick gasps. "What are you doing over here? Run away. I don't want to see you, Oh God—every other woman can have her children and my boy is gone!"

Janey was frightened at first. But at the sight of Aunt Consuelo's grief, her purpose only strengthened. She would put an end to all this needless suffering.

"Aunt Consuelo," she said sweetly, going straight to the side of the hammock, and looking directly at her aunt with big, wistful, compassionate eyes, "I have something to tell you. Something nice that you'll like to hear."

Aunt Consuelo buried her face in her hands an instant and shuddered. When she looked at Janey again, her face had softened. Janey was encouraged, and laid one plump hand on Aunt Consuelo's white cheek.

"I know you're ill, Aunt Consuelo, an' I'm most very sorry, an,' an' that's why I came,—to make you well, an' I want to tell you that God knows best, an' that's why He took Hubert 'sted of me." She hurried on,—"An, an' that's why he took the little Spanish boy to be an angel. He makes angels out of all the little children He takes, an' sends them to other ladies who haven't any children and who want some."

Aunt Consuelo was rocking back and forth now with her hands over her face, but Janey went on bravely. "He wants to make everybody happy; so He takes little boys from people who have lots of other children. See, you have six children left. Don't you remember how you laughed when the Spanish lady's little boy died, and you went to the ball afterwards, and danced, and Lovely-Mother said it was right 'cause people shouldn't cry when their little boys died, 'cause God takes them away to make everybody happy. God knows best."

"Happy!" cried Aunt Consuelo, flinging herself back on the cushions, and tearing the hammock covering. "God! There is no God. Do you suppose if there were a God He would have taken Hubert,—my Hubert of all the children in the world? Don't talk to me of God."

"But you said yourself, Aunt Consuelo," pleaded Janey, wonderingly, "that what was one little child more or less, an' an' an' when the Doctor offered you Donjon you said you had too many children already. Now maybe you have just enough."

"Too many children!—do you think if I had a hundred children I could have spared Hubert. Hubert, Hubert, Hubert, my son!"

Aunt Consuelo was screaming and sobbing wildly now. "Hubert, Hubert, Hubert, oh why did they take my little boy from me, why,—why, why?"

Some one snatched Janey from behind, and rushed her downstairs. Afterwards she remembered being taken home, and looked at very queerly by Lovely-Mother and the Secretary, and very much hugged, and petted after that, but no one ever spoke of her visit and after awhile she ceased to think of it herself. But she never forgot.

Later they told her that Aunt Consuelo and Uncle Lamar had gone far away. Not long afterward the children went too, and the big, old-fashioned Spanish house stood silent, and deserted—its many long green blinds all closed.

For the first few years afterwards, the children returned each winter to their home, and Janey played blithely with them, but after a time these yearly visits ceased, and they came no more. Aunt Consuelo never came back.

JUANITA V. HARRISON

From *My Great, Wide, Beautiful World*

Jerusalem, October 18
Wynham House, The street of the Prophet
I left my suite case* at the Ticket office at Baalbec† with a man that speak French. When I went to leave for Damascus the agent teased me and said that He had not seen it and I should have left it with a man in unforme. The Mayor and His family from Damascus was there and the wife asked me what was the Trouble. I told her and said there was no trouble I only felt sorry about the pictures and Postal cards I had collected and anyway I would not have to bother with a suite case anymore. For while I was standing there I had planned to get two nice dresses at Damascus and roll them in a paper. they all was amused and admired me when I did not seem worry. the Mayo an Aribian Gentleman spoke perfect English and the beautiful young Lady wife with their first baby and nurse. Then I asked for my ticket and the gentleman would give it to me and I got angry and told Him I would buy one on the Train. Then he sent a boy to bring the case and the Mayo said He see I am quite cable of taken care of myself. then we all had a good laugh. The 5 student Boys of the best Familys were leaving on the same train for their college at Beirut. One of them had seen me the day before and laugh at me when he saw me climb up

Source: Excerpted from Juanita V. Harrison, *My Great, Wide, Beautiful World*, Mildred Morris, ed. (New York: Macmillan, 1936), pp. 67-75. Originally published in *The Atlantic Monthly* (October 1935): 434-443; (November 1935): 601-612.

*Harrison had no formal education. The spellings and punctuation are her own, and Macmillan editors chose to publish them without correction.

†In Lebanon.

on a high fence to look over into a yard. 3 of them spoke a little English the Youngest of them a Handsome Boy of 14 showed me a scalp wound he got in a auto accident and His father were killed He was a Hundred Had been married twice His eldest son was 65 and His youngest two years. he was active as a 35 year old we found each other very interesting. then on the Train Two nice looking Syrian women one with two little girls got into my compartment and the train started off without the two girls and they ran to get on and I caught the youngest and pulled her on and the other was nocked down by the open door but she got up and we saw her running. Well the mother cried and went on it made me cry she grabe me and hug and Kissed me because I got one in. The condoctor sent a telegram at the next stop. anyway I got to see their pretty but pale faces for they threw back the vail.

We reach Damascus at dark. after visiting 7 Hotels I choosed the eight I wanted one over a stream as that is the Arabic idea of Paradise it was so pleasant and clean I just loved the room and bed and also the view. the Arabic food are so good and I liked so much the Cabarets the men were such Gentleman the dancing girls tryed to talk to me the dancing are very lady like they served delicious things in small butter plates water melon seed that had been boiled in salt also punkin seeds they laugh at me because I did not know the nack of getting the nut out but I know as well as they do now. at Twelve midnight when I was ready to go a Handsome Policeman went with me. At Damascus are many ruins from the 1925 fighting.

I left the next morning for Afoulah Israel where you get off for Nazareth. An Arabian man got on at a station where He had been to buy Groceries for a village and geting his things on the train cut his finger and it bled ever so much and he did not have anything to stop it. I tore my handkerchief in half and gave it to him. I did not have time to get anything to take on the train to eat and the things they sold at the station they had on the groun. they have wonderful large white grapes so sweet the syrup are all on the outside and they are covered with bees. so I offered to buy some tomatoes and grapes from him. He said to the lovely Syrian couple in the compartment the wife spoke Spanish and French that I had tyed up his cut finger so he could not sell me any but gave me so much I would not eat it all. I always have salt and pepper so had a feast. It was late when we arrived at Afoulah so I stayed the night it is a new Village that were open by the American Jewish accocation the River

Jordan passes in half a mile of Afoulah. the train stop is called the Jordan Holt the only Hotel were filled. I spoke to a Gentleman he spoke a little English and were the Village Doctor and from Poland. I knew I had found a friend so I left all the worry for him. He was afraid He couldnt find a place for me I told Him not to worry I would be delighted to spend the night sitting on my suite case on the Porch of the Hotel and He wanted to know How I could be so happy when I had no shelter for the night. and would say to himself how interesting I could hear him say it. He asked me if I was hungry. Then I thought how hungry I am. He took me to an elderly German Jewish couple where he have his meals but he had a room in the Hotel. The couple were Two Dears. She gave us soft boiled eggs cheese fresh butter milk and such good bread I keep them buisy bringing bread and butter. I noticed them smiling but I did not think about what they was smiling at until I got filled and I said to the Doctor I cant eat any more. then I said to Him may be the couple would let me sleep in the Dinning room He said I will ask. and the lady said Yes. everything was clean as a pin. She put a couch in the dinning room for the Husband and She and I slep in the bed room. All she could say in English was. and It was good. then I would answer that it was good. the next morning she repeated the supper and the Doctor came and we had Breakfast together. I left at 9 A.M. for Nazareth. She kissed both of my cheeks and gave me a bag of grapes and ask me to write to Her. everybody are very buisy in the little place some have good houses and some just shacks but everything clean.

The Lady who keep the Hotel in Nazareth were born there but her parents are from Germany and built the Hotel many years ago. I went right out and got acquainted with several Nazareth women and went to the home of the prettis one. I meet them at a Bakery the Boy that put the bread on a long poll into the oven spoke a little English. My Friend lived on the side of a hill. She had been married just long enough to have a baby a few months old. Her to rooms were clean and had light and air. In this country are many places that are much like dunjons. Like the Japanese they have matresses they take up every morning and place on shelves. the windows have iron bars like Cuba and brick floors. on the floor by the window she had a little chorcoal stove and she sqart down to cook. Her eldest sister live with Her and did the hard work. She dressed like the Nazareth. Her Husband and boy living in Detroit and Her Mother with a brother in Havana so I felt quite near them. She was cooking something that smelt good but I did not stay when she ask me because

I had seen the markets and how they let the flies feast on everything. I ate only what I could get that had been wrapped in some Switzerland or French Factory and fruit I would take to my room and wash with soap and water. I thought I would have dinner at the Hotel so tipped into the Kitchen to have a look and saw many flies over what was perparein I left by auto for Jerusalem in the car were a young Swedish man a Fine looking colored Arabican Gentleman that wore a red turban and a cream colored silk kimono and a long gray overcoat like they use here. He had a thomos bottle with delicious hot tea in it and gave me some the other Gentleman was a captain in the Worlds war. He pointed out all the interesting things about the Bible times and the war times. He showed me the remains of Herods Temple and where John the Baptist were beheaded also Jacobs well. He and his family had lived many years at Nablous the place of the well and the most prettiest Valley town in Palestine. at Nazareth the night before I had wished it would rain as it was so dusty and a very good shower came the Lady at Hotel said she have never known them to have such a nice shower at that season. so it was delightful next day as the dust was laid.

Jerusalem, October 23
Y.W.C.A.
I have a single room at the Y. it is so lovely here about 4 blocks from the main Gate of the old city. I take my meals at a very nice Jewish Restaurant. it is cheaper than the Y. and I dont hafter wash and pray before I can eat. they cook very much like we do and always have good icecream. When we are in our own country we get more Holiness out of the Holy Land than when we are Here. One have so much to overlook and I have to think hard to get down to the Days of Our Lord. Last Friday was the first time I could really live in the Days of Christ and then there was always something happen in the streets to make you forget. Every Friday at 3 P.M. from the Armenian Monastery built on the site of Caiaphas House start the Procession along the way of the Cross lead by Priests their monks nuns children from the Convent and Christians the Police keep the way clear. We went on stoping at each Station of the Cross but through the winding up and down covered old streets are many things to take your mind off. but most of the time I tryed to picture the day of Our Lord. on the way you meet a donkey loaded with tins of water or a drove of black goats and there are the Moslems making noise at their tin making and

the Jews selling their ware. I got the best part inside of the Church then it were only about 20 in the Procession and it was 53 when it were over I had a scarf over my head and looked so nun like. At the end I felt I would go right home and remember it as a Holy afternoon but on leaving the Church an Arabican Friend meet me and insisted that I go to the Movie and to the Hotel to the Dance. I went to the Movies but not to the Dance.

I was sitting outside the Holy Sepulcher waiting until some tourists come so I could fall in line. a young man that speak English said would I like a guide. I said Im a guide myself I've been guiding myself around Europe for over a year. He was so amused at my answer. then he told me he was not a guide but He were born inside the old city and would like to show me about. He had grey eyes and such a nice expression. then he introduce me to his Rich Cousin who has a car. the Cousin had fair curly hair and spoke English like an Oxford graduate. He took me to the Dead Sea I found it different from what you read It was nothing that made it look dead. not near so heavy and salty as Salt Lake. I spent one hour in the water did not want to come out. 3 Priest that had never had their hair cut nor their beards went in bathing they undressed on the shore and wrapped a white cloth around their waist until they got into the water then I thought How nice it must be in that warm sea without a Bathing suite. On the Banks are a refreshment place I was hungry but they only had Libby's corn beef. I was just full of brine and felt just like Lot's wife so I couldn't eat any. Then we went to the River Jordan. on the Banks are a very Cuban like House with a long shelter of polls and a grass covering where you can eat. Hundreds of Turkeys geese chicken and Black goats are there with a few young boy and three dogs. We had a lovely Arabican dinner the man that own the place wares a blue and white striped homespun kimono and a red turban. This young man have met wealthy American women travelling alone but I am the poorest girl that ever travelled alone. I spend a day in a town as though I was going to spend my life there this is for my own consciance and I find men are always willing to treat you nice. I have a very Oriental looking scarf I ware most of the time on my head everyone think I am Arabian but are puzzled to see me with such a short french dress and the first thing they ask My Friend if I am Arabaian. then when I ware my little French cap they take me for Jewish. I am willing to be what ever I can get the best treatments at being.

PART 7

HARLEM'S GLORY: A WOMAN'S VIEW

The decade of the Roaring Twenties marked an unprecedented flowering of black culture in America, encompassing literature and all the arts. Looking for opportunity, African-Americans had begun to move north, especially to New York, as early as the post-Reconstruction period. Harlem, an uptown area of Manhattan where blacks had been residing since the beginning of the century, became the hub of black cultural activity. To African-Americans nationwide, Harlem seemed to be "the center of all the glory, all the wealth, and all the freedom in the world."[1] Like a magnet, Harlem's fame drew aspiring black writers into its precincts. As a character in a novel by Claude McKay says, "Oh, to be in Harlem again after two years away. . . . The deep-eyed color, the thickness, the closeness of it. The noises of Harlem. The sugared laughter. The honey-talk on its streets. And all night long, ragtime and 'blues' playing somewhere . . . singing somewhere, dancing somewhere! Oh, the contagious fever of Harlem."[2]

The phenomenon known as the Harlem Renaissance lasted for almost two decades, from 1917 to 1935.[3] Black women usually played a subordinate role as promoters behind the scenes during this period, but a few were more active participants. Literary gatherings and parties and contests sponsored by black magazines energized writers and provided them

---

1. The poet Paul Laurence Dunbar, cited in Jervis Anderson, *This Was Harlem: A Cultural Portrait, 1900–1950* (New York: Farrar, Straus and Giroux, 1982), p. 51.

2. Anderson, *This Was Harlem*, p. 144.

3. Scholars are not in agreement on the dates. Bruce Kellner proposes 1917 to 1935 (*Harlem Renaissance: An Historical Dictionary for the Era* [Westport, Conn.: Greenwood Press, 1984]), while other scholars cite the 1920s only.

with a shared repertory of themes, including the excitement of the city experience, the exploration of African-American identity, and the alienation and anger evoked by segregation and discrimination.[4]

In her column in *Opportunity,* "The Ebony Flute," Gwendolyn Bennett heralded the efforts being made by African-Americans to express themselves on the arts scene in New York and around the country. Helene Johnson published poems that extol ordinary black people, linking them with a proud African heritage; her work exemplifies the themes of the Harlem Renaissance.[5] Other women writers offered depictions of Harlem life from a perspective quite different from that of their male counterparts, who played up the Harlem street and night scene. Eunice Hunton Carter describes the Harlem that she observes from the window of a friend's home. For her, the essence of Harlem is to be sought elsewhere, perhaps among the schoolgirls in short fur coats returning from the movies, or in the rapt audiences listening to soapbox speakers or the sellers hawking new patent medicines.

Elise Johnson McDougald (her name sometimes appears as "Elsie"), a social worker and an educator, focuses on the lives of Harlem women—the privileged as well as the disadvantaged—and the stratifications within the community itself. Celebrating "the multiform charm, beauty and character of Negro women," McDougald astutely exposes some erroneous stereotypes that obscure the realities of black women's lives. But McDougald makes no bones about the obstacles that black women face: "daily contempt," economic exploitation, and exclusion from the ideals of beauty promoted by advertising.

Zora Neale Hurston, the best known of the black women writers of this period, captures the sound of street talk in Harlem. Drawing on her expertise in black folklore, she created characters who manipulate language as a way to survive. Women easily prove themselves to be the match of men in such linguistic games and wiliness. Here, too, we see the flip side of Harlem high life—the many newcomers who scarcely have the price of a meal in their pocket.

Hazel Vivian Campbell's story "Part of the Pack" raises pointed ques-

4. See Nathan Huggins, *Voices from the Harlem Renaissance* (New York: Oxford University Press, 1976).

5. See Gloria T. Hull, *Color, Sex and Poetry* (Bloomington: University of Indiana Press, 1987). See also T. J. Bryan, "The Published Poems of Helene Johnson," *The Langston Hughes Review* 6 (Fall 1987): 11–21.

tions about social protest, providing a counterpoint to the prevailing myth of a carefree Harlem. In order to eat, the characters resort to stealing; in order to protest injustice, they resort to looting and violence—even as they debate militant versus pacifist forms of resistance to deprivation. Campbell's story is complemented by "Tar," written by Shirley Graham (who later became Shirley Graham Du Bois when she married W. E. B. Du Bois). Set ten years later than "Part of the Pack," Graham's story offers a sense of the promises as well as the disappointments ushered in by America's entrance into World War II. Ann Petry's "Solo on the Drums" captures a mood of disappointment even as it rescues an image of the power and beauty of the jazz music created in that era.

The Harlem Renaissance ended in the wake of the stock market crash of 1929 and the Great Depression. Literary patronage dried up, and riots in Harlem kept audiences away. Zora Neale Hurston, returning for a visit from her ethnographic researches in the South, commented on the devastation of the literary scene in a letter dated May 31, 1930: "I was in Harlem yesterday for the first time [in a long while]. Some of my friends are all tired and worn out—looking like death eating crackers. All of them cried to me to come and put some life into the gang again. I don't feel any older or tired a bit. Perhaps the hectic life of Harlem wore them out fast while I was in the South getting my rest as well as getting some work done."[6]

Some black women participants, including Hurston, nonetheless continued to write, and some came into their prime much later, after 1935, the date often used to delimit the Harlem Renaissance era.

6. Zora Neale Hurston to Larry Jordan, May 31, 1930. Manuscript Division, Schomburg Center for Research in Black Culture, The New York Public Library (Astor, Lenox and Tilden Foundations).

The Corner

My friend lives in the house on the corner. She lives high above the street in a doll's house of white enamel and soft blues with lovely old furniture and oriental rugs of faded brilliance on dark polished floors; in a miniature home with a real fireplace and polished glasses and flowers all about in crystal bowls. She lives high up there but below are the street and the avenue. And one Fall night as I waited for her in the loveliest room of all, I turned from watching the fire flicker and dart across the room and great chrysanthemums casting sleeping shadows on the wall. I turned from this and watched the street. It was alive with light and sound, the light and sound of the city, the black city. Motor cars whizzed by carrying throngs of pleasure seekers, aliens many of them, in search of novelty and thrill, come to the black city for something new. And in the small morning hours they went back to their homes in Westchester and the Bronx, on Park Avenue and Riverside Drive, back to their haunts on Broadway and thereabouts, serene in the belief that in Harlem cabarets they had found something new, that in black and tan replicas of downtown cabarets, roofs and supper clubs, promoted by quacks of every race, they had seen life in the black city.

In reality as their cars swept past the corner, they were passing life by. They had missed a chance of seeing life when they didn't stop and watch the boy on the corner who for clapping companions in front of the drug store was doing a dance that was a bit of Buck and Wing, a bit of "Charleston" and many other things. They didn't hear the errand boy

Source: *Opportunity* 3 (April 1925): 114–115.

who came out of the drug store singing a song that had drifted out of the cabaret to come from him purified by the sheer joy and spontaneity of his singing.

Around the corner on the Avenue, a man mounted on a soap box was making a political speech in which he was putting race first and country after and the crowd around him was eager and interested—until a pair of detectives passed leading a troupe of gypsies toward the police station.

A group of school girls, bright felt hats perched jauntily on sleek bobbed heads, with short fur coats from which bright scarves fluttered in the night, passed by linked arm in arm, chattering as they went home from a late moving picture. To me, from my high perch, they looked like school girls the town over, but a passerby would have seen skins of olive, tan and copper beneath the bright felt hats.

A man without legs wheeled himself along on a wooden platform and with an instrument or two gave the effect of a whole brass band as he attracted attention to the box for largess fastened onto his platform. A girl of the town dropped a coin or two as she went on her way but [a] slim brown girl and boy passed him by unheedingly as with eyes locked, they walked on into the night.

Across the street the crowd around an automobile from which a swarthy man in morning clothes and a fez was displaying gruesome pictures and dispensing patent medicines parted to let a girl, glitteringly shod and swathed in furs, enter a waiting taxicab.

Beneath the window a crowd of youths were in heated argument gesticulating fiercely. I leaned from the window and listened. For want of a better meeting place a group of college youths were discussing philosophy.

Inside the lovely room the fire had burned low. The silver chimed clock on the mantle struck many times. I decided not to wait longer for my friend. I took my hat and coat and went down into the street and turned into the Avenue. I started to cross. A taxicab filled with alien pleasure-seekers crossed my path. As they passed the tower, they heard nothing but their own maudlin laughter, they saw nothing but their own vacuous faces. They passed on to the cabarets, illegitimate offspring of their own resorts, looking for life, Harlem life, and blindly, feverishly, rushing by it.

The Double Task:
The Struggle of Negro Women
for Sex and Race Emancipation

Throughout the long years of history, woman has been the weather-vane, the indicator, showing in which direction the wind of destiny blows. Her status and development have augured now calm and stability, now swift currents of progress. What then is to be said of the Negro woman today?

In Harlem, more than anywhere else, the Negro woman is free from the cruder handicaps of primitive household hardships and the grosser forms of sex and race subjugation. Here she has considerable opportunity to measure her powers in the intellectual and industrial fields of the great city. Here the questions naturally arise: "What are her problems?" and "How is she solving them?"

To answer these questions, one must have in mind not any one Negro woman, but rather a colorful pageant of individuals, each differently endowed. Like the red and yellow of the tiger-lily, the skin of one is brilliant against the star-lit darkness of a racial sister. From grace to strength, they vary in infinite degree, with traces of the race's history left in physical and mental outline on each. With a discerning mind, one catches the multiform charm, beauty and character of Negro women; and grasps the fact that their problem cannot be thought of in mass.

Because only a few have caught this vision, the attitude of mind of most New Yorkers causes the Negro woman serious difficulty. She is conscious that what is left of chivalry is not directed toward her. She realizes that the ideals of beauty, built up in the fine arts, exclude her almost entirely. Instead, the grotesque Aunt Jemimas of the street-car

Source: The Survey 53 (March 1, 1925): 689–691.

advertisements proclaim only an ability to serve, without grace or loveli-ness. Nor does the drama catch her finest spirit. She is most often used to provoke the mirthless laugh of ridicule; or to portray feminine vicious-ness or vulgarity not peculiar to Negroes. This is the shadow over her. To a race naturally sunny comes the twilight of self-doubt and a sense of personal inferiority. It cannot be denied that these are potent and detri-mental influences, though not generally recognized because they are in the realm of the mental and spiritual. More apparent are the economic handicaps which follow her recent entrance into industry. It is conceded that she has special difficulties because of the poor working conditions and low wages of her men. It is not surprising that only the determined women forge ahead to results other than mere survival. The few who do prove their mettle stimulate one to a closer study of how this achieve-ment is won in Harlem.

Better to visualize the Negro woman at her job, our vision of a host of individuals must once more resolve itself into groups on the basis of activity. First, comes a very small leisure group—the wives and daughters of men who are in business, in the professions and in a few well-paid personal service occupations. Second, a most active and progressive group, the women in business and the professions. Third, the many women in the trades and industry. Fourth, a group weighty in numbers struggling on in domestic service, with an even less fortunate fringe of casual workers, fluctuating with the economic temper of the times.

The first is a pleasing group to see. It is picked for outward beauty by Negro men with much the same feeling as other Americans of the same economic class. Keeping their women free to preside over the family, these women are affected by the problems of every wife and mother, but touched only faintly by their race's hardships. They do share acutely in the prevailing difficulty of finding competent household help. Negro wives find Negro maids unwilling generally to work in their own neigh-borhoods, for various reasons. They do not wish to work where there is a possibility of acquaintances coming into contact with them while they serve and they still harbor the misconception that Negroes of any station are unable to pay as much as persons of the other race. It is in these homes of comparative ease that we find the polite activities of social exclusiveness. The luxuries of well-appointed homes, modest motors, tennis, golf and country clubs, trips to Europe and California, make for social standing. The problem confronting the refined Negro family is to know others of the same achievement. The search for kindred spirits gradually grows less difficult; in the past it led to the custom of visiting all the large cities in order to know similar groups of cultured Negro people.

A spirit of stress and struggle characterizes the second two groups. These women of business, profession and trade are the hub of the wheel of progress. Their burden is two-fold. Many are wives and mothers whose husbands are insufficiently paid, or who have succumbed to social mal-adjustment and have abandoned their families. An appalling number are widows. They face the great problem of leaving home each day and at the same time trying to rear children in their spare time—this too in neighborhoods where rents are large, standards of dress and recreation high and costly, and social danger on the increase.

The great commercial life of New York City is only slightly touched by the Negro woman of our second group. Negro business men offer most of their work, but their number is limited. Outside of this field, custom is once more against her and competition is keen for all. However, Negro girls are training and some are holding exceptional jobs. One of the professors in a New York college has had a young colored woman as secretary for the past three years. Another holds the head clerical position in an organization where reliable handling of detail and a sense of business ethics are essential. For four years she has steadily advanced. Quietly these women prove their worth, so that when vacancy exists and there is a call, it is difficult to find even one competent colored secretary who is not employed. As a result of opportunity in clerical work in the educational system of New York City a number have qualified for such positions, one being appointed within the year to the office work of a high school. In other departments the civil service in New York City is no longer free from discrimination. The casual personal interview, that tenacious and retrogressive practice introduced in the Federal administration during the World War has spread and often nullifies the Negro woman's success in written tests. The successful woman just cited above was three times "turned down" as undesirable on the basis of the personal interview. In the great mercantile houses, the many young Negro girls who might be well suited to salesmanship are barred from all but the menial positions. Even so, one Negro woman, beginning as a uniformed maid, has pulled herself up to the position of "head of stock."

Again, the telephone and insurance companies which receive considerable patronage from Negroes deny them proportionate employment. Fortunately, this is an era of changing customs. There is hope that a less selfish racial attitude will prevail. It is a heartening fact that there is an increasing number of Americans who will lend a hand in the game fight of the worthy.

In the less crowded professional vocations, the outlook is more cheerful. In these fields, the Negro woman is dependent largely upon herself and her own race for work. In the legal, dental, medical and nursing professions, successful women practitioners have usually worked their way through college and are "managing" on the small fees that can be received from an underpaid public. Social conditions in America are hardest upon the Negro because he is lowest in the economic scale. This gives rise to demand for trained college women in the profession of social work. It has met with a response from young college women, anxious to devote their education and lives to the needs of the submerged classes. In New York City, some fifty-odd women are engaged in social work, other than nursing. In the latter profession there are over two hundred and fifty. Much of the social work has been pioneer[ing] in nature: the pay has been small with little possibility of advancement. For even in work among Negroes, the better paying positions are reserved for whites. The Negro college woman is doing her bit in this field at a sacrifice, along such lines as these: in the correctional departments of the city, as probation officers, investigators, and police women; as Big Sisters attached to the Children's Court; as field workers and visitors and for relief organizations and missions; as secretaries for travelers-aid and mission societies; as visiting teachers and vocational guides for the schools of the city; and, in the many branches of public health nursing, in schools, organizations devoted to preventive and educational medicine, in hospitals and in private nursing.

In New York City, nearly three hundred Negro women share the good conditions in the teaching profession. They measure up to the high pedagogical requirements of the city and state law and are, increasingly, leaders in the community. Here too the Negro woman finds evidence of the white workers' fear of competition. The need for teachers is still so strong that little friction exists. When it does seem to be imminent, it is smothered away, as it recently was at a meeting of school principals. From the floor, a discussion began with: "What are we going to do about this problem of the increasing number of Negro teachers coming into our schools?" It ended promptly through the suggestion of another principal:

"Send all you get and don't want over to my school. I have two now and I'll match their work to any two of your best whom you name." One might go on to such interesting and more unusual professions as journalism, chiropody, bacteriology, pharmacy, etc., and find that, though the number in any one may be small, the Negro woman is creditably represented in practically every one. According to individual ability she is meeting with success.

Closing the door on the home anxieties, the woman engaged in trades and in industry faces equally serious difficulty in competition in the open working field. Custom is against her in all but a few trade and industrial occupations. She has, however, been established long in the dressmaking trade among the helpers and finishers, and more recently among the drapers and fitters in some of the best establishments. Several Negro women are themselves proprietors of shops in the country's greatest fashion district. Each of them has, against great odds, convinced skeptical employers of her business value: and, at the same time, has educated fellow workers of other races, doing much to show the oneness of interest of all workers. In millinery, power sewing machine operating on cloth, straw and leather, there are few Negro women. The laissez-faire attitude of practically all trade unions makes the Negro woman an unwilling menace to the cause of labor.

In trade cookery, the Negro woman's talent and past experience is recognized. Her problem here is to find employers who will let her work her way to managerial positions, in tea rooms, candy shops and institutions. One such employer became convinced that the managing cook, a young colored graduate of Pratt Institute, would continue to build up a business that had been failing. She offered her a partnership. As in the cases of a number of such women her barrier was lack of capital. No matter how highly trained, now how much speed and business acumen has been acquired, the Negro's credit is held in doubt. An exception in this matter of capital will serve to prove the rule. Thirty years ago, a young Negro girl began learning all branches of the fur trade. She is now in business for herself, employing three women of her race and one Jewish man. She has made fur experts of still another half-dozen colored girls. Such instances as these justify the prediction that the foot hold gained in the trade world will, year by year, become more secure.

Because of the limited fields for workers in this group many of the unsuccessful drift into the fourth social grade: the domestic and casual workers. These drifters increase the difficulties of the Negro woman suited to housework. New standards of household management are forming and the problem of the Negro woman is to meet these new business-like ideals. The constant influx of workers unfamiliar with household conditions in New York keeps the situation one of turmoil. The Negro woman, moreover, is revolting against essential domestic service. It is a last stand in her fight to maintain a semblance of family life. For that reason, principally, the number of day or casual workers is on the increase. Happiness is almost impossible under the strain of these conditions. Health and morale suffer, but how else can her children, loose all afternoon, be gathered together at night-fall? Through her drudgery, the women of other groups find leisure time for progress. This is one of her contributions to America.

It is apparent from what has been said, that even in New York City, Negro women are of a race which is free neither economically, socially, or spiritually. Like women in general, but more particularly like those of other oppressed minorities, the Negro woman has been forced to submit to over-powering conditions. Pressure has been exerted upon her, both from without and within her group. Her emotional and sex life is a reflex of her economic station. The women of the working class will react, emotionally and sexually, similarly to the working-class women of other races. The Negro woman does not maintain any moral standard which may be assigned chiefly to qualities of race, any more than a white woman does. Yet she has been singled out and advertised as having lower sex standards. Superficial critics who have had contact only with the lower grades of Negro women, claim that they are more immoral than other groups of women. This I deny. This is the sort of criticism which predicates of one race, to its detriment, that which is common to all races. Sex irregularities are not a matter of race, but of socio-economic conditions. Research shows that most of the African tribes from which the Negro sprang have strict codes for sex relations. There is no proof of inherent weakness in the ethnic group.

Gradually overcoming the habitual limits imposed upon her by slave masters, she increasingly seeks legal sanction for the consummation and dissolution of sex contracts. Contrary to popular belief, illegitimacy among Negroes is cause for shame and grief. When economic, social and biological forces combined bring about unwed motherhood, the reaction is much the same as in families of other racial groups. Generally the married aunt, or even the mother, claims that the illegitimate child is her own. The foundling asylum is seldom sought. Schooled in this kind of suffering in the days of slavery, Negro women often temper scorn with sympathy for weakness. Stigma does fall upon the unmarried mother, but perhaps in this matter the Negroes' attitude is nearer the modern enlightened ideal for the social treatment of the unfortunate. May this not be considered another contribution to America?

With all these forces at work, true sex equality has not been approximated. The ration of opportunity in the sex, social, economic and political spheres is about that which exists between white men and women. In the large, I would say that the Negro woman is the cultural equal of her man because she is generally kept in school longer. Negro boys, like white boys, are usually put to work to subsidize the family income. The growing economic independence of Negro women is causing her to rebel against the domineering family attitude of the cruder working-class Negro man. The masses of Negro men are engaged in menial occupations throughout the working day. Their baffled and oppressed desires to determine their economic life are manifested in over-bearing domination at home. Working mothers are unable to instill different ideals in their sons. Conditions change slowly. Nevertheless, education and opportunity are modifying the spirit of the younger Negro men. Trained in modern schools of thought, they begin to show a wholesome attitude of fellowship and freedom for their women. The challenge to young Negro womanhood is to see clearly this trend and grasp the proffered comradeship with sincerity. In this matter of sex equality, Negro women have contributed few outstanding militants. Their feminist efforts are directed chiefly toward the realization of the equality of the races, the sex struggle assuming a subordinate place.

Obsessed with difficulties that might well compel individualism, the Negro woman has engaged in a considerable amount of organized action to meet group needs. She has evolved a federation of her clubs, embracing between eight and ten thousand women, throughout the state of New York. Its chief function is to crystallize programs, prevent duplication of effort, and to sustain a member organization whose cause might other-

wise fail. It is now firmly established, and is about to strive for conspicuous goals. In New York City, one association makes child welfare its name
and special concern. Others, like the Utility Club, Utopia Neighborhood,
Debutante's League, Sempre Fidelis, etc., raise money for old folks' homes,
a shelter for delinquent girls and fresh air camps for children. The Colored
Branch of the Y.W.C.A. and the women's organizations in the many
churches, as well as in the beneficial lodges and associations, care for the
needs of their members.

On the other hand, the educational welfare of the coming generation,
has become the chief concern of the national sororities of Negro college
women. The first to be organized in the country, Alpha Kappa Alpha, has
a systematized and continuous program of educational and vocational
guidance for students of the high schools and colleges. The work of
Lambda Chapter, which covers New York City and its suburbs, is outstanding. Its recent campaign gathered together nearly one hundred and fifty
such students at a meeting to gain inspiration from the life-stories of
successful Negro women in eight fields of endeavor. From the trained
nurse, who began in the same schools as they, these girls drank in the
tale of her rise to the executive position in the Harlem Health Information
Bureau. A commercial artist showed how real talent had overcome the
color line. The graduate physician was a living example of the modern
opportunities in the newer fields of medicine open to women. The vocations as outlets for the creative instinct became attractive under the
persuasion of the musician, the dressmaker and the decorator. Similarly,
Alpha Beta Chapter of the national Delta Sigma Theta Sorority recently
devoted a week to work along similar lines. In such ways as these are
progressive and privileged groups of Negro women expressing their
community and race consciousness.

We find the Negro woman, figuratively, struck in the face daily by
contempt from the world about her. Within her soul, she knows little of
peace and happiness. Through it all, she is courageously standing erect,
developing within herself the moral strength to rise above and conquer
false attitudes. She is maintaining her natural beauty and charm and
improving her mind and opportunity. She is measuring up to the needs
and demands of her family, community and race, and radiating from
Harlem a hope that is cherished by her sisters in less propitious circumstances throughout the land. The wind of the race's destiny stirs more
briskly because of her striving.

ZORA NEALE HURSTON

Story in Harlem Slang:
Jelly's Tale

Wait till I light up my coal-pot and I'll tell you about this Zigaboo called
Jelly. Well, all right now. He was a sealskin brown and papa-tree-top tall.
Skinny in the hips and solid built for speed. He was born with this
rough-dried hair, but when he laid on the grease and pressed it down
overnight with his stocking-cap, it looked just like that righteous mass,
and had so many waves you got seasick from looking. Solid, man, solid!

His mama named him Marvel, but after a month on Lenox Avenue, he
changed all that to Jelly. How come? Well, he put it in the street that when
it came to filling that long-felt need, sugar-curing the ladies' feelings, he
was in a class by himself and nobody knew his name, so he had to tell
'em. "It must be jelly, 'cause jam don't shake." Therefore, his name was
Jelly. That was what was on his sign. The stuff was there and it was mellow.
Whenever he was challenged by a hard-head or a frail eel on the right of
his title he would eyeball the idol-breaker with a slice of ice and put on
his ugly-laugh, made up of scorn and pity, and say: "Youse just dumb to
the face, baby. If you don't know what you talking 'bout, you better ask
Granny Grunt. I wouldn't mislead you, baby. I don't need to—not with
the help I got." Then he would give the pimp's sign and percolate on
down the Avenue. You can't go behind a fact like that.

So this day he was airing out on the Avenue. It had to be late afternoon,
or he would not have been out of bed. All you did by rolling out early
was to stir your stomach up. That made you hunt for more dishes to dirty.

Source: American Mercury 55 (July 1942): The "Glossary of Harlem Slang" appended to
the story has been edited from the original version.

The longer you slept, the less you had to eat. But you can't collar nods all day. No matter how long you stay in bed, and how quiet you keep, sooner or later that big gut is going to reach over and grab that little one and start to gnaw. That's confidential right from the Bible. You got to get out on the beat and collar yourself a hot.

So Jelly got into his zoot suit with the reet pleats and got out to skivver around and do himself some good. At 132nd Street, he spied one of his colleagues on the opposite side walk, standing in front of a café. Jelly figured that if he bull-skated just right, he might confidence Sweet Back out of a thousand on a plate. Maybe a shot of scrap-iron or a reefer. Therefore, Jelly took a quick backward look at his shoe soles to see how his leather was holding out. The way he figured it after the peep was that he had plenty to get across and maybe do a little more cruising besides. So he stanched out into the street and made the crossing.

"Hi there, Sweet Back!" he exploded cheerfully. "Gimme some skin!"

"Lay de skin on me, pal!" Sweet Back grabbed Jelly's outstretched hand and shook hard. "Ain't seen you since the last time, Jelly. What's cookin'?"

"Oh, just like de bear—I ain't nowhere. Like de bear's brother, I ain't no further. Like de bear's daughter—ain't got a quarter."

Right away, he wished he had not been so honest. Sweet Back gave him a top-superior, cut-eye look. Looked at Jelly just like a showman looks at an ape. Just as far above Jelly as fried chicken is over branch water.

"Cold in hand, hunh?" He talked down to Jelly. "A red hot pimp like you *say* you is, ain't got no business in the barrel. Last night when I left you, you was beating up your gums and broadcasting about how hot you was. Just as hot as July-jam, you told me. What you doing cold in hand?"

"Aw, man, can't you take a joke? I was just beating up my gums when I said I was broke. How can I be broke when I got de best woman in Harlem? If I ask for a dime, she'll give me a ten dollar bill; ask her for a drink of likker, and she'll buy me a whiskey still. If I'm lying, I'm flying!"

"Gar, don't hang out dat dirty washing in my back yard! Didn't I see you last night with dat beat chick, scoffing a hot dog? Dat chick you had was beat to de heels. Boy, you ain't no good for what you live."

"If you ain't lying now, you flying. You ain't got de first thin. You ain't got nickel one."

Jelly threw back the long skirt of his coat and rammed his hand down into his pants pocket. "Put your money where your mouth is!" he challenged, as he mock-struggled to haul out a huge roll. "Back your crap with your money. I bet you five dollars!"

Sweet Back made the same gesture of hauling out nonexistent money. "I been raised in the church. I don't bet, but I'll doubt you. Five rocks!"

"I thought so!" Jelly crowed, and hurriedly pulled his empty hand out of his pocket. "I knowed you'd back up when I drawed my roll on you."

"You ain't drawed no roll on me, Jelly. You ain't drawed nothing but your pocket. You better stop dat boogerbooing. Next time I'm liable to make you do it." There was a splinter of regret in his voice. If Jelly really had had some money, he might have staked him, Sweet Back, to a hot. Good Southern cornbread with a piano on a platter. Oh, well! The right broad would, or might, come along.

"Who boogerbooing?" Jelly snorted. "Jig, I don't have to. Talking about me with a beat chick scoffing hot dog! You must of not seen me, 'cause last night I was riding 'round in a Yellow Cab, with a yellow gal, drinking yellow likker and spending yellow money. Tell 'em 'bout me, tell 'em!"

"Git out of my face, Jelly! Dat broad I seen you with wasn't no pe-ola. She was one of them coal-scuttle blondes with hair just as close to her head as ninety-nine is to a hundred. She look-ted like she had seventy-five pounds of clear bosom, guts in her feet, and she look-ted like six months in front and nine months behind. Buy you a whiskey still! Dat broad couldn't make the down payment on a pair of sox."

"Sweet Back, you fixing to talk out of place." Jelly stiffened.

"If you trying to jump salty, Jelly, that's your mammy."

"Don't play in de family, Sweet Back. I don't play de dozens. I done told you."

"Who play in de dozens? You trying to get your hips up on your shoulders 'cause I said you was with a beat broad. One of the lam blacks."

"Who? Me? Long as you been knowing me, Sweet Back, you ain't never seen me with nothing but pe-olas. I can get any frail eel I wants to. How come I'm up here in New York? You don't know, do you? Since youse dumb to the fact, I reckon I'll have to make you hep. I had to leave from down south 'cause Miss Anne used to worry me so bad to go with me. Who, me? Man, I don't deal in no coal. Know what I tell 'em? If they's white they's right! If they's yellow, they's mellow. If they's brown, they can stick around. But if they come black, they better git way back! Tell 'em 'bout me!"

"Aw, man, you trying to show your grandma how to milk ducks. Best you can do is to confidence some kitchen-mechanic out of a dime or two. Me, I knocks de pad with them cackbroads up on Sugar Hill, and fills 'em full of melody. Man, I'm quick death and easy judgement. Youse just a home-boy, Jelly. Don't try to follow me."

"Me follow *you!* man, I come on like the Gang Busters, and go off like The March of Time! If dat ain't so, God is gone to Jersey City and you know He wouldn't be messing 'round a place like that. Know what my woman done? We hauled off and went to church last Sunday, and when they passed 'round the plate for the *penny* collection, I throwed in a dollar. De man looked at me real hard for dat. Dat made my woman mad, so she called him back and throwed in a twenty dollar bill! Told him to take dat and go! Dat's what he got for looking at me 'cause I throwed in a dollar."

"Jelly, de wind may blow and de door may slam; dat what you shooting ain't worth a damn!"

Jelly slammed his hand in his bosom as if to draw a gun. Sweet Back did the same.

"If you wants to fight, Sweet Back, the favor is in me."

"I was deep-thinking then, Jelly. It's a good thing I ain't short-tempered. Tain't nothing to you, nohow. You ain't hit me yet."

Both burst into a laugh and changed from fighting to lounging poses.

"Don't get too yaller on me, Jelly. You liable to get hurt some day."

"You over-sports your hand you ownself. Too blamed astorperious. I just don't pay you no mind. Lay de skin on me!"

They broke their handshake hurriedly, because both of them looked up the Avenue and saw the same thing. It was a girl and they both remembered that it was Wednesday afternoon. All of the domestics off for the afternoon with their pay in their pockets. Some of them bound to be hungry for love. That meant a dinner, a shot of scrap-iron, maybe room rent and a reefer or two. Both went into the pose and put on the look.

"Big stars falling!" Jelly said out loud when she was in hearing distance. "It must be just before day!"

"Yeah, man!" Sweet Back agreed. "Must be a recess in Heaven—pretty angel like that out on the ground."

The girl drew abreast of them, reeling and rocking her hips.

"I'd walk clear to Diddy-Wah-Diddy to get a chance to speak to a pretty li'l ground-angel like that," Jelly said.

"Aw, man, you ain't willing to go very far. Me, I'd go slap to Ginny-Gall, where they eat cow-rump, skin and all."

The girl smiled, so Jelly set his hat and took the plunge.

"Baby," he crooned, "what's on de rail for de lizard?"

The girl halted and braced her hips with her hands. "A Zigaboo down in Georgy, where I came from, asked a woman that one time and the judge told him ninety days."

"Georgy!" Sweet Back pretended to be elated. "Where 'bouts in Georgy is you from? Delaware?"

"Delaware?" Jelly snorted. "My people! My people! Free schools and dumb jigs! Man, how you going to put Delaware in Georgy? You ought to know dat's in Maryland."

"Oh, don't try to make out youse no northerner, you! Youse from right down in 'Bam your ownsclf!" The girl turned on Jelly.

"Yeah, I'm *from* there and I aims to stay from there."

"One of them Russians, eh?" The girl retorted. "Rushed up here to get away from a job of work."

That kind of talk was not leading towards the dinner table.

"But baby!" Jelly gasped. "Dat shape you got on you! I bet the Coca Cola Company is paying you good money for the patent!"

The girl smiled with pleasure at this, so Sweet Back jumped in.

"I know youse somebody swell to know. Youse real people. You grins like a regular fellow." He gave her his most killing look and let it simmer in. "These dickty jigs round here tries to smile. S'pose you and me go inside the café here and grab a hot?"

"You got any money?" The girl asked, and stiffed like a ramrod. "Nobody ain't pimping on me. You dig me?"

"Aw, now, baby!"

"I seen you two mullet-heads before. I was uptown when Joe Brown had you all in the go-long last night. Dat cop sure hates a pimp! All he needs to see is the pimps' salute and he'll out with his night-stick and ship your head to the red. Beat your head just as flat as a dime!" She went off into a great blow of laughter.

"Oh, let's us don't talk about the law. Let's talk about us," Sweet Back persisted. "You going inside with me to holler 'let one come flopping! One come grunting! Snatch one from de rear!'"

"Naw indeed!" the girl laughed harshly. "You skillets is trying to promote a meal on me. But it'll never happen, brother. You barking up the wrong tree. I wouldn't give you air if you was stopped up in a jug. I'm not putting out a thing. I'm just like the cemetery—I'm not putting out, I'm taking in! Dig?"

"I'll tell you like the farmer told the potato—plant you now and dig you later."

The girl made a movement to switch on off. Sweet Back had not dirtied a plate since the day before. He made a weak but desperate gesture.

"Trying to snatch my pocketbook, eh?" She blazed. Instead of running, she grabbed hold of Sweet Back's draping coat-tail and made a slashing gesture. "How much split you want back here? If you feets don't hurry up and take you 'way from here, you'll *ride* away. I'll spread my lungs all over New York and call the law. Go ahead. Bedbug! Touch me! And I'll holler like a pretty white woman!"

The boys were ready to flee, but she turned suddenly and rocked on off with her earrings snapping and her heels popping.

"My people! My people!" Sweet Back sighed.

"I know you feel chewed," Jelly said, in an effort to make it appear that he had had no part in the fiasco.

"Oh, let her go," Sweet Back said magnanimously. "When I see people without the periodical principles they's supposed to have, I just don't fool with 'em. What I want to steal her old pocketbook with all the money I got? I could buy a beat chick like her and give her away. I got money's mammy and Grandma change. One of my women, and not the best one I got neither, is buying me ten shag suits at one time."

He glanced sidewise at Jelly to see if he was convincing. But Jelly's thoughts were far away. He was remembering those full, hot meals he had left back in Alabama to seek wealth and splendor in Harlem without working. He had even forgotten to look cocky and rich.

Glossary of Harlem Slang

Astorperious—haughty, biggity
Bam, and down in Bam—down South
Beating up your gums—talking to no purpose
Bull-skating—Bragging
Coal scuttle blonde—black woman
Cold—exceeding, well, etc., as in "He was cold on that trumpet!"
Collar a nod—sleep
Collar a hot—eat a meal

Cruising—parading down the Avenue. Variations: *oozing, percolating,* and *freewheeling.* The latter implies more briskness.

Diddy-wah-diddy—a far place, a measure of distance. (2) another suburb of Hell, built since way before Hell wasn't no bigger than Baltimore. The folks in Hell go there for a big time.

Frail eel—pretty girl

Free schools—a shortened expression of deprecation derived from "free schools and dumb Negroes," sometimes embellished with "free schools, pretty yellow teachers and dumb Negroes."

Ginny Gall—a suburb of Hell, a long way off

Granny Grunt—a mythical character to whom most questions may be referred

Jelly—sex

Jig—Negro, a corrupted shortening of zigaboo

July jam—something very hot

Kitchen mechanic—a domestic

Mammy—a term of insult. Never used in any other way by Negroes.

Miss Anne—a white woman

My people! My people!—Sad and satiric expression in the Negro language: sad when a Negro comments on the backwardness of some members of his race; at other times, used for satiric or comic effect

Pe-ola—a very white Negro girl

Piano—spare ribs (white rib-bones suggest piano keys)

Pimp—In Harlemese, *pimp* has a different meaning than its ordinary definition as a procurer for immoral purposes. The Harlem pimp is a man whose amatory talents are for sale to any woman who will support him, either with a free meal or on a common law basis; in this sense, he is actually a male prostitute.

Playing the dozens—low-rating the ancestors of your opponent

Reefer—marijuana cigaret, also a *drag*

Righteous mass or *grass*—good hair

Russian—a Southern Negro up north. "Rushed up here," hence a Russian.

Scrap iron—cheap liquor

Solid—perfect

Stanch, or *stanch out*—to begin, commence, step out

Sugar Hill—northwest corner of Harlem, near Washington Heights, site of newest apartment houses, mostly occupied by professional people.

(The expression has been distorted in the South to mean a Negro red light district.)

The bear—confession of poverty

Thousand on a plate—beans

What's on the rail for the lizard?—suggestion for moral turpitude

Zigaboo—a Negro

Zoot suit with the reet pleat—Harlem style suit, padded shoulders, 43 inch trousers at the knee with cuff so small it needs a zipper to get into, high waistline, fancy lapels, bushels of buttons, etc.

GWENDOLYN B. BENNETT

From "The Ebony Flute"

December 1926

New Yorkers have a way of thinking that after Gotham nothing is. I suppose because the city itself is the very door of the Nation, even the name of the place becomes the synonym for the center of the world . . . evident then that we should come to think of New York as the great book-publishing, book-consuming ogre. Needless to say, gossip of this and that thing concerning books and their makers would tend by centripetal force alone to precipitate into what groups in the great Metropolis are doing and thinking . . . it is ever so refreshing to be brought sharply up against the fact that here and there in other less motley cities are little knots of people writing, and reading . . . perhaps hoping and certainly thinking. So when came a letter from Emma Lue Sayers of Los Angeles, California—

"This is just a line from the Far West to tell you how much we enjoy 'The Ebony Flute.' And when I say 'we' I mean a Saturday non-writer's organization, which Charles S. Johnson was good enough to help us form, when he was in Los Angeles a few weeks ago. We call ourselves the Ink Slingers."

. . . And from Boston comes the word that Thomas L. G. Oxley's *Souls of Colored Poets* soon to be on the market including three hundred poems selected from eighty-five poets . . . Mr. Oxley is the Director of the Colored Poetic League of the World . . . also one of the Quill Club

Source: "The Ebony Flute" was Bennett's column in *Opportunity.* The selections here are from *Opportunity* 4 (December 1926): 391; 6 (February 1928): 55–56; and 6 (April 1928): 122.

devotees . . . which reminds me that Dorothy West and Helene Johnson are spending the winter in New York . . . I believe they are studying Journalism at Columbia University.

This month's geographical check-up presents an interesting aspect . . . Jean Toomer off for Chicago for Gurdjieff work; Abram Harris in New York . . . he is now assisting Dr. Melville Herskovits; Frank Horne gone down Georgia-way to dip his intellectual finger into the publicity of the Hunt Industrial School . . . Langston Hughes divides his time very nicely between Lincoln University and New York City; Countee Cullen permanently located in the "City of Skyscrapers" is now the Assistant Editor of *Opportunity* . . . which by the way, gives me splendid opportunity to extend to him the right hand of fellowship and welcome upon the advent of his column, "Thoughts from a Dark Tower." Both of these two last named young men deserted their several ways around the twenty-first of November to go to Columbus, Ohio, where they read at a meeting similar to the one held in New York called *The New Negro Speaks*. [. . .]

With the passing of "Deep River" and "Black Boy" we have the arrival of the Negro concert season . . . Roland Hayes again holds American audiences motionless and breathless with music silver sweet; again Paul Robeson's immense voice shall boom forth to the delight of his listeners . . . Rosamond Johnson and Taylor Gordon are again at team-work on the spirituals; from the warm suns of Southern France comes Lillian Evanti who after a tour of the United States will return to Europe, there to begin a continental tour in December. So music will go close on the slinking heels of mimicry and drama. Louis Gruenberg, a young white American composer living in Paris, has made a setting of James Weldon Johnson's poem "The Creation." This was performed for the first time at a concert of the League of Composers given at the Town Hall on November twenty-seventh. The conductor was Koussevitzky, who conducts the Boston Symphony Orchestra.

With surprising surety American Negroes who go to the European capitals as entertainers in the fashionable night clubs and cafes become endeared to the French pleasure-seeker. "The Chocolate Kiddies," "La Revue Negre," Josephine Baker, and Florence Mills . . . each caught and held the admiration of first Paris and later other cities on the continent. At the opening of "Les Nuits du Pardo," the most chic cabaret Paris has yet seen, Nora Holt Ray entertained in inimitable way . . . she accompanies herself at the piano and her voice has a touching appeal in it . . . she was immediately engaged to sing in Monte Carlo . . . and now has come the offer to be starred by the Champs Elysee management . . . this theater is accepted as one of the best Music Halls in Europe . . . the French are in happy consternation over the miracle of "La Blonde Negresse" . . . strange, we live here side by side by many members of the black race whose skins are fairer than some of their white neighbors. [. . .]

February 1928

[. . .] The second issue of *Black Opals*, the voice of the New Negro group in Philadelphia, was out for Christmas. . . . Folks interested in the literary output of the young Negro writers will be glad that this word-child continues to thrive. I had the rare pleasure of being asked to be their guest editor for this issue and so I watched it grow from the first stages of manuscript infancy to its present happy debut before its readers . . . I understand that the Black Opals have been asked to visit the Quill Club in Boston in the spring of the year. Such interchange is good . . . and mayhap some year both of these groups with one or two of New York's younger, newer Negroes will get together and go to visit the Ink Slingers in California. Which gives us an opportunity to make a pretty bow of thanks for the lovely card with "Greetings from California" which Julian Bagley sent to "The Ebony Flute" for its Christmas.

April 1928

We hasten to welcome another group of creative workers to the fold . . . Book and Bench, comprising four writers of verse, five prose writers, two composers of music and one painter, has been organized in Topeka, Kansas, since last fall. They plan publishing a year-book, entitled "Urge," early in May. . . . The number grows . . . The Quill Club in Boston, The Ink-Slingers in California and Black Opals in Philadelphia . . . to say nothing of the many groups in New York. [. . .]

My Race

Ah, my race,
Hungry race,
Throbbing and young—
Ah, my race,
Wonder race,
Sobbing with song—
Ah, my race,
Laughing race,
Careless in mirth—
Ah, my veiled unformed race,
Fumbling in birth.

Source: Opportunity 3 (July 1925): 196.

Metamorphism

Is this the sea?
This calm emotionless bosom,
Serene as the heart of a converted Magdalene—
Or this?
This lisping, lulling murmur of soft waters
Kissing a white beached shore with tremulous lips;

326

Blue rivulets of sky gurgling deliciously
O'er pale smooth stones—
This too?
This sudden birth of unrestrained splendor,
Tugging with turbulent force at Neptune's leash;
This passionate abandon,
This strange tempestuous soliloquy of Nature,
All these—the sea?

Source: Opportunity 4 (March 1926): 81.

Bottled

Upstairs on the third floor
Of the 135th Street library
In Harlem, I saw a little
Bottle of sand, brown sand
Just like the kids make pies
Out of down at the beach.
But the label said: "This
Sand was taken from the Sahara desert."
Imagine that! The Sahara desert!
Some bozo's been all the way to Africa to get some sand.

And yesterday on Seventh Avenue
I saw a darky dressed fit to kill
In yellow gloves and swallow-tail coat
And swirling a cane. And everyone
Was laughing at him. Me too,
At first, till I saw his face
When he stopped to hear a
Organ grinder grind out some jazz.
Boy! You should a seen that darky's face!
It just shone. Gee, he was happy!

And he began to dance. No
Charleston or Black Bottom for him.
No sir. He danced just as dignified
And slow. No, not slow either.
Dignified and *proud!* You couldn't
Call it slow, not with all the
Cuttin' up he did. You would a died to see him.

The crowd kept yellin' but he didn't hear,
Just kept on dancin' and twirlin' that cane
and yellin' out loud every once in a while.
I know the crowd thought he was coo-coo.
But say, I was where I could see his face,
And somehow, I could see him dancin' in a jungle,
A real honest-to-cripe jungle, and he wouldn't have on them
Trick clothes—those yaller shoes and yaller gloves
And swallow-tail coat. He wouldn't have on nothing.
And he wouldn't be carrying no cane.
He'd be carrying a spear with a sharp fine point
Like the bayonets we had 'over there.'*
And the end of it would be dipped in some kind of
Hoo-doo poison. And he'd be dancin' black and naked and
    gleaming.
And he'd have rings in his ears and on his nose
And bracelets and necklaces of elephants' teeth.
Gee, I bet he'd be beautiful then all right.
No one would laugh at him then, I bet.
Say! That man that took that sand from the Sahara desert
And put it in a little bottle on a shelf in the library,
That's what they done to this shine, ain't it? Bottled him.
Trick shoes, trick coat, trick cane, trick everything—all glass—
But inside—
Gee, that poor shine!

Source: Countee Cullen, ed., *Caroling Dusk: An Anthology of Verse by Negro Poets* (New York: Harper, 1927), p. 221.
    *Refers to World War I.

SHIRLEY GRAHAM

Tar

It was the moan of the saxophones that did it—deep down, lingering and warm. Mary turned abruptly and began pushing her way towards the door. "Easy there, honey. What's the hurry?" "Lady, can I . . .?" "Hands off, Alabama, I seen her first!" "Some chick!" "Tall, slim mamma!"

No good. She had to get out. As usual, on Saturday night, the place was crowded, but nobody seemed to mind. Deep red leather, black lacquer, smooth floors, laughter, smoke and good music. No mistake about the music! The U.S.O. down the street offered no competition to the Savoy. Week ends there were always plenty of men in uniform. Plenty of men—not in uniform. Why should there be so many? Why weren't they in the army with—Tom?

Down on the street Mary drew a deep breath that hurt. Lenox Avenue was rakish without being tawdry. The air was good, touched lightly with the pungent odor of barbecue, and there were sounds of loud and easy friendliness. But without a glance either way, Mary turned off the avenue into 140th Street, gradually leaving lights and haunting saxophones behind.

This was the way they usually went home—she and Tom—clinging to each other, shadowed by the trees. Then the throb of the saxophones was part of all the breathless night. No—it was pain.

Crazy idea—going to the Savoy without Tom. She had thought to run into some lonely soldier from down home. They were all over Harlem—gawky, slow-speaking dark boys from Mississippi, Alabama and Georgia—

Source: Date and place of publication unknown.

anxious and defiant, crude and proud. They turned to Mary like cornflowers to sunshine. Mary was one of them. She wasn't long come from Georgia herself.

That's why she could never get over the wonder of Tom. He was so sure of himself. He knew so well what he was going to do—had everything figured out. Nothing was going to stop him. And she had fitted into all his plans. "You're the missing link," Tom had grinned. "Right out of heaven into my arms! Oh, Baby!" Imagine calling Georgia heaven! Tom, who had made heaven for her. Smart Tom, who went downtown to school all day and worked nights. (All except that one night a week when he took her dancing at the Savoy.) Georgia and heaven, Tom and music and the bridges he told her he was learning to build, the shining clean home they were going to have—all mixed up like molasses—sweet!

Then the dirty Japs dropped bombs on Pearl Harbor!

Lord, Tom was mad! "Just like that. Right out of the sky on Sunday morning. Few more months and I'd be finished—set to build all the roads and canals and bridges in the world. But the army needs engineers *right now!*"

Just before Christmas he had come in all excited. The entire class was going to be commissioned—wouldn't have to wait till June. All the fellows were going into the army right away! He was going to be an officer! And Mary didn't say a mumbling word.

But there seemed to be some delay, and Tom fussed and fumed. Then for several evenings he was very quiet. Mary's heart ached. She recognized the look. She'd seen it on the face of a child who had been slapped *hard*. She even remembered it in the eyes of a kitten, which had been kicked. You see, Tom had been so sure! One night he was downright glum until unexpectedly he said, Aw hell, he was going to the army anyway. Wouldn't take long—he'd soon get to officers training camp. They'd see, he had muttered darkly. He'd build bridges yet!

Now he was gone.

The odor of burnt hair assailed Mary's nostrils when she let herself into the walk-up apartment. Cleo was home—had converted the tiny kitchen into a beauty salon. Bits of hair still clung to the sink. With smoking iron she was transforming the thick, spongy mass of her head into a carefully designed and glistening coiffeur.

Cleo was not, however, happy. Her Saturday evening had been a total loss. Washing and pressing her own hair was a chore to which she had been forced only through dire necessity. For Cleo sang in the Abyssinian Baptist Church choir. Attendance at morning service was obligatory. Nor dare she fall below the high standards set by Brother Powell. She sang second alto and intended "to shine for Jesus"—literally. Now, her voice was aggrieved.

"Two hours—two hours I wait at Maybelle's for this shampoo and curl. Then—what you think happens?"

"What?" asked Mary, knowing it must have been terrific.

"In walks that great big balook of a sailor of hers, and she goes wild! Not nary another head tonight—said I didn't have no appointment—walks right out leavin' two customers. Would you believe it? After two hours!"

"Well . . ." began Mary, doubtfully, "if he was here only one evening I guess . . ."

"This dam [*sic*] war is ruinin' the country—just ruinin' it." Cleo's voice was bitter.

Mary paused long enough to cluck sympathetically, then sidled into the living room and threw up the window.

"Say," called Cleo, "Mrs. Van Dyke phoned. Wants you to come in Monday."

Mary didn't answer, and Cleo appeared in the doorway, hot iron poised.

"You hear what I said. Mrs. Van Dyke . . ."

"I heard you."

Mary had thrown herself down on the couch and was fumbling with the radio. She added without spirit[,] "Fat old thing!" Cleo eyed her suspiciously.

"Where you been?" A direct question.

"I stopped by the Savoy."

Mary didn't look up. She didn't need to. Tom might just as well be standing there on the rug. Through the pregnant silence the radio began to sputter.

Cleo hadn't liked Tom. She considered him "uppity." And Cleo felt responsible for Mary. There was some sort of vague relation between the two families. It was Cleo who had suggested that Mary come north. Mary, she said, had a future.

For Mary sewed. Ever since she was a little girl she had been putting pieces together in striking and unusual patterns. And her tiny stitches were perfect. Now, what she could do with a length of cloth was something. She had a feeling for colors, too. The white folks in Maxwell were crazy about her. They all said Aunt Ross' gal was a well-mannered little thing.

"But," Cleo had urged, "why stay in such a dump workin' your fingers to the bone for fifty cents a day when you can come to New York and in a little while have your own shop on Seventh Avenue. Look at Madame Walker!"

Mary couldn't very well look at Madame Walker—but she got the point. So did Aunt Ross, for that matter. There wasn't anybody else to consult. So that's how Mary came to be in Harlem sharing an apartment on West 136th Street with the veteran New Yorker, Cleo. And she was doing very well. Cleo had mentioned Mary's abilities to her boss. All her friends were delighted to find such an "unspoiled" seamstress.

Cleo cooked. She was a good cook, but she had no illusions about *her* future. She refused to live in—got what she could out of her nights as she went along, and accepted her fate. But Mary was different. Mary had talent!

And a girl with talent didn't have to get gaw-gaw over the first fast talker who came along. For all his big talk about bridges, the only work that "engineering student" did was odd job man around the Taft Hotel—nights.

Mary had protested. "But Tom's putting in all his time studying. He's going to . . ."

"Bridges!" Cleo had snorted. "Don't make sense for a colored man—no future!"

No, she had not approved. And him going to the army hadn't helped matters. Mary had wanted Tom to marry her before he left. He had explained to a tight-lipped Cleo, "Engineers get in mighty tough spots. Wouldn't be fair to her. When I come back . . . if everything's okay . . . I mean—if I'm all here—you know . . . then we'll . . ." He had turned away from Mary's hungry eyes.

That was six months ago. And look at her now! Limp as a rag—no ambition—not interested in good customers—Mrs. Van Dyke, for instance . . . and her living on Central Park, South!

"This night," Cleo told herself, "I gotta speak my mind!"

But Mary didn't hear a word of it.

For Mary was listening to the radio. Thousands of other people heard that same announcement. They didn't know the man was talking straight to Aunt Ross' Mary—was telling her what she could do—how she could join up with Tom and help get this war over—quickly.

No, she didn't hear a word Cleo said. After she had written down an address she leaned far out the window and watched the blinking lights of a mail carrier high over head. The throbbing of its engines was music. She thought again of the saxophones, but now it was sweet. For she was feeling the beauty of a plane—all silver in the sunlight. How wonderful it would be to make even the tiniest part of a great plane!

It had never occurred to any of Mary's satisfied customers that she knew a war was going on. She said nothing the next afternoon until the job was finished. Then stooping over to pick up a long basting thread from the thick rug she announced in her husky, honey-thick drawl, "I won't be comin' next week."

The lady was annoyed. These girls, so utterly unreliable.

"I signed up for a defense course."

When the lady remonstrated, Mary was a bit apologetic. (Cleo had told her bluntly she was a fool.)

"I figured I ought do somethin' to help. I . . . I . . . don't think this," she lifted the silken folds, "is awful important. You reckon 'tis?"

Because Mary was skilled in cutting cloth on a bias and fitting uneven edges, she did exceptionally well in the sheet metal class. She took the advanced course. Then showed her certificate proudly.

"Now what?" Cleo asked.

"I'm going into the plane factory."

But Mary didn't get into that factory. Nothing daunted, she tried another and another and another. She stood in long lines day after day— clutching her certificate. At night she had crazy dreams about flying and dropping through clouds—of her color fading out when she blew a saxophone. One night she dreamed she was green! After a while her face did get sort of ashy. She couldn't just keep on living on Cleo. She put her certificate away.

The customers welcomed her back gladly. "After all," they said. One lady mentioned the circumstances to her husband. "She's so *disappointed*. I thought there was a shortage of help." The husband thought so too and immediately gave Mary a letter to a friend of his. Mary took the letter gratefully. It asserted that she was "honest" and "a personable negress."

Mary got a job—filling vats with tar. She stood and poured tar all night—going on at twelve and returning in the morning spattered with tar.

"For heaven's sake," Cleo asked, "must you push in the tar with your nose?"

"Seems like I'm awful clumsy. It's so thick. I'll move up soon. Everybody has to start with tar."

The folks for whom Cleo cooked went south for the winter. Because Cleo's flesh yearned for the golden warmth of Texas sunshine, she went with them.

It was cold and damp the April morning Cleo returned. She shivered in the dark hallway as she fitted her key. Inside, water was running. From the bath room door she surveyed Mary vigorously scrubbing tar from her forearms. Mary was thinner.

"Look," Cleo demanded, "you still pourin' tar? Ain't you been promoted?"

Mary shook her head.

"The old-so-and-so . . ." Cleo began, but Mary stopped her.

"Just had a long letter from Tom." Her eyes were shining.

Cleo was trying to stuff her coat into the tiny hall closet. Perhaps the state of that closet rendered her voice acid as she commented,

"Naturally Tom's awful busy right now buildin' bridges over the Rhine."

"Tom didn't say nothin' 'bout bridges this time." Then why was Mary's voice singing? "That morning they'd been unloading a ship when . . ."

"Unloading ships—Tom?" Cleo experienced a grim satisfaction. Engineers and their "tough places," indeed!

". . . planes come. Tom said they was rushin' the stuff to cover when machine fire riddled the wharf."

"Was he . . .?"

"Not Tom! The tank he was rollin' was shot to pieces—and tar gushed all over him—knocking him down—burying him in tar. He said nothing could have hit him. And when they was gone and he managed to get up . . . Lord, he mustta been a sight!" And Mary laughed.

Cleo found herself moistening her lips as she finally managed to close the closet door. Then she turned back to Mary, who asked,

"Can't you just see Tom in that tar?"

She shook the soap from her eyes, leaned over and carefully removed a bit of tar from behind her left ear.

Cleo grinned. "You don't do so bad yourself."

"I'll get it all off. I'm stopping by the Savoy tonight. Count Basie's there."

Mary studied a spot just above her right elbow and frowned slightly.

"I reckon it'll take a heap of tar for all the new roads we gotta make. Yeh—a lotta tar!"

ANN PETRY

Solo on the Drums

The orchestra had a week's engagement at the Randlert Theater at Broadway and Forty-second Street. His name was picked out in lights on the marquee. The name of the orchestra and then his name underneath by itself.

There had been a time when he would have been excited by it. And stopped to let his mind and his eyes linger over it lovingly. Kid Jones. The name—his name—up there in lights that danced and winked in the brassy sunlight. And at night his name glittered up there on the marquee as though it had been sprinkled with diamonds. The people who pushed their way through the crowded street looked up at it and recognized it and smiled.

He used to eat it up. But not today. Not after what happened this morning. He just looked at the sign with his name on it. There it was. Then he noticed that the sun had come out, and he shrugged, and went on inside the theater to put on one of the cream-colored suits and get his music together.

After he finished changing his clothes, he glanced in the long mirror in his dressing room. He hadn't changed any. Same face. No fatter and no thinner. No gray hair. Nothing. He frowned. Because he felt that the things that were eating him up inside ought to show. But they didn't.

When it was time to go out on the stage, he took his place behind the drums, not talking, just sitting there. The orchestra started playing

Source: John Clark, ed. *American Negro Short Stories* (New York: Hill and Wang, 1966), pp. 165–169.

softly. He made a mental note of the fact that the boys were working together as smoothly as though each one had been oiled.

The long gray curtains parted. One moment they were closed. And then they were open. Silently. Almost like magic. The high-powered spots flooded the stage with light. He could see specks of dust gliding down the wide beams of light. Under the bands of light the great space out front was all shadow. Faces slowly emerged out of it—disembodied heads and shoulders that slanted up and back, almost to the roof.

He hit the drums lightly. Regularly. A soft, barely discernible rhythm. A background. A repeated emphasis for the horns and the piano and the violin. The man with the trumpet stood up, and the first notes came out sweet and clear and high.

Kid Jones kept up the drum accompaniment. Slow. Careful. Soft. And he felt his left eyebrow lift itself and start to twitch as the man played the trumpet. It happened whenever he heard the trumpet. The notes crept up, higher, higher, higher. So high that his stomach sucked in against itself. Then a little lower and stronger. A sound sustained. The rhythm of it beating against his ears until he was filled with it and sighing with it.

He wanted to cover his ears with his hands because he kept hearing a voice that whispered the same thing over and over again. The voice was trapped somewhere under the roof—caught and held there by the trumpet. "I'm leaving I'm leaving I'm leaving."

The sound took him straight back to the rain, the rain that had come with the morning. He could see the beginning of the day—raw and cold. He was at home. But he was warm because he was close to her, holding her in his arms. The rain and the wind cried softly outside the window.

And now—well, he felt as though he were floating up and up and up on that long blue note of the trumpet. He half closed his eyes and rode up on it. It had stopped being music. It was that whispering voice, making him shiver. Hating it and not being able to do anything about it. "I'm leaving it's the guy who plays the piano I'm in love with him and I'm leaving now today." Rain in the streets. Heat gone. Food gone. Everything gone because a woman's gone. It's everything you ever wanted, he thought. It's—everything you never got. Everything you ever had, everything you ever lost. It's all there in the trumpet—pain and hate and trouble and peace and quiet and love.

The last note stayed up in the ceiling. Hanging on and on. The man with the trumpet had stopped playing but Kid Jones could still hear that last note. In his ears. In his mind. The spotlight shifted and landed on Kid Jones—the man behind the drums. The long beam of white light struck the top of his head and turned him into a pattern of light and shadow. Because of the cream-colored suit and shirt, his body seemed to be encased in light. But there was a shadow over his face, so that his features blended and disappeared. His hairline receding so far back that he looked like a man with a face that never ended. A man with a high, long face and dark, dark skin.

He caressed the drums with the brushes in his hands. They responded with a whisper of sound. The rhythm came over but it had to be listened for. It stayed that way for a long time. Low, insidious, repeated. Then he made the big bass drum growl and pick up the same rhythm.

The Marquis of Brund, pianist with the band, turned to the piano. The drums and the piano talked the same rhythm. The piano high. A little more insistent than the drums. The Marquis was turned sideway on the piano bench. His left foot tapped out the rhythm. His cream-colored suit sharply outlined the bulkiness of his body against the dark gleam of the piano. The drummer and the pianist were silhouetted in two separate brilliant shafts of light. The drums slowly dominated the piano.

The rhythm changed. It was faster. Kid Jones looked out over the crowded theater as he hit the drums. He began to feel as though he were the drums and the drums were he.

The theater throbbed with the excitement of the drums. A man sitting near the front shivered, and his head jerked to the rhythm. A sailor put his arm around the girl sitting beside him, took his hand and held her face still, and pressed his mouth close over hers. Close. Close. Close. Until their faces seemed to melt together. Her hat fell off and neither of them moved. His hand dug deep into her shoulder and still they didn't move.

A kid sneaked in through a side door and slid into an aisle seat. His mouth was wide open, and he clutched his cap with both hands, tight and hard against his chest as he listened. The drummer forgot he was in the theater. There was only he and the drums and they were far away. Long gone. He was holding Lulu, Helen, Susie, Mamie close in his arms. And all of them—all those girls blended into that one girl who was his wife. The one who said, "I'm leaving." She had said it over and over again, this morning, while rain dripped down the window panes.

When he hit the drums again it was with the thought that he was fighting with the piano player. He was choking the Marquis of Brund. He was putting a knife in clean between his ribs. He was slitting his throat with a long straight blade. Take my woman. Take your life.

The drums leaped with the fury that was in him. The men in the band turned their heads toward him—a faint astonishment showed in their faces.

He ignored them. The drums took him away from them, took him back, and back, and back, in time and space. He built up an illusion. He was sending out the news. Grandma died. The foreigner in the litter has an old disease and will not recover. The man from across the big water is sleeping with the chief's daughter. Kill. Kill. Kill. The war goes well with the men with the bad smell and the loud laugh. It goes badly with the chiefs with the round heads and the peacock's walk.

It is cool in the deep track in the forest. Cool and quiet. The trees talk softly. They speak of the dance tonight. The young girl from across the lake will be there. Her waist is slender and her thighs are rounded. Then the words he wanted to forget were all around Kid Jones again. "I'm leaving I'm leaving I'm leaving."

He couldn't help himself. He stopped hitting the drums and stared at the Marquis of Brund—a long, malevolent look, filled with hate.

There was a restless, uneasy movement in the theater. He remembered where he was. He started playing again. The horn played a phrase. Soft and short. The drums answered. The horn said the same thing all over again. The drums repeated it. The next time it was more intricate. The phrase was turned around, it went back and forth and up and down. And the drums said it over, exactly the same.

He knew a moment of panic. This was where he had to solo again and he wasn't sure he could do it. He touched the drums lightly. They quivered and answered him.

And then it was almost as though the drums were talking about his own life. The woman in Chicago who hated him. The girl with the round, soft body who had been his wife and who had walked out on him, this morning, in the rain. The old woman who was his mother, the same woman who lived in Chicago, and who hated him because he looked like his father, his father who had seduced her and left her, years ago.

He forgot the theater, forgot everything but the drums. He was welded to the drums, sucked inside them. All of him. His pulse beat. His heart beat. He had become part of the drums. They had become part of him.

He made the big bass rumble and reverberate. He went a little mad on the big bass. Again and again he filled the theater with a sound like thunder. The sound seemed to come not from the drums but from deep inside himself; it was a sound that was being wrenched out of him—a violent, raging, roaring sound. As it issued from him he thought, this is the story of my love, this is the story of my hate, this is all there is left of me. And the sound echoed and re-echoed far up under the roof of the theater. When he finally stopped playing, he was trembling; his body was wet with sweat. He was surprised to see that the drums were sitting there in front of him. He hadn't become part of them. He was still himself. Kid Jones. Master of the drums. Greatest drummer in the world. Selling himself a little piece at a time. Every afternoon. Twice every evening. Only this time he had topped all his other performances. This time, playing like this after what had happened in the morning, he had sold all of himself—not just a little piece.

Someone kicked his foot. "Bow, you ape. Whassamatter with you?"

He bowed from the waist, and the spotlight slid away from him, down his pants legs. The light landed on the Marquis of Brund, the piano player. The Marquis' skin glistened like a piece of black seaweed. Then the light was back on Kid Jones.

He felt hot and he thought, I stink of sweat. The talcum he had dabbed on his face after he shaved felt like a constricting layer of cement. A thin layer but definitely cement. No air could get through to his skin. He reached for his handkerchief and felt the powder and the sweat mix as he mopped his face.

Then he bowed again. And again. Like a—like one of those things you pull the string and it jerks, goes through the motion of dancing. Pull it again and it kicks. Yeah, he thought, you were hot all right. The jitterbugs ate you up and you haven't any place to go. Since this morning you haven't had any place to go. "I'm leaving it's the guy who plays the piano I'm in love with the Marquis of Brund he plays such sweet piano I'm leaving leaving leaving—"

He stared at the Marquis of Brund for a long moment.

Then he stood up and bowed again. And again.

HAZEL V. CAMPBELL

Part of the Pack:
Another View of Night Life
in Harlem

Steve Hall opened the door of his basement home on East 133rd Street. The wooden door cried under its labor. Sucking his teeth the tall black man bent low and stepped into the dark hallway. The door closed behind him with a bang and a lone picture hanging on the wall fell to the floor amid a bed of broken glass. The four room apartment was odorous with the smell of stale cabbage and boiled beef. Steve moistened his lips with one sweep of his tongue and walked back to the cheerless kitchen.

His wife, a tall mulatto woman, was standing over the gas stove stirring a black pot from which steam was issuing.

"You have been stealing again, Lu?" he asked wearily and knitting his brow.

"Sure. Where the hell you think I got this food from?" she answered indifferently, still stirring the pot.

"Aw, we've got to quit this sort of living, Lu. We've got to quit. I'm tired of eating stolen goods," and Steve's voice was strained.

"Ain't satisfied? You don't have to eat it if you don't want to," she snapped turning toward him. "That will be all the more for tomorrow," she finished.

Steve shifted on his feet. His lean face took on a hurt expression. His pride had been injured and his heart beat heavily against the ragged shirt covering his bony breast. It hurt him that he could not live up to the word of his promise to her mother, to provide for her in the proper way. Here she was now stooping to the degrading thing of stealing food so that neither he nor she might starve.

Source: Opportunity 13 (August 1935): 234–237, 251.

"Lu, I wish you wouldn't talk so. Why don't you talk human anymore? You do nothing but snap and snarl like a dog from morn till night." Steve spoke dully.

"Well, what if I do snap and snarl? Maybe I am a dog. I'm part of the pack ain't I, fighting for food and life against the odds," she yelled throwing a wooden spoon on the table.

"Lu, please," he coaxed raising his hands as if to quiet her.

"Please, hell! I'm tired of please this and please that. I'm tired of this damn Yankee town anyway. I'm tired of all these black Yankees who do nothing but put on airs with their bellies thinking their throat is cut. Yes, look at me! You and these damn gin soaked, gun-toting, razor pulling niggers," and Lu's voice rose to a scream.

"Hush, Lu. Please!" he begged raising his hand.

"Hush! Hush! Hush! That's why we are where we are today cos it is always hush! hush! hush! I tell you I am tired. I am tired of everything from that damn jazz that beats in your ears like the tom-tom of the jungles to the false prophets who walk up and down these streets crying to have faith. Faith in what? I'm going back to the Delta. I'm going back where the music is dull and heavy and kind like the people. At least down there you won't have fight with dogs and cats over a piece of meat," she finished, her voice growing calmer under memories of pleasant days in the Delta basin.

"It will be only for a while, dear," he tried to say cheerfully but his voice cracked. "Only for awhile. Then there will be plenty of work. In the meantime, dear, why can't you put your pride aside and go to the Home Relief: We just can't go on like this. I hate to see you sneaking like a cat stealing food. You don't have to steal it," and Steve sat on the three legged stool and hung his head.

"Charity? Did you say charity?" she scoffed.

"Why yes. Yes, of course," he said looking up.

"Charity! Who the hell wants charity?" she screamed. "A pinch here and a pinch there, and a look of contempt written on everyone's face. Hell, who you think is going to stand for that? I'm going back to the Delta, if I have to crawl on my hands and knees to get there."

"All right! All right!" he said, waving her aside.

"I'd rather steal than take the white man's so-called charity," she snapped.

Steve rubbed his head with both of his hands and shifted in his seat.

Someone was knocking at the door. Neither of them moved.

Again the knock. Lu looked at Steve and Steve looked at Lu.

A look of dismay passed between them. For a while only the tick tock of the clock was heard.

"Well, what you looking at me for?" Lu spoke firmly, pressing her lips together. "You can answer the door, can't you?"

"Yes," Steve spoke slowly, rising from the seat.

"Well, answer it," she said waving her hand. "You ain't afraid are you? We've been dodging the landlord and bill collectors for the last few months, so I guess we can face the music now. If it is the landlord bring him back here so I can give him a piece of my mind. The damn cheat."

Steve walked away from her. His knees felt weak and useless under him. Suppose it was the landlord and he had come to put them out. Where would they go? No rent paid for three months and no outlook of paying any rent for the next twelve months. He could go to charity, but Lu would rather walk the streets and die from hunger. Queer woman. He opened the door slowly. A short bow-legged man was standing before him. Steve gave a deep sigh as recognized his best friend, Bradford Hardy.

"Hi, Steve," Brad spoke warmly.

"Come in, Brad. Glad to see you," and the tone of Steve's voice was sincere.

Brad followed Steve to the rear where Lu was still standing.

She had not moved from her position. Her eyes opened in relief as Brad came toward her.

"Hi, Brad," she greeted.

"Hi, Lu."

"Did you have any luck with that job you went after?" she asked.

"Hell, no," he answered shortly, and taking off his cap he placed it on the table.

"Gee, that's tough. I'm sorry, old boy," Steve said, patting Brad on the back. "I wonder just what is wrong?"

"What's wrong, man?" sneered Brad looking at Steve in contempt. "If you must know what is wrong, it is this," and Brad pointed a dirty brown finger to his face. "Just this," and taking the three legged stool he sat down.

"You ought to know just what is wrong, Steve, without asking. There is one thing I hate more than poverty and that is a dumb nigger," Lu spoke sharply. "You've been black long enough to know what is wrong. Even a baby could have guessed it was his skin," and Lu looked at him with an air of superiority.

"Not that I couldn't do the work. I've had good training in that field," and a deep frown formed in Brad's forehead. "They always have to give lame excuses," and his voice shook. Steve caught a hint of anger in the tone of his friend's voice. Steve knew that anger. It was revengeful anger, rising slowly and then suddenly bursting like an eruption. Brad was talking again. "Damn, how long you think this is going to keep up?" and Brad banged his fist on the table. "I'm damn tired of it. Damn it to hell I wish I were white—hell, no! I wish I were a yaller, bless my soul if I wouldn't cross the line and fool all these old 'ofays.'* I'd get the best kind of job, and marry the best kind of them, and fool the hell out of them. Then I'd laugh."

"Would you?" Lu looked at him in amusement. "There would be that something in your blood that would hold you back, and, Brad, you wouldn't be able to get away from it."

"Aw, hell!" and Brad put his head on the cupboard.

"Hungry, Brad?" Steve asked.

"Well, I'd be lying if I said no, and I don't want to lie," he laughed, looking up.

"We thought you were the landlord at first and we had made up our minds to make the best of his verdict," Lu said, going to the dish closet, taking three cracked dishes from the closet and setting them on the table. Brad moved his hat.

"If he came in my place I'm afraid I'd go in for cannibalism," Brad spoke watching the dishes on the table.

"You'd go in for what?" laughed Lu.

"Cannibalism."

"Well, as long as you have friends like Steve and I, you won't have to sink that far. Count on us sharing our meager blessings with you," Lu answered. Taking the pot from the stove she placed it on the table, and began filling each plate, giving each a generous portion. When each dish had been filled she sat down.

"I wish to hell I knew how to pray," Brad spoke mournfully.

"Well, why don't you learn?" Lu asked looking up from her plate and brushing a long strand of hair from her face.

"Then I'd pray to God from the bottom of my heart, and I'd pray and pray and pray." And Brad jumped from his seat, upsetting the food onto

*White people.

the floor, "and I'd pray to God to give me food, and a job, and to send a Moses to lead us to the land of milk and honey."

Neither Steve nor Lu answered him.

"And I'd pray to God. God I'd pray to you," went on Brad. "God! oh God! I'd pray for justice, for fairness, and God, I'd pray. Oh hell, I wish I knew how to pray," and Brad tore at his ragged shirt and beat his bony hand against his hairy breast. "God! My God!" he said sitting down. His foot slipped on the food on the floor. He looked down. His eyes became bewildered.

"Food! God, I'm stepping on food. Good food!" and Brad bent down and picked up the dirty cabbage and beef, scraping the food in his plate. Picking out the splinters and dirt he could see he began eating again. Lu watched him thoughtfully, as she counted how many times his Adam's apple worked up and down, and his lean face twitched nervously.

When the meal was finished, Brad washed the dishes, Steve dried them, and Lu put the rest of the food on the window sill.

Above them a woman's voice arose clear and strong.

> It's me, it's me, it's me, oh Lord
> Standing in the need of prayer,
> It's me, it's me, it's me oh, Lord
> Standing in the need of prayer.

Lu put her hands on her hips, and looked at the ceiling. "Listen to that damn black woman. She's been singing that song all day." Steve and Brad wiped their hands on a soiled handkerchief. They too listened.,

> Tain't mah brother
> Tain't mah sister
> But me, oh Lord,
> Standing in the need of prayer.

"She's right. She's standing in the need of prayer. We all are," Steve said putting the dishes on the wash tub.

"Well, she doesn't have to shout it from the house tops. What if she is standing in the need of prayer, who the hell she thinks is going to pray for her. Sure, we all are standing in the need of prayer, but are we letting everyone know it? No, we're keeping our hard luck to ourselves, and if we can take it on the chin, and not cry to the whole world, that cat up there can too," Lu answered Steve.

"We can't keep it to ourselves much longer," put in Brad.

"Damn right. Damn right." Lu agreed.

Somehow or other they were glad when Brad left them. The afternoon wore on. The woman above them still sang the same song. Out on the river the boats cried and whistled. In the streets the children's laughter and cries shrilled above the noise of the traffic. The clock in the kitchen struck four. Steve paced the rooms in disgust, his wife watching him. Finally he threw himself on the bed and fell asleep. Lu walked to the window and watched with amusement two kittens tumbling over each other. Both of them fighting for supremacy, she thought. For a long time she sat by the window. Steve was snoring, and from her boredom she made a song from his snoring.

Then evening came, and the children in the streets had gone, and the woman above her had ceased her singing. Lu fell across the couch in the living room and slept. It was after nine when she was awakened by someone, knocking at the door. She sat up. She heard Steve rise from the bed and his heavy footsteps falling on the wooden planked floor. By the tone of the voices she knew Brad had come back. She went to the front door.

"Back again?" she smiled in the dark.

Brad was out of breath.

"What's the matter?" Steve asked, pulling his friend into the living room.

"Race riot," he gasped.

"What?" Lu yelled, opening her eyes wide.

"Fighting down on 125th Street," he went on.

"How's it start?" Lu asked excitedly.

Brad shrugged his shoulders. "I ran up here as fast as I could in case you all want to join the battle. You can hear the noise clean up here."

Lu grabbed Steve's arm.

Brad tugged at the other arm of Steve's. "Come, old man."

Steve knitted his brow, and looked at Brad. "Where?"

"To the battlefield. I guess the mob is up near 130th Street by now. They were coming uptown when I came up."

Steve freed his arms, from Lu and Brad. "Who wants to fight?"

"Man alive, they are busting windows like hot cakes. The niggers have gone plumb mad. Nigger heaven* has turned into a living hell now. Come on Steve, we can at least get some of the food from those stores where windows are broken. I'm not in for the fighting either, but if I can get some food and clothes without paying for it, I'm just raring," Brad finished.

"Go on, Steve. You and Brad go out and get food. Keep away from the mob as much as you can, and if you have to fight—damn it, fight. Fighting will make a man of you, Steve. A fighting man, who can snap and snarl along with the pack," Lu said, pushing him from her.

Steve did not answer. He played with the one remaining button on his shirt.

"Go on, Steve. Tain't no sin no more nohow to steal. The Lord knows we've got to eat and if we can't get it honestly, we'll have to take matters into our own hands," Lu was coaxing.

"I'm not going," he said sharply, turning on her. "What's the sense of fighting when you don't have to."

Lu threw back her head. "Well, damn it if you don't go, I will," she shot at him. "I'll show you, you big coward. I'll be the fighter in this family. I'll get food, and I'll get clothes, and bring it back. You can stay here and nurse your petty feelings. I'll go out and fight and I'll fight like a man, and that is more than you can boast of, you—you, you coward," and switching past him she took a soiled coat from a nail behind the door, and together she and Brad left him standing in the dark hallway.

Steve did not know what to think. Outside he could hear the murmur of angry voices, mingling with tramping feet. He scratched his head. He wondered why he had let Lu go. She had no business out there. It was his place to fight the battles, if there was any need to fight. Lu could be a regular spit-fire when she wanted to be. She was a woman, and nice women never fought, and Lu was an nice woman. She was his wife. She was good, even though she did drink, and smoke and steal and cuss. He'd go and bring her back. Clenching his fist he slipped his overcoat on and left the house. The street was crowded. Lu and Brad were nowhere to be seen. He knew they were swallowed up in the crowd. He half walked and half ran toward Lenox Avenue, his eyes fastened on the mob ahead of him, hoping to catch a glimpse of Brad's broad shoulders or the tall figure of Lu. A woman had taken his arm. He looked down and saw that she was

Nigger Heaven was the title of a controversial novel by Carl Van Vechten (1926).

a gray-headed woman. She grinned up at him. "We have to go with our men to war," she laughed coarsely. He could smell stale gin coming from her mouth. He did not answer her. She was talking again: "Have you ever fought battles for your rights?"

"Naw," he answered with a shrug of his shoulders.

A crash of glass sounded behind hem. A cry went up. "Kill him!"

"Take that 'ofay' and string him up a pole. Kill that cracker," and the cry ran down the street. Steve was glad the man escaped. The street was more crowded now with men and women battling with uniformed men on foot and horse. Knives flashed, guns barked, clubs swung, fists flew and blood flowed freely in a tumult of misunderstanding and revenge.

All around was broken glass and more glass being broken rang in his ears. He found himself in middle of the battle and he began to fight blindly, and wondered what he was fighting and why he was fighting. Something heavy struck him on the head. Blood gushed down his face . . . running into his eyes . . . blinding him. He felt darkness engulfing him . . . his head began to spin—he could feel his legs slipping from underneath him. Wiping the blood madly from his face, he groped his way clear of the mob, and slumped in a doorway. He could hear tramping feet and angry voices far in the distance.

Lu and Brad came home long after two that morning. Their eyes were blackened and their clothes were torn to shreds, but they were happy. In their arms was food. Lots and lots of food, and more if they wanted to go through the same ordeal they just came through. No one stopped them on their way home. In fact no one would dare, for Lu and Brad would fight.

Lu stumbled in the doorway.

"Steve," she cried.

Silence.

"Steve, wake up." Only the echo of her voice came back to her from the darkness.

"Hey, you lazy, good for nothing character, awaken yourself and see what your mama has brought home to her baby."

Silence.

"Hey, Brad, wake that lazy nigger up," she commanded from the kitchen.

Brad tipped into the bedroom. Turning on the light he gasped in surprise.

"He ain't here," he yelled.

"Who, Steve?"

"Ain't a sign of him."

"Thank God, he went out to fight. Come in here and get me some cold water. I want to fix this eye before he comes back."

Morning came. Brad came in late bringing with him the morning paper.

"Steve ain't come home yet," she greeted him.

Brad did not answer.

"What's the matter?" she asked suddenly.

"Steve ain't coming back any more, Lu," he said giving her the paper.

"What you mean, he ain't coming back any more?" she asked, not looking at the paper.

"He just ain't coming back," and Brad shook his head. "I took this paper from the stand," and he shook the paper so that she would take it. "Here," and Brad's voice cracked under the strain he was trying to control.

Lu looked at him, then at the paper. Tears blinded her eyes, but she blinked hard and fast. "Brad—Brad—do you mean—he—is dead. Do you mean the white people killed him? Why he can't be dead. He was here only a little while ago. Don't you remember? You do remember, Brad . . . why we left him right out there in the hallway right out there—remember he was standing there all alone—and we left him just like that."

Brad said nothing. He bit his lips, and his face had become grave.

"Brad, do something," Lu screamed all at once. "Oh God! My God!! Bring Steve back to me. White papers say you are dead, but Steve, they lie, they lie, they lie," and Lu was sobbing. Overhead a voice clear and strong was singing:

> It's me, it's me, it's me, oh Lord
> Standing in the need of prayer.

PART 8

IN THE
LOOKING GLASS

"In the Looking Glass" contains the reflections of black women writers on their lives as women and as blacks, and on their struggle to separate their self-perceptions from the images projected on them by society. Hollywood and the nascent film industry led the way in portraying black women in ways injurious to their advancement: as "mammies," cleaning women, cooks, washerwomen, prostitutes, and so on; the concept of African-American women as writers was not a part of these figurations. Unable completely to elude the world's mirror or to deny its effect on how they saw themselves, they nevertheless committed themselves to challenging those images.

Anne Spencer's poems and her life itself are models of commitment to writing as a craft of aesthetic control and to a refinement that does not exclude the possibility of fierce criticism of racial inequality. Other authors in this section contemplate the many cultural differences and the variety of experience that constitute "the black experience"—a phenomenon easily overlooked if perception ends where skin pigment begins. The protagonist in May Miller's "'Bidin' Place" registers shock at her first encounter with a culture that, though black, seems totally alien. Zora Neale Hurston's story "Black Death" deals with folk beliefs about the retribution exacted for violations of sexual honor codes. As both an anthropologist and a native southerner, Hurston is in a unique position to describe cultural practices on the fringes of Western society and beliefs.

Aloise Barbour Epperson seeks insight through her belief in a compassionate and responsive God. Through her poetry she reflects on what freedom means, arriving at an idealistic, nonmaterialistic answer. The example of an excoriated Jesus sustains her, infusing her poems with inspiration and determination. In contrast, (Lucy) Ariel Williams Holloway is by turns introspective and mocking. Her poems include social satire and meditation. Margaret Walker's poems speak in two voices: personal and collective. Like other female poets of her time, Walker shared her thoughts on various aspects of African-American existence, often hoping to strike a universal chord in the reader.

Prelude

I know how a volcano must feel
With molten lava
Smoldering in its breast.
Tonight thoughts, wild thoughts,
Are smoldering
In the very depths
Of my being.
I would hold them within me
If I could.
I would give them form
If I could.
I would make of them
Something beautiful
If I could.
But they will not be formed;
They will not be shaped.
I must pour them out thus,
Like molten lava.
Shape them into beautiful dreams
If you can.

I know how a volcano must feel.

Source: Ariel Williams Holloway, *Shape Them into Dreams* (New York: Exposition Press, 1955), p. 9.

Memory of a "Jim Crow" Car

I am riding tonight
In a "Jim Crow" car—
Old, steam-engined
"Jim Crow" car:
Cinders falling,
Odors mingling,
Noise—
Laughter—
Lunches—
Flies—
Stocking caps,
And bedroom slippers.

"Where you gwine, Daughter?"

Source: Ariel Williams Holloway, *Shape Them into Dreams* (New York: Exposition Press, 1955), p. 14.

My Temple

I stopped today for meditation
In a tiny temple—
The sanctuary
Of my own soul.
All parts of my being were there:
My sinful self,
My wilful self,

My selfish and unselfish selves,
That part of me
Which longeth overmuch,
And myriad parts
Which love,
And hate,
And wonder,
And regret.
It was the smallest chapel,
But the greatest communion
I have ever known.

Source: Ariel Williams Holloway, *Shape Them into Dreams* (New York: Exposition Press, 1955), p. 25.

To One Who Would Be Great

You wish that you were great?
Then, if giving is for asking,
Take the sorrows
To be hidden through long years,
Without complaining,
From a world that can be cruel
Save to him who overcometh.
Take the million little heartaches
That will lock arms with achievement
And rush in with smiles and handclasps,
Leaving pain instead of gladness.
Take the years of toil unnoticed;
And the hour, so swiftly coming,
When the bell that tolls your parting
Will mean curtain for another.
Taking this, you'll have as booty:

Precious memories of struggle,
One true friend whom you can count on,
Brief applause,
And briefer glory.

Source: Ariel Williams Holloway, *Shape Them into Dreams* (New York: Exposition Press, 1955), p. 37.

His Life and Mine

(To my husband)

I wonder why did Fate entwine
His life and mine?
He is so carefree;
I so weighted down
With every tiny care.
We are a mismatched pair.

'Tis thus I muse
In noonday's busy heat.

But when the evening comes with twilight gray,
And in the distance far away
I see him coming,
My heart forgets my brain's cold reasoning
And leaps to meet his beckoning smile.
I know then, Heaven did entwine
His life and mine.

Source: Ariel Williams Holloway, *Shape Them into Dreams* (New York: Exposition Press, 1955), p. 43.

Problems Facing Negro Young Women

A brown girl sits in the closely packed employment office waiting room. Every piece of her cheap clothing has been put on with care, and the perk of the little green hat is a brave defiance. But despair is in the dark eyes, a little too deeply sunk, and ever so often the set smile must be fastened again upon her lips. No job today So back to the sister-in-law's again, and taking from the children the little they all have from relief.

It is ten o'clock at night. Perhaps by hurrying the tired dark woman bending over the sink of dishes can have them all washed and the kitchen put to rights by ten-thirty. Then the trolley ride home across town. A tub of things to be washed for the children. That will be twelve-thirty. One. Then up again in time to be back on the job at seven. Three dollars and fifty cents a week!

A woman stands in the doorway of a shack. Almost up to the very door come the stripped cotton plants. Bare. That is the word for the autumn world without, and the bleak world of her thoughts. The cotton gathered, but no profit to her and hers. Children nearly naked. Almost no food, and what there is [is] part of the burden of debt. This hovel of a home. And the threats of the boss that even this will be taken from them if there is any more talk of "rights." Rights of croppers, indeed!

* * *

Source: Opportunity 14 (February 1936): 47–49.

In her smart little bungalow a busy young housewife hurries to get lunch ready before the children storm in from school. It is a good thing that her hands know their tasks so well, for all morning the riveting of the same thought has hammered in her head. What if he *did* lose his job! Mail carriers' jobs have always been ones to count on. Uncle Sam! Are Negro men to be driven from these, too? What if he *did* lose his job!

Because she always ran down the school steps the trim little teacher does so now, but she is really tired this afternoon. Nearly six, and just getting away from the building. Records must be kept, and now with unemployment, undernourished children, and private and public agencies to work with on it all, what a welter of detail, and checking and re-checking. Well, tonight is the bridge party, and she can forget about it all. But can she, and the other young women of her club, they of the good jobs and the good clothes? Is not part of the time at almost every club meeting now taken up with talking about *conditions?*

The committee meeting breaks up and the social workers hasten back to offices scattered all over the city. Some important little victories have been won today, and of them none more important than the opening up of the new work to Negro people. The young woman who has made the fight returns to her own office. She closes the door behind her and drops a weary head upon her arms. Exultation slips away and she is just a tired woman knowing that this is gain, yes, but so small, so small. For tomorrow, and all tomorrows, it must be fight, fight, fight.

There is no possibility of picturing even so sketchily as is here done the army of Negro women who march with the on-drive of life in our modern world. Sifted with a heavy hand over the whole land is the silt of the dark race. Here it piles up in great masses. There it thins out, and there again the scattering is so scant it is almost lost. But whether it be where her own kind group in thousands and tens of thousands, or where they are few among all the other peoples of our country, the Negro woman stands up under the terrific burden of child bearer, home maker, and toiler. For more than any other group of women in the country is she a toiler outside her home.

Hoeing the fields, stripping the tobacco plants, performing the endless round of household tasks in the homes of others, cleaning shop and office, waiting and serving. And for smaller numbers nursing, making clothing, tending machines, teaching, serving as social workers, working in stores and offices. At these things the Negro woman works.

There is no need to elaborate here upon the fact that the Negro woman suffers from the double discrimination of sex and race. The important thing to make clear is that as she holds her own as a worker the precarious footing of the Negro group is that much more secure; as she is pushed back, because she is so greatly the contributor to the whole group, all lose with her. The loss of work opportunities by Negro women is not compensated for by work gains on the part of Negro men.

There is a subtle deference on the part of Negro men to their women. This is not the remnants of a feudal chivalry, although as much of that as still exists anywhere operates within the westernized dark group; but it is the deference of a comradeship, and a tribute to a great courage. Too many black men owe part or all of what they are to the toil of mothers; too many men today see wives set forth with them daily to earn bread for their children; too many young, unmarried women gallantly carry on for a whole family group. The conditions of life in this country obliterated early any chattel relationship as between women and Negro men, and with women as free as men within the group, there could be the attack by both upon that enslavement coming from without. Considering the terrific oppression of the black people in this country and the little headway made in spite of it, the fact that [that] attack upon the problem of existence was shared by all of the adults of this minority is in large part the answer as to how this bit of headway has been made.

But these are days for Negro women to think again of how they keep the little hold they have on work opportunities, and through these their opportunities for participation in the life and thought of the country. Perhaps "think again" is too pretentious a term to apply to that tenuous process by which dark women have clung to life and fought for expression and expansion. For their way has been that of the vine, clinging to every jut, leafing toward the sun, struggling up and up.

Today, however, demands a more conscious process. The last few years have witnessed the dropping away of much of the tinsel of our boasted wealth, and the sharp outlines of our necessity stand clearly revealed. It is against this stark outline that the Negro woman measures herself and asks herself what must be her way in the immediate years to come.

First of all, the present day has brought a sense of union that could not have been true of the old days, when except for such community contacts as a woman had, she felt herself very much the individual woman struggling alone. But all the modern forms of communication, plus the network of organizations of various kinds, combine now to give actuality to the fact that the individual is part of the mass. This realization does not have to be any passion for mass as mass, but it is the knowledge of the hundreds and thousands who, caught in the same situations, struggle in the same fashion, and for the same ends. Nor is it again the bleak cheer of the love of misery for company. It is a plain knowledge of numbers, of the enormity of the situation, of multiple odds that must be faced.

Now from this sense of union can be born a consciousness of what strength can come of union. The Negro woman today is beginning to realize that she is a worker. The few who hold what are called the good jobs know that so slender is their security that the breath of chance, to say nothing of the winds of economic change, can topple almost any of them from this security. Moreover, in compensation there is a limit in range. A few at the very top have salary or income above what has been set as the living wage of the country, but there is a middle point where the job preferred in name or actuality has nothing to distinguish it, as far as compensation is concerned, from the less desired kinds of work.

Here, then, is a truth that gives direction to the course the Negro woman must pursue. She is a worker. She must throw her lot with workers. Nor will an increasingly large number consider this a counsel of hysteria. To labor, to look upon one's self as one who toils and who is justified in asking for adequate rewards for that toil, is not necessarily to run shrill-voiced in the face of the moving currents of life.

But it does mean learning to know something of work and rewards, of the production of goods and their consumption, of the ambitions of wealth, and the self-seeking of nations. And it means also a knowledge that goes deep enough to help one stand firm in that inevitable time when as a group, or as an individual, there must be a demand for the decencies of civilized living for all.

There is a second sense of union that is of great significance at the present time, and that is the unity between women as women, regardless of race and color. This feeling of women for women might spring from something deep in the very biological nature of women. For they who must give birth know the intimacies of pain. Or this feeling may be the result of woman's long battle for her freedom. Or again, sensitivity may be heightened today because woman sees the old terrors of war and the lusts of war threaten all she has made of order in the world.

The Negro woman knows that she can turn to white women, to some of them, for an appreciation of her problems, and that some, they may not be many, but some of them will stand by her in the hour of necessity.

There is scoffing in some quarters that some Negro and white women assert a large measure of trust in each other, for they who scoff believe that here is pretty sentiment and nothing more than that. But there is more. Women as women have more to lose by mankind's periodic indulgences in the major follies. And they know it, that is all. It is this knowledge of what is lost by separateness that may bring the working groups, regardless of race, to a solidarity in our country. Womankind has no perfect knowledge on this point as yet, but there are evidences that they sense the fundamental truth of the strength of union; and there is little evidence that to some degree they are able to act upon it.

Here, then, is a second truth to give direction to the course that Negro women must pursue. They must understand what is involved in the liberal movements among women. For all that is mere sentiment, or shallow thinking in these movements it is their right, as of any others, to prove the weakness, to expose that which is defective.

It will be no mere friendly acquiescence that will cause Negro women to join with white women in the fight to stop the driving of women back to the kitchen. The Negro woman knows that for years to come, it would seem, she must be a paid worker if her children are to have even the half chance a life that this dual toil of parents makes possible. Nor is it, again, mere friendly gesture that she joins with white women [so] that law may be made real sanctions of the state and operative. Too often have Negro women seen their husbands and sons mobbed by fiends; too often have they seen their daughters despoiled.

It is not likely that in the years of struggle that lie ahead of her the Negro woman will lose her charm of ready sympathy, of understanding born of suffering, of that joy that breaks through when oppression is lifted ever so little. For she has been through much in the years gone by. It is her sensing of the inner character of life, her patience with its varied and often vagrant forms, her belief in its ultimate possibilities for good, that shall remain to her a staff no matter what the road down which she travels. And as such gifts do not come by mere asking, so they do not flourish by mere possession. There is promise that in the days that lie ahead, as in days past, these gifts will be called upon for use, and in the using serve her well.

DOROTHY WEST

Mammy

The young Negro welfare investigator, carrying her briefcase, entered the ornate foyer of the Central Park West apartment house. She was making a collateral call. Earlier in the day she had visited an aging colored woman in a rented room in Harlem. Investigation had proved that the woman was not quite old enough for Old Age Assistance, and yet no longer young enough to be classified as employable. Nothing, therefore, stood in the way of her eligibility for relief. Here was a clear case of need. This collateral call on her last employer was merely routine.

The investigator walked toward the elevator, close on the heels of a well-dressed woman with a dog. She felt shy. Most of her collaterals were to housewives in the Bronx or supervisors of maintenance workers in office buildings. Such calls were never embarrassing. A moment ago as she neared the doorway, the doorman had regarded her intently. The service entrance was plainly to her left, and she was walking past it. He had been on the point of approaching when a tenant emerged and dispatched him for a taxi. He had stood for a moment torn between his immediate duty and his sense of outrage. Then he had gone away dolefully, blowing his whistle.

The woman with the dog reached the elevator just as the doors slid open. The dog bounded in, and the elevator boy bent and rough-housed with him. The boy's agreeable face was black, and the investigator felt a flood of relief.

The woman entered the elevator and smilingly faced front. Instantly the smile left her face, and her eyes hardened. The boy straightened, faced

Source: Opportunity 18 (October 1940): 298–302.

front, too, and gaped in surprise. Quickly he glanced at the set face of his passenger.

"Service entrance's outside," he said sullenly.

The investigator said steadily, "I am not employed here. I am here to see Mrs. Coleman on business."

"If you're here on an errand or somethin' like that," he argued doggedly, "you still got to use the service entrance."

She stared at him with open hate, despising him for humiliating her before and because of a woman of an alien race.

"I am here as a representative of the Department of Welfare. If you refuse me the use of this elevator, my office will take it up with the management."

She did not know if this was true, but the elevator boy would not know either.

"Get in then," he said rudely, and rolled his eyes at his white passenger as if to convey his regret at the discomfort he was causing her.

The doors shut and the three shot upward, without speaking to or looking at each other.

The woman with the dog, in a far corner, very pointedly held the small harmless animal on a tight leash.

The car stopped at the fourth floor, and the doors slid open. No one moved. There was a ten-second wait.

"You getting out or not?" the boy asked savagely.

There was no need to ask who he was addressing.

"Is this my floor?" asked the investigator.

His sarcasm rippled. "You want Mrs. Coleman, don't you?"

"Which is her apartment?" she asked thickly.

"Ten-A. You're holding up my passenger."

When the door closed, she leaned against it, feeling sick and trying to control her trembling. She was young and vulnerable. Her contact with Negroes was confined to frightened relief folks who did everything possible to stay in her good graces, and the members of her own set, among whom she was a favorite because of her two degrees and her civil service appointment. She had almost never run into Negroes who did not treat her with respect.

In a moment or two she walked down the hall to Ten-A. She rang, and after a little wait a handsome middle-aged woman opened the door.

"How do you do?" the woman said in a soft drawl. She smiled. "You're from the relief office, aren't you? Do come in."

"Thank you," said the investigator, smiling, too, relievedly.

"Right this way," said Mrs. Coleman, leading the way into a charming living-room. She indicated an upholstered chair. "Please sit down."

The investigator, who never sat in overstuffed chairs in the homes of her relief clients, plumped down and smiled again at Mrs. Coleman. Such a pleasant woman, such a pleasant room. It was going to be a quick and easy interview. She let her briefcase slide to the floor beside her.

Mrs. Coleman sat down in a straight chair and looked searchingly at the investigator. Then she said somewhat breathlessly, "You gave me to understand that Mammy has applied for relief."

The odious title sent a little flicker of dislike across the investigator's face. She answered stiffly, "I had just left Mrs. Mason when I telephoned you for this appointment."

Mrs. Coleman smiled disarmingly, though she colored a little.

"She has been with us ever since I can remember. I call her Mammy, and so does my daughter."

"That's a sort of nurse, isn't it?" the investigator asked coldly. "I had thought Mrs. Mason was a general maid."

"Is that what she said?"

"Why, I understood she was discharged because she was no longer physically able to perform her duties."

"She wasn't discharged."

The investigator looked dismayed. She had not anticipated complications. She felt for her briefcase.

"I'm very confused, Mrs. Coleman. Will you tell me just exactly what happened then? I had no idea Mrs. Mason was—was misstating the situation." She opened her briefcase.

Mrs. Coleman eyed her severely. "There's nothing to write down. Do you have to write down things? It makes me feel as if I were being investigated."

"I'm sorry," the investigator said quickly, snapping shut her briefcase. "If it would be distasteful—. I apologize again. Please go on."

"Well, there's little to tell. It all happened so quickly. My daughter was ill. My nerves were on edge. I may have said something that upset Mammy. One night she was here. The next morning she wasn't. I've been worried sick about her."

"Did you report her disappearance?"

"Her clothes were gone, too. It didn't seem a matter for the police. It was obvious that she had left of her own accord. Believe me, young woman, I was relieved when you telephoned me." Her voice shook a little.

"I'm glad I can assure you that Mrs. Mason appears quite well. She only said she worked for you. She didn't mention your daughter. I hope she has recovered."

"My daughter is married," Mrs. Coleman said slowly. "She had a child. It was stillborn. We have not seen Mammy since. For months she had looked forward to nursing it."

"I'm sure it was a sad loss to all of you," the investigator said gently. "And old Mrs. Mason, perhaps she felt you had no further use for her. It may have unsettled her mind. Temporarily," she added hastily. "She seems quite sane."

"Of course, she is," said Mrs. Coleman with a touch of bitterness. "She's old and contrary. She knew we would worry about her. She did it deliberately."

This was not in the investigator's province. She cleared her throat delicately.

"Would you take her back, Mrs. Coleman?"

"I want her back," cried Mrs. Coleman. "She has no one but us. She is just like one of the family."

"You're very kind," the investigator murmured. "Most people feel no responsibility for their aging servants."

"You do not know how dear a mammy is to a southerner. I nursed at Mammy's breast. I cannot remember a day in my life without her."

The investigator reached for her briefcase and rose.

"Then it is settled that she may return?"

A few hours ago there had been no doubt in her mind of old Mrs. Mason's eligibility for relief. With this surprising turn there was nothing to do but reject the case for inadequate proof of need. It was always a feather in a field worker's cap to reject a case that had been accepted for home investigation by a higher paid intake worker.

Mrs. Coleman looked at the investigator almost beseechingly.

"My child, I cannot tell you how much I will be in your debt if you can persuade Mammy to return. Can't you refuse to give her relief? She really is in need of nothing as long as I am living. Poor thing, what has she been doing for money? How has she been eating? In what sort of place is she staying?"

"She's very comfortable, really. She had three dollars when she came uptown to Harlem. She rented a room, explained her circumstances to her landlady, and is getting her meals there. I know that landlady. She has other roomers who are on relief. She trusts them until they get their relief checks. They never cheat her."

"Oh, thank God! I must give you something to give to that woman. How good Negroes are. I am so glad it was you who came. You are so sympathetic. I could not have talked so freely to a white investigator. She would not have understood."

The investigator's smile was wintry. She resented this well-meant restatement of the trusted position of the good Negro.

She said civilly, however, "I'm going back to Mrs. Mason's as soon as I leave here. I hope I can persuade her to return to you tonight."

"Thank you! Mammy was happy here, believe me. She had nothing to do but a little dusting. We are a small family, myself, my daughter, and her husband. I have a girl who comes every day to do the hard work. She preferred to sleep in, but I wanted Mammy to have the maid's room. It's a lovely room with a private bath. It's next to the kitchen, which is nice for Mammy. Old people potter about so. I've lost girl after girl who felt she was meddlesome. But I've always thought of Mammy's comfort first."

"I'm sure you have," said the investigator politely, wanting to end the interview. She made a move toward departure. "Thank you again for being so cooperative."

Mrs. Coleman rose and crossed to the doorway.

"I must get my purse. Will you wait a moment?"

Shortly she reappeared. She opened her purse.

"It's been ten days. Please give that landlady this twenty dollars. No, it isn't too much. And here is a dollar for Mammy's cab fare. Please put her in the cab yourself."

"I'll do what I can." The investigator smiled candidly. "It must be nearly four, and my working day ends at five."

"Yes, of course," Mrs. Coleman said distractedly. "And now I just want you to peep in at my daughter. Mammy will want to know how she is. She's far from well, poor lambie."

The investigator followed Mrs. Coleman down the hall. At an open door they paused. A pale young girl lay on the edge of a big tossed bed. One hand was in her tangled hair, the other clutched an empty bassinet. The wheels rolled down and back, down and back. The girl glanced briefly and without interest at her mother and the investigator, then turned her face away.

"It tears my heart," Mrs. Coleman whispered in a choked voice. "Her baby, and then Mammy. She has lost all desire to live. But she is young, and she will have other children. If she would only let me take away that bassinet! I am not the nurse that Mammy is. You can see how much Mammy is needed here."

They turned away and walked in silence to the outer door. The investigator was genuinely touched, and eager to be off on her errand of mercy.

Mrs. Coleman opened the door, and for a moment seemed at a loss as to how to say good-bye. Then she said quickly, "Thank you for coming," and shut the door.

The investigator stood in indecision at the elevator, half persuaded to walk down three flights of stairs. But this, she felt, was turning tail, and pressed the elevator button.

The door opened. The boy looked at her sheepishly. He swallowed and said ingratiatingly, "Step in, miss. Find your party all right?"

She faced front, staring stonily ahead of her, and felt herself trembling with indignation at this new insolence.

He went on whiningly, "That woman was in my car is mean as hell. I was just puttin' on to please her. She hates niggers 'cept when they're bowin' and scrapin'. She was the one had the old doorman fired. You see for yourself they got a white one now. With white folks needin' jobs, us niggers got to eat dirt to hang on."

The investigator's face was expressionless except for a barely perceptible wincing at his careless use of a hated word.

He pleaded, "You're colored like me. You ought to understand. I was only doing my job. I got to eat same as white folks, same as you."

They rode the rest of the way in a silence interrupted only by his heavy sighs. When they reached the ground floor, and the door slid open he said sorrowfully, "Good-bye, miss."

She walked down the hall and out into the street, past the glowering doorman, with her face stern and her stomach slightly sick.

The investigator rode uptown on a northbound bus. At One Hundred and Eighteenth Street she alighted and walked east. Presently she entered a well-kept apartment house. The elevator operator deferentially greeted her and whisked her upwards.

She rang the bell of number fifty-four, and visited briefly with the landlady, who was quite overcome by the unexpected payment of twenty dollars. When she could escape her profuse thanks, the investigator went to knock at Mrs. Mason's door.

"Come in," called Mrs. Mason. The investigator entered the small, square room. "Oh, it's you, dear," said Mrs. Mason, her lined brown face lighting up.

She was sitting by the window in a wide rocker. In her black, with a clean white apron tied about her waist, and a white bandanna bound around her head, she looked ageless and full of remembering.

Mrs. Mason grasped her rocker by the arms and twisted around until she faced the investigator.

She explained shyly, "I just sit here for hours lookin' out at the people. I ain' seen so many colored folks at one time since I left down home. Sit down, child, on the side of the bed. Hit's softer than that straight chair yonder."

The investigator sat down on the straight chair, not because the bedspread was not scrupulously clean, but because what she had come to say needed stiff decorum.

"I'm all right here, Mrs. Mason. I won't be long."

"I was hopin' you could set awhile. My landlady's good, but she's got this big flat. Don't give her time for much settin'."

The investigator, seeing an opening, nodded understandingly.

"Yes, it must be pretty lonely for you here after being so long an intimate part of the Coleman family."

The old woman's face darkened. "Shut back in that bedroom behin' the kitchen? This here's what I like. My own kind and color. I'm too old a dog to be learnin' new tricks."

"Your duties with Mrs. Coleman were very slight. I know you are getting on in years, but you are not too feeble for light employment. You were not entirely truthful with me. I was led to believe you did all the housework."

The old woman looked furtively at the investigator. "How come you know diff'rent now?"

"I've just left Mrs. Coleman."

Bafflement veiled the old woman's eyes. "You didn' believe what all I tol' you?"

"We always visit former employers. It's part of our job, Mrs. Mason.

Sometimes an employer will re-hire our applicants. Mrs. Coleman is good enough to want you back. Isn't that preferable to being a public charge?"

"I ain't a-goin' back," said the old woman vehemently.

The investigator was very exasperated. "Why, Mrs. Mason?" she asked gently.

"That's an ungodly woman," the old lady snapped. "And I'm God-fearin'. 'Tain't no room in one house for God and the devil. I'm too near the grave to be servin' two masters."

To the young investigator this was evasion by superstitious mutterings.

"You don't make yourself very clear, Mrs. Mason. Surely Mrs. Coleman didn't interfere with your religious convictions. You left her home the night after her daughter's child was born dead. Until then, apparently, you had no religious scruples."

The old woman looked at the investigator wearily. Then her head sank forward on her breast.

"That child warn't born dead."

The investigator said impatiently, "But surely the hospital—?"

"'T'warnt born in no hospital."

"But the doctor—?"

"Little sly man. Looked like he'd cut his own throat for a dollar."

"Was the child deformed?" the investigator asked helplessly.

"Hit was a beautiful baby," said the old woman bitterly.

"Why, no one would destroy a healthy child," the investigator cried indignantly. "Mrs. Coleman hopes her daughter will have more children." She paused, then asked anxiously, "Her daughter is really married, isn't she? I mean, the baby wasn't—illegitimate?"

"Its ma and pa were married down home. A church weddin'. They went to school together. They was all right till they come up N'th. They *she* started workin' on 'em. Old ways wasn't good enough for her."

The investigator looked at her watch. It was nearly five. This last speech had been rambling gossip. Here was an old woman clearly unoriented in her northern transplanting. Her position as mammy made her part of the family. Evidently she felt that gave her a matriarchal right to arbitrate its destinies. Her small grievances against Mrs. Coleman had magnified themselves in her mind until she could make this illogical accusation of infanticide as compensation for her homesickness for the folkways of the South. Her move to Harlem bore this out. To explain her reason for establishing a separate residence, she had told a fantastic story that could not be checked, and would not be recorded, unless the welfare office was prepared to face a libel suit.

"Mrs. Mason," said the investigator, "please listen carefully. Mrs. Coleman has told me that you are not only wanted but very much needed in her home. There you will be given food and shelter in return for small services. Please understand that I sympathize with your—imaginings, but you cannot remain here without public assistance, and I cannot recommend to my superiors that public assistance be given you."

The old woman, who had listened worriedly, now said blankly, "You mean I ain't a-gonna get it?"

"No, Mrs. Mason, I'm sorry. And now it's ten to five. I'll be glad to help you pack your things, and put you in a taxi."

The old woman looked helplessly around the room as if seeking a hiding place. Then she looked back at the investigator, her mouth trembling.

"You're my own people, child. Can' you fix up a story for them white folks at the relief, so's I could get to stay here where it's nice?"

"That would be collusion, Mrs. Mason. And that would cost me my job."

The investigator rose. She was going to pack the old woman's things herself. She was heartily sick of her contrariness, and determined to see her settled once and for all.

"Now where is your bag?" she asked with forced cheeriness. "First I'll empty these bureau drawers." She began to do so, laying things neatly on the bed. "Mrs. Coleman's daughter will be so glad to see you. She's very ill, and needs your nursing."

The old woman showed no interest. Her head had sunk forward on her breast again. She said listlessly, "Let her ma finish what she started. I won't have no time for nursin'. I'll be down on my knees rasslin' with the devil. I done tol' you the devil's done eased out God in that house."

The investigator nodded indulgently, and picked up a framed photograph that was lying face down in the drawer. She turned it over and involuntarily smiled at the smiling child in old-fashioned dress.

"This little girl," she said, "it's Mrs. Coleman, isn't it?"

The old woman did not look up. Her voice was still listless.

"That *was* my daughter."

The investigator dropped the photograph on the bed as if it were a hot coal. Blindly she went back to the bureau, gathered up the rest of the things, and dumped them over the photograph.

She was a young investigator, and it was two minutes to five. Her job was to give or withhold relief. That was all.

"Mrs. Mason," she said, "please, please understand. This is my job."

The old woman gave no sign of having heard.

MAY MILLER

'Bidin' Place

I had never intended stopping in Bladen County; in fact, I had never heard of Bladen County before that autumn night the engine of my three-year-old "lizzie" coughed, spit and died on a spot located somewhere in the corner of the county. It was, I learned, a far deserted corner opposite the end that the railroad runs through and cuts off from its less fortunate environs.

The whole county doesn't boast of one good-sized town. As for the Negro element, generally it devotes itself to prayer, memories and song, tolerating the few prescribed months of education and the onus of farm labor when it becomes inescapable. The young people move away early or remain to dry-rot in the company of their elders who familiarize them with the spots where antebellum mansions once stood, and fill their ears with tales heard from great grandparents of Sherman's march through to the sea. All rather complacently, almost ecstatically await death. Cypress Creek, as this particular section is called, had undoubtedly died before the World War; it is doubtful whether it had really lived since the Civil.

This information, to be sure, I gained later. All I knew at the moment my car refused to budge was that I was alone late at night on a dreary road which some miles back had picked up the Dismal Swamp that still dogged its path. The moonlight was pitiless in clarifying the eerie road that stretched like a band of tinsel ribbon into the distant mistiness. With full light, too, it exposed the ghostly company of tall, dark cypresses, hung with web-like moss, that rose from the swamp beside the road. A phalanx

Source: The Arts Quarterly (April–June 1937): 5–6, 31.

of patient brides waiting, they stood bedecked in their moss veils that caught the shimmering light and were turned into silver patterns beyond daylight realization. Spectres of beauty to haunt the mind and elude expression.

I had time to study them and be terrified by my own uncanny thoughts as I trudged down the road in search of friendly lamp light filling a window—anybody's window. By this time it was quite clear that the car had stopped to keep company with the skeleton brides and that it was unwholesome for me to pass the night in a cramped position in this dark, weird atmosphere.

It is not easy to efface from memory a walk such as I took that night. Sticks cracking beside me and behind me; unexplained movement more significant than the wind; and always the droning chorus of insects from the swamp. An occasional howl of a dog sometimes made me expectant; but if the dog belonged to a home, the house was too far removed from the road for me to distinguish its outline. Finally I stumbled into the assuring ray of a lamp from a mean hovel that not even the sportive moonlight could trick into semblance of a decent abode.

The man who answered my knock, a large black fellow in over-alls, was sullen and forbidding. "No," he responded shortly to my request, "ain't no place heah foh nobody nor nothin'. Ah's up 'cause mah wife's sick an' two o' the chilluns got it, too."

"Got it—got what?" I blurted out.

"Doan know. Doan 'xactly nobody know but it's sumpin' hell awful. It taken one chile o' mines las' week. Plenty folks here bouts has died."

"Can I help?" The offer was sincere. Disappointed though I was in my welcome, I was sorry for this big troubled man, for I also felt the need of human company and comfort.

"You bes' git away from heah," he shook his head positively.

"Can't tonight. My car's stalled. I was just going to ask where I can stay if you won't keep me. I haven't seen a light for a mile or more."

"Well, ah tell you," the man passed a big knotty hand over his brow. "It's right late but Ma Grady keeps huh lamp burnin' the night through so as folks kin fin' huh easy. She's a mid-wife. You'd reach huh right easy on 'count o' it's the next house a step 'er two up the road. She might could put you up wid huh Mose. There ain't nobody but huh an' Mose."

And that's how I happened to spend the night at Ma Grady's. It was a sojourn that has since taxed my credulity and intelligence, for to this day I never return to that night without questioning my own sanity and marvelling at man's ingenuity.

I found the house readily enough—only Cypress Creek's "step or two" lengthened out to what seemed to me endless distances. At last I reached the welcome light and knocked on the door. After a repeated knock and a few minutes of silence, came slow, wary footsteps and a cracked, reedy voice. I explained my predicament through a discreet crack, begging the shadow that cautiously held the door to study my honest face. However, it was a five-dollar bill waved before her that proved the open-sesame. Eager claw-like fingers closed greedily over the bill, and the door swung open.

Once inside the squalid room I breathed more freely, thankful for the friendliness of mellow lamp-light and shelter from the penetrating damp-ness that had clung to my clothes, chilled my bones and gripped my chest. I could see my hostess now. Ma Grady was a wizened gray woman—kinky hair, crackled skin and filmy eyes harmoniously blending in a washed-out neutral tone. The rusty black shawl, which might have introduced a bit of contrast, was so soiled and dusty that it, too, faded into gray inconspicu-ousness. She was quick of decision and short of answer.

"Ah needs five dollars," she muttered, "and you needs a place to 'bide. Ah ain't trustin' you none 'cause ah ain't got no cause to, but you kin stay."

She bustled about the room and returned from one of the corners with a bottle. "Drink this." She spoke in a quiet not unfriendly voice, but there was command in her tone. "There's so much sickness in these heah parts, an' you's chilled clean through; Ah sees you shakin'." She thrust the bottle into my hesitant hands, watched me drink and left the room.

I sank on a packing box and covered my eyes with my hand. I must have dozed from fatigue and the effect of the strong potion. I was shaken to a groggy consciousness by Ma Grady's bony hand.

"A bed's a bed," she muttered under her breath. I didn't know whether she was talking to me or herself, but I quite agreed. A bed was a bed, and I was sleepy. "Ah gotta put you up wid Mose," she explained. "Ah jes' can't put 'im out o' his bed yet, but you doan trouble 'im an' he ain't gonna bother you none."

With or without Mose the thought of a bed was more than welcome. I rose with alacrity and followed the woman into a damp, chilly room. "You'll call me first thing in the morning, won't you?" And I added by way of explanation, "I want to have the car fixed and get an early start. I'm due in Durham tomorrow."

"Yeah, 'bout daybreak Ah'll git you up. Jes' 'fore light." The last words were pronounced so thoughtfully, so emphatically that they had the force of a threat. The woman lingered a minute or two unnecessarily, eyeing the bed uncertainly. Reluctantly she took the lamp from a big box in the corner where she had set it and went out, leaving the room in darkness save for the moonlight that streamed in through a crude opening.

By that light I tried to discover just how much sleeping space had been left to me. My bed fellow was just a hulking straight figure under the ragged covers and fortunately lay very still with his face turned toward the wall. I remember thanking some providence that he didn't snore. I pulled off my coat and vest, loosened my collar, yanked off my shoes and climbed in. Sleep was upon me almost immediately.

True to her word, before light broke Ma Grady called me; and before the sun was well up, I was at the cross-roads store soliciting the aid of the two men about whom she had told me. They tended the gas tanks at the store and were, it seemed, the only ones for miles around who knew anything about repairing a car. In their efficient bus the trip to my own car seemed two short city blocks, impossible that the distance had seemed so endless the night before. Arriving at the recalcitrant car, the mechanics lifted the hood and went to work.

"Good the d——d thing stopped this near a shop," one called from somewhere under the car.

"Yes, and near enough for me to walk to shelter. Though, as warm as it is today, I can't realize how damp and chilly I got from sitting here a few minutes last night."

"Tain't no beatin' the fog that comes out o' that Dismal Swamp. Death chills we call it." The man under the hood explained.

"Tain't no man wid sense gonna spend a night camped heah, nohow. The swamp does things to you. Where'd you stay las night?" He laid down his wrench and coming around to the side of the car, planted one foot on the running board to have a good chat.

"I believe they called her Ma Grady," I answered briefly, anxious about the progress of the repairs.

"Oh yeah. Too bad 'bout huh trouble; ain't it?"

"I don't know. What was her trouble? She didn't say." The old woman had been kind to me in her way and I was concerned. "Why, she lost huh boy Mose yistiddy. He, huh onliest chile too; an' she that crazy 'bout 'im she'd drink the creek dry foh 'im."

"Lost her boy Mose! What do you mean?"

"He died sudden-lak yistiddy wid the sickness lak them others is dyin' wid."

"When? When did this Mose die?"

"Yistiddy 'bout sundown. Ah seen Doctor James a-coming 'way an' he tole me."

"Has she another son? Who is the other man who lives there?" I didn't recognize my own voice as it stumbled over the words.

"'Nother son? No, folks 'round heah doan even so much as 'member Mose's pappy. Doubt if'n he had one. Ain't never been no one else in the house—jes' Mose an' Ma Grady. Kinda strange she let you in. Ah ain't never heard o' nobody but them two stayin' there."

"And you say Mose died yesterday at sundown?" Surely I had not heard right.

"Yistiddy at sundown," the man repeated calmly.

"Did she raise 'nouf to bury him? None but the best was good 'nouf foh huh Mose." The voice from the ground called up.

"Late las' night ah heard the folks say as how she still needed five dollars. Ah wonders whether she got it."

A swig of strong liquor; a straight mound-like figure under the bed clothes, face to the wall; a rising before day-break, an insistent "'fore light"; five dollars, five dollars for a 'bidin' place.

"Yes, she got the five dollars," I said slowly. "I know she did."

The men went back to their work. I turned and studied the swamp. Cypress trees look so different in the daylight.

MARGARET WALKER

Since 1619

How many years since 1619 have I been singing Spirituals?
How long have I been praising God and shouting hallelujahs?
How long have I been hated and hating?
How long have I been living in hell for heaven?

When will I see my brother's face wearing another color?
When will I be ready to die in an honest fight?
When will I be conscious of the struggle—now to do or die?
When will these scales fall away from my eyes?

What will I say when days of wrath descend:
When the money-gods take all my life away;
When the death knell sounds
And peace is a flag of far-flung blood and filth?

When will I understand the cheated and the cheaters;
Their paltry pittances and cold concessions to my pride?
When will I burst from my kennel an angry mongrel,
Lean and hungry and tired of my dry bones and years?

Source: Margaret Walker, *For My People* (New Haven: Yale University Press, 1942), p. 26.

Lineage

My grandmothers were strong.
They followed plows and bent to toil.
They moved through fields sowing seed.
They touched earth and grain grew.
They were full of sturdiness and singing.
My grandmothers were strong.

My grandmothers are full of memories
Smelling of soap and onions and wet clay
With veins rolling roughly over quick hands
They have many clean words to say.
My grandmothers were strong.
Why am I not as they?

Source: Margaret Walker, *For My People* (New Haven, Conn.: Yale University Press, 1942), p. 25.

People of Unrest

Stare from your pillow into the sun.
See the disk of light in shadows.
Watch day growing tall.
Cry with a loud voice after the sun.
Take his yellow arms and wrap them round your life.

Be glad to be washed in the sun.
Be glad to see.
People of unrest and sorrow
Stare from your pillow into the sun.

Source: Margaret Walker, *For My People* (New Haven, Conn.: Yale University Press, 1942), p. 27.

We Have Been Believers

We have been believers believing in the black gods of an old land, believing in the secrets of the seeress and the magic of the charmers and the power of the devil's evil ones.

And in the white gods of a new land we have been believers believing in the mercy of our masters and the beauty of our brothers, believing in the conjure of the humble and the faithful and the pure.

Neither the slavers' whip nor the lynchers' rope nor the bayonet could kill our black belief. In our hunger we beheld the welcome table and in our nakedness the glory of a long white robe. We have been believers in the new Jerusalem.

We have been believers feeding greedy grinning gods, like a Moloch demanding our sons and our daughters, our strength and our wills and our spirits of pain. We have been believers, silent and stolid and stubborn and strong.

We have been believers yielding substance for the world. With our hands have we fed a people and out of our strength have they wrung the necessities of a nation. Our song has filled the twilight and our hope has heralded the dawn.

Now we stand ready for the touch of one fiery iron, for the cleansing breath of many molten truths, that the eyes of the blind may see and the ears of the deaf may hear and the tongues of the people be filled with living fire.

Where are our gods that they leave us asleep? Surely the priests and the preachers and the powers will hear. Surely now that our hands are empty and our hearts too full to pray they will understand. Surely the sires of the people will send us a sign.

We have been believers believing in our burdens and our demigods too long. Now the needy no longer weep and pray; the long-suffering arise, and our fists bleed against the bars with a strange insistency.

Source: Margaret Walker, *For My People* (New Haven, Conn.: Yale University Press, 1942), pp. 16–17.

Black Death

We Negroes in Eatonville know a number of things that the hustling, bustling white man never dreams of. He is a materialist with little care for overtones. They have only eyes and ears, we see with the skin.

For instance, if a white person were halted on the streets of Orlando and told that Old Man Morgan, the excessively black Negro hoodoo man, can kill any person indicated and paid for, without ever leaving his house or even seeing his victim, he'd laugh in your face and walk away, wondering how long the Negro will continue to wallow in ignorance and superstition. But no black person in a radius of twenty miles will smile, not much. They know.

His achievements are far too numerous to mention singly. Besides, any of his cures of "conjures" are kept secret. But everybody knows that he put the loveless curse on Bella Lewis. She has been married seven times but none of her husbands have ever remained with her longer than the twenty-eight days that Morgan had prescribed as the limit.

Hirma Lester's left track was brought to him with five dollars and when the new moon came again, Lester was stricken with paralysis while working in his orange grove.

There was the bloody-flux that he put on Lucy Potts; he caused Emma Taylor's teeth to drop out; he put the shed skin of a black snake in Horsos

Brown's shoes and made him as the Wandering Jew; he put a sprig of Lena Merchant's hair in a bottle, corked it and threw it into a running stream with the neck pointing upstream, and she went crazy; he buried Lillie Wilcox's finger-nails with lizard's feet and dried up her blood.

All of these things and more can easily be proved by the testimony of the villagers. They ought to know.

He lives alone in a two-room hut down by Lake Blue Sink, the bottomless. His eyes are reddish and the large gold hoop ear-rings jangling on either side of his shrunken black face make the children fly in terror whenever they meet him on the street or in the woods where he goes to dig roots for his medicines.

But the doctor does not spend his time merely making folks ill. He has sold himself to the devil over the powerful black cat's bone that alone will float upstream and may do what he wills. Life and death are in his hands—he sometimes kills.

He sent Old Lady Crooms to her death in the Lake. She was a rival hoodoo doctor and laid claims to equal power. She came to her death one night. That very morning Morgan had told several that he was tired of her pretenses—he would put an end to it and prove his powers. That very afternoon near sundown, she went down to the lake to bathe, telling her daughter, however, that she did not wish to go, but something seemed to be forcing her. About dusk someone heard her scream and rushed to the lake. She had fallen in the shallow water at the edge. The coroner from Orlando said she met her death by falling into the water during an epileptic fit. But the villagers *knew.* White people are very stupid about some things. They can think mightily but [illegible in original manuscript].

But the undoing of Beau Diddely is his masterpiece. He had come from up North somewhere. He was a waiter at the Park House over in Maitland where Docia Boger was a chamber-maid. She had a very pretty brown body and face, sang alto in the Methodist choir and played the blues on her guitar. Soon Beau Diddely was with her every moment he could spare from his work. He was stuck on her all right, for a time.

They would linger in the shrubbery about Park Lake or go for long walks in the woods on Sunday afternoon to pick violets. They are abundant in the Florida woods in winter.

The Park House always closed in April and Beau was planning to go North with the white tourists. It was then Docia's mother discovered that Beau should have married her daughter weeks before.

"Mist' Diddely," said Mrs. Boger, "Ah'm a widder 'oman an' Doshy's all Ah got, an' Ah know youse gointer do what you orter." She hesitated a moment and studied his face. "'Thout no trouble. Ah doan wanta make no talk 'round town."

In a split second the vivacious, smiling Beau had vanished. A very hard vitriolic stranger occupied his chair.

"Looka heah, Mis' Boger. I'm a man that's travelled a lot—been most everywhere. Don't try to come that stuff over me—what I got to marry Docia for?"

"'Cause—'cause"—the surprise of his answer threw the old woman into a panic. "Youse the cause of her condition, ain'tcher?"

Docia, embarrassed, mortified, began to cry.

"Oh, I see the little plot now!" He glanced maliciously toward the girl and back again to her mother. "But I'm none of your down-South-country-suckers. Go try that on some of these clod-hoppers. Don't try to lie on *me*—I got money to fight."

"Beau," Docia sobbed, "You ain't callin' *me* a liah, is you?" And in her misery she started toward the man who through four months' constant association and assurance she had learned to love and trust.

"Yes! You're lying—you sneaking little—oh you're not even good sawdust! Me marry you! Why I could pick up a better woman out of the gutter than you! I'm a married man anyway, so you might as well forget your little scheme!"

Docia fell back stunned.

"But, but Beau, you said you wasn't," Docia wailed.

"Oh," Beau replied with a gesture of dismissal of the whole affair. "What difference does it make? A man will say anything at times. There are certain kinds of women that men always lie to."

In her mind's eye Docia saw things for the first time without her tinted glasses and real panic seized her. She fell upon her knees and clasped the nattily clad legs of her seducer.

"Oh Beau," she wept, struggling to hold him, as he, fearing for the creases in his trousers, struggled to free himself—"You said—you—you promised—"

"Oh, well, you ought not to have believed me—you ought to have known I didn't mean it. Anyway I'm not going to marry you, so what're you going to do? Do whatever you feel big enough to try—my shoulders are broad."

He left the house hating the two women bitterly, as only we hate those we have injured.

At the hotel, omitting mention of his shows of affection, his pleas, his solemn promises to Docia, he told the other waiters how that piece of the earth's refuse had tried to inveigle, to force him into a marriage. He enlarged upon his theme and told them all, in strict confidence, how she had been pursuing him all winter; how she had waited in ambush time and again and dragged him down by the lake and well, he was only human. It couldn't have happened with the *right* kind of a girl, and he thought too much of himself to marry any other than the country's best. The worst sin a woman could commit was to run after a man.

So the next day Eatonville knew; and the scourge of tongues was added to Docia's woes.

Mrs. Boger and her daughter kept strictly indoors, suffering, weeping, growing bitter.

"Mommer, if he jus' hadn't tried to make me out a bad girl, I could look over the rest in time, mommer, but—but he tried to make out—ah—"

Docia broke down weeping again.

Drip, drip, drip, went her daughter's tears on the old woman's heart, each drop calcifying a little the fibers till at the end of four days the petrifying process was complete. Where once had been warm, pulsing flesh was now cold heavy stone that pulled down, pressing out normal life and bowing the head of her. The woman died, and in that heavy cold stone a tiger, a female tiger—was cut by the chisel of shame.

She was ready to answer the question Beau had flung so scornfully at her old head: "Well, what are you going to do?"

Docia slept, huddled on the bed. A hot salt tear rose to Mrs. Boger's eyes and rolled heavily down the quivering nose. Must Docia awake always to that awful desolation? Robbed of *everything,* even faith? She knew then that the world's greatest crime is not murder—its most terrible punishment is meted to her of too much faith-too great a love.

She turned down the light and stepped into the street.

It was near midnight and the village slept. But she knew of one house where there would be a light; one pair of eyes still awake.

As she approached Blue Sink she all but turned back. It was a dark night but the lake shimmered and glowed like phosphorous near the shore. It seemed that figures moved about on the quiet surface. She remembered that folks said Blue Sink the bottomless was Morgan's grave-yard. All Africa awoke in her blood.

A cold prickly feeling stole over her and stood her hair on end. Her feet grew heavy and her tongue dry and stiff.

In the swamp at the head of the lake, she saw Jack-O-Lanterns darting here and there and three hundred years of America passed like the mist of morning. Africa reached out its dark hand and claimed its own. Drums, tom, tom, tom, tom, tom, beat in her ears. Strange demons seized her. Witch doctors danced before her, laid hands upon her alternately freezing and burning her flesh. She cried out in formless terror more than once before she found herself within the house of Morgan.

She was not permitted to tell her story. She opened her mouth but the old man chewed a camphor leaf or two, spat into a small pail of sand and asked:

"How do yuh wanta kill 'im? By water, by a sharp edge, or a bullet?"

The old woman almost fell off of the chair in the amazement that he knew her mind. He merely chuckled a bit and handed her a drinking gourd.

"Dip up a teeny bit of water an' po' hit on de flo',—by dat time you'll know."

She dipped the water out of a wooden pail and poured it upon the rough floor.

"Ah wanta shoot him, but how kin ah' 'thout . . .?"

"Looka heah" Morgan directed and pointed to a huge mirror—scarred—and dusty. He dusted its face carefully. "Look in dis glass 'thout turnin' yo' head an' when he comes, you shoot tuh kill. Take good aim!"

Both faced about and gazed hard into the mirror that reached from floor to ceiling. Morgan turned once to spit into the pail of sand. The mirror grew misty, darker, near the center, then Mrs. Boger saw Beau walk to the center of the mirror and stand looking at her, glaring and sneering. She all but fainted.

Morgan thrust the gun into her hand. She saw the expression on Beau Diddely's face change from scorn to fear and she found it in herself to laugh.

"Take good aim," Morgan cautioned. "Yor cain't shoot but once."

She leveled the gun at the heart of the apparition in the glass and fired. It collapsed; the mirror grew misty again, then cleared. "You'll find things alright when you git home," Morgan said.

In horror she flung both money and gun at the old man who seized the money greedily, and she fled into the darkness, dreading nothing, thinking only of putting distance between her and the house of Morgan.

The next day Eatonville was treated to another thrill.

It seemed that Beau Diddely, the darling of the ladies, was in the hotel yard making love to another chamber-maid. In order that she might fully appreciate what a great victory was hers, he was reciting the Conquest of Docia, how she loved him, pursued him, knelt down and kissed his feet, begging him to marry her,—when suddenly he stood up very straight, clasped his hand over his heart, grew rigid and fell dead.

The coroner's verdict was death from natural causes—heart failure. But they were mystified by what looked like a powder burned directly over the heart. Probably a cigarette burn.

But the Negroes knew instantly when they saw that mark, but everyone agreed that he got justice. Mrs. Boger and Docia moved to Jacksonville where she married well.

And the white folks never knew and would have laughed had anyone told them. He who sees only with the eyes is very blind.

ANNE SPENCER

Letter to My Sister

It is dangerous for a woman to defy the gods;
To taunt them with the tongue's thin tip,
Or strut in the weakness of mere humanity,
Or draw a line daring them to cross;
The gods own the searing lightning,
The drowning waters, tormenting fears
And anger of red sins.

Oh, but worse still if you mince timidly—
Dodge this way or that, or kneel to pray,
Be kind, or sweat agony drops
Or lay your quick body over your feeble young;
If you have beauty or none, if celibate
Or vowed—the gods are juggernaut,
Passing over . . . over . . .

This you may do:
Lock your heart, then quietly,
And lest they peer within,
Light no lamp when dark comes down
Raise no shade for sun;
Breathless must your breath come through
If you'd die and dare deny
The gods their god-like fun.

Source: Charles S. Johnson, ed., *Ebony and Topaz: A Collectanea* (New York: National Urban League, 1927), p. 94. Revised version of "Sybil Warns her Sister."

At the Carnival

Gay little Girl-of-the-Diving-Tank,
I desire a name for you,
Nice, as a right glove fits;
For you—who amid the malodorous
Mechanics of the unlovely thing,
Are darling of spirit and form.
I know you—a glance, and what you are
Sit-by-the-fire in my heart.
My Limousine-Lady knows you, or
Why does the slant-envy of her eye mark
Your straight air and radiant inclusive smile?
Guilt pins a fig leaf; Innocence is its own adorning.
The bull-necked man knows you—this first time
His itching flesh sees form divine and vibrant health,
And thinks not of his avocation.
I came incuriously—
Set on no diversion save that my mind
Might safely nurse its brood of misdeeds
In the presence of blind crowd.
The color of life was gray.
Everywhere the setting seemed right
For my mood!
Here the sausage and garlic booth
Sent unholy incense skyward;
There a quivering female thing
Gestured assignations, and lied
To call it dancing;
There, too, were games of chance
With chances for none;

But oh! Girl-of-the-Tank, at last!
Gleaming Girl, how intimately pure and free
The gaze you send the crowd,
As though you know the dearth of beauty
In its sordid life.
We need you—my Limousine-Lady,
The bull-necked man, and I.
Seeing you here brave and water-clean,
Leaven for the heavy ones of earth,
I am swift to fell that what makes
The plodder glad is good; and
Whatever is good is God.
The wonder is that you are here;
I have seen the queer in queer places,
But never before a heaven-fed
Naiad of the Carnival-Tank!
Little Diver, Destiny for you
Like as for me, is shod in silence;
Years may seep into your soul
The bacilli of the usual and the expedient;
I implore Neptune to claim his child to-day!

Source: James Weldon Johnson, ed., *The Book of American Negro Poetry* (New York: Harcourt Brace and Company, 1922), pp. 169–170.

Lady, Lady

Lady, Lady, I saw your face,
Dark as night withholding a star . . .
The chisel fell, or it might have been
You had borne so long the yoke of men.
Lady, Lady, I saw your hands,
Twisted, awry, like crumpled roots,

Bleached poor white in a sudsy tub,
Wrinkled and drawn from your rub-a-dub.
Lady, Lady, I saw your heart,
And altared there in its darksome place
Were the tongues of flames the ancients knew,
Where the good God sits to spangle through.

Source: Survey Graphic 53 (March 1, 1925): 661.

Black Man o' Mine

Black Man o' Mine,
If the world were your lover,
It could not give what I give to you,
Or the ocean would yield and you could discover
Its ages of treasure to hold and to view;
Could it fill half the measure of my heart's portion . . .
Just for you living, just for you giving all this devotion,
Black man o' mine.

Black man o' mine,
As I hush and caress you, close to my heart,
All your loving is just your needing what is true;
Then with your passing dark comes my darkest part,
For living without your love is only rue.
Black man o' mine, if the world were your lover
It could not give what I give to you.

Source: J. Lee Greene, *Time's Unfading Garden: Anne Spencer's Life and Poetry* (Baton Rouge: Louisiana State University Press, 1977), p. 183.

White Things

Most things are colorful things—the sky, earth, and sea.
　Black men are most men; but the white are free!
White things are rare things; so rare, so rare
They stole from out a silvered world—somewhere.
Finding earth-plains fair plains, save greenly grassed,
They strewed white feathers of cowardice, as they passed;
　The golden stars with lances fine,
　The hills all red and darkened pine,
They blanched with their want of power;
And turned the blood in a ruby rose
To a poor white poppy-flower.

They pyred a race of black, black men,
And burned them to ashes white, then,
Laughing, a young one claimed a skull,
For the skull of a black is white, not dull,
　But a glistening awful thing
　Made, it seems, for this ghoul to swing
In the face of God with all his might,
And swear by the hell that sired him:
　"Man-maker, make white!"

Source: The Crisis 25 (March 1923): 204.

The Wife-Woman

Maker-of-Sevens in the scheme of things
From earth to star;
Thy cycle holds whatever is fate, and
Over the border the bar.
Though rank and fierce the mariner
Sailing the seven seas,
He prays as he holds his glass to his eyes,
Coaxing the Pleiades.

I cannot love them; and I feel your glad,
Chiding from the grave,
That my all was only worth at all, what
Joy to you it gave,
These seven links the *Law* compelled
For the human chain—
I cannot love *them;* and *you,* oh,
Seven-fold months in Flanders slain!

A jungle there, a cave here, bred six
And a million years.
Sure and strong, mate for mate, such
Love as culture fears;
I gave you clear the oil and wine;
You saved me your hob and hearth—
See how *even* life may be ere the
Sickle comes and leaves a swath.

But I can wait the seven of moons,
Or years I spare,

Hoarding the heart's plenty, nor spend
A drop, nor share—
So long but outlives a smile and a silken gown;
Then gaily reach up from my shroud,
And you, glory-clad, reach down.

Source: James Weldon Johnson, ed., *The Book of American Negro Poetry* (New York: Harcourt Brace and Company, 1922), pp. 171–172.

Freedom

A man is free that has no things;
Free to stretch his earth-bound wings
Free to tramp the sun-kissed sod;
Free indeed to worship God.

A man is free that has no things,
No weight of sod that owning brings;
He'll feel no pang of deep regret
When train shall end and last sun set.

A man is free that has no things
To awaken greed for more that brings
No satisfaction with the best,
And batters down his will to rest.

Yea, he is free that has no things,
No bulging purse with narrow strings,
Yet owns as far as eye can see
Hill and sky and rolling lea.

A man is free that has no things;
Free as a lightsome bird that sings,
Amid the blue of widening cloud,
A homeless minstrel, gay and proud.
A man is free that has no things.

Source: Aloise Barbour Epperson, *The Hills of Yesterday and Other Poems* (Norfolk, Va.: J. A. Brown, 1943), p. 70.

A Negro in a Dime Store

Bronze of skin and strong of limb,
He straightly stood amid the crowd
Of petty things that swirled about,
A king of men, patient and proud.

Here and there were scorn and jibe.
He neither knew nor hearing cared,
But eye of mystery, deeply veiled,
Saw hidden deeps we little shared.

My heart contracted swift with pain
And pity, that the Black Man there
Should be the sport of idle fools
Because his skin could not be fair.

And then I thought, what boots the thing?
His is the better part and way.
Once, another Man was scorned
Because a shadow on him lay.

All roads end as time speeds on,
Gladness and tears, darkness and day,
Fair skin and black each in its hour
Shall shrivel and shrink and wither away.

Go, my black Brother, fare you on!
Patient and brave as you have gone,
Leaving this pettiness, soon you shall step
Out of the darkness into the dawn.

Source: Aloise Barbour Epperson, *The Hills of Yesterday and Other Poems* (Norfolk, Va.: J. A. Brown, 1943), p. 71.

Heard on an Atlantic City Bridge

"Want to die, Corine?
Jump over dere."
"Is you asking me?
No! I swear
I don't want to die!
I know what's here.
Funny thing to me
This suicide!
When there's plenty of good wittles [*sic*]
An' the world is wide.
Jump over dere
In that black flow!
Is you asking me?
No! child, No!
I don't want to die!
I likes it here
An' the doings over dere
Ain't somehow clear.
Nobody can prove
'Bout dem great things,
'Bout golden shoes,
An' Angel's wings,
An' us being white,
With time to spare,
An' nobody ordering us
To sit over dere.
It might be true,
What de preachers say
But Corine's where
She wants to stay!"

Source: Aloise Barbour Epperson, *The Hills of Yesterday and Other Poems* (Norfolk, Va.: J. A. Brown, 1943), p. 64.

PART 9

CRISIS

Editors of *The Crisis*, a periodical sponsored by the National Association for the Advancement of Colored People (NAACP), described their era as "a critical time in the history of the advancement of men" when "bigotry and prejudice" would lead to violence if "reason and forbearance" did not prevail.[1] The notion of "crisis" embodies the sense among black Americans that they were living at a time in which significant changes were impending. By 1917 black women were at "the cusp of a new era" of tangible accomplishments and advances.[2]

Many were to challenge the "Jim Crow/Jane Crow"[3] laws segregating blacks from whites, because of which, in their daily lives, blacks were treated differently from their white counterparts and were denied access to many public places, including libraries, cafeterias, and hotels. Angelina Weld Grimké's story tells what it felt like to be the object of such humiliation. Black women opposed segregation with equal ferocity to black men, both collectively and personally.

The selections presented here include accounts of some of the more traumatic experiences with the color line during a turbulent period in African-American history. In these works the "crisis" is not simply physical atrocities, such as rapes or lynchings, but also their symbolic consequences for all Americans—whether black or white, male or female. In Florida Ruffin Ridley's "He Must Think It Out," a man discovering that he

---

1. *The Crisis* 1 (November 1910): 10.
2. V. Paula Giddings, *When and Where I Enter: The Impact of Black Women on Race and Sex in America* (New York: Bantam, 1985), p. 138–139.
3. See C. Vann Woodward, *The Strange Career of Jim Crow* (New York: Oxford, 1966).

has a black forebear is forced for the first time in his life to contemplate the benefits of white privilege in the context of American racism. Horrified to learn that he is, in some small way, black, he contemplates giving up a great fortune and even considers murder to keep his ancestry a secret.

Marion Cuthbert's "Mob Madness" focuses on the conscience of a southern white woman unwittingly caught up in the consequences of racial violence. These consequences, as Cuthbert relates, could go so far as to be fatal. Esther Popel's poems concretize the horror and brutality of lynching and articulate the depth of her determination to escape such a death.

Marita Bonner's narrator in "—And I Passed By" wrestles with her personal code of ethics, and in her own eyes she fails a spiritual test when she realizes she has engaged in reverse racism. This piece demonstrates the complexity of the relationship between women of color and white women, as sisters in struggle. In Bonner's story "One True Love," a domestic's encounter with a white female lawyer stimulates such a strong desire to secure a successful career of her own that she forges blindly ahead, forgetting that she stands at the disadvantageous intersection of race and gender. And Elise Johnson McDougald, who in real life found the professional success that Bonner's character was seeking, relates in her autobiographical "The Women of the White Strain" that this was not enough to make her life a happy one.

MARITA BONNER

One True Love

When Nora came through the swinging doors between the kitchen and the dining room with the roast, she was just a butter-colored maid with hair on the "riney" side hurrying to get through dinner so she could go to the show with the janitor's helper, Sam Smith.

By the time Nora had served dessert, though, she had forgotten the show, forgotten Sam—forgotten everything but this: she was going to be a lawyer!

"They" had company to dinner. ("They" in Nora's family were a Mr. and Mrs. This is not their story—so they are merely "They.")

Company came often enough, but this time everything had been different.

"We are having a noted lawyer to dinner tonight, Nora," Mrs. had said.

Nora had expected a bay window, side-chop whiskers and a boom-boom voice.

When she backed through the door with the roast she saw sitting at the table in the guest's place, a woman. She had been beautifully but simply dressed in black velvet: her hair was cut short, worn brushed up in curls: every inch of her had been smart and lovely.

"This must be the lawyer's wife. Maybe he couldn't git here!"

But then "they" began talking. "Is your law practice as heavy as it was two years ago or do you devote more time to lecturing?" he asked.

"We hear you've been pleading at the Supreme Court!" "she" cut in.

Nora nearly gaped.

This was the lawyer!

Source: The Crisis 48 (February 1941): 46–47, 58–59.

All through dinner she noted how nicely the lawyer ate, how pleasant her voice was when she spoke—how direct her eyes were when she looked at you.

"I'm going to get in some kind of school and be a lawyer, too!" Nora declared to the dishes as she washed them.

A knock at the back door cut into her thoughts.

Nora opened it and Sam bristled in.

"Why ain't you through? It's quarter to nine!"

"Whyn't you say good-evenin' and ask me how I feel?" Nora shot back at him. "You always act so ignorant!"

"What you got to talk so mean to me for? Ain't you glad to see me?"

"Can't say that I am if you always going to act so ignorant and degrading!"

"De-who?? S'matter with you, Nora?"

"Nuthin' cept I'm tired and I'm not going to be bothered going to no show tonight!"

"Well who—!" Sam staggered back from the choice of two words to follow his who: "cares" and "wants," decided he did not want to use either. "Well, good night, then!" he finished instead. "Maybe Sadie Jones would like to see a show!"

"Maybe so! She's your kind! Two ignorants together!" Nora flashed back at Sam.

"And maybe I don't need to come back here no more! I won't be seeing you!"

Nora did not even turn around to close the door after Sam. He had to close it himself.

Now Sam was a runty, bowlegged dark brown janitor's helper with a shiny scalp on which his hair grew in kinked patches.

That is what Sam was to the world.

And Sam was just that to Nora, too.

But to Sam, Nora was elegant and beautiful and more desirable than anything ever had been to anyone at anytime.

His, "Maybe I don't need to come back here no more!" frightened him.

Nora forgot it.

He had said it on Wednesday.

He stayed awake all Wednesday night, all Thursday night—all Friday night—hearing himself say over and over again: "Maybe I don't need to come back here no more!"

Suppose Nora thought he really meant just that!

Suppose Nora would never see him anymore!

By Saturday morning, his eyes were so red it upset your stomach just to look at him.

"You ain't taking to drink, is you Sam?" the head janitor asked. "Cause if you is, then I needs another helper 'stead of you!"

"Naw I ain't drinking! Don't feel good!"

"Take a good physic! Do something! You look right bad!"

Sam had said "Maybe I won't be seeing you any more" on Wednesday.

So Saturday night he bought a box of flour water and cocoa chocolates and came and knocked humbly on Nora's back door.

"Want to go to the show?" he asked anxiously as Nora opened the door. "They got that 'Kiss in the Dark' down to the Dream World."

"I don't mind," Nora answered mildly. "I have a lot of things to talk over with you!"

Sam's heart turned completely over. "You mean we—going to get— you going to give up working here and we going to get married? That guy keeps telling me he'll rent them two rooms on Rommy Street for twenty dollars and Levack's got some swell new furniture real cheap!"

Sam was breathless.

Nora was not listening to him. She knew vaguely that Sam was talking so she merely waited until his voice ceased before she began to tell him what was in her mind.

"I've enrolled in the night classes at the City College! I'm taking law!"

"You taking law! How come you taking law?"

"I mean I'm going to study to be a lawyer!"

"You ain't! When we going to get married?"

"I been telling you never! I got to get some education first anyhow!"

"Aw you don't need no education! You know enough to get along with me!"

"Aw Sam! Wait'll I get my hat on!"

As they walked toward the town center, Nora gossiped a bit, "'They' surely was having a terrible fuss tonight! She really cussed and damned him off the boards!"

"Yeah? What's the trouble?"

"Oh, she went down town and tried to buy up the stores and he got to hollering but she out-cussed him! I don't see why they don't get along lovely! Everything so lovely in their home and he and she both educated."

"What makes you talk so much 'bout this education business now? That ain't what makes a man and woman git on together!"

"Aw Sam you so ignorant! If you are educated you know how to do everything just right all the time."

"Everything like gettin' along with a husband? Naw! You got to love folks! A guy really got to love a girl so he kin pass by the beer gardens and the hot mamas and the sheeny what wants him to lay a dollar on a suit and watch and a diamond and a God-knows-what-all—and bring the paycheck home to her so they kin go in on it together!"

"Aw paychecks ain't everything!"

"And edjucation ain't everything! You got to love folks more than books!"

"And more than money!"

"Yeah! You got to love folks more than everything to git along and live fifty years with 'em!"

"Who said anything 'bout staying married fifty years?"

"Me!" Sam retorted stoutly. "My grandma did and I'm going to too!"

"You ain't going to do nothing your grandmother didn't do! That's ignorant!"

They reached the theater and no conclusion to the argument, so they went in.

Nora kicked off her shoes and munched chocolates and lived the picture. She felt comfortable and happy in a remote way that there was somebody with whom she could talk and argue good-naturedly—someone who knew enough to pass you his handkerchief at the cry parts.

She was glad—dimly—about all this.

What gave her feelings a real edge was that Monday night she was going to her first class at City College to study law.

City College was not particularly glad to receive Nora.

They endured a few colored students there but they had always been men—men whose background of preparation made professors and students of the lesser type keep their sneers under cover.

But after it was seen that Nora got her superlatives mixed and "busted" when she should have "broken" and "hadn't ought to" came out when she meant "should not have"—quite a few sneers came out in the open.

People like to place you and your desires and tastes where they think your particular color and hirsute growth belong. They do not like to feel

that Something-greater-than-themselves can give you the feel for the er-
mine and satin of living; the air for silver services and a distinct love of
beauty that sets you quietly aloof—truly poised beyond the rough wood
of living.

If they are above you—culturally—sometimes they shower sneers
down at you, forgetting all the while that the thick coats of culture which
surround them began once with one coat—thinly applied—sometimes—
somewhere—on their own family tree.

If they are below you—culturally—they try to stone you to death—
sneer at you until you reach the point where you gladly smother all your
ideas and ideals and crawl into a protective shell of sameness so that the
mediocre mob will let you alone.

Nora had a touch of this something that made her struggle to get
beyond a stove, a sink, a broom and a dust-mop and some one else's
kitchen.

She worked hard at her books. She stayed up late to struggle with
books full of pages that she had to read ten times over to even begin to
get a glimmer of sense from them.

Professors demand more than a glimmer of information. They want
things presented as they are and a bit more grafted on to it to show you
are really getting an education.

Came the mid-year exams.

Nora snapped at Sam—burnt two steaks and had to buy a third one
out of her own pocket one night—trying to untangle torts and contracts.
Haggard with overwork and bewildered with subjects for which no
preparatory steps had ever been laid in her, Nora flunked all her exami-
nations.

Sam came one Sunday night to carry her over to the colored section
of town for a special celebration.

Nora met him at the back door and began to cry.

"They flunked me, Sam! I didn't pass! No need to go celebrating."

"You mean those old fools didn't give you no good mark? Much
studyin' and stewin' and strivin' and worryin' and stayin' up nights as you
did? S'matter with them folks? I bet if I'se to go down there they'd pass
you or sumpin!"

Nora's anger flared: "Why you always have to talk so ignorant, Sam?
You can't do nothing! I didn't know enough to pass, that's all."

"Tain't no need to bellow at me all the time! I 'clare you got to feelin' right important since you got your feet inside of that City College! Good enough for you! You bound to fail! You too bigitty!"

"You get out of here! You no kind of friend! Rejoicing at my downfall!"

"Wouldn't fall down if you'd a married me 'stead of learnin' law all the time!"

"Don't need your love! I can lean on law and be a lawyer too if I wants to, Mr. Sam Smith!"

"Well go on leaning on your busted crutch, then!"

"Aw go on home Sam! My head's achin' fit to bust!"

Sam backed out in a huff.

When he came back the next night and knocked at the door no one answered.

The kitchen was dark.

"Gone to bed! Still mad! Let her stay mad!" Sam growled as he left.

The next night he came again and no one opened the door.

Sam did not come back for two whole days.

When he knocked at the door a strange colored woman opened it.

"Where's Nora?" Sam gasped in surprise.

"Nora? Oh you mean the maid what was here? Oh she sick!"

"Sick?" Sam shouted and bounded into the kitchen. "Where she at? Whyn't nobody tell me?"

"Who you anyhow?"

"I'm the man what's going to marry huh! Marry Nora! Where she at?"

"Well don't yell so and don't come running in here that-a-way! She ain't here! She in some hospital. Wait'll I ask the lady."

When the woman came back to the kitchen Sam was already running down the back stairs!

"She got pneu-monyer in the City Hospital," the woman called down the stairs after him.

"And you might have shut the door if you couldn't wait."

Sam tore up the gangway between the buildings and hired the biggest taxi lurking in front of the apartment house where they worked.

"Steppin' out for a big night, Boy?" the driver jibed as he pushed down the meter.

"I'm going to City Hospital to get my wife—what is going to be. Got to bring her home and take care of her!"

It took a while to find Nora. She was in a public ward somewhere and since pneumonia cases were coming in at that particular season faster than the registrar could list them, no one could locate her for a full half hour.

Beads of real agony dropped from Sam's face when the nurse showed him the elevators.

He found the ward.

And he found a white screen around Nora's bed.

He could not believe this grey-faced woman who lay panting—panting was Nora. Her nostrils flared wide—too wide. Her teeth stuck deep in her lower lip and her eyes stared straight at nothing.

If "they" had said a little more—if someone had said that they would pay for Nora—she would not have been shoved aside and forgotten in a public ward.

Sam raced frantically back to the hall where the night nurse sat.

"Could Nora Jones be put in one of these here rooms to herself? I got every bit of four hundred dollars! Couldn't nobody set by her?"

The nurse glanced at a paper on her desk.

"She can't be moved right now! Perhaps—if she's better tomorrow—maybe!"

You could tell all this meant that nothing nobody could do would help Nora anymore.

Sam went back to the bed and sat behind the white screen. He laid his head beside Nora's and cried.

His love must have reached her somewhere.

Nora's eyes focused on him for a second. "Sam! Sam—" he could hardly hear her. "I've got l—— I've got l——!"

It sounded as if she said "law," her breath rasped so and her lower jaw seemed to fall away from the work.

Sam wiped his eyes and grabbed her hand.

"I know Nora! I know you got that old law to lean on! Ef you could of just want something I could a helped you git. Just get well! I'll help you get that law!"

Nora tried to shake her head.

Couldn't he understand!

She had waited and waited to tell Sam that down deep somewhere where she had been lost in pain for so long—there was nothing about books and what they gave you. The only thing she had remembered had been that there was someone who loved her enough to love her even when she was snappish and cross—who came back again and again—no matter what.

And she was glad!

So glad she wanted to tell Sam that she loved him—had love enough for the two rooms he wanted on Rommy Street and enough to try to understand how his grandmother came to stay married fifty years.

Right now Nora was too tired to try to tell him again.

She closed her eyes.

But she closed her eyes carrying with her the love that was in Sam's eyes.

She thought she smiled.

The doctor said the death agony had set her face at that angle.

He wondered too, why that little colored man just sat by that empty bed crying so long. The nurses wanted to prepare the bed for another case.

And Sam sat crying—wishing he had been elegant and wonderful enough to match the wonder in Nora—trying to take something out into his empty world from an empty bed.

MARITA BONNER

—And I Passed By

I used to take so much of Life for granted. Enough to eat—enough sleep—enough rest—not too much to do—the schools I wanted—the things I wanted—friends with the things they wanted.

I had even been pit-pat too. Took the Natural-Trickery-of-the-White-man to be an indelible streak in the breed. An indelible streak that only called for enough distrust on my own part to get along.

I used to take so much of Life for granted. But once the Wing—the WING of Death—swept across my home. Swept across my home twice in two short years.

It swept twice. It made sure that all of my heart beneath was the two pieces of the world that men call graves.

I used to take so much of Life for granted. When the Wing had swept clean the halls of my home, people came and talked. Came to talk, to tell me how to face two spaces that were empty forever. Empty spaces that ached. Then the talk and the people flowed back around me like blood from around a wound.

The Empty Spaces ached. I was the flesh around the wound—the Empty Spaces, the wound.

I cried to high Heaven—"Is God really good—?"

But I should have bowed and cried low—"Yet—somehow—God is really good."

Source: Charles S. Johnson, ed., *Ebony and Topaz: A Collectanea* (New York: National Urban League, 1927), pp. 158–160. Written under the name "Joseph Maree Andrew."

I had taken too much for granted, you see. The Wing swept clean. It swept away the scales from my eyes, too. I began to soften.

—Soft, you will see what I mean.

The scales left my eyes. I decided I could again see and talk once more without dropping out of things into my own abyss.

Thus I set out on a winter's evening with a friend to dinner. Cold air pooled around us as we stepped out of the door.

I took a deep sniff—drew in as much as I could—pressed my cheeks deeper in the fur around me—appreciated my friend's well-clad appearance—sniffed her perfume—and let my pulse race ahead to the click of our heels on the pavement.

Nothing troubled us. Absolutely nothing at all. School and its work lay behind us. A home we could really enjoy lay ahead.

We pattered. Light talk pattered with our heels.

"Let's walk all the way." I had to skip a step as I said [it]. It was so good to be freely alive.

"I want to walk for once," replied the girl beside me.

The hill mounted. Our blood pounded. Our heels clicked. Our tongues raced—I could breathe deeply and I could only know it was cold by the whiffs of the air across my nose (which is strangely tender in winter).

The hill veered sharply. We would either have to prolong the jaunt or take a short cut.

"Are you afraid to cut through ——— Street?" asked my companion. She mentioned a street that is not supposed to be safe after dark.

It has sad houses, sad stores in every available space, and people, white and colored up and down it. It is sad. The white and colored people fight pitched battles and hate each other as if each blamed the other for being there.

"No! of course I am not afraid." My pulse made me say that.

We struck out. I really was a bit afraid. That made my pulses race harder. We crossed an intersection. I stumbled over the car tracks and hopped the curb. Then I turned to look back.

"Not buttered fingers but buttered toes," I explained.

The other girl did not answer. She looked beyond me. I turned the other way to look too.

Something soft brushed against me. A girl—slender, dead-white—in a light blue dress with a low round neck—and with bed-room slippers on her feet—staggered against me.

I welched away. She fell in a sort of confusion against the building behind us. The street light lay full in her face. Her eyes were half closed, her mouth slightly opened.

Something made me catch hold of my throat. The girl staggered and stumbled. She went around the corner.

"Oh—." It sounded futile even to me, but I said it. We both stared at one another. I rambled on: "She did not have a coat!" I started toward the corner. "She is sick!"

"You'd better let that cracker alone! You do not know this place! This is ——— Street!" cried the girl with me.

I wavered. This was ——— Street.

That sent us on up the hill. A weight fell on me. The sidewalk made me stumble. I felt burdened. I was stumbling.

I sat at the table. Food, talk, good fellowship flowed around me, bathed me about.

"Come to and answer my question!" someone said beside me.

"Mustn't let yourself worry, my dear," the hostess whispered in the kindly warmth of motherly middle-age.

Tears wavered in my eyes. She thought I was rooting back.

Digging beneath my wound. Filling my Empty Spaces with dreams that hurt. But—

—Cold. A blue voile dress. Bed-room slippers. Eyes half-opened. But she was white. She would have pushed me away if I had touched her and she had seen my brown flesh.

What did I have to do with it? She would have spat in my face.

Still a white face swam before me. It swam between me and my plate. A pale blue voile dress. I only knew it was cold by the touch of wind across my face.—

I tried to blot it out then. I tasted food. Tasted ideas. Talked. Listened. Gave in [to] talk. Shut it out.

—Shut out the cry within me. Shut out the cry—What had I to do with it? What had I to do with it?

Played. Played the piano to shut it out.

"You always play so beautifully for me!" the hostess purred.

Beautifully for her! I was trying to send out the warmth my fingers should have had to a thin pale body in a blue voile dress. Trying to make myself hard. Playing down the fight that was within me.

—You should have gone back!

What had I to do with the—

With thee! Jesus of Nazareth—

I was too soft. It was the Empty Spaces that made me soft. People forget things that have nothing to do with them, why could not I? Why could I not let it alone?

Empty Spaces. She was sick. The dress was blue voile.—

A room full of warmth and easy pleasant lovable folk.

The room was warm—bare arms—Empty Spaces. She would leave a space empty. Someone else would become the Flesh-Around-the Wound. Aching around an Empty Space. Empty. Aching.—

And I had gone up the hill.

Jesus of Nazareth! What had I to do with Thee?—

I took my hands off the keys and laid one quickly over my lips.

"Does your tooth ache?" someone queried behind me.

I had to leave then.

Someone else was talking in the room next to me as I put on my hat. "She takes her sorrow too hard. She must give them up!"

I knew they meant me—that was it. I thought of myself so much—so much for granted—that everyone knew I only thought of Things as they related to me.

—Always me. I had not gone back. She hated my kind. I would not let her "Spit in my face." Me.—

Sometimes I think I see her white face and feel her brush by me.

What had I to do with Thee, Jesus of Nazareth?

God forgive me. Forgive me for letting You stumble by me—alone.—In a thin white body this time; into the dark—in a dress that was no dress—no shoes—into the dark of a winter night.

Forgive me for letting hate send me up the hill while You went down. I wonder where You went then?

I do not know why I did not go back to You. Today I cannot say why. Someday, though, God, I shall have to tell You why.

ELISE JOHNSON McDOUGALD

The Women of the White Strain

Let me think back to that woman, my grandmother, from the part of England known as Sussex. What I know of her I learned pieces of from my own mother. There was not a full picture because this grandmother of mine succumbed to her physical illness or maybe broken heart and left my mother at the age of three. My mother never really knew her mother. There was one brother, much older. When my mother and father brought this brother and his family to America when I was in my teens, I was struck with the great difference in appearance and refinement between this brother and my mother.

My mother had told me that her mother was a lady. She had fallen in love with a carpenter and had paid dearly for marrying "beneath her class." Her family had ostracized her and she had to bear the burden of her choice with no sympathy from anyone. The "lower" classes in England frown as much upon such social "mistakes" as do the "upper." This sketchy touching upon my unusual grandmother gave me a deep understanding, but I was even as a young girl fascinated by it. I now know that this grandmother, whose maiden name I never knew, must have been greatly endowed. She must have been a woman who could love deeply and truly if not wisely. She must have been a social rebel and very

Source: Unpublished manuscript, Manuscripts, Archives and Rare Books Division, Schomburg Center for Research in Black Culture, The New York Public Library, Astor, Lenox and Tilden Foundations, n.d. Several sentences have been moved for the sake of continuity. Proportionately, only a few lines have been deleted that are either redundant or not necessary for the import of the text. Our aim was to protect the integrity of the text and the cadence and voice of the piece while making it easier to follow.

411

courageous. And, I'm sure, stubborn and wilful. For in that Victorian day, girls were constrained to do what their parents—especially their fathers, required them to do. Because being rich in emotions is not often balanced by practicality and common sense and some self-interest, her "mistake" left a little girl of 3 at the mercy of fate. My mother told me that her brother and she were separated almost at once. He was unattractive but she was a beautiful little girl. I remember her blonde hair, her clear skin of fine texture, her blue eyes and her beautiful hands of a lady and her refinement under the most trying ordeals. My mother said that some ladies of wealth saw her and took her away to live with them. Though my mother never said so, they probably knew my grandmother's story or they may have been even closer to the situation but my mother evidently did not know.

In the 1850s when my mother was born, general education did not exist in England. In fact, it's within the last decade or so that England has laws requiring the education of the masses and then only basic elementary schooling. So, these ladies trained my mother to be acceptable in the houses of the upper classes and to be a lady in the sense of being a "lady's maid." That was her position. She taught herself to read and was intelligent. From the constant travelling that her benefactor did, she gained real education. She could talk interestingly about visiting Venice, Paris, etc. She loved to travel.

However, she was cut off from normal family life. She had the status of a servant but the inheritance of the upper class. This doubtless caused conflict within her. And no one seemed to have desired for her real happiness. She spoke of having one proposal of marriage by an ardent Frenchman who was distracted* when she left him in England and came to America as a lady's maid for a wealthy American family—the Phelps-Stokes. I asked her why she hadn't found it possible to marry the Frenchman—wouldn't she have been happier. She showed the fatal romantic and sentimental attitude of the English, which runs through the English character. She said, "I didn't love him," never thinking that she could have learned to love this man, whom she said was good and kind and loving. I am only supposing, because she wasn't given to philosophizing, that he wasn't up to her ideal in intellect or position—the qualities she had been able to observe in the gentlemen of the families where she worked. The

*Distraught.

emotions of the men she could not observe as the English do not let servants see much of their emotions. And her employment kept her inferior, which attitude and feeling were no doubt carefully nurtured by her benefactors as she was growing up.

And so she arrived in America. The first colored woman friend she met was a Mrs. Theresa Cooper—a dressmaker to wealthy people. I remember her well. Hers was the only house my mother permitted us to visit when we—my brother and I—were about 10 & 12 yrs. Mrs. Cooper's son was my brother's age and we 3 had good times in Mrs. Cooper's cluttered kitchen on 32nd Street. (I was born in 142 W. 32nd Street.) Mrs. Cooper told me what a beauty my mother was—her hair was the deep blond color of pure gold and thick and luxurious. Mrs. Cooper a shrewd woman—whose parlor and upstairs rooms were full of beautiful furniture and bric-a-brac that I can still visualize. She was the business woman of the family. I remember her husband, a stout man with sideburns who let the wife run the house. There were few if any places where important colored people could stay in N.Y. and of them, Mrs. Cooper's was known as the outstanding place. She dressed elegantly and yet couldn't read. But she could figure and save. She told me that she pleaded with my mother when she saw a romance developing between my father and mother. She talked about the color bar existing in America about which my mother had known nothing. My mother seemed to care less. In fact, like her mother before her, she was a rebel against arbitrary social distinctions. Mrs. Cooper impressed [me] as a child with her sincere love for my mother. I couldn't understand it all but it made me like Mrs. Cooper. Mrs. Cooper's practicality and her admiration for my mother made her start match-making for me. She started much too soon in my development to speak of my marrying her son. He was the apple of her eye. She called him "Booty"—baby-talk for beauty. He was a good-natured stupid "marvy" boy and I liked to romp and play with him but I, even then, thought him stupid in contrast to my brother who was so smart. Mrs. Cooper was a friend to us until she died.

Now—my father.

In the meantime, my father was the protégé of the immensely rich Fred Stevens family of New York City. His mother had been the expert cook for various branches of that family for years. Only recently I learned, from her death certificate among old legal papers, that her maiden name was Martha Frazier. She came from Morristown N.J. and, as the tintypes

I have [show], she [was] clearly mostly of American Indian blood. She and her husband and his brother had bought the land near Eatontown in the 1850s and early 1860s.

Again, one of the Stevens family noticed that Peter my father was superior to his brothers. Evidently, the cook was allowed to keep her children with her. Her husband had died and she had been left with 5 sons to support. She became a cateress and worked and served in such still-existing fine hostelries as the Hathaway House at Elberon, N.J. Her sons, perforce, grew up in the backwoods, mischievous, without the example of a father in a family. Fortunately, there were some uncles and cousins on adjoining acres who exercised some supervision, so the 5 boys went to the one room school at Pine Brook and never got records of delinquency. But, the main point is that they would not be trained to be good loving husbands for they had no example. And their mother, a strong but stern capable woman, was too pressed to feed and clothe the brood to be able to stay at home and do a complete family job.

Also, Eatontown is in what is still called "horse country." The Homestead of the Johnson family was on the edge of estates of the wealthy where fine horses were and are still bred. Long Branch and Elberon were the Newports of early days. The Monmouth Race Track was and is again on the edge of Eatontown. Understandably, the 5 Johnson boys touched opulence through their mother and through environment. My father especially liked to be around horses. He learned to like the races. This, in his middle age, became a hobby and then a habit. Betting and losing at the races and later owning a stable of horses—with all its retinue and hangers-on—became the cause of his family's doing with less and less. My mother's devotion, thrift and resourcefulness [were] taxed to the limit to counteract the worst effects.

To get back to their courtship and the emotional implications. I've learned to think of the emotions most of all. These are the undoing or the saving forces of personalities. Where not disciplined—lives are ruined.

I now see that my English grandmother must have had compelling emotions that drove her head-long into love affairs. All caution and wisdom cast aside. Her daughter must have had the same compelling emotional make-up.

When she came to America, she lived in one of the great houses in the Washington Square district. One of the servants in the same house was a colored girl. To call on this girl comes a young colored medical student who worked as footman for the Stevens family. It seems that he was quite good-looking—large brown eyes and regular refined features. He was intelligent. The girl he came to see had another beau she liked better. One night, she asked my mother to come down (my mother lived upstairs, being a lady's maid) to the servant's sitting room to entertain Peter Johnson while the other girl slipped out with her beau. That was the beginning. Peter thereafter came to see Bessie and my mother fell head-over-heels in love. My father no doubt was flattered by this English beauty's interest because he was a vain man. This I well know and women were attracted to him. Later it was reason for bitter unhappiness for my mother.

But nothing could deter my mother. Never having loved, the emotion was so compelling she could not resist. Mrs. Cooper advised her. When this unheard of romance reached the ears of their employer, they called in [four illegible lines in original manuscript]. At any rate it was on that order. The employer begged her to let them send her on vacation back to England. There she could think things over. The more they talked about the real problems of marrying a man of a different background and experience and of the horrors of marrying into the Negro race back in the 1880s the more this rebel against convention became determined. Nothing could stop her. So, when my father graduated from Long Island Medical College they married secretly. My father knew he was also going to meet obstacles because of this marriage but he really was spoiled and self centered and was flattered. He wore his marriage lightly and went on living his life without much sacrifice on his part.

I think from what my mother said there was at least one colored woman who thought she was the one he would marry. This was the reason they secretly married. Though pregnant in a short time he shipped her to Chichester,* England, to have her baby in her brother's house. My father's early home life made him unfeeling. He was never affectionate to my mother or to my brother or me. [My mother and father] were married, keeping it secret until my brother was on the way. In the meantime my father was becoming a social "catch."

My mother confided a lot in me when I was old enough. She desperately needed some one to unburden herself to. She told me how rough

*In West Sussex.

the Atlantic was as she went along, ill in the last stages of pregnancy. How deserted she felt that her husband didn't put her and her welfare ahead of the gossips. I can still feel how miserable she must have been. And, all through her marriage, he still showed that he came first. He did not try to make her happy; women always ran after him and as a Dr. he never remained a loyal devoted husband. My mother took what was left and that wasn't much either in love or money. He never fought her battles and she had many. As I grew older, I fought them for her. I remember pushing out a woman who my mother said was only posing as a patient. What a bitter life—she had burned her bridges behind her. She was regarded with contempt by white neighbors until a few learned to respect her for her fine character and behavior. While all the time the hardest work was her lot while her husband used his large earnings for his own sport with horses and women.

Many times, school girls (and the school I attended on 28th Street had all kinds of round [?] girls) would say, "Your mother won't let you go to dances or go out with boys! Some mother. Why don't you kick one"[?] or "I saw you washing windows. How come? Your father's a doctor. Mine isn't and I wouldn't wash windows." I'd answer that I liked to. As a matter of fact, I really never disliked any job. It was always a challenge and I was always trying to work out a better way of doing even menial tasks. I was devoted to and happy with my mother who kept us close to her. As I see now she feared prejudice would wound us. This over-protection was well-meant. She felt it was the least she could do after she had brought us into a hostile world. She fought the idea to the end that she had thus done wrong. But she took all the steps she could to implement a restitution.

While I was helping in the housework I didn't know the reason my mother had to let me do it. I swept and scrubbed and in those days the tools were not vacuums, polishers. A carpet sweeper was the tops. Everything was hard. Later my mother said she had 9 pregnancies altogether. My father was a doctor and he should have known that a dropsical condition causing miscarriages and still-births meant pregnancies should have been prevented. But he was a self-indulgent man all around. My mother was sturdy and strong for many years or she would have died early. I now look back and see that my hard work meant much to her in those trying times. She couldn't help herself. But I do remember that I wasn't resentful to either my mother or father. I even didn't resist the fact that I had to sleep in a small, cold extension that was built out on the back of the house. It was so small that a single bed and a dresser filled the room. It was impossible to keep it as clean as it should be. I always had a cold. I only realized how bad it was when 1 of my "friends" I had allowed in my naivete to see it, brought another of my "friends" to see it. The motive for their visit was made plain by a direct request for me to take them away up 3 floors with no particular reason. Then the quality of the room struck me! How unaware and naive can one be! To this day a bath is not something I look forward to with anticipation and pleasure as many do. It was a necessity. The bathroom was underneath my bedroom in the same cold, exposed extension. It could never be heated properly. No houses were too well heated in those days, except those of the wealthy.

My mother, pinched for money after being reared around wealth and luxury, found in my disposition her main hope. Her English "class" training had led her to marry an educated man. She probably subconsciously felt she was not "throwing herself away" as others who could be objective told her. In England, a doctor is a man to be highly respected. That she knew and she thought it applied here to a colored doctor too. The situation was indeed complex and her life up to her time of marriage (26 years) hadn't fitted her to understand. In fact, she couldn't guide me as I surely needed to be. I remember when I was about to graduate from h.s. my French teacher, only recently over from her native Paris asked me: "Now what are your mother's plans for you?" I told her she hadn't told me. My teacher said: "What can she be thinking of. She surely wouldn't let you stay in this country. Why doesn't she take you to the West Indies." Naive as I still was, I wasn't upset when my mother's reaction was simply silence to my relaying of the above. Now, I can see that she didn't know which way to turn to help her children. She had gone to another country and married. Having to deal with a husband where social customs and values were so different was an insurmountable obstacle. His rearing in America also was so different from hers in England. Why take her daughter, she must have mutely asked herself, to the West Indies? There she'd marry into alien social customs and values. There she'd meet color prejudice when black people become bitter and want to get away and live in emotional revolt. There the status of women makes the man the overbearing master and women mostly for use and convenience. By this time my mother silently realized her ignorance but proudly refused to admit it. Instead she kept saying: "Be proud of yourself. Be the best in this, your race. Help them. It's your duty. You can get ahead here."

Being English, in my mother's plans the son of the family took precedence. He must have the better education and be a gentleman. I can't recall her having made him bear her burdens. He shared a warm room with a lodger. The latter did much to guide my brother in neat habits. 4 other rooms in the house were rented out. My mother and father slept in the room that served also as family parlor and also as waiting room for patients. My father's office was a tiny room under the bath-room—totally inadequate and poorly heated as the rooms above it. Yet he was such a good doctor and so charming to outsiders that in spite of all he had a fine practice. In those days standards of patients and doctors were low as compared to now.

On the other hand my father did not have to struggle to live or get an education. He was a footman to the Stevens family but he didn't work as a footman. He went to school in Newport, Rhode Island. He ate well and had no worries. He spent his time studying and pleased his benefactors. Then they paid his tuition all through L.I. Medical School letting him be a part-time footman in name only. When he graduated, the Stevens family set up his office. Had they known he was secretly married they may not have done so. But his outstanding intelligence intrigued them. The Stevens family connections helped my father too. He was the 3rd colored doctor to practice here. [illegible sentence] The white doctors were glad to turn over all their colored patients to them. My father soon prospered. I look, however, at the property we rented for so long on 33rd Street opposite Penn Station and think of the opportunities he threw away. When he died he left my mother not 1 cent. He left us children the land in N.J. and [an] $800 debt which we paid. It was a bitter thing to my mother and she didn't regret that circumstances had necessitated her being in N.J. when he died. He had brought her no joy. Her spirits were nearly crushed but her head [was] high.

My father's self-centeredness made him indifferent if not hostile to my marrying. He would pilot young doctors (who really came to meet me I learned afterward) into his office at the end of the front hall, talk medicine to them and pilot them out the door. Never once did he say "I'd like you to meet my family." Guess I got an aura of untouchability around me. No telling how many good men I failed to meet. Maybe only those who sized him up dared to venture and they turned out to be the least desirable.

Hard as it is to believe, he permitted one beau to borrow money from him knowing the man wanted it to give me a present. This shiftlessness didn't condemn the man in his eyes. This man was an intellectual—I fell in love with that quality—I realize now that was a failing. I was immature or stunted when it came to knowing about what emotions were desirable in a husband. I thought for many years only of a man's mind and also of his intellectual or professional prestige and accomplishment. I now see what a serious mistake that is. A good husband is a man who makes the most of his capabilities to earn a living. Also, and most important, one whose emotions are healthy. (Very few men or women have wholly healthy and mature emotional development or we wouldn't have such marital misery.)

So my mother turned to me to help. At the end of my h.s. career she suddenly realized I had been trained in the confused and emerging h.s. system of N.Y.C. to be a stenographer and bookkeeper. She said I'd be exposed in office work to unscrupulous employers (of the poor working girl). She repeated often: "Never trust a white man—he means you no good." I remember my first real opposition to my mother came when she emphatically put her foot down and said, "You must be a teacher." I wasn't prepared, but I pushed myself and passed the entrance exam to NY Training College. [illegible words] But my opposition melted in the face of our financial needs. My father said he never wanted me to be a nurse or teacher. But, he made conditions such that I must work—so I took my mother's advice. I liked children and have found the profession a challenge. I found classroom work exhausting and later determined to get into the more rewarding work of vocational guidance and administration. I have really never regretted following my mother's advice.

My first paycheck caused me to stop and ponder. My mother asked me to pay my board. I now realize she had reached the point of breaking. This made me "grow up." I knew then I must be ready to rely upon myself.

Not only that, my brother was making a brilliant record in City College where only a few colored boys had entered. He finished in 3 yrs. My mother dinned in my ear that if my father died (or continued to waste his money) I must stand ready to put my brother through Medical School. I can remember feeling that I was not the favored child but this left no deep wound. I always had the way of handling the problem that was immediate. That is, I crossed the bridge when I came to it. I now realize that a map of the road and a plan would be a better kind of way but that was my disposition. It had served me until then and I never had to help my brother other than relieving my family of my support. My father paid his way in school and I guess was proud of us. Later, when my brother graduated with honor as the first of his race from Columbia University's College of Physicians and Surgeons, he felt rewarded. And my mother's anxieties were relieved and her feeling changed that her life had after all been worth while. He applied to become an intern at Lincoln Hospital but was told by the Board of Directors: "Johnson—we know that you can pass any exam with your record but the time is not right for a colored intern." And the hospital was named after Lincoln! Then his teachers at Columbia began urging him to go into research. They told him he was too brilliant to take on routine practice of medicine.

Here is where my father fatally failed my brother. He wanted him to get to the business of earning money and even more to take over that part of his father's practice which didn't pay well or was pure charity. He resented my brother's up-to-date knowledge. He felt his ego offended when my brother wanted a well appointed office. My father didn't want to deny himself his hobbies and luxuries. This was my brother's undoing. In his rounds as doctor with one charity organization he met the woman who set her cap to get my brother for her daughter. They were white but had found advantages in moving among colored. She was the director of a neighborhood nursery. The marriage was a failure and fatal. My mother now knowing the bitterness of a mixed marriage implored him to wait. But, true to his mother's traits, he went headlong into it. Nothing could stop him. While his wife saw only a "good thing" with a handsome colored fellow whom she treated as an inferior. He was a struggling idealist intellectual and she a gold digger. She used their son as a hostage. In a few short years she had wrecked him with infidelity and greed. He died in 1917 under circumstances that made the light fade entirely from my mother's life. She had had all she could bear.

My father had died in 1914. In the meantime, I had to stand by, helpless to come to the rescue. I had married in 1911. Only my brother had opposed my marrying.

After the wedding plans had been announced, [a] woman had come to my parents to try to stop the marriage. She had loaned McDougald all her savings on his promise to marry her. She shows signs of irrationality in her anger [illegible line]. They faced McDougald and he denied the truth as a lie out of whole cloth.

My leaning toward intellectuals and men with professional prestige was still unchanged. I didn't realize or in fact know much if anything about his background. The time was so short before the wedding, the excitement and scandal surrounding the announcement confused me. I should have listened to my brother and not my parents. But I went into it with a foolhardy bearing, thinking I was loyal to the one I had promised (though my compulsive emotions had been wounded). I felt I could by my endurance and example bring all the factors to a good end and a successful marriage. Here, true to my inheritance, I was naive and unrealistic. The background of McDougald was as foreign to my N.Y.C. environment as was America to my mother or as might have been the West Indies that my French teacher suggested. He was the creature of a crude and cruel back country farm upbringing. His appraisal of women was low—they were work-horses and to be breeders of children. The men in his environment were self-indulgent both as to work and sex life. The latter colored their thinking. And, their thoughts about sex had nothing in them of kindness and graciousness and tenderness. Mistreatment was to be accepted and endured. I had to continue to work, as he was in debt, not to that 1 woman but several others—all of the humble domestic type. I had loaned him all I had saved in my 6 years of teaching. This he felt was his due—sort of a dowry like African men expected.

But I, even in my predicament, began to think of the meaning of things. I had to earn a living—my brother said he was so disgusted he wouldn't help me because McDougald would get the benefit and sit down completely. My parents helped by having me come home to have the 1st baby. But there was no love any more. McDougald had no training in love. He had grown up unsupervised in a back country. He showed no evidence of having lived in a well-ordered house with a mother, tenderly treated and cared for. But, somewhere, the whole family had gotten pride in their superiority in that particular environment. And, in that superior feeling, they had all cultivated meanness and base thoughts. They gave me enough hints of this by an unfriendly attitude toward the marriage. I met only one brother, the doctor, and one half brother who was in N.Y.C when I married. The others I avoided like the plague.

My mother stood by me—she had nowhere else to turn. I regret to this day that my burdens had to be shared with her in her old age. I regret that I did not bring a husband to her that could have eased the pain and loss of her son. Instead, my husband treated her with scorn, bedded in his southern customs toward white women who married colored. I regret that my children did not have the care and protection of a mature and responsible father. And too that I could not be a complete full-time mother but a bread-winner, harassed and tormented by a wicked and selfish foolish man.

I am proud of the accomplishments of my daughter and my son. Their happiness and welfare were what I strived for. Every effort I've made—to push toward conserving what [little] was left me—toward not being a burden to them and toward saving my earnings—has had them in mind.

And, I married again at the urging of my widowed mother. She grieved that she would—when she died—leave me alone with no relatives at all. That helped me fall in love again. And of course with an intellectual and a doctor with prestige of family and upbringing. Though devotion to his divorced mother has been almost neurotic, he has been an honorable disciplined man whose kind attitude, at least, to my children has been a source of comfort.

The Handicapped

Jocelyn Jessups stood in the swaying doorway of the Jim Crow car as the train was slowing down for the next halt at Pinewood. All the prettiness had been wiped out of her face, leaving it glowering, youthless. Save, now and then, for a faint flickering just under the skin in the left cheek, it was immobile.

Her eyes were not pleasant to remember afterwards. As a rule, the disillusionment of youth is a gradual and a comparatively painless process. In less than one hour, Jocelyn had met life, naked—face to face—and her eyes were not pleasant to remember.

Behind her stretched the now empty length of the car. To her over-wrought and obsessed mind, it was no longer a car but a malignant personality; and although she kept her face painfully to the front, she could feel its presence behind her. She could feel its breath, its covert and obscene touch along her spine. A sudden nausea left her clinging, shuddering and shut-eyed, to the door jamb.

In front of her with her new bag (that no longer looked new) on the platform beside him the porter stood with his not over-clean grey uniformed back to her. He was a short, black man who clearly took himself very seriously. He balanced himself with his slipshod feet rather wide apart[,] above his yellowed collar there was a disgusting yet fascinating bulge of fat and above that a deep crease. These being on a level with her eyes demanded her reluctant attention. Above the slowing down noises

---

Source: Unpublished manuscript, Moorland-Spingarn Research Center, Howard University, n.d. Text has been abridged to delete repetitious sections.

of the train she could hear him whistling. Like many of his race he whistled beautifully—so beautifully in fact that it hurt to hear him. Strange to say, he intruded this as an assumption of equality—with her.

"Dere ain't no yaller wimmin goin' to put it ova me," he said [to himself]. "Ah'll show'em. Gib me tin centses will ya, to kerry yo' bags. Huh! Ahm'nt use to ten centses, ah ain't. Ah deals in quarters, masef. No cheap yaller wimmin in mine."

Jocelyn, recovering from her vertigo could not help smiling, if palely, at the aggressive disapproval of herself expressed in every line of that shabby back. It would have been hard to misunderstand it.

"Why you funny, little fat-necked man," she thought, "If you only knew how very much I needed that ten cents you'd give me a nice shiny quarter and your blessing. Imagine a porter tipping and blessing the passengers. Stranger things than that have happened as I am still alive to prove. Oh, well, as the funny papers would say, 'Cheer up, little Jocelyn, perhaps the worst is yet to be.'"

Between the two cars, in the space to right and left, could be seen stretches of pine woods, brassy sunlight, and orange colored earth. The straight slim trunks whizzed by so swiftly that they made her blink and turn her eyes away.

[She] had forgotten the flies. They had hounded her during the early morning and now were engaged in taking a most affectionate farewell of her. They buzzed around her, lit, and stuck to the flesh. The porter was plentifully sprinkled with them but he did not seem to mind them much. She noticed with loathing that they enjoyed the hill of fat above his collar.

The cinders fell in a sharp rain upon her bag and the platform. Now and then one struck her on the cheek. She narrowed her eyes defensively. If she dared not look back at the empty car within [nor] did she dare to look down at her badly mussed and wrinkled waist* and skirt. One glance had been enough. She had not the courage to look again. Months of small savings had gone to the buying of this suit. Carefully and reverently it had been put away and kept for this journey. It was as though the Jim Crow car had soiled and shriveled body and soul, even the very clothes she wore. To one who is constitutionally immaculate, the shadow of uncleanness is a source of positive unhappiness. What then would be the suffering of such a one thus mercilessly exposed? And this is only one of the small humiliations of the Jim Crow car.

*Shirtwaist, or blouse.

The train's pace grew slower. There was a different sound and looking out to the right Jocelyn saw a rough wooden platform. There was a jolting, sudden stop that threw her and her sharp-handled umbrella forcibly against [the porter's] back.

To her quick, "Oh! Excuse me, please," there was no response. Insult was now added to injury. Carelessly dragging and bumping her precious bag along the steps he swung himself off the car and threw it down with a thud. He made no attempt to help her alight.

Out on the hot platform Jocelyn looked around swiftly; but there was no one to meet her, an utter stranger. With a great effort she checked a wave of pity for herself. Pride stood her friend.

"I probably was right," she thought, "the worst is yet to be."

Besides herself and the train man, there was no one on the platform. From the baggage coach just ahead, her trunk was literally thrown out. She congratulated herself that it was strong, and the strap, new. A stream of tobacco juice followed the trunk and just missed it.

Diffidently and rather wistfully, she turned towards the now animated porter who was extremely busy grinning and making unintelligible sounds to another porter leaving from a car below.

"Could you . . ." she began in a faint little voice.

"Deed ah couldn't," he answered drawling and swung himself back onto the car. He ostentatiously took a seat on her side near the window (without, however, looking at her) and proceeded to give his face and neck a most thorough mopping into a much abused handkerchief. How much industry did she expect for ten cents[?]

The conductor looked up and down the platform importantly and fussily. He was a short, apoplectic-looking man with puffy eyes, a listless clay-colored mustache, much in need of trimming, a heavy rope-like watch chain and a gold ring on his left hand. He was wearing a blue suit into which he had forced the lumpiness of his body with much seam-stretched difficulty. As the train began to move, he caught sight of Jocelyn.

"Some looka theah for a nigger," he wheezed jocosely to the brake-man. "Eyah! She'll pass."

They leered condescendingly at her as they passed. Their eyes wandered over her desirously from her head to her feet.

The insult of it all sent the hot red into her cheeks.

"Oh! no, I'm not to miss anything, it seems," she said bitterly, "not even that."

The train was gone. She and her trunk were alone.

Presently the square end of the last car was only a diminishing speck down the straight bright rails. There was certainly no one to meet her.

"My! There isn't any place anywhere any hotter than this," she said aloud, for overhead out of a cloudless, very-blue sky, the September sun was pouring down in a perfect deluge. The air was humid and heavy with the scrub of the pines. There was no breeze; and it was very quiet. At first the heat and the stillness, so pronounced after the buffeting train sounds and motion, left her somewhat dazed. Then she looked around.

Beside her a space had been cleared of trees from the platform to a dusty highway running parallel to it and some twenty yards distant. Pine woods began again at either end of the platform, proceeded along the edge of the clearing, jumped the road, and marched on thickly again along the opposite side of the way. They formed the sides of a hollow square, the platform being the fourth. The road plunged out of the gloom and then into it again. The space was decidedly nasty in appearance, the hacked faces of the trees protruding everywhere—disfigured nodules. For some reason one partially dead pine tree had been left near the center of the square.

On the opposite side of the double rails was another pinewood platform and midway on it an extremely crude little box of a building, evidently the station, for over the one door was a large sign upon which was painted "Pinewood." Behind this was the loop of a very dusty orange-colored road. Beyond this again was a hill covered completely with nothing but very dead yellow grass. There on the side of the hill Jocelyn saw the strangest little house her New England eyes had ever seen. It was whitewashed, shot up for two brief storeys and stood on stilts. From underneath it as she watched, a yellow, harassed, yelping dog appeared, an extremely dirty child in pursuit.

This eruption started a tremendous squawking and cackling also beneath the house, followed presently by something of a whirlwind of flapping wings and feathers and flying fowls of all ages and conditions. Two rather small black animals with much grunting and swift aimless spurts of running added their part to the general uncomfortable confusion. She later learned that these last animals were Southern pigs.

Suddenly Jocelyn found she was not alone. A tall lanky man holding a white flag in his only hand came out to see what the outburst of noise meant. He was just in time to see the yellow dog bolting for the protection of the stilts again and the child still in pursuit scattering the now thoroughly outraged fowls. The man was clad in a dark undershirt and dark blue jeans with suspender attachments. The right arm was gone from the shoulder. He was trying to hold up the white flag by wrapping it around the stick. His face, bare left arm, and stringy hair were all [the color] of an unhealthy saffron tea.

"Golly, that boy," he said spitting much and evincing great pride. A wad of tobacco appeared and disappeared in either cheek as he ponderously worked his lean jaws.

"Golly, that boy," she heard him [again] say proudly. After quiet was restored to the house on the hill [the man] turned and gave her a cursory glance. After much expectorating and lazy eyeing of her he said, in a colorless flat drawl,

"School?"

"What?" she said sharply, again abruptly on the defensive.

More chewing and expectorating followed now and then. The hot rail hissed back as he aimed true.

"School?" he asked again adding this time the double gesture of jerking his head and thumb backward.

"Oh," she said, finally enlightened. "Am I going to school?"

There followed another animated pause. Finally he vouchsafed.

"Uh huh."

"Do you—can I—do you think—I could walk there?"

He grinned.

"How far is it?" she asked quickly.

"A long about ten miles."

"How am I to get there, then?"

"Know'd you comin'?"

"Yes."

"Better wait then. Some one come for you, I reckon, afore sundown."

They eyed each other. Finally she leaned over wearily and picked up her bag. Just as she started to cross the rails he said,

"Say."

"Yes."

"Where you goin'?"

"Isn't there a chair in the—in the station?"

"Ahuh!"

"Well, I'll wait there until someone comes."

"No, you won't."

"Why?"

"Cause why? Tain't for niggers. Dat's why."

He watched her warily, but still indifferently. Jocelyn paled.

"Where may I wait, then?" she said in a hard, quiet voice.

"Uh," he said slowly, "round."

"What do you mean by around?"

"Theah seem to be plenty of nice soft tree trunks ovah yondah, and lots of pine needles, and far as I can see, lots of ground." He waved his one scrawny yellow hand around aimlessly. "You can tek your chice. Come to think on it, I reckon that ain't no law agin you'h setting undah that pine tree back of you. He had indicated the lone tree in the clear space. Hep yer sef. Say, air you a teacher up at that school? Huh? If you are, you're the only good lookin' yaller woman I ever seen goin' thrah. Say . . ."

"Are you sure," Jocelyn interrupted in a sharp, tremulous voice, "that this pine tree is a Jim Crow tree? I should hate to make a mistake."

"Ho! Ho! Ho!" greeted her. "That's good, that sure is good. Jim Crow tree! Yeah, that's a Jim Crow tree, all right. You ask who comes for you if that ain't a Jim Crow tree. Say! You say to 'um Mister Benson tole yer to ask. Ho! Ho! Ho!"

The "Ho! Ho! Ho!" was muttered in a loud, toneless round expulsion out of a perfectly expressionless face. Such laughter Jocelyn had never heard and prayed never to again. She took off her hat, [sat down], and leaning her head back against the tree shut her eyes. It was very quiet, and sweet-smelling and soothing under the pine tree and soon Jocelyn was falling asleep.

Suddenly an abhorrent but distant "Ho! Ho! Ho!" startled [her] into a bundle of taut nerves again. She looked around quickly and found she had an audience of four at the house on the hill; Mister Benson, Mrs. Benson, young Master Benson and even his royal highness the mongrel, yellow dog. They were all watching the new "nigger" teacher under the Jim Crow pine. A slow scorching hatred welled up in her soul and overflowed into her eyes.

"They're not worth it," she said grimly and leaning back again closed her eyes. Several tears slipped out from under the closed lids. There were only five of them. Would, by any chance, God record those five tears? Probably not, certainly not America's God. The little yellow mongrel dog could have gone into that box of a station and might have set carefree on the chair. Jocelyn Jessups, a refined, cultivated woman might have been lynched for such a presumption. No, America's God would not record those tears and the millions upon millions of tears shed by a dark race since the year 1619* Anno Domini—in the year of our Lord.

An hour afterwards, or perhaps less, a sound aroused her. She peered around the tree trunk. A man, but not Mister Benson, was standing in front of the station. He was Indian-brown in color, tall, large of frame, not over burdened with flesh. His Scotch Tweed suit was well made, but not new and in need of a pressing. He was mopping first the sweat band of his straw hat and then his forehead. In the meantime he was plainly looking for somebody, and without doubt that somebody was herself. Over and over again this eyes made the same circular journey, beginning and ending with the trunk. He did not see her behind the tree. Finally he put on his hat, crossed the tracks to the trunk and examined the name on the end. Reassured as to its identity he looked around again. And then suddenly his eyes came straight at her. Both stiffened under that look and neither was pleased at the fact. With face grim and with very apparent reluctance he approached her.

"I am very sorry," he said patiently, "to have been so late. You see, the principal intended to send someone else; but at the last moment he found that I was the only one who could come. I was rather busy but finally . . ."

"Oh! Never mind," she cut him off irritably. "Don't make any more excuses, please. I understand. Your overanxiety—to meet me is rather apparent. Do we walk the ten miles—and which one of us carries the trunk?"

"We ride. Some one is coming for your trunk now. My name is James Martin."

They proceeded silently side by side to the station on the opposite side of the rails. He climbed [into the buggy] and sat beside her. [They began moving.]

"Now, Mr. Martin, would you mind driving around the corner there to the very best and most expensive restaurant in town?"

"Are you hungry?" he demanded sharply.

"I ate all I had brought with me then and . . ."

"Yes."

"I couldn't get any more."

*The year the slave trade began in the United States. See John Hope Franklin, *From Slavery to Freedom: A History of American Negroes* (New York: Knopf, 1947),chap. 6.

"Why?"

"They wouldn't serve me at the station where I had to change trains. And they very thoughtlessly neglected to add a diner to the Jim Crow car. Inconsiderate of them, wasn't it? I didn't know very much about being colored before yesterday. I think I do now."

He lifted up the warm buggy cushion and began feeling around in the space beneath the seat. Presently he brought to light a large white shoe box neatly tied up with cord. He replaced the cushion.

With trembling fingers Jocelyn lifted off the cover. For a few minutes she could say nothing. Her lips quivered and her lashes were again wet. In the box were three large brown-shelled hard-boiled eggs, a bottle of creamy coffee, six delicious looking crustless bread and butter sand-wiches, and a little spotlessly white fringed napkin.

"I hope," she said at last rather tremulously, although she was smiling, "for your sake I'm not going to c-cry. I don't w-want to, but nothing ever looked so good b-before. Kindness never made me silly like this before. I'm s-so glad this shoe box belonged to someone with awfully b-big feet."

[Gaining her composure she remarked,] "And this is the glorious South, is it? What are those trees there?"

"Where?—Oh, those are the live oak."

"What is that growing on them?"

"Moss."

"I have read about that. It is beautiful."

They were both silent for a while; both were thinking. Each, so early in their acquaintance, could pay the tribute of a comfortable silence to the other. Both faces had the sad, long-suffering expression common to their race where the face is in repose.

Abruptly he turned finally and almost flung at her the question:

"Why did you come?"

"I had to," she said simply. "I'm poor."

"You have no relatives?"

"No." There was a pause.

"My mother died three years ago. I tried," she went on presently, "to get a position in the North. I had studied Domestic Science; but although there was plenty of demand for teachers in that line, they didn't seem to need me. That was the beginning of my education as a colored girl. I was born and brought up in a little New England village; there wasn't much prejudice there, virtually none. Business competition opened my eyes to it. Well, I managed to get little things to do. Then I read of this school and applied for a position and was accepted. Now you know why I came."

"It's the same old story," he said half to himself.

"What do you mean?"

"I mean most of us at the school could tell about the same story. They could tell it at all the hundreds of Southern schools too, I daresay. The story may differ in the details but the main facts are the same."

"Is that your story?" she asked softly.

"Yes. I'm an electrical engineer—and a good one. That isn't conceit either. One of the professors who was noted for his eccentricities and plain speaking said to me once, "Martin, you're a fool to study this profession. There is no square deal in it for you." And then he added, "It's a damned shame too." I was young and hopeful and wouldn't believe him. I graduated at the head of my class. Oh! they had to acknowledge that much. And then I started answering applications. As with you when they saw me I wasn't needed. Some were polite and nervous; some were brutally rude; some evinced a vulgar curiosity concerning me, tried to patronize me.

One man said he couldn't employ a colored man in such a position, he didn't believe in encouraging a race to climb above its place. He offered me a good position as his butler, though. He seemed hurt and surprised at my curt refusal. As I was leaving he put a pudgy hand on my arm and said unctuously, "Young man, you are making a great mistake—a great mistake. You must take your haughty spirit and your ambition to the good Lord in prayer. You must pray to him to make you humble. The negro race was made to be a servant for the white race. You must ask the Lord to teach you that." I shook off his hand and looked him up and down. He cowered away. "Damn your God then," I said and turned and left. I was afraid to stay longer. There was murder in my heart. He paused.

Jocelyn now understood all the bitterness and grimness in his face.

"As with you I finally did anything I could. When I had only ten dollars left I bought a revolver. I thought I was in a blind pocket. I had no relatives, as far as I know. I was a foundling. One morning while I was looking at the revolver the landlady called up that there was a letter for me. It was from Mr. Bishop and offering me a position here in his school. We had been friends of a sort. I wrote back telling him I couldn't accept because I hadn't the car fare. He loaned me the money, and here I am. I teach grammar and geography and arithmetic. I have been here ten years. Some day they'll bury me and the farce will be over.

"It sounds inadequate to say I'm sorry; but you understand. It's worse for you than for me. I didn't really love domestic science and you did your profession."

"It was all I had," he said simply.

"Do you know Mr. Benson?" [Jocelyn ventured.]

"The station master?—I do." The "I do" was grim.

"What did he mean by telling me to ask whoever came for me why this pine tree I was sitting under was a Jim Crow pine?"

"Did he say that?" he said slowly.

"Yes."

"I don't know what he meant," he said, but he did not look at her.

"Why [don't] you tell the truth?"

"Well," he said, "the truth isn't a pretty story."

"I can stand anything now."

"A young and good looking colored girl who lived in one of those houses we passed a half mile or so from the station accused Mr. Benson of insulting her. She was excited, I suppose, and said a good many things. One night Mr. Benson and some of his cronies went to the house, dragged her out of bed and carried [her] down to the station. They saturated her night clothes with kerosene oil and set her on fire. They tied her so she couldn't get away. A colored woman who lived within hearing distance has been a raving maniac ever since. Then they strung her up to the tree. Mr Benson, I understand that he has one of her ears put away as a memento. Also, I hear others say the same. I told you it wasn't a pretty story."

"Oh!" Jocelyn said and then after a long time, "Oh."

"You shouldn't have insisted," he said kindly.

"I don't regret knowing. It's not that but why didn't the law interfere?"

"Mr. Benson is a sheriff, Miss Jessups."

"There is no redress, then?"

"None, whatever."

"And her story was true?"

"Undoubtedly."

"I wonder," she said slowly, "whether I shall ever be able to pray again. How can God let such things happen?"

"God has forgotten us, Miss Jessups."

There was no attempt made to lighten the gloom this time. They rode along, their faces set and bitter and dark. For twenty minutes at least there was not a sound, save the thud of the horse's hoof and the creak of the harness.

At last he turned to her.

"Shan't I laugh now?" he suggested.

She shook her head. "Oh no! Not after that. And that was only one case, I suppose there are hundreds like that aren't there?"

He assented sadly.

"How do we laugh at all, I wonder," she said in a low voice. "The horror of it."

"And I thought," she said with a twisted little smile "my experience in the station at B—— and in the Jim Crow car could not possibly be any worse. Why, I was lucky."

"You had an unpleasant time?" His voice was tense though quiet.

"I did," she [breathed] and shut her mouth tightly.

"Tell me," he said gently.

"When I reached B—— I was hungry. My head ached. I had not eaten since eleven or twelve as I told you. I walked into the restaurant and took a seat. The place was thrown into consternation. They were so astounded at first that they couldn't even move. Then the cashier, I judge, beckoned to a waiter. They were both terribly excited. Finally the waiter came to me and said loudly and brutally, 'What are you doing in here? Don't you know we don't serve your kind?' Well, there was nothing to do but go out. I remember nothing but unfriendly and horror-stricken eyes. They were everywhere. I was afraid I would faint before I reached the door, but I didn't. I couldn't have eaten anyway. So much for B——.

"When the train was ready I was of course directed to the Jim Crow car. There was a woman with a sick baby there and four men. The men had been drinking. The train started. I had always been used to clean things. Every bit of that car was unspeakable—but then you know. I tried to help the woman with the sick baby all I could. It kept calling for water. There was no water in the tank at the end of the car. I spoke to the porter and then to the conductor. They both said it was not possible to get any then. 'But,' I said to the conductor, 'the child may die.'

"'Good thing,' he said, 'one nigger less.'

"I didn't say any more. The woman and I were both thirsty too. The four men were having a hilarious time. They were drinking. I had to pass them once and one offered me a drink. They didn't say anymore. The woman and I were both thirsty too. They didn't mean to be rude, they were too drunk." I did take some for the baby though. It didn't do any good, for it died. The rest of the time that heart-broken woman held the child in her arms. She covered its face and whenever the conductor or porter went by she talked to it and hushed it. She said she was afraid that if they found out it was dead they might throw them both off.

"About twelve o'clock the poor dazed woman and her dead boy and the four men all got off. I was left entirely alone. As I was trying to make myself comfortable and get a little sleep something made me look at the door. A white man was lurking outside and eyeing me. I tell you that man's eyes made me afraid. He was well-dressed, middle-aged, and what I suppose the whites would call a gentleman. He opened the door and strolled by me still eyeing me. I heard the door shut at the other end and believed him gone. Presently he strolled by me again and looked back as he passed. He took his position again outside the door in front of me and watched. Again he opened the door and passed. He was still smoking. Once he paused beside me but only to use the spittoon. The more I saw of his eyes the more afraid I became. When the conductor went by I complained to him. He laughed: 'You're lucky,' he said, 'he's a big gun. Better make the most of it.' I was sick with shame. Well, he must have passed me some twenty times when he finally stopped and spoke. I can't tell you what he said. When he had finished I took this hat pin out of my hat and I said, 'Now you had better go, for if you don't go away, as God is my witness I'll kill you.' He saw that I meant what I said and slunk away. He didn't bother me any more. But when you tell me about that poor girl, I wonder that I am here."

"Sometime—, sometime—," Martin said. He spoke with difficulty and his nostrils were dilated. He said no more.

"What are those other buildings on the hill there?" Jocelyn asked [changing the subject suddenly.]

Martin was in a deep study and he started.

"Oh! That is Lakewood. We are almost there."

"I don't think I shall ever forget this ride," she said.

"Nor I."

"So you don't like women, Mr. Martin," she said. She was smiling again.

"How did you guess?"

"Ask me something easy."

"But you will like me," she said confidently and sweetly.

"I am afraid so," he said to himself.

ESTHER POPEL

Flag Salute

(Note: In a classroom in a Negro school a pupil gave as his news topic during the opening exercises of the morning, a report of the Princess Anne lynching of October 18, 1933. A brief discussion of the facts of the case followed, after which the student in charge gave this direction: pupils, rise, and give the flag salute! They did so without hesitation!)

"*I pledge allegiance to the flag*"—
They dragged him naked
Through the muddy streets,
A feeble-minded black boy!
And the charge? Supposed assault
Upon an aged woman!
"*Of the United States of America*"—
One mile they dragged him
Like a sack of meal,
A rope around his neck,
A bloody ear
Left dangling by the patriotic hand
Of Nordic youth! (A boy of seventeen!)
"*And to the Republic for which it stands*"—
And then they hanged his body to a tree,
Below the window of the county judge
Whose pleadings for that battered human flesh
Were stifled by the brutish, raucous howls
Of men, and boys, and women with their babes,

Brought out to see the bloody spectacle
Of murder in the style of '33!
(Three thousand strong, they were!)
"One Nation, Indivisible"—
To make the tale complete
They built a fire—
What matters that the stuff they burned
Was flesh—and bone—and hair—
And reeking gasoline!
"With Liberty—and Justice"—
They cut the rope in bits
And passed them out,
For souvenirs, among the men and boys!
The teeth no doubt, on golden chains
Will hang
About the favored necks of sweethearts, wives,
And daughters, mothers, sisters, babies, too!
"For ALL!"

Source: The Crisis 41 (August 1934): 231.

Blasphemy—American Style

Look, God,
We've got a nigger here
To burn;

A goddam nigger,
And we're goin' to plunge
His cringin' soul
To Hell!

Now watch him
Squirm and wriggle
While we swing him
From this tree!

And listen, God,
You'll laugh at this
I know—

He wants to pray
Before we stage
This show!

He's scared
And can't remember
What to say—

Imagine, God,
A nigger tryin'
To pray!

Lean over, God,
And listen while we tell
This fool

The words
He couldn't even
Spell!

"Our Father
Who art in Heaven,"
(Say it again!)

"Thy will be done
On earth . . ." (Laugh, God!)
"Amen!"

To Hell with him!
Come on, men,
Swing him high!

A prayin' nigger,
Golly—
Watch him die!

Source: Opportunity 12 (December 1934): 368.

October Prayer

Change me, oh God,
Into a tree in autumn
And let my dying
Be a blaze of glory!

Drape me in a
Crimson, leafy gown,
And deck my soul
In dancing flakes of gold!

And then when Death
Comes by, and with his hands
Strips off my rustling garment
Let me stand

Before him, proud and naked,
Unashamed, uncaring,
All the strength in me revealed
Against the sky!

Oh, God
Make me an autumn tree
If I must die!

Source: Opportunity 11 (October 1933): 295.

MARION VERA CUTHBERT

Mob Madness

Lizzie watched Jim stir his coffee. Her eyes were wide with fever and horror. Around and around he stirred, and the thin stuff slopped over and filled the saucer. But he did not notice because he was talking to their son.

"Shore, we got 'im at the very spot I showed you and Jeff. Lem would 'o slit his throat right then, but the fellers back on the pike was waitin' an' wanted to be in on it, too, so we drug 'im out o' the brush. The boys wanted ter git at 'im to once, but some o' the more experienced on 'em cooled us down. You was there last night, so you know as much o' that end o' it as anybody."

He turned to the neglected coffee now and downed it in great gulps. The thirteen year old boy watched, his face set in a foolish grin of admiration and wonder.

"Jeff said he heard a man down to the square say you all got the wrong nigger. Said this one didn't do it."

"Guess he did it all right. An' if he didn't, one of the black ——— stretched out Ole Man Dan'l, an' the smell o' this one roastin' will teach the rest o' em they can't lay hands on a white man, b'Gawd!"

"Les see the toe again."

The man took a filthy handkerchief out of his overalls pocket, and unwrapped carefully a black object.

Lizzie swayed, and fearing to fall against the hot woodstove, sank into a chair.

Then Jim and the boy finished breakfast and went out.

Source: The Crisis 43 (April 1936): 108, 114.

For a long time Lizzie sat in the chair. After a while she got up shakily and went in the other room. Little Bessie was still sleeping heavily. She was ailing and her mother had been up with her most of the night.

But she would have been up all of that night, that terrible night, anyway. Neighbors had run in on their way to the square to ask her if she was not going too.

She was not going.

Jim had come in long past midnight, little Jim with him. His eyes were bloodshot. She would have believed him drunk, but there was no smell of liquor on him. The boy was babbling incoherently.

"Maw, you should a seed it!"

Big Jim shut him up. The two fell into bed and slept at once.

After a time it was day, and Lizzie moved like a sick woman to get breakfast.

She stood looking down now on little Bessie. The child's yellow hair had fallen across her face. This she brushed back and looked for a long time on the thin little oval of a face. The purple veined eyelids were closed upon deep blue-gray eyes. Lizzie's own mother had said she was the living image of little Bessie when she was a child. Delicate and finicky. But when she was sixteen she had married six-foot, red-faced Jim. He was always rough, but men seemed all like that. She did not know then that he would . . .

After a little while the child awoke. She gave her some breakfast, but would not let her get up. Allie Sneed from next door ran in.

"Everything's as quiet as kin be this mornin'. Not a nigger on the street. Lizzie you missed it last night!"

Jim drove the truck for the store. He had gone to Terryville and did not come for lunch. Little Jim came in, swallowed his food and was off. It was cold, so Lizzie kept the woodstove going smartly. She held little Bessie in her arms and rocked back and forth. All day she had not eaten, but she was not hungry. She rocked back and forth.

. . . they got it down in the brush on the other side of the branch. . . . They took It into the woods . . . at dark they tied It to a car and dragged It back to the town . . . at the square they piled up a huge bonfire . . .

. . . Jim had helped by bringing crates from the store . . .

. . . they had cut parts of It away . . .

. . . Jim had something black in a handkerchief . . .

. . . then they put what was left of It on the fire . . . their house was quite a way from the square, but she had heard the shouting. Every house around was emptied . . .

. . . once her brother had had an argument with another man. They fought, and pulled knives on each other. Both were cut pretty badly and they feared the other man would die. But she never shrank from her brother after that. All hot words and anger. He did not shout, crazy. Afterwards he did not brag . . .

. . . they did not fight It . . . they caught It like an animal in the brush . . . if It had been an animal they would have killed It at once . . . but this they took in the woods . . . before they killed It outright they cut off Its fingers and toes . . . Jim had something black in a handkerchief . . .

She put the child back in bed and went out in the yard to pump some water. She leaned her hot face against the porch post. In the dark by the fence something moved. It came nearer.

"Mis' Lizzie? O my Gawd, Mis' Lizzie! Dey burned me out las' night. Ah bin hidin' in de shacks by de railroad. Waitin' fo' de dahk. You allays good to us po' cullud people. Hope yo' Jim put me in de truck an' take me to Terryville tonight. Tell 'im he'p me, Mis' Lizzie, tell 'im he'p me!"

She could only stare at her. The voice of the black woman seemed far away, lost in the shouting in her head.

Their home was quite a way from the square, but she had heard the shouting.

The voice of the black woman seemed to go away altogether. So Lizzie went inside and began supper.

Soon after Jim came home and ate his supper. He was weary and dour. As soon as he was through he went to bed, and the boy, too.

Lizzie sat by the fire. Little Bessie was better and sleeping soundly.

. . . if Jim had not been so tired he would have come to her.

. . . he did not yet know she was going to have another child. This child, little Bessie, and little Jim, and a father who helped catch a Thing in the brush . . . and cut off the quivering flesh. It seemed that all the men in the town had thought this a good thing to do. The women, too. They had all gone down to the square. . . .

. . . little Jim was like his father. The other day he had spoken sharp to her. As big Jim so often did. He said she was too soft and finicky for her own good. Most boys were like Jim. When little Bessie grew up she would marry a boy like this . . .

. . . when little Bessie grew up . . .

. . . some boy who could touch her soft, fair flesh at night, and go forth into the day to hunt a thing in the brush, and hack at its flesh alive . . .

Lizzie looked and looked at the child. She remembered things which she had thought were true when she was a child. She was a woman now, and she knew that these things were not true. But she had thought they were true when she was a child.

The fire in the stove went down, then out. She made no effort to replenish it. Toward morning she went to the table drawer and took something out. She went into the other room and looked down on the uncouth figures of the sprawling man and boy. It was over the boy that she finally bent, but she straightened at once remembering that the man and boy were one. So she turned to the little girl, and the lifted blade of steel did not gleam any more.

Jim had had a good rest and awakened early. He found the bodies, already cold.

When the shock of the first terror let him find his voice he declared he would kill with his own hands every black man, woman and child within a hundred miles of town. But the sheriff made him see that it was not murder. All this she had done with her own hand.

"She didn't touch me ner the boy. When they go mad like this, some-times they wipes out all."

Out in the yard Allie Sneed said to an awestruck group, "I know it was somethin' wrong with her when she held back from seein' the burnin'. A rare, uncommon sight, that, and she hid in her house, missin' it."

OTTIE B. GRAHAM

Slackened Caprice

Coming home from a long journey, I stopped with Carlotta at a southern city to visit an old friend of her mother's. The trip had been wearisome and we were glad of the few hours to stretch our limbs and rest. The place we wanted was easily reached, and when we arrived there it was so beautiful and still that a feeling of rest came over us in spite of our fatigue.

On the porch was a man standing before a bird cage. He was quiet, with his hands behind him, and he saw only the bird. We walked up the steps and spoke to him before he turned to notice us. He was too old to be young and too young to be even middle-aged. His eyes were soft, very kind and soft, and his smile was slow. He started to speak, but a woman came hurriedly out of the house, interrupting with a laugh and a greeting. She was his mother and the friend Carlotta had come to see. She welcomed us and led us to a sitting-room; then she asked us to excuse her for a few minutes. Her girl was burning something.

As she left the room by one door, her son entered by another. He had us make ourselves comfortable and brought us a cool drink of fruit juice. He sat and talked with us, saying himself very little but making us say much. I believe we were talking about a relative of his or about somebody's new position when he asked very abruptly, "How do you find people as you travel? Are they at all care-free?" His question was directed to Carlotta, but she had chance only for a philosophical, "Well," before he had apparently forgotten that the question was ever in his mind.

Source: Opportunity 1 (November 1924): 332–335.

"Do you like music?" he asked quite as suddenly as he had made the first query. We said yes, of course.

"Then I shall play for you," he announced very quietly, and without more ado went to the piano. Once seated, he thought no more about us, and his long, bony fingers lifted and sped across the keyboard. For a moment they reminded me of slender, swiftly driven horses. I remember smiling inwardly as I thought that, because the idea seemed far-fetched; but there was something about him that made me draw far-fetched figures. He trilled and lilted through passages as light and airy as flying fairy down. There was something of Grieg wonder in them, but they were not Grieg. Glad, laughing measures repeated themselves, splashing in patches of sharp brilliancy throughout the ascending movement. Then, with what seemed something of reluctance in the long, bony fingers, the allegro stopped its prancing and quieted to a soberer swing. It did not cease descending; it came down, down, losing its gay fire, until only a sweet, crying melody remained. This melody was not at all akin to the start of the composition. Sweet and soft, even yearning, as though it would dance but could not, it merely sang. Here was something of Taylor plaintiveness, but it was not Taylor. And the slender fingers, stopped in their fleet gallop, caressed now tenderly the keys over which they had just sped.

This change of tone and tempo, though beautiful, was to me unusual and I wondered about it as I listened. So engrossed in his rendition was the man, he seemed actually to suffer from his tenseness. His brows raised in despairing frowns which wavered and settled again. He began to sway so that I looked at Carlotta and she at me, both afraid that he would fall from his seat. Just then his mother called to him, cheerily and as though she would check his sad song. Somehow I had imagined he would not leave the instrument even if he stopped playing to answer, but he did. He whirled from the piano, stood a moment, and passed through the door with what seemed a single stride. He said nothing to us—nothing whatever; but before we got over the shock of his leaving he had returned by the other door. He appeared to be annoyed—exceedingly annoyed, and he made a slight glance in our direction as he took his seat again.

The bony, long fingers rested once more upon the keys, impatient to be driven; and the light, dashing measures arose once more—arose and danced away. Then again came the gradual downtoning, and the slackening of the pace, down, down, until a mere song remained. A mere song, but a sad one, which sang since it could not dance. The man, as he played on, suffered again, losing himself in the strains that went floating away. This time his mother came into the room, cheerily interrupting him at the place where she had called before. He turned, slowly this time, excusing himself, and quietly left our presence.

The woman made some passing mention of her son's absorbing fondness for the piano, and with an apology for her delay, set upon other conversation. We had well launched upon some interesting thing when the son returned again. He sat close by listening but saying little, and smiling here and there his slow smile. A woman was mentioned, a master of some instrument, and we turned to talking of music. This made for our hostess' son a livening interest. In a short while he had taken the discussion into details of execution, and arrested the whole with his offer to play again. As though he had not touched the piano for us before, he said very simply, "I will play for you."

His mother seemed a bit nervous as he arose and approached the piano; but he was seated, we were forgotten, and the slender steeds were ready again to obey the will of their master. So splendid a musician was the man, we found ourselves too firmly held by his skill to become amused. A third time he set out upon the same thing—the thing which started in swift beauty and descended, down, down, to a simple, plaintive song.

His mother wanted to stop him again. It was easy to see that she wanted to, but a third time would be significant of the strange uneasiness which lay behind her son's playing, this thing beyond a certain point. Here again I wondered, as I listened, about the gradual, depressing change in the composition, and I wondered whether it pleased me. It was beautiful, to be sure, but I decided that I did not like it. There came then the end of the number. Quite suddenly it ended, and with a crash! A crash in high treble, like a quick, shrill scream. It did something to me that I could never explain; I will never forget that crash.

The son staggered from the piano and out to the porch. He murmured as he went, clutching at his breast and his head. When his mother reached him, he had stopped at the bird's cage. He was standing still, very still, as though he had never been unsteady. To the bird he talked confidingly, saying low things we could not understand. But when he saw Carlotta and me, he lifted the cage down, quietly excused himself and walked away, down the veranda steps and out to the back of the lawn. All the way he talked to the bird.

"He's been this way now for sometime," his mother said resignedly, looking after him. "He went with the army—volunteered. He came back to me a wreck from gas. His nerves were almost gone, and sometimes his head was wrong; but he began to get back to normal after a while. His music helped a lot—dear boy. He started on his composing again and became wrapped up in a Caprice. That was what he just played. Oh, he was doing so well and I was so proud of him, and one little incident ruined everything. It's strange how it affected him." She stopped a minute as it all came back to her, and when she started again her southern drawl seemed sweeter and sad.

"He went walking one day with me down through the grove. We were just a'laughing and talking, and he kept singing snatches of his Caprice. We stopped to watch a group of children playing in a pretty little park. My boy said that he would work better on his Caprice now that he had seen them. Oh, they were happy little mites. They ran and skipped about and fell over one another, and laughed and sang as though nothing was anything but their little game. I picked out one who reminded me of the way my boy used to look—brown face and brown curls—brown eyes full of sparkle. Oh, my!" she said, and she sighed.

"Then just as we started to move away, we noticed a sudden hush come over them. There stood a big, burly white man, a watchman or keeper or something, snarling at them and telling them they couldn't stay there. 'No niggers in there.' Well, the poor little things just sauntered away. Nothing else to do. It was mean. Children are such lovely things—who could hurt them? As they moved away down the grove, one tried to start the others skipping again. They tried it, but it didn't do. They went along their way, several trying to stop the youngest little fellow from crying. He wanted to play in the park."

"Well, my boy didn't talk any more all the way home. He was like something hit in the face. I found him looking at his khaki next day, and later saying something to the bird about his song. He said the cage took something from the bird's song. Then he worked on his Caprice, but it wouldn't go. The first part kept up, but it would just change, it seemed, of itself. My poor boy, he couldn't do a thing with it. It stopped on him every time. Then he got so his head was wrong again. The doctors didn't do much good. They still come, but what's the use? I'm afraid it's all over with him. He can't play anything else. Nothing else but that half Caprice. Funny how one little thing can do so much harm."

Soon we left, as best we could, trying to smile again. Carlotta said later that always within her she could hear that woman saying, "Children are such lovely things—who could hurt them?" And I could hear, and can hear now, the scream in that final crash!

Last year I returned to that city for a longer visit, this time alone. Soon after my arrival there I inquired about the Jaimesons. The mother had died of grief sometime back, upon the son's failure to return home. He had wandered away five years ago without saying anything at all. His mother had stood talking to visitors, bidding them good-bye. The son, bearing a bird in a cage, and gone off through the back garden gate and had not been seen since. This, of course, was like the firing of a cannon to me. I was completely stunned to know that I had figured unknowingly in so grave a tragedy. Had Carlotta and I not been there to take the good woman's time, she might have kept better watch over her demented son.

I asked about their home. It had been sold at auction and torn down, and a theatre now stood in its place. I expressed a desire to see the structure—to attend the theatre, and I was surprised to learn that it was actually possible for me to be admitted. This was the South, and no place in America was any too kind. Always they said the Negro had little or no culture; yet they closed to him, as a rule, all roads to culture. Soon there was to be a concert at this theatre, held through the efforts of a certain music club. Anybody could go. A brown face could not appear on the main floor, to be sure, but a brown face could *appear*. I would go.

I sat, on the night of the concert, awaiting the beginning of the program. To a friend I talked of the Jaimesons. The theatre was pretty— just pretty. It seemed a great shame that so beautiful a home as that of the Jaimeson's should have been destroyed. Oh, well. My friend seemed not to mind. Soon she opened her program and I remembered that I had not looked at mine. The artist of the evening was a well known pianist. He would give a group of his own arrangements of rare and unfinished compositions. In a footnote the name Jaimeson caught my eye. Then I could not believe what I read. An unfinished Caprice by a little known Negro composer had furnished the theme of a number which was very dear to the artist. This thing was next to the last number, and I could scarcely enjoy what went before it. I tried to feel ashamed of not becoming sufficiently absorbed in what at some other time would have taken me from the earth. But I wanted now only to hear this Caprice—to see it executed—and I was not at all ashamed. It was only natural that the rest of the numbers were minor to Jaimeson's.

Finally the Caprice was played and encored. I almost choked to keep from screaming. The old picture came before me, and all that this thing had meant and had failed to mean to its composer whirled round and round in my brain, and I could hear the crash before it came. I waited for the crash. This man did not make it. Then it had not been written in the manuscript. Why should I have thought it had?

The last rendition was a tremendous thing. I tried to concentrate upon it, but instead I sat and wondered about what had gone before it. I supposed that the manuscript of the Caprice had fallen into the hands of the music club during the moving and auctioning of the household goods of the Jaimeson home. Through them it had come into the hands of this artist, no doubt. Thus I pondered and listened at intervals until the music ceased. The artist refused an encore, so the audience started filing out. Now I was wondering why monsieur would not play again. We had reached the lower floor, when there broke upon the air that Caprice.

It was not the artist of the evening. One knew that immediately. I heard three men half whisper, "My God!" I may have said it too. Everyone turned back into the auditorium—also we, even we. Downstairs. Jaimeson sat at the piano. Jaimeson himself. I knew him as soon as I looked. He was like a ghost, long kept from some material thing which he had needed. He was taller, it seemed, and gaunt. His hair had grown long and his profile keener. Like a rail he looked as he leaned forward, driving once more the thin, fiery steeds, his fingers. Nobody stopped him—nobody dared. He played with the frenzy of madness—played as though he were trying to atone for an ill-given rendition of this thing which was his.

The pianist of the concert stood midway the stage, staring and bewildered. Almost the entire audience had returned. They stood staring and astounded. Nobody stopped the player. Midway its dashing course, as five years before it had done, the Caprice checked its wild capering. It changed to something slower, softer, yearning—then came the crash! Like a great mark of exclamation in the midst of the sad, smoothly flowing voice it came. It smote the dazed listeners and I could feel them start—a shortened breath, quickly drawn *en masse.*

Jaimeson had obeyed his urge; it had taken all his strength; now he collapsed. No one had noticed the bird cage on the floor beside him until he reached for it at the end of his playing. He must have intended to leave as suddenly as he had come, but he missed the cage (it was empty now), and crumpled to the floor.

There was great and immediate excitement, of course. It was not until special appeals were made to the curious crowd by both the manager and the artist that peace and quiet were secured. Then the curtains were drawn and the onlookers cut off from the little scene. But I held a feeling of intimacy for this poor, crazed soul, hurt forever beyond cure, and I ran, almost unconsciously, to him. Somehow I found my way backstage where they had taken him. The friend who was with me had thought me daring, but I had dismissed her, not caring what she thought. This man was alone and I would help him.

Someone I took to be a doctor asked who I was. "His sister," I answered.

"This fellow was an only child. I knew the family." Here was a tangle. The person speaking was sure of what he said. I knew that certainly.

"Wife, huh?" from someone else, and the words meant more than they asked.

They ignored the glance of defiance I had flashed and accepted my silence for affirmative response. I made no answer, but went to the couch where Jaimeson lay. No one forbade me to touch him, so I sat beside him and rested his head on my breast. He stirred and looked at me, and tears stole down my face. He reached up and fingered a loose ringlet of my hair. I found myself gazing at a man who stood beside me. I was hardly aware of his presence, yet I was speaking to him. "Children are such lovely things—who could hurt them?"

"Was he injured when he was a child?" the man inquired.

"No," I said, "but such a little thing caused it. *Not* a little thing either."

"What was it?" the man asked quickly, and I knew that I had better cease talking while I could.

"Please don't ask me now," I whispered. "It will upset him again." Then, laying Jaimeson's head back upon the couch, I stood up.

"How did he get here tonight? Why wasn't he more closely watched?" the man continued. I had known this question was coming, though I had not prepared an answer.

"I don't know how he came," I said. "I thought he was safe in bed." I felt my face burn, and dropped down upon the couch again beside my strange charge. "I think I can move him now," I ventured, "if you will get a cab." Heaven knows where I would have taken him. I had not the faintest idea.

"Better wait until the doctor gets here. We've sent for him." Just slightly I trembled.

"Where has he been all these years? In a sanitarium?" the man asked. He seemed wound up to ask questions forever.

"Yes," I whispered again. Anything which sounded plausible would do.

Just then Jaimeson sat up and stared across the room. A piano stood in the corner. Again he was like a ghost. I moved that he might arise. He wanted to. And I motioned to the others not to interfere. I must show some authority, and it would satisfy him to play, even if the result were adverse. So he moved to the instrument, two of the men and I keeping close behind him. He did not notice us. Once seated, he leaned forward to play. He started the Caprice and stopped. Started again and stopped. Something was wrong. Something wrong. The steeds would not obey their master. First time. First time? I wondered. They started on their dash; then stopped. Started; then stopped. The man looked at me. There was something he knew, yet something he could not understand. He smiled his slow smile and shook his head. Then he played. But it was not the first part he played. That part he could not do. Instead he brought forth the sad, low singing melody which seemed not at all a part of the Caprice.

Over and over this thing he played, his head sometimes dropped low and forward—sometimes pitched back and high. I stood behind him, and a little to the side. His mouth was partly open. His mouth watered. With a soft, silk kerchief I wiped his watering mouth. Over and over he played the softly wailing measures, his head sometimes dropped low and for-ward—sometimes pitched back and high.

The others stood watching—simply watching. No one spoke. Finally an arrival was announced.

"Here's the doctor," someone called.

Jaimeson stopped short. I imagined he wanted the bird cage, for he looked around for something. However, he turned and clung to me. He knew that I was someone who cared.

The doctor came toward us. Jaimeson's hold on me relaxed. The doctor spoke lightly. "What seems to be the trouble?"

Jaimeson slipped down and crumpled again to the floor. I answered the doctor. "Nothing now."

I knew without the doctor's word, that the man was dead. I just knew somehow. Just knew. And I was glad for him. It was better that he escape. The others straightway looked to me. I had seen it this far, I would finish. I sold my rings and paid for the burial.

FLORIDA RUFFIN RIDLEY

He Must Think It Out

Henry Fitts took up Gray's letter. It was the last in his mail to be reached and he had avoided the big document largely because of its bulkiness. With pressing financial adjustments to make, Fitts was in no mood for discursiveness in any form.

While he was frowningly considering his mail, Henry's daughter Irene had interrupted. Fitts had resignedly pushed aside the disturbing literature to look upon his daughter, equally disturbing in her way, and now bound upon an expedition of "week-ending."

Irene had found her father in a familiar attitude, and had rallied him, as was her habit.

"Cheer up, darling!" she had said, as with calm assurance she had swept the sheets from before him and established herself upon his desk. "This outfit is not entirely to the bad. I expect it to land me on Hazard's staff. I have a hunch it made a big impression on Minnie Hazard at the class luncheon today. I'd like to embrace you, but haven't time to trifle with my make-up. Now, brace up, dearest. You were nice to marry early so as to have many years to enjoy the prosperity to be achieved by your wonder child!"

Although Irene had drawn the usual caressing smile, her banter had slipped off the edge of her father's mood. There was quiet, approving fondness in his eyes, as he watched the youthful figure whose vitality and poise were so clearly revealed in its costuming.

Irene was talking now seriously but practically and vividly, talking of

Source: *Saturday Evening Quill* 1 (June 1928): 5–8.

her plans, but Fitts was not following her, although his mind and heart were absorbed in her.

What had it meant to produce this clear-cut, adorable young thing, this vigorous, healthy body in its absurd yet fascinating clothes, the clear, responsive mind, the cultivated taste? It had cost more than money, and money had never come easily to him. It had cost frayed nerves and anxious days. But her ambition was no greater than his. He was proud of his children—how proud!—how fondly proud! Irene, the eldest, the best beloved, she was his gift to posterity.

It had been nearly closing time when Irene had taken her affectionate and lively departure from his office. Fitts took up the letter and saw with surprise that it was from Gray, Ephraim Gray. Why should Gray, whose office was in the same building, whom he ran across in or out of court, almost any day—why should he send a letter, a long letter in long hand, and in his own hand, at that?

In the growing quiet he began to read. The outer office was by now deserted. His own stenographer had long since clicked daintily down the corridor. The doors of the elevators had given their last clank, and a few belated passengers were running down the stairs.

Fitts glanced at his watch as he picked up Gray's letter. It was time to go home, and he would take the letter with him; and yet, somehow, he would rather read it here. Besides, it would take only a few minutes to run it over.

What the deuce, anyway, had Gray to say on paper? True, they had been thrown together, in a way, on government cases, but Gray was counted in another race; was, in fact, a Negro, and except in the courts, very seldom seen.

In a way, Fitts had been an admirer of Gray. He had admired the strong personality of the big man whose deep, arresting voice carried an irresistible human, as well as logical, appeal. He had wondered at the poise which held through circumstances of so persistently tragic a flavor. They had been drawn together in a certain kind of restricted companionship, and Fitts had enjoyed the dry and genial humor of the man. It had been only a few days ago that they had laughed together over an old photograph, which Fitts produced, of one of his forebears wearing the strained expression and painful best clothes called for in photographs of the "sixties."

"If they could only have caught him unawares, Gray. By George, he has the same lion head as yourself!"

He had lingered as Gray had told some incidents of his own life and experiences, a field which the man had seemed loath to enter, but from which, under the spell of Fitts' sympathy, he drew tales of tragic interest. They had sat late that day, so late that Fitts had a passing regret, more or less poignant, that it was not possible to take the man home with him, to eat dinner with them, to charm Bella and Irene. But of course that was unthinkable; the idea had been hurriedly, almost frantically, dismissed!

Harassed as Fitts had been, and was, by the many demands of a growing family, he naturally had his ears open for any current tale of opportunities for big money; although it had never happened, he was always hoping for some ideas, some suggestions that might be grasped for his own benefit; so when Gray had approached him a short time before with a tale of possible wealth for a client of his, Fitts had been an interested listener.

Gray's story had been about a recently-built highway leading to a newly-developed manufacturing center which had brought some old forgotten woodlots and their to-be-found owners into prominence and prosperity. During the telling it had been impossible for Fitts to suppress a twinge of envy and a surge of bitterness. Of course Gray's clients must be Negroes—Negroes inheriting American land! While he, Fitts . . . It was a damned shame that he had no help. With the hope of getting, without reading the letter, an idea of what it was all about, Fitts began to glance hastily through the many sheets he had taken from the envelope. There were enclosures. There were arresting phrases. He snapped on his desk light and sat down to read:

My Dear Fitts:
The information which I am passing on to you, in this statement, I have withheld until I was absolutely sure of its validity; more than this, I have not brought myself to give you these facts until I had become convinced myself that it was the right and proper step for me to take.

I have been weeks in coming to this conclusion, and now that the decision that you should have the facts has been reached, I shall not weary or annoy you by beating around the bush.

In investigating my client's claim to the tract of woodland whose ownership has recently come into dispute and of which we have so often talked, I found that there was an adjacent lot in demand and waiting the appearance of a legal owner. Naturally I interested myself in an endeavor to trace the ownership of this property. So successfully have I done this that I tracked the original owner to Texas, and then identified him as the original owner of a tract of land there on which oil wells were afterwards discovered, and which lately has gained much notoriety as the "Garden Oil Fields."

Stephen Griggs, in whose name the title of the Ardley Woodlots (those of which we have talked) rests, was the brother of Eben Griggs, who owned adjoining lots, those claimed by my client as a descendant of Eben Griggs. Stephen Griggs disappeared while a young man,—in fact, while a boy,—and was entirely lost sight of by relatives and friends. Eben Griggs had two daughters, both of whom left the lonely homestead. One appears to have dropped out of sight, after taking service in a distant city; the other moved away upon her marriage, but her descendants never lost sight of their claim to Eben Griggs' property, for the title was redeemed by his grandson in recent years. This grandson, in the absence of other known heirs, had also claimed title to the lots left by his great-uncle Stephen.

In settling this claim for my client, who is the great-grandson of Eben Griggs, I have given much time to an effort to track and locate the descendants of Stephen Griggs, should he have any. It has been a long and tiring process, the details of which I will submit to you at another time. Here and now I will briefly outline the results.

I have found that Stephen Griggs never married, and that he wandered by degrees into the far southwest. Then he evidently took up a small tract of land of little apparent value, but which probably kept him alive. At his death he left his little property to be held by the courts until a legal claimant should appear.

For many years those sixty lonely acres of Stephen Griggs went almost unnoticed. At one time they were rented in order to obtain land fees, but in the main they were overlooked. Recently a tenant discovered oil upon this land and made a frenzied attempt to purchase and obtain a clear title. It was through the broadcasting of this sensational news that my attention was attracted, and that, after a long investigation, I connected the owner of the land upon which these oil wells were located with the original unknown owner of the Ardley Woodlots, whose sale I was negotiating. I am now convinced that Stephen Griggs was the owner of both and that the collateral descendants of Stephen Griggs can claim title not only to his share in the Ardley woods, but also to one of the best yielding oil fields now operating. You may be asking of what interest this can be to you?

Simply this, I have found through my investigations that you are indisputably a lineal descendant of the brother, and, with one other, the only legal heir, of Stephen Griggs!

You will recall my interest in an old portrait of your great-grand-father's which you showed me, your sole heirloom, you said. My client has its duplicate. It is his great-grandfather, also, which would make him (my client) your cousin one degree removed. Further proof will be found in enclosed papers and in those which I am forwarding, which are copies of birth and death and marriage certificates that have been secured to prove your claim.

If there should seem to be impropriety in my using our acquaintance to help obtain this knowledge, you must lay it to a lawyer's propensity to investigate, and my natural desire to push my client's interest.

At this, Fitts threw down the sheets and leaped excitedly to his feet.

"My God, man, make no excuses! You've saved my life!" He spoke aloud, the words tumbling from his lips.

With hands trembling and blood pounding in his temples, he went back to his reading.

Among the papers I am sending you, you will find description of both properties and of the great potential wealth within your grasp.

Before allowing you to publicly investigate and corroborate this claim, there is one other piece of information which I must pass on to you. I do it reluctantly, for although it is so, yet it is dastardly that these facts should be a matter of such vital import. However, there is no course open to me but to tell you that my client, co-heir with you, the great-grandson of your great-grandfather, the son of your mother's cousin and the great-nephew of Stephen Griggs is, myself, Ephraim Gray!

With bulging eyes Fitts read again and yet again. "The son of your mother's cousin"—what did the man mean? What was he driving at? How could Gray, who was almost black in color, be the son of *his* mother's cousin? Was this a fool joke? Was it possible that Gray was trying to blackmail him?

"The black rascal! How dare he?" He almost shouted the words.

Then he stopped short, stabbed with a remembrance of Gray's impressive sincerity. Suppose it were true—impossible of course, but just suppose . . . Tied up with a black family!

"No, no!" he almost shrieked, as he threw down the papers and rushed to open the window. "Damn him, no, no!"

So violent was his instinctive protest that a feeling of nausea overcame him as he leaned against the open window seeking air. For some minutes he stood there, fighting down the mental and physical surge which was becoming chaos within him.

Regaining, after a while, a measure of composure, he stumbled back to his desk and attempted to take up the disordered sheets of Gray's letter, but the full sense of the hideous implications again overwhelmed him. He—"a nigger" and Irene, his Irene, his gay, lovely daughter . . . It was a lie! a *lie!*

He flung his arms over his desk, and in doing so uncovered a snapshot of Gray,—one taken in the corridor by an amateur photographer in the building. Glancing at it with eyes dulled by pain and anguish, his slow gaze was caught by something familiar in the picture: the outline, the poise of the body, the set of the head suggested some one—he hadn't noticed it before, but there it was. Yes, the resemblance was there—no need to bring out the portrait of old Eben.

Fitts tore the card in two and sank his head into his hands. Well, it might be true. No, not *really* true, never, *never,* but how to keep down any suspicion that any one had thought it to be true. It was Gray that must be handled. He must be made to swallow his words, they must be forced down his throat.

He fumbled for Gray's letter and steeled himself to go on.

I will not, for obvious reasons, make extended comment upon the situation; the papers accompanying will make clear many things which may seem inexplicable. At any rate, it may not be out of place to emphasize the fact that there were many unions in the backwoods of our state, and that these mingled the blood of Indians, Negroes and whites, and many cases are on record where traces of Negro blood have grown faint with subsequent white infusions. Lois Griggs, your grandmother and sister to Nancy Griggs, my grandmother, seems, as I said, to have left home early in life to take service with a family in a distant city. Her movements were never checked by her family, but you will find among the papers a true record which leads straight to your birth, the son of a white mother and a supposedly white man; but, really, the grandson of old Eben Griggs, Negro and Indian.

After the signature came a postscript:

It is no reflection upon my regard for you or on the sincerity of our intercourse that from the first I have had an idea of our relationship. In fact, from letters which were left by my father and which you will be allowed to examine, I judged that just such a situation would develop. I confess I have been on the outlook, ready to follow any and every clue. America's attitude in such relationships made it impossible for me to be more open with you. Even now, whatever may be your future plans, they may be made without reference to me.

Fitts straightened himself stiffly. The impressiveness of Gray's personality was too strong upon him to allow a complete rejection of the whole matter. He arose from his chair and dragged himself to the door of his coat closet, stumbling over a chair in his way. He turned on the light and consulted the mirror sunk in the door.

Yes, he had the same face, a face which was even a little whiter than it was before he had received the staggering news that he was no longer a white man. If this thing proved to be true, what was he, and where did he belong? Where would he look for friends? He gave himself a prolonged stare. He was the same man identically, the same man that he was at this time yesterday, and yet he must be damned by what—for what . . .

And what about his family? Fitts' eyes grew wild as the thought of Bella, of Irene, came into his mind, and then he laughed at his reflection in the glass. Was it not ridiculous for him to be afraid to face facts? But his laugh cracked. He *was* afraid, miserably afraid! He shivered as his imagination leaped forward and tortured him with the pictures it drew. Doors closed on Irene, his loved and lovely Irene, so adequately prepared and so gallantly facing a friendly world—doors closed everywhere and on every side—in schools and stores and churches and homes!

And then, that Jim Crow business, with sheriffs waiting for objectors! He would shoot, kill! Let any one dare insult his daughter! Yes, he would show how this thing should be met! But how absurd to imagine that Irene would be treated like a common black girl! And he laughed again, and again the laugh broke.

There was that incident of last winter. He had seen the girl in Gray's office—a girl as fair as his Irene. It was a judgment against him that he hadn't been more outspoken. But now—he would cry their crimes from the house tops.

Of all persons why should this curse come upon *him,* upon him who had always been tolerant and sympathetic? Why hadn't some of those ugly fanatics, Negro-haters,—why hadn't they been the ones to suffer?

It wasn't fair—it was unjust that a good man, that a sweet girl, should be so punished. Punished? *Cursed!* Talk about a merciful God! Hadn't he been a Christian—hadn't he been upright? And God had let this come upon him. He would not submit—he would maim, he would murder! He would rather see Irene dead!

"Better dead!" he whispered as, spent with emotion, he slumped into a nearby chair. His overwrought feelings gave way, and for a while he sprawled motionless and blessedly thoughtless. Into this lethargy other thoughts began to creep. Why need the truth be divulged? Why couldn't that be managed? It shouldn't be hard!

Fitts jerked up straight, his head lifted, the light returned to his eyes. He was foolish to despair. There was always a way.

Gray was leaving America. He would get Gray's promise of secrecy. He would not appear as a claimant of the fortune. He would pay *that* price for secrecy. Gray could be trusted! And Fitts laughed again. He threw up the window and drew deep breaths of the cool night air. The world was all right again—everything was all right—all right! What a fool he had been to give way! To let himself get worked up to such a frenzy! It was a good thing no one had seen or heard him.

The thing to do was to swear Gray to secrecy and to avoid all contact with him or people of his kind.

And now for home and his delayed dinner. Get away, get away—The phrase persisted in his mind! But if he was to get away, why not take the money? Think what it would do! If he didn't take the money, Gray would know the secret just the same. Would there be any advantage not to take the money? In either case, he would be at the mercy of Gray. *Could* Gray be trusted? And if he could, why couldn't they manage together that the world shouldn't know the truth?

What would happen should Gray die? That would have to be arranged; could it be arranged?

Would it be better to refuse the money, after all? What difference would it make, except that he would be poor instead of rich? He was getting confused again; but another gleam shot through his confusion.

"Bella!" he almost shouted in his relief. "I'll talk with Bella! She'll know what is best. She always does." Why hadn't he thought of her before? She always saw light in the darkest problems. Why, of course.

But he stopped short again. Tell Bella what?—that in marrying him she had been deceived, betrayed, condemned? No, he could not tell Bella. Even that comfort was denied him. Fate was giving the last twist to the implements of torture!

Well, what was it he was trying to decide?

He must concentrate!

He must think it out before he saw Bella.

He must think it out.

He must think it out alone.

The bell of the telephone shrilled again and again, unheard in the darkened room.

Henry Fitts was thinking it out—and alone!

PART 10

THE OFFERING

While individuals of all backgrounds have made sacrifices for their children or their community, the sacrifices made by African-Americans are
unique in the context of historical experience. A number of the pieces
in this section center on the dilemma faced by black Americans, when,
in April 1917, the United States entered World War I. Blacks were among
those who thronged to the recruiting stations before a general draft was
instituted. Black women—relegated to the sidelines because of their
gender—grappled with many questions: Should black men enlist to fight
for a country that discriminated against them and segregated them even
in the armed forces? Should the struggle for freedom elsewhere preempt
the struggle for civil rights at home? Sarah Collins Fernandis called the
decision to give up black men for the war "the offering." She asks in her
poem of the same name about the dilemma of black mothers: whether
"the vision of the whole / Intent of Freedom" outweighs the accumulated
burden of prejudice.

Often, as can be seen in May Miller's "One Blue Star," women—in this
case the mother of a young draftee—were called upon to support their
enlisting men. Miller's character not only offers her encouragement as the
greatest gift she can give, but she also envisions herself as one with others
in Africa and elsewhere, in other times, who have made similar sacrifices.

Other offerings—money, love, devotion—are also represented in this
section. Octavia Beatrice Wynbush's story "The Return of a Modern Prodigal" tells of a son who chooses to conceal his identity from long-lost
parents for their sake, and so must forgo a reunion with them. Anna Julia
Cooper writes of a widow whose devotion to her husband makes her

unable to accept his death and live her own life. Dorothy West's story of a little girl's attempts to help her mother camouflage deceit underlines the moral ambiguities inherent in the concepts of sacrifice and loyalty. In each of these pieces, the reader is left to ponder the experience of women who often sowed with little expectation of reaping any tangible reward.

MAY MILLER

One Blue Star

He did not give me a chance to open the door. Even as I hesitated there separating from the ring the right key to fit into the lock, he swung the door vehemently inward and barred the way, waving exultingly in his hand a letter. I knew without questioning its import. Not recognizing one symbol, I read each word as though it had been magnified tenfold.

The President of the United States

To ———. Greetings:

Transfixed, I attempted to utter no sound, to make no movement. His strong arms encircled me and drew me into the hallway. I stood convulsively clutching him, digging frantic fingers into his firm young flesh. And I, who had but once conceived, who had for one brief period only felt life within my womb, knew the stirring of generations within me, suffered the agony of multitudinous birth. Life of dim eras, of far-flung continents swept through and over me, engulfing my entity. I was one with timelessness—I became the black mother of the fighters of the ages.

I was Zipporah, the black wife of Moses, standing amid the alien corn of my mate's new land of adventure, cuddling my wounded dark boy from the taunts of Miriam. I experienced with him the hurt and bewilderment of childhood and held back the puny arms that would have struck at his tormentors, the young of Hazeroth who found his dark skin strange.

Source: Opportunity 23 (Summer 1945): 142–143.

"Hush, my beautiful golden boy, your brothers of tomorrow, older and far wiser than you, will fight that your tawny head shall not be bowed in shame."

With Simon of Cyrene, my strong fighter offspring, born to lead insurrectionist slaves, I dreamed a dream of freedom, of freedom snatched through blood and burning. Then by his side climbing the hill to Golgotha, I glimpsed with him for one brief second the light in a doomed man's eyes; and I felt the bitterness and rebellion die in my son's soul as he humbly shouldered the cross and trudged beside his Saviour.

"Don't hear their jeers, Simon—Don't look up to the gaunt cross now fixed against a leaden sky. The crown of thorns is there; the purple robe lies in a crumpled heap on the ground; the torn bleeding form hangs limp now; but we know—you and I—that it has housed the secret of the ages—love of human kind."

In my frail body I have cradled the sperm that [brought] forth dark heroes of distinction. Down the ages, I marched, rode and tented with them—my warrior sons. I call the roll and from the dim corridors of time they answer century after century, from continent to continent:

Antar the Lion—Arabia's black warrior bard, conquering with artful lance and nursing in his soul a poet's vision.

Angelo Soliman—defender of the Holy Roman Empire, snatched from his African hut to be at last courted by Emperor Francis I, himself.

Henrique Diaz—invincible general in the Portuguese army,—on his breast the "Cross of Christ" and in his heart the hope of a free Brazil.

Toussaint L'Ouverture—native governor general of Haiti, whose rule the mighty Napoleon could break only by cheap chicanery.

Chaka—stern military chieftain of the Zulu tribes, building of the uncivilized one of the most effective fighting machines in history and leaving unto his unheeding native land, one rule—"Conquer or die!"

Antonio Maceo—Negro general and hero of Cuba's wars of independence, whose deeds the imposing monument in Havana calls a free people to honor.

"Stand there in life, my generals, my chieftains, my rulers, robed in your odd vestments and babbling your many tongues, and hear me. Know you that neither time nor space, nor greed, nor prejudice can snatch your prestige nor eradicate from your countries' histories the names you have etched there for immortality."

On these shores of my native Africa I stood when the strange ravishing horde bore down and snatched my strong young sons. With them I traversed an ocean in the stench hole of a slave ship. I huddled near them on the auction block, their great strength bound in irons, their firm gleaming bodies naked for appraisal and barter.

I watched them bend their backs in foreign fields beneath another stretch of sky, toiling to bring the soil to flower. Down to the swamp they crept when stars were hazy and the moon dripped blood—there to nurse a faint hope and seek a God who seemed to have forgotten them.

"Make your plans. They will fail, for even your own may prove traitors and bloodhounds have keen scent. But never, never forget that swamp flowers bloom too."

Blood of my blood spattered on the dignified sod of Boston Common to christen a baby country in its first stretch for liberty. Crispus Attucks, bound though he was by shackles of color, died to bring to liberty a new meaning, a breadth that must eventually encompass a continent and all thereon.

"Crispus, the shot that fell you penetrated to the bowels of a nation. Rest well in your honored grave."

That lank, lean thing that dangles grotesquely on the gallows in yonder clearing—he's mine too. That's Nat Turner—my poor impatient Nat.

Where's the proud army he raised, armed with makeshift weapons, and fired with the promise of freedom? Some captured and punished; others deserted and gone back sniveling to their masters. And now he hangs there alone with only me lurking in the shadows and around him the wise wind howling, "Too soon! Too soon!"

"It's all right, Nat. They have yet to stifle a dream by killing the dreamer. A dream such as yours never ended a broken limb on a skeleton tree."

* * *

And here again I am, my dark form silhouetted against a vast white amphitheatre, marble columns rising behind me and below me flowing the lazy Potomac; but I see none of this. The omnipresent thing is the severe white sepulchre, and I claw and claw to scratch my way to the carrion flesh within.

Can he be mine, too? He might; he well might; and I have a message:

"Son of mine, or son of fairer hue, you are mine too. Do you not lie here because you believed in a world safe for democracy? That bond at once makes you mine. It mustn't be for naught that you gave up the acrid smell of soil, the feel of soft flesh in the moonlight, the laughter of children at play, even though your brothers returned to a land still shackled by fear, want, and prejudice.

"Time slid rapidly over your alabaster box; and so soon they are at war again, for oppression is a cancer that eats at the vitals of mankind. They are fighting again, mark me, with the word freedom whizzing around them and filling the air.

"Murmuring Potomac, don't drown my whisper; let him hear me."

Dig, dig—I can reach him. Claw, claw—the hard stone softens.

"Hey, Ma, you're scratching me. You're not going to faint are you?" Gently my son shook me, bringing me back to the stark reality of the present with all my fears and self agony—my yesterdays and todays and all time hereafter bound up possessively in his eighteen-year-old body.

"No, son," I answered steadily, "I don't think I am."

"You were standing there looking queer, staring through me out into space."

"Yes. I know. I saw things; I had a vision."

"Come on, Ma, don't carry on like that. You're not sick, are you? You want me to fight, don't you—fight for those four freedoms we live for, don't you?"

"Yes, son, yes I do." I studied his unlined face marked by the conflict that was tearing him between solicitude for me and the age-old yearning for vindication, for accomplishment. I knew he bore in his young heart the harvest of all those others:—their fierce pride, their feel for power and the inward knowledge of their own capabilities and the relentless yearnings to realize the world that Simon had envisioned when the scourged Man had spoken.

And he bore their burden too—their burden of frustration and rebellion, for now he was boastfully announcing as if to quiet his own secret misgivings, "And this time there'll be no quibbling. We mean those four freedoms for everybody, everywhere—for Negro boys like me right here in America."

His voice faltered; the grand pronouncement dribbled to a pitiful personal plea; and I felt a gnawing pain for the doubt that clouded his great vision. He must go to the battle freed from nagging doubt. He must keep throbbing within him the promise of a better world. His untried youth must nurse a dream, if he is to fight for fulfillment. And eager to quell his inward questioning, I answered quickly, "And that's something well worth fighting for. I shall be proud of you, my son." I had given him up, and spent from the wrenching effort, I sank on the hall seat.

His eyes cleared; the dear swagger returned as he reached in his pocket to draw out a bit of cloth. "Look," he said boyishly, "after I got the letter, I went out and bought this for you to hang in our window."

He tossed in my lap a tiny white silken banner bearing in its center a single blue star.*

---

*A banner used to indicate that a member of the household was fighting in the war.

DOROTHY WEST

The Five Dollar Bill

Judy could read before she was seven. Mother said that when she was four she could read the weather reports to her father. The only one she fell down on was the variable wind one. Only she didn't really fall down, for when she came to that difficult word and got it out somehow, the father caught her up in his arms and hugged and kissed her hard.

Judy loved the father. She did not know very much about him. She guessed he was her relative because they had the same name. She would have liked to know if this kinship were closer than an uncle; or was it like a grandfather, for the father was much older than mother, with the top of his head broken and wrinkled around his kind eyes.

But Judy was a shy child who did not like to ask questions, for either the grown-up people said, Run and play, or gave you ridiculous answers with superior smiles.

Judy could answer the little questions herself. It was the big questions about babies and God, and telling a lie for your mother that grown-up people were never truthful about.

The stork did not bring babies. It was not true about a stork flying over clouds and dropping babies down chimneys. Santa Claus could come down a chimney because he was a man and wouldn't get hurt. But would God let a stork drop a dear little baby down a dirty chimley?

No, a woman prayed God very hard for a baby. Then it began to grow in her stomach. When it was quite grown a doctor cut a hole in her side

---

Source: Challenge: A Literary Quarterly 1 (June 1936): 35–40. Written under the name Mary Christopher.

and the baby came out. After that the woman stayed in bed until the hole healed up. In that moment of the baby's birth the woman became a mother. But how a man became a father Judy did not know.

And about God: did He really punish people in a fire with a pitchfork? Did he stick them with the pitchfork *Himself?* Why Judy could not have hurt a fly. She could kill a mosquito all right because it was tinier. Sometimes though when you killed a mosquito a lot of blood squished out. That made your stomach feel queer for a minute. But then mother said beamingly, Got him good, didn't you darling, and everything was all right.

Mother could kill anything without feeling queer. She killed flies and ants and even big roaches, and put down traps for mice. She said anything that belonged outdoors should stay outdoors if it didn't want her to kill it. And she would grab up a wad of paper and go banging at a fly, which was fun to watch if you did not think too hard about the fly's fambly.

God was supposed to be gooder than mother. God was not supposed to have mother's temper. Mother said damn and sometimes Goddamn. If Judy overheard she would frown and have a temper. She would say Goddamn to the father. Then she would have a temper when the father reproached her for saying such words before Judy.

They would begin the queer thing called quarreling. The words would fly between them and it would seem to Judy that her mother's words hit hardest. Yet at such times, as fond as she was of the father, she would want to run to her mother, saying protectively, there, there, my darling.

Judy often wondered if the father lived with them. She always went to bed while he was still sitting up, and he was never there in the morning like her mother. There were only two bedrooms, hers and her mother's. And once she had heard her mother say to the college man, Jim and I have not lived together as man and wife for months.

Mother was careless with money. She was always losing it. Judy never saw her lose it really, but she would tell Judy about it and after a while Judy would remember exactly how it happened. When the father sat down to dinner, mother would tell him about it, too, adding, Judy remembers. Judy would say proudly, yes mother.

Mother always lost the money on the day the college man came. Mother said he was poor and came to sell things to help him through college. She said Judy had better not tell the father because he was not a college man and got mad if anybody mentioned college men to him.

Judy did not know what the college man sold and she would not ask her mother. It always cost just what the father had left for the gas bill or the milk bill, and once even what the father had left for a birthday frock for Judy.

When the college man came, mother would let Judy take her dolly out in its carriage. But it would not be the same as on other days. She would dress her doll hurriedly, and it would not seem to be a real baby, but just an old doll. She would feel silly, and would just want to get away from the college man and his teasing voice.

Then one night the father and mother had a terrible quarrel about mother losing money. You could hear their voices all over the house, only this time it was the father's words hitting hardest. Neither Judy nor her mother had ever mentioned the college man to him, but he knew all about him just the same, and called himself a fool and the college man a rat and said he was going to divorce mother and take Judy away from her.

Judy did not know what divorce meant, but when the father said he would take her away from her mother, she knew that as mad as he was he would take her for keeps, and never let them see each other.

She got out of bed and ran into the kitchen, and threw herself into her mother's arms. She was sobbing wildly and saying hysterical things. Her mother held her close and began to cry, too, saying, there, my precious, just like Judy had always wanted to say to her.

After a long time she felt the father's hand on her head. She heard him say something about the child's sake, and knew he meant he would let her stay. All in a moment she fell asleep, with her hand sliding down her mother's soft cheek.

After that the father did not leave any more money for bills. The college man came once and said where was the money for his books. He looked very scornful while he said it, and he kept his hat in his hand.

Mother forgot about Judy and cried and clung to the college man. He pushed her away and said she knew where to reach him when she had the money for his books. The outer door slammed after him.

Then Judy knew that the college man sold books and was mad because mother would not pay him. Still it was strange. She had never seen her mother so heartbroken. Even with the father it had not been like that. For she had never heard her proud mother plead. She had never seen her stalwart mother cling to anyone.

Judy had to say it. Give him back his old books.

Her mother stopped in the midst of a sob. You go and play, she said coldly.

After a while Judy almost forgot about the college man and the money her mother owed him. It was only when her mother walked up and down and around the room looking burningly beautiful, that Judy felt sick and afraid and saw the college man's image.

Then it was that Judy, who could read almost anything at seven, read in the Sunday supplement about the moving picture machine. You sent away for some reproductions of famous paintings. When they came you sold them. When you had sold them all you sent the money to Mr. Fisher in Chicago, and he sent you a moving picture machine. If you put up a sheet and charged a penny to all the children in the neighborhood once a week, pretty soon you'd have enough money to give your mother to pay that old college man for his old books.

Judy talked it over with the father, except the part about the college man. He said he was proud of his little business woman and helped her write the letter to Mr. Fisher. He took her out and lifted her up to the mailbox so she could post it herself.

In less than a week the pictures came. The father said they were beautiful and made the first purchase himself. There were twenty to dispose of at a quarter apiece.

Judy sold one to her teacher, one to the barber who cut her hair, one to the corner grocer, at whose store they had an account, one to kind Mr. McCarthy who ran the poolroom, one to an uncle, one to an aunt, and two to company ladies. The father said she had done simply wonders and took the rest of the pictures to the office building, where he was super-intendent, and sold them. He brought her the money in silver. Judy was very excited. She counted out her money and wanted to have [it] all changed to a five dollar bill.

Mother got up and said she would take Judy to the corner grocer's right now. And tomorrow they would go to the post office where Judy was to send the money order herself.

Mother held out her hand and was radiant. Judy slipped her small palm into hers. They smiled at each other and shut out the male, their husband and father. In this moment Judy was saying, It is for your sake, my darling. Her mother's mounting excitement answered, I know it, my sweet, my precious.

They went to the corner grocer's, still holding hands. Judy skipped along. It was seven o'clock of a winter's evening. The stars were shining. The snow crunched under her feet. Everything was dear and familiar, the car line, the icicles on the cables, the signboards with their bright illustrations luminous under the electric lights, the vacant lot with the snowmen silent and stout, the fire alarm, the post box. All things good, and best of all her mother's bright and beautiful face, her mother's parted red-lipped mouth, with her breath on the winter night.

The corner grocer rang up No Sale and gave Judy a five dollar bill. Judy said, You take it for me, mommy, with the same indulgence that mothers use in saying to small children, You may carry the package, dear.

Mother opened her purse and fished around in it. After a while she looked her amused surprise at Mr. Brady and gave him a lovely humble smile, full of sweet pleading. She took Mr. Brady into her confidence and said she must make an urgent call. Would Mr. Brady give her a nickel and put it on the bill.

All of a sudden Judy felt sick. She knew her mother's burning beauty had not been for her, nor was it for Mr. Brady. She did not want to hear her mother make the telephone call. She went and stood at the door and stared up at a little star snug among its elders. The star began blinking so hard that it made her eyes water.

When she heard the nickel ring in the telephone box, she began to sing shrilly and kept on singing until her mother came out of the booth and bade Mr. Brady a wonderful good night.

All the way home Judy would not look at her mother. She played a skipping game that kept her a pace ahead. Her mother kept saying loving things, but Judy pretended not to hear and would give no loving answers.

At the door her mother reminded her, My precious, don't bother to mention to your father about the telephone call. I dialed the wrong number and lost my nickel, so I didn't really make it after all.

When Judy went in she said, Good night father, with her head hanging down. She hated him, too, and ran off to bed without once begging to stay up.

In the morning Judy made herself believe that last night had been a bad dream. She ran all the way home from school. Her mother greeted her with a hug and kiss. She looked very alive and kept smiling at Judy, with the blood flooding her cheeks and her eyes star bright in her head.

Judy ate her lunch. The table was pretty, but there was unwashed company china in the sink. The plate her mother placed before her was not a company plate.

The lunch was soft things but they stuck in Judy's throat. She felt excited and sad. Suddenly her mother was saying, Darling, I sent your money off myself. I was passing the post office this morning, and it seemed rather silly to make a second trip this noon. You won't tell your father, will you? He thought it would please you to send it yourself. But you're mother's big girl, aren't you, my precious? And you aren't disappointed, are you?

No'm, said Judy, and she never said No'm. Her heart was standing in her throat. She thought it would burst.

That night she went to bed before the father came for dinner. She said she felt sick in her stomach, and in fact she did. She did not want the light, nor a book, nor her doll. She shut her eyes tight. The father tiptoed into the room. She lay very still. His lips brushed her forehead. He tiptoed out. She put her mouth in the pillow and sobbed herself to sleep.

It was not so bad the first week. After every mail she would make herself believe the moving picture machine would surely come on the next. But the week passed. Another week began. The father said, It ought to come this week anyway. Her mother added cheerfully, Oh, yes.

The second week ended. The third week began. Then the father said, Shall I help you write them a letter, Judy?

Her eyes met her mother's bright unwavering ones. I forgot the address, she said.

Thereafter the father did not speak of the matter again. He said Judy must just consider it an unfortunate experience and profit by it.

Saturday morning of the fourth week it was Judy who got the mail that the elevator boy had pushed under the door sill. There was a letter addressed to herself. It bore Mr. Fisher's return address. The other letters fell from her hand. She stumbled blindly into her room and opened the envelope.

It was not really a letter. It was a newspaper page. There was a picture of a little girl and a story with easy words about how she had kept some pictures that belonged to Mr. Fisher, though he had written her twice to return them. The police had come and taken her to jail, where she had stayed forever and ever. Her mother got sick and died from worrying. Her father lost his job because his daughter was a thief and had to beg on the streets.

Judy was so terrified she could not stir. Her eyes dilated. She could not swallow. She began to itch all over.

After a long time she folded the newspaper page and hid it under her mattress. She flung herself across the bed, quivering and unable to cry. She would suffer like this at the peal of a bell, at an unfamiliar voice, at an unexpected sound, and she would share this pain with no one. For she knew even if she screwed up the courage to go to a grown-up, she would get the untruthful answer, children don't go to jail, when there was that picture of that little girl which proved that they did.

The doorbell jangled. Judy jumped off the bed, scuttled under it, and drew herself up into a ball, banging her head against the floor, and holding her breath hard.

God, she prayed, let me die.

But children do not die. They grow up to be the strange things called mothers and fathers. Very few parents profit by childhood experiences. When they look back they do not really remember. They see through a sentimental haze. For childhood is full of unrequited love, and suffering, and tears.

ANNA J. COOPER

The Tie That Used to Bind:
A Mid-Victorian Negro Marriage

She did not cry. Her eyes were dry and her lips trembled and twisted just a little as she tried to smile.

With native courtesy she bent at the waist to greet me. How-you do, Sis Annie. Whe'eh's Ander? I told her as gently as I could that the body could not have come through on the same train with me, although I had thought that every arrangement was complete and the station master at Old Point assured me when I bought the tickets for myself and—*the box,* that it would be put in the baggage car of my train to Raleigh. She asked only one question:

"Does he look po?"

"Oh no," I answered with brave cheerfulness. "He looks all right."

At the same time visions of the shrunken figure in army blue trousers, long rows of metal file cases like compartments of a huge oven, drawer upon drawer, drawer upon drawer, all ticketed and provided with knobs so that the efficient attendant could conveniently pull out one or shove in another as easily as the baker man looks into the compartments of his huge stacks of browning bread. And when the right one ticketed "Andrew J. Anderson; disease pneumonia; department—" and so on and so on [was found], I said quietly: "His wife wants me to bring him home for burial."

"You will have to see an undertaker over in town for that. We provide just the plainest interment here at the Home."

I choked back my visions and dwelt only on how natural and peaceful he looked. She turned to the kitchen to prepare a meal for me in spite

Source: Unpublished manuscript, Moorland-Spingarn Research Center, Howard University, n.d.

of my repeated insistence that I wanted nothing. I heard her mutter to herself: "Dat po' soul out dere in all dis rain by hisself."

She went through the funeral with the same more than natural calm. Chose the hymns herself from the Hymnal: No. 660. "Oh for a closer walk with God" and "How firm a foundation" "cause," she said, "Ander always liked dat one."

I had slipped to the undertakers and ordered suitable clothes and a handsome casket so that he would not *"look po."* Friends sent flowers— not stiff set pieces from florists, but familiar loving blooms from home gardens and friendly yards; and the little front room of that humble cottage where her Ander lay in state was as dignified and solemnly beautiful as a millionaire's castle could have been made. The impressive burial service of the Prayer Book, the same alike for prince or peasant, the rich harmony of full throated voices unspoiled by instrumental ac- companiment, the simple dignity of that silent form lying there seemed to await and claim as its just and fitting due the final homage and ultimate tribute of reverential adoration from all the living.

I had to get back to my work almost immediately and in Washington busied myself at once to secure a pension for her as a Spanish American War Widow. As the cottage in which she lived free of rent was mine and she seemed physically fit to look after herself, I felt the pension though small was sufficient for her simple wants the rest of her natural life. To prove her marriage I had the frayed and yellow leaves of the family Bible: *Andrew J. Anderson married to Caroline McPherson Jan. 1, 1867.* No need, for every citizen of Raleigh, white or black, knew her and could testify that from the time that memory runneth not to the contrary she had always been a faithful and devoted wife, a loyal and even ostenta- tiously proud supporter and defender of her liege lord as any medieval vassal. For 50 years they had lived together in an ideal union and not even the vilest ever dared a breath of suspicion against her fidelity to her marriage vows. Though wise gossips would shake slanderous heads with "Calline's plum crazy 'bout her Ander as she calls him, and he aint no better'n he ought to be. She'd sell her soul to de debble jes' to please him. Jes' look a'dat bastard o' his'n she took to raise." "Aint he de very spit o' Ander?" Caroline would say proudly. "Jes' look a' de way he walks and de way he th'ows his hands. And dem eyes—jes' Ander right over again." Then she would chuckle to herself and hang her head self consciously: "Well I reckon de Lawd took dat chile to punish me. Hit dont do to set your heart too much on nothin' nor nobody in dis worl'."

In an altercation once with a very important personage she was told "You must remember, Caroline, I am Mrs. So and So." "Yes sum," she replied bending at the waist as always in her courtly fashion, "An,—an' you mus' member, Ma'am, Dat I am Mrs. Ander Anderson," which was no joke for this Mrs. So and So could have consigned both Mr. and "Mrs." Ander Anderson to the poor house by the flick of a pen. In the way that love begins as often happens she had pitied and mothered Andrew—who was several [years] younger than she, through a spell of sickness in a hospital for contagious diseases in a lonely deserted spot outside the city limits. She was not a nurse and of course not allowed to enter. But love finds a way and Calline would take her knickknacks to the woods and give the signal by firing a pistol. If by any chance she was caught, she was shooting at a big black snake that "Jes' run right under dem bushes there."

Absorbed in my own affairs I dismissed this case from my mind, easily assuming that with the house and garden (she was fond of gardening) and her regular pension money for food and simple necessities her life would resume its even tenor—neither poverty nor riches, the happiest ideal. But one day a letter from a social worker at Raleigh brought a shock to my smug satisfaction. "Aunt Calline was surely not herself. Found wandering in the woods looking for 'Ander.' Obviously demented." I wrote Dr. —— and tried every expedient to avoid a trip to Raleigh for myself. When finally I had to go I found her to all appearances so docile and simply childlike, I concluded the symptoms of insanity that had alarmed the neighbors must have been due solely to lack of normal social contacts and that what she needed was the renewal of her accustomed associations in an ordinary comfortable home wherein her presence would be taken as a matter of course and where she would encounter only kind looks and loving words. I was not unaware of a District Law which forbids the bringing of insane persons from the States into Washington. I did not at all believe her to be insane but knew that she could be quickly rendered so by being put into an asylum with crazy people and less quickly, but perhaps just as surely, if left to the solitary life she had been leading since her husband's death. Again I suppose with the conceit which I hope is pardonable in an inveterate School Marm, I may have overestimated the efficacy of my own powers of suggestion and mental control. I thought that kind treatment in an ideal environment and constant companionship of a potential psychiatrist would keep her as well as most minds commonly considered simply morbid. I brought her into the bosom of my own family, ministering personally and directly to her wants physical and mental. I bathed her, dieted her, coiffured her hair becomingly, took her out for walks and sight seeing, to church every Sunday—and at night when she had a nice warm dip in the big tub, her face shiny with the clean smell of good wholesome toilet soap and she was cozily tucked in bed, together we would repeat the good old 23rd Psalm, her voice trembling naturally and pathetically with the emphasis: "The Lord's my Shepherd *I shall not want;* He rest'ith my soul—" and after my cheery "Good night, Sleep tight" she would sink peacefully and happily into a restful, natural, childlike sleep.

Indeed as I remember her in those early days in our home, she seemed perfectly normal, tractable as a sweet and trustful child, responsive, ready to obey, kindly and open minded to guidance. Those were to me the happy days of fulfillment of a teacher's task with a mind under apparently perfect control, a mind less distracting than a group of youngsters, however intelligent,—more challenging to originality of method, more inspiring to the urge for experimenting on a *tabula rasa* with a new untried method, more satisfying from the unexpected thrill of having met a real human need and at the same moment receiving adequate and grateful appreciation. True I recognized at times a confusion of places and persons between Raleigh and Washington—a blending of present and past associations that did not always yield to treatment. One day for instance when Griffith Stadium was mentioned as the Base Ball Park, she startled me by saying knowingly "Oh yes; That's where Ander, my husband, works." I said, "You mean he used to work at the Park in Raleigh. This you know is Washington." "Yessum, I know but Ander is at the Park right up the street here. I been there many a time. Oh yes ma'am I understan. But Ander aint dead. He works up here at the Base Ball Park. I been intendin' to go up dere and see him but I been sort er sick and kept puttin' it off." Then without arguing the point I tried to call to mind the day of the funeral. "Don't you remember the hymns you chose for the service that day and the beautiful long stem chrysanthemums Miss Phoebe sent and how we laid him to rest beside Grandma and Big Brother. I'm sure you remember how sweetly your Miss A—— sang *'Oh rest in the Lord; Wait patiently for him.'* You said it was the sweetest thing you had ever heard."

"Yes'm. I know there's some says Ander's dead, but—" and after that she would watch her chances with the utmost cunning and steal out of the house to find the Base Ball Park. That one expression seemed to stick. The chance change on a word had upset the entire fabric I thought I was building. I seemed to have lost all power to start her over again. I pled with her to stay in the house, telling her that the City Fathers would not leave her to stay with me if she kept running away and had to be brought home by the police. Thinking to convince her that this was not Raleigh and that the Ball Park in Washington was not the place where "Ander" had worked I let her follow her bent one day and meekly walked beside her without trying to direct or in any way hinder her route. She stopped a strange man to ask if "this wasn't the right way to the Base Ball Park" and added didactically: "de place where de teams come to play Ball." He pointed to the Park which wasn't far and she kept on triumphantly. Our roles had changed completely. She was the teacher and naturally enough mistook my silence for docility. "You see Sis Annie" and she would go on into details of Ander's history and why she hadn't been up to see him etc., etc. Finally we reached the Park and went inside. "They've changed it," she said and pitifully, "They've sent Ander somewhere else to work." I took the whip hand again and made her promise to give up these excursions to the Base Ball Park. I told her honestly that they would say she was crazy and send her to the Asylum and I would be powerless to keep her any longer. She seemed to understand for the time being and promised sweetly as ever that she would stay in the house till I came from work every day and then we would take our walk together. This promise, however, she was wholly incapable of keeping. The police were very considerate and brought her home several times, but finally she was taken to Gallinger, adjudged insane by the Court, and sent to St. Elizabeth's, and after that to the hospital for the colored insane in North Carolina, her native State.

The nurse who brought her in on my first visit to her there whispered: "She is such a nice patient. Such a perfect *lady*." So clean and comfy she looked—and there was the same unforgettable bending at the waist curtsey. "How you do, Sis Annie. I never can fergit you." We sat holding hands for a while and repeated together our old familiar Psalm while the hospital attendant stood at a respectful distance with moist sympathetic eyes. "*I shall not want. He leadeth me beside—Yea though I walk—He resto'ith my soul—*" then breaking off she pinned me with a piercing look: "Sis Annie there's jes one thing I want to ask you." It was the look a judge might give a culprit with the command to tell the truth, the whole truth and nothing but the truth: "I wants to know is Ander dead or is he not?"

OCTAVIA B. WYNBUSH

The Return of a Modern Prodigal

The Illinois Central Flyer spun along the gleaming steel rails, farther and farther from the chill, blustering shores of Lake Michigan, deeper and deeper into the balmy warmth of the southland. Past Memphis, past rich fields of cotton, sugar cane and rice, deep, threatening swamp, and romantic vistas of old plantation mansions dating 'way before the days of the Civil War, rushed the train, while the wheels hummed and sang to the steel rails.

To Slim Sawyer, reared back in the Jim Crow smoker, his hat on the side of his head, a huge cigar in his mouth, and his feet planted comfortably on the cushion of the seat in front of him, the wheels spinning on the steel rails were singing, "Going home, Going home!"

There was a pleasurable exhilaration in listening to their steely song, an exhilaration mixed at the same time with a heaviness and an apprehension that was growing momentarily with the shortening of the miles between him and his destination. Slim was wondering. Would his folks know him after twenty-five years? He would know them, without a doubt.

His hand strayed to the side of his head uncovered by his hat, and felt the close-curled hair that covered it. He smiled as he had smiled a hundred times after performing the same act. A crop of hair felt good after a man had been forced to keep his head clean-shaven for nineteen years. Slim jerked himself out of his reverie and looked around with the air of one who fears he has whispered a secret too loudly. No one was paying him any attention. Evidently nobody had heard his thoughts.

Source: The Crisis 44 (October 1937): 300–301, 306, 311.

Staring out the window at the fields, trees, mules and cabins that went spinning by, Slim saw back and beyond them all, the panorama of his own life unrolling. It had been boyish restlessness and dissatisfaction that had shaped his life into what it now was.

He saw himself as he must have looked at fifteen—like that youngster out there, leaning against the fence, watching the train rush by. He must have been like that—a tall, slim youngster out of whose face blackened by the intimate acquaintance with the Louisiana sun, shone two eyes eager and alive with the dreams and longings of youth. Many a time when unobserved by his father, he had let the mules stand idle in the field at plowing time while he leaned against the fence and stared down the road that wound away into the distance. It always fascinated him, that road, yellow with powdery dust in the dry season, churned into black, sticky mud in the wet.

There, somewhere at the end of that road was a railway station where trains came puffing in three times a day and once a night. And these trains carried people away from the never-ending toil of the plantation. Somewhere in the great unknown these trains stopped at New Orleans, Memphis, Chicago and God only knew where else in that heaven called the North.

One day in plowing time the lure of the road had proved too strong for his boyish imagination. As he came opposite the fence on this particular day, he had dropped the reins of the mules, bolted over the fence, and taken to the road. His action was entirely unpremeditated, and was simply the result of dreams, and the day which had beckoned him with teasing finger ever since he had risen at dawn.

Once on the road there was no turning back. Too many things lured him on. Every curve in the road, hidden by trees and clumps of bushes, hinted of something more alluring around the bend. That night he had slept in the station where he hid behind a pile of old boxes. At day-break he had started on his trek to New Orleans. Slim smiled as he pictured the dirty ragged black boy who had ventured from house to house begging food, and who had slept in field corners at night, and had stolen from those fields under the shadow of night what he needed to eat.

The man's smile was sadly reminiscent as his mind flew back over the many vicissitudes through which he had passed during the following years spent in New Orleans, in Memphis, in Chicago and Detroit. His mouth twisted wryly as he thought of Detroit. That city had been the scene of his undoing. A cloud of sadness and of shame descended upon him. Drink—a fight—fumes of poisonous whiskey clearing away from his brain to reveal to him the still, dead form of a man they said he had killed—the trial—the cold pronouncement of the sentence by the judge—nineteen wasted years in the penitentiary, his time had been shortened to nineteen years because of his good behavior. He had spent the year following his release trying to lose the prison traces. His hand involuntarily went back to the hair on his head.

He wondered how the old folks would take his return. He did not wonder whether they were still alive. His first concern after leaving prison was to find that out by devious secret means. They were just as poor now as they were the day he had walked off. Certainly they were feebler. The years and the hard, back-breaking, spirit-grinding toil had taken care of that.

Slim smiled broadly. In an inside belt he was carrying enough money to put his parents on Easy Street the rest of their lives. Bootlegging had been the easiest and the most profitable business he had found open to him after his release. He had saved nearly every penny of his profits for the old folks.

The shadows cast by the coaches were gradually lengthening; the sky was growing less and less light. Evening was coming, quickly to be followed by the night. One more night in the uncomfortable coach, with his long body doubled "S" fashion on two seats in lieu of a berth, and he would be in New Orleans. From that point a local would carry him by slow, perspiring stages to the station in which he had slept the night he had run away.

The lights in the coach flared up. Night had fallen. Slim's preparations for retiring were simple. He removed his hat and placed it in the rack above him. Then he threw the remaining part of his cigar out of the window, removed his shoes and accommodating his long body to the two seats drew over him a lightweight overcoat to keep out the chill of the night.

It was six o'clock the next morning when the train pulled into the station in New Orleans. As he stepped from his coach Slim saw the local on the next track, getting up steam to pull out. Quickly he was aboard and settled in a seat. This train did not move with the speed of the flyer had he just quitted. The wheels, however, sang, "Going home," but with a difference.

It was like a funeral dirge now. "I feel more like a corpse than a livin' man," Slim muttered, wiping his face with a large fancy silk handkerchief.

The day was exceedingly warm and as the local crept from station to station, stopping often for a longer period than it was in motion, the oppressive heat weighed on Slim to such an extent that it gave an oppressed feeling.

Somehow, the nearer he was borne to his home, the farther away he felt from all that home represented. His mother, a saintly, well-meaning woman; his father, a practical, hard-headed man who worshipped his God and measured mankind by the Ten Commandments.

The utter simplicity of their faith, the purity of their lives, the shining whiteness of them served only to make his misspent years stand out boldly black and ugly. His hand surreptitiously patted the money belt. How would those dollars be received? He had concocted a tale that to his ears had seemed plausible enough when he boarded the train in Chicago. But now at the thought of looking into his mother's calm, trusting eyes and telling the carefully planned lie, a feeling of nausea swept over him. Under the keen, shrewd, soul-scrutinizing eyes of his father, the best planned tale would seem weak and futile.

The tortuous hours crawled on. Noon had enveloped and smothered the passengers with its heat, and the slight breeze that had sprung up drove clouds of smoke and showers of cinders into the windows of the Jim Crow car. Slim noted with increasing irritation that his cuffs, collars and shirt front were growing momentarily dingier. Every now and then he removed his hat and carefully flicked the soot and cinders from its surface. He sighed with relief when the conductor shouted the name of the station.

Gathering his luggage, Slim made his way to the platform and sprang to the ground as soon as the train stopped. He looked around him. The dingy unpainted shed of a station that had once sheltered him was gone. In its place arose a trim bright yellow building bearing on one side the legend, "Laurelville." There were two waiting rooms, also, one bearing the sign "White Waiting Room," the other, "Colored Waiting Room."

The next question was how to get to the plantation on which his father lived. Slim did not relish the long walk through the yellow dust. Surely there must be someone with a wagon and mule, who wouldn't mind earning a dollar by carrying him up that road.

He walked around the corner of the station, and there came upon a crowd of young men lolling and sprawling in all degrees of idleness and inertia. Looking at their dull, stagnant, yellow, brown and black faces, Slim reflected that here, but by the grace of chance, was Slim Sawyer. Singling out one of the group he walked up to him and spoke.

"Buddy, do you know where I can get a wagon to carry me out to Logan's plantation?"

The fellow questioned spat carefully into the dust beyond Slim, wiped his mouth on his ragged shirt cuff and answered, "Sho'. I'll take y' in my ole flivver. It's jes' aroun' the cornah behin' de station. Come, git in."

Slim followed his guide to the rear of the station, where stood the great, great grandfather of all flivvers. Battered, dented, with great gaping wounds in the top, and every shred of upholstery vanished from the interior, it looked entirely incapable of motion. Gingerly Slim deposited himself on the front seat through which a broken spring protruded. He made an effort to keep the spring between the owner and himself.

After much cranking, kicking and coughing, the ancient chariot started off with the noise of a cannon shot. Its bounds and leaps at the starting made Slim think of a passage his father had once spelled out in the family Bible—something about horses pawing in the valley.

The light yellow dust rose in clouds from the dry road, sprinkling the vehicle and its occupants with a fine yellow film. It seeped between Slim's lips, making his mouth feel rough and gritty. He was thankful for the dust, though, for it kept his companion from asking the very personal questions that every native felt privileged to ask every newcomer.

The heat and the dust played havoc with Slim's freshly washed face and clean clothes. He cursed inwardly for not having kept on the clothes he had worn during his journey on the train. The handkerchief with which he swabbed his face came away streaked with dirt and perspiration. His silk shirt grew stickier and stickier. A longing to exchange his summer weight woolen suit for the airy tatters of his companion overcame him. The car engine seemed to add twenty degrees to the temperature of his feet.

At last the car turned a bend in the hot unshaded road and entered a narrow lane lined on either side with magnolias, live-oaks, and a sprinkling of pecan trees. Slim sighed with relief for their shade. He knew that in a few minutes his ride would be over. The thought brought a flood of conflicting feelings.

"Well, hyah you is," drawled the owner of the car, bringing it to a standstill in front of a gate in a barbed wire fence.

Slim climbed out and took the luggage which the man handed him from the car.

"How much do I owe you?" he asked.

"O, 'bout two bits, I reckon."

Reaching into his pocket, Slim drew out a dollar and handed it to the fellow, saying with a smile, "Keep the change for lagniappe."*

Ignoring the voluble thanks that followed his generosity, Slim turned and opened the gate. He stood just within it until the car had hiccoughed out of sight. He suddenly felt bewildered, frightened and very small-boyish. Strangely enough his mind flew back to a day in his childhood—a day when, often having disobeyed his father's injunction to stay out of the creek because the water wasn't warm enough yet, he had stood at that same gate, making up his mind to go to the house. He remembered wondering whether all signs of his disobedience were destroyed, and feeling then exactly as he felt now.

Slowly closing the gate behind him, he advanced up the path, merely a ribbon of trodden grass threading through a grove of trees similar to those lining the lane. A few moments of slow walking brought him to the end of the path and into an open grassy space. There, under the wide-flung branches of a live-oak whose Spanish moss dipped and touched the much patched roof, stood the little cabin. It was black, now, with the wind and the sun and the rains. The same flower beds were flung out in front of it. The same little path led to the cabin steps. The railing around the porch supported wooden flower boxes similar to those Slim had seen there in his boyhood.

He halted again. Sudden panic overcame him. He wanted nothing so much as to run away. But any such intention was quickly put to an end by the appearance in the doorway of an old woman. The short, thin gray hair, the spectacles, the deep furrows on her brow and thin cheeks and the stoop that comes of old age and labor could not disguise her. It was his mother. His heart quaked into stillness. Would she know him? Did he want her to know him?

The old woman looked at him questioningly yet with a smile of unmistakable hospitality.

---

*Louisiana slang for "tip."

"Good evenin', sah," she said in a somewhat thin tremulous voice.

"Good evening, ma'am." Slim accompanied the words with a sweeping bow. His mind was made up as to the course he would pursue until she recognized him, or until he decided to drop his disguise.

At the beginning of his journey he had hoped for instant recognition. Now, somehow, he was glad it had not come. In a few words he established his assumed identity. His name was Adams, Lee Adams, and he was on a long journey from Chicago to a point still farther away. He wanted to break the trip by stopping somewhere tonight. On the train from New Orleans someone had told him of Mr. and Mrs. Sawyer as nice people to stop with, and here he was. Would she put him up overnight? He would pay her well for her trouble.

With true Louisiana hospitality Sarah Sawyer invited him into the house.

"Sho' you kin stay. We ain't much of a place, but ef you kin put up with it, why we'll be glad to have you. 'Tain't often strangers draps aroun' heah."

Slim followed her into the cabin. How familiar everything was! The oven of the big cook-stove in the center of the wall opposite the outside door, was sending forth fragrant whiffs of something baking. On the stove were a sauce pan, a kettle and a big black iron pot. In a corner of the room, near an open window was the table spread with a neatly patched blue checked table cloth, and laid for two people. Slim thrilled to think that soon another place would be there for him. The willow rocker that he had helped his father make sat turned toward the door, as if Sarah had been sitting in it looking out when the stranger came up the path.

She led him across the kitchen to a door on one side of the stove. Opening this door she stood aside with fine courtesy to let Slim enter.

"I'm sho' it ain't what you is used to, sah," she apologized, "but sech as it is, you is welcome to it. Jes' mak yo' se'f comfatible. I'll bring you some hot watah so you kin wash de dus' off yo'se'f. Dis Looziana dus' sho' sticks. My husban'll be in f'm de fiel' soon, an' we kin have suppah."

She walked out, closing the door behind her, and leaving Slim to look around him. He was in his own room once more. The rafters were darker now than they were when he used to lie in the white covered bed and look up at them at night. Vivid colored pictures from magazines, posters and newspapers were pasted on the walls. He fingered some of the prints tenderly, realizing the fact that he had often helped his mother paste such on the walls when he was a boy. White barred dimity* curtains hung at the two windows. A rag carpet covered most of the floor. Near the door through which he had just come stood an old-fashioned washstand with a large tin bowl and pitcher.

"Heah's yo' watah."

Stepping to the door Slim opened it and received a bucket of cold water and a kettle of hot water from Sarah.

When he reappeared in the kitchen, he was rewarded with a smile and an appreciative glance from Sarah.

"Son, yo' sho' looks a heap bettah sence gettin' shet of some of dat dus'. Dey ain't no dus' nowheres else in de whole worl' lak dis Looziana dus'. It sticks lak leeches. Set down an res' yo' se'f. My husban' be comin' any time now. Set in de willow rocker."

"But won't I be robbing you?" Slim's whole being was throbbing with a strong ache at sound of that word "son." But he realized that it was only a term of kindness and friendliness, nothing more.

"Shucks! A woman don' have time to set down near meal-time," he heard Sarah say, as she stooped to open the oven door.

Slim sat in the rocker, his eyes on his mother. She was so much thinner than he had ever known her. Already the trembling, uncertain movements of old age were creeping upon her. The spryness, while not altogether gone, was somehow less dynamic, less vital. A step on the porch. Slim looked up into the eyes of his father. Involuntarily he rose to his feet.

Sarah had heard the step, for she came forward.

"Andrew, dis is Mr. Lee Adams. He come frum Chicago an' is on his way to Baker, an' he ast to stop heah ovah night. Mr. Adams, dis is my husban', Mr. Andrew Sawyer."

Feeling the shrewd, close scrutiny of the tall, straight old man's eyes, Slim felt a chill as he stretched out his hand to meet the other's. As their hands clasped, Slim's thumb doubled under his finger in a movement he had not made since leaving home. He felt a sudden fear. This little trick was one his father had taught him. It was their sign of sticking together

*A thin cotton fabric, white, dyed, or printed, woven with a stripe or check of heavier yarn.

in any plot conceived and carried out against the wishes of Sarah. Slim looked searchingly into Andrew's eyes, but they were the unfathomable, scrutinizing eyes of one meeting and appraising a stranger.

After a few words of formal greeting, Andrew withdrew to another room opening out of the kitchen. Slim remembered again. No matter how hungry or tired her men-folks, Sarah always made them "fresh up" before eating their evening meal.

By the time Andrew appeared once more, the supper was sending out tantalizing odors from the table. The three sat down and began to eat. Little was said, except by Sarah, full of womanly curiosity as to the ways of city folks. Andrew ate in silence, but Slim knew that the old man was mercilessly scrutinizing, analyzing and classifying him.

When the meal was over the two men repaired to the porch, Andrew to smoke, and Slim to watch the advancing night as it slowly conquered the west and spread up the heavens. Finally Sarah joined them, and began to speak.

"I put Mr. Adams into the little room, Andrew."

"Uh huh," grunted Andrew between puffs at his pipe.

Sarah leaned toward Slim.

"You know, Mr. Adams, it's our boy's room. He lef' us twenty-five years ago."

"Dead, you mean?"

"No. He runned off. Jes' lef' one day 'thout rhyme or reason."

Slim expressed his sympathy. Encouraged by his words Sarah poured out the whole story of her fears, her sorrow and her sleepless nights.

"Hain't a night passed sence then what I don' pray for him. I ast God to let me see my baby boy once mo'. We ain' nevah knowed why he runned away. Lawd knows we was as kin' to him as we knowed how to be."

"Perhaps he'll come back some day, rich an' able to help you," suggested Slim.

"Dat's what I tells Andrew all time," answered Sarah, lookng in the direction of the glowing pipe embers, "but he say de boy is daid, or good as daid."

"Good as dead?"

"Yes, he say ef his tuhned out to be a worthless no-count rascal, his good as daid to him."

"An' I'm right!" exclaimed Andrew, and the glowing embers in his pipe came to rest with a slight thud on the railing. "A man what don' say nothin' in twenty-five years to his parents what done all they could to find him, is daid or a no-count rascal."

"He may have been hindered in getting in touch with you. Maybe he couldn't send you anything. That is—something may have—"

"Ef he's lived de right kin' o' life, he'd write to his folks even ef he ain't got nothin' to send em."

"Andrew, go in an light de lamp," Sarah's tone was peevish. She didn't want Andrew giving this stranger the wrong impression of her boy.

Slim leaped up. "Let me!" he exclaimed, "I know where it is."

In the darkness he walked across the porch into the kitchen. Unconsciously as he crossed the porch, there was a slight dragging sound as if one of his feet had gone suddenly lame, or was moved with difficulty because of a heavy weight.

As he placed the chimney on the lighted lamp, a cold sweat broke out on him. He realized what he had done. After a year of practicing and being on his guard, he had gone back to the habit burned into his blood by nineteen years of wearing the ball and chain. Cautiously, every nerve on guard, he walked back to his seat in the far corner of the porch. In passing, he cast a glance at Andrew's face, dimly visible in the faint reflection of the lamp in the kitchen. The old man was looking off into the darkness, smoking away. Slim fancied that the muscles of his mouth quivered an instant, and then set in a granite line.

Sarah took up the conversation. "My boy wouldn't do nothin' whut wuzn't right," she declared stoutly, "ez hard ez we tried to raise him right."

"But it might be easy for a young lad to get into trouble. Maybe he did go wrong, but if he was sorry an' wanted to come back—"

"He could come, bless God," cried Sarah, "but my baby wouldn't do no wrong. He's alive, too, somewhere an' he'll come back yet. I don' believe he's daid—"

"It would be too bad," murmured Slim.

Removing his pipe once more, Andrew remarked in low, tense tones.

"I'd rather believe he's daid than come to some things I can think of. Some things is worse than death."

A slow tightening around Slim's throat and chest. "What, for instance?" he asked, after a thick silence.

"Servin' time in the pen," returned the old man.

"No mattah whah he is, or what he done, he's my own little baby whut I borned into dis worl'. He kin come to his mammy f'um any place he's at," sobbed Sarah.

With an effort Slim spoke again. "Suppose he had—served time—an' had got out—an' made money an' come back to take care o' you—"

Andrew bit in savagely, "Ef he done made his peace with God an' made his money clean, he be welcome. Ef he ain't, he could take hissel'f an' his money and an' hit de highway. We kep' de family name clean an' clear fo' lo dese many yeahs, an' we don' what was right in de sight of de Lawd. We ain't gwine be disgraced an' made ashame in ouah ol' age. Honest want is bettah dan dishonest plenty."

The yellow moon was now shining directly upon their faces. To hide whatever his countenance might betray, Slim leaned back in the shadow of the vines covering one side of the porch. He knew too well that old man. Arguing with him was about as effective as using one's fists to beat a way out of a tomb of solid granite. His mother, rocking softly, had covered her face with her apron and was sobbing softly.

At last Slim arose, said goodnight and went to his room. Locking the door he sat on the side of the bed. Dejectedly his head sank into his hands. For a long time he sat there. Finally he arose, walked to the chair upon which his bag rested, opened the bag, and took [out] a writing case. After taking out an envelope and a piece of paper he closed the bag and seated himself beside the lamp stand. Slowly he began writing:

> Dear Mrs. Sawyer,
>   I have decided to take the three o'clock morning train. So when you get up I'll be gone. I'm leaving a little gift in the letter. Think of me sometime.
>   Thank you,
>   Lee Adams.

From his money belt he counted out some of the currency—fifty ten dollar bills, twenty fives and twenty twenties—$1,000 in all—placed it in the envelope with the letter, and stood the sealed letter against the bowl on the washstand.

The stars dimming in the early morning sky looked down upon a man trudging through the dusty road leading back to the railroad station. His well-tailored clothes and expensive luggage were covered with a film of yellow, clinging dust.

A Blossom in an Alley

A blossom in a window, in a city's alley dark—
I see it, and my smoldering faith leaps to a glowing spark.
For I can read its message of all-pervading good,
Its earnest of a sweeter life, a closer brotherhood.
For the same urge that guided the rough hand that placed it
  there,
Inspired wealth's richest garden, teeming with exotics rare,
And Beauty, answering, reck'd* not of hovel or of hall—
But that a human soul had craved and she had felt its call!

O, ye who, patient, seek the eternal verities
'Mid intricate mazes of our life's diversities
Of creed and caste calling, and perchance have failed the mark,—
Go see a blossom growing in a city's alley dark!

Source: Sarah Collins Fernandis, *Poems* (Boston: Gorham Press, 1925), p. 10.
  *Reckoned, i.e., told.

The Torch Bearer

To the Late Booker T. Washington,
Founder of Tuskegee Institute

Up from the portals dark of slavery's night,
  The dusky, untried youth, emerging came;
His feet set on the trail, his heart aflame
  With a great purpose: He would reach the light
Freedom held forth, and for his needy race
  Would touch his torch and bear it forth to teach,
To lead his people till they rose to reach
  The goal where progress needs must give them place.

Ah! woe for us, the once uplifted hand
  Lies nerveless; that a hush the world can feel
Reigns where erstwhile a voice with strong appeal
  Rang out for righteous standards in our land!
O, Washington, thy light we ill can spare,
  And thy great leadership, the strength, the grace
Of thy rich life spent to uplift a race
  With self-effacement, and achievement rare!

Source: Sarah Collins Fernandis, *Poems* (Boston: Gorham Press, 1925), p. 38.

The Offering

I was not keen to offer up my son—
  E'en when I saw white mothers give their all
Proudly to Freedom, answering the call
Of our common country. For, upon
  My soul heavily pressed the galling load
Of prejudice's mass accumulate.

Though I had stifled bitterness and hate,
  And rendered true allegiance while the goad
Of race-thrusts hurt, I could not give my boy.
'Twas thus I writhed, when, lo, my strugglin soul,
  illumined by a vision of the whole
Intent of freedom, offered him with joy!

Source: Sarah Collins Fernandis, *Poems* (Boston: Gorham Press, 1925), p. 35.

Biographical Notes

REGINA M. ANDREWS (1901–1993)

Regina Andrews was the daughter of Chicago attorney William Grant and Margaret Simons. Raised in a middle-class Chicago home and educated at Wilberforce University and the University of Chicago, she received her master of library science degree from Columbia University and served as librarian for many years at various branches of the New York Public Library, including what is now the Schomburg Center for Research in Black Culture. A promoter of theater in Harlem through such organizations as the Crisis Guild of Writers and Artists, in 1929 she cofounded the Negro Experimental Theatre with Dorothy Peterson and worked tirelessly behind the scenes to give new life to black theater. She was a sustaining member of a literary circle: the apartment she shared with Ethel Ray Nance (assistant to Charles Johnson) on Sugar Hill was a gathering place for writers in Harlem, and she helped to organize such events as the 1924 Civic Club dinner that honored black literary talents like Gwendolyn Bennett, Countee Cullen, Langston Hughes, and Jessie Fauset. In 1926 she married William T. Andrews, an attorney who later became a New York City councilman, and they had one daughter, Regina Ann.

Among the plays she wrote were *Climbing Jacob's Ladder* and *Underground*. They were performed in New York and well received, yet most of her work remains unpublished. *The Man Who Passed* is undated; it was probably written in the mid-1920s.

DELILAH LEONTIUM BEASLEY (1871–1934)

Delilah Beasley was born in Cincinnati, Ohio, and eventually became a journalist and a historian, although she had little formal education. After her parents died, she supported herself as a maid, a masseuse, and eventually as a physical therapist, all the while pursuing historical research and journalism, first in Ohio and then in California.

In a column entitled "Activities among Negroes," written for the *Oakland Tribune* (in California), she constantly advocated the elimination of the derogatory terms for African-Americans that were in common usage in the print media at that time. In her 1919 book, *The Negro Trailblazers of California,* compiled from records in the Bancroft Library at the University of California at Berkeley and from diaries, photographs, and letters, Beasley documented the existence of black Californians as far back as the Spanish explorers.

GWENDOLYN B. BENNETT (1902–1981)

The only child born to Joshua and Maime Bennett of Giddings, Texas, Gwendolyn Bennett moved to Washington, D.C., with her parents at the age of five so that her father could study law and her mother could train to be a manicurist and beautician. After high school in Washington, Bennett enrolled as a fine arts student at Columbia University in New York. She transferred to the Pratt Institute after two years. Following her graduation in 1924, she was awarded Delta Sigma Theta's $1,000 foreign scholarship. Bennett used this money to go to Paris, where she studied with Parisian artists and at the Sorbonne.

After returning to the United States, Bennett moved to New York. During the 1920s' cultural renaissance of the African-American in New York, she played several roles: assistant editor of *Opportunity* and author of "The Ebony Flute" column in that magazine, lyricist and poet, and one-time director of the Harlem Community Art Center. In "The Ebony Flute," she told of the social and cultural goings-on of the Harlem scene. Bennett worked and socialized with the celebrated figures in Harlem's art and literature world. Her own artwork appeared on the covers of *Opportunity* and *The Messenger,* and her poetry and essays were published in various periodicals and anthologies of the 1920s and 1930s. The story anthologized here ("Wedding Day") was written, like the bulk of her work, in the mid-1920s.

MARITA BONNER (1898–1971)

The youngest of three children, Marita Bonner grew up in Boston and was educated in the Brookline public schools. Bonner was admitted to Radcliffe College and graduated in 1922. At Radcliffe, she was active in the school's mandolin, music, German, and English clubs; she also wrote her class song and reportedly founded the Radcliffe chapter of the black sorority Delta Sigma Theta.

After graduation, Bonner taught in Bluefield, West Virginia, and Washington, D.C. A writer whose plays, short stories, and essays appeared in such magazines as *Opportunity, Black Opals, Black Life,* and *The Crisis* from 1924 to 1941, Bonner was an active participant in Washington's literary salons. She identified the triple jeopardy of being black, female, and excluded from the upper class, and her writings often dealt with that struggle. One such piece, "On Being Young—A Woman—and Colored" won first prize in a 1925 *Crisis* literary contest.

After marrying William Almy Occomy, Bonner moved to Chicago, where the couple raised their three children. Chicago became the backdrop for Bonner's writing. Several of her pieces published in the 1930s won first- and second-place prizes in *Opportunity* and *Crisis* literary contests, some written under the pseudonym Joseph Maree Andrew. In 1941 Bonner and her husband became Christian Scientists. In 1987 their daughter, Joyce Occomy Stricklin, published a posthumous volume of her mother's collected writings, *Frye Street and Environs: The Collected Work of Marita Bonner,* in which "One True Love" appears.

NELLIE R. BRIGHT (1902–1976)

Nellie Rathborne Bright was born in Savannah and raised in Philadelphia by parents who had emigrated from the Virgin Islands. Her father was an Episcopal clergyman, and his profession placed the family in the black middle class. She attended the Philadelphia School of Pedagogy and the University of Pennsylania, where she earned a bachelor's degree in 1923 and a master's degree in 1925. She studied at Oxford University from 1925 to 1926 and at the Sorbonne from 1926 to 1927 before returning to Philadelphia to write and to teach in the Philadelphia public school system.

Bright was a frequent contributor to *Black Opals,* the short-lived magazine published by Philadelphia's New Negro literary circle in the 1920s. In fact, Bright's poem "Longing," published in the debut issue, gave the publication its title: "I want to look deep in a pool at night, and see the stars / Flash flame like the fire in black opals." Her essay "Black" won third prize in the 1927 literary contest of *Opportunity* magazine. It was published by *Opportunity* and by *Carolina Magazine,* a literary publication of the University of North Carolina.

HALLIE QUINN BROWN (c. 1845–1949)

Teacher, writer, librarian, elocutionist, and civil and women's rights advocate Hallie Quinn Brown was born in Pittsburgh. The daughter of former slaves Thomas Arthur Brown and Frances Jane Scroggins Brown, she was the fifth of six children.

Brown's parents became free before 1865, and Thomas Arthur Brown accumulated some real estate prior to the Civil War that permitted the Browns to live relatively well and to provide their children with an education. Hallie Quinn Brown received her bachelor's degree in 1873, an honorary master of science degree in 1890, and an honorary doctorate in law from Wilberforce University in 1936.

While Brown was growing up, her father

was employed as a steward and an express agent on the riverboat route between Pittsburgh and New Orleans; through this job he actively assisted the Underground Railroad. Brown retells some of the episodes her father shared in her book *Tales My Father Told and Other Stories* (1925).

HAZEL V. CAMPBELL (?–?)

Almost nothing is known about Hazel Vivian Campbell. When she published two short stories in *Opportunity* in the mid-1930s, the short biography of her in the magazine revealed only that she was living in New Rochelle, New York.

EUNICE HUNTON CARTER (1899–1970)

Born in Atlanta to activist and author Addie Waites Hunton and Young Men's Christian Association (YMCA) national executive William Alphaeus Hunton, Eunice Hunton moved to Brooklyn with her family after the Atlanta race riots of 1906. She spent two years in a school in Strassburg, Germany (now Strasbourg, France), while her mother attended Kaiser Wilhelm University. Hunton received both a bachelor's and a master's degree in political science in 1921 from Smith College.

In New York Hunton worked for various family service organizations while taking courses at Columbia University. After marrying Lisle Carter, a dentist, in 1924, she took night school classes at Fordham Law School and received her law degree in October of 1932. She was admitted to the New York Bar Association in 1934. When New York Special Prosecutor Thomas E. Dewey named her deputy assistant district attorney for the state of New York, she became the first black woman to attain such a position.

Carter was a charter member of the National Council of Negro Women, served as that organization's legal council, and was a member of, and one-time chair of, its board of trustees.

Carter published four short stories and six book reviews in *Opportunity* magazine during the 1920s.

ETHEL CAUTION DAVIS (1880–1981)

Born in Cleveland Ethel Caution was orphaned at an early age and was adopted by a Mrs. Davis of Boston. She used the Davis surname until her adoptive mother died, after which time she became Ethel Caution Davis. She attended Girls' Latin School in Boston and graduated from Wellesley College in 1912.

After graduation, Caution Davis taught in Durham, North Carolina, for two years, subsequently moving to Kansas City, where she taught at Summer High School, worked for the Young Women's Christian Association, and served on the executive committee of the Citizens' Forum of the Kansas branch of the National Association for the Advancement of Colored People (NAACP). She was appointed dean of women at Talladega College, a post which she held for three years before moving to New York City to work for the public assistance program.

Caution Davis's writing was first published while she was in college, when some of her short poems and essays appeared in *Wellesley* magazine and the Wellesley *News.* After graduation, her poetry was published in *The Crisis,* the *Durham Advocate,* and *The Brownies' Book* for children.

In later years, Caution Davis was the director of Club Caroline, a residence club for women, before she retired to New Jersey. Though by then almost blind, she tended a garden and kept up with literature through a volunteer reader and audio books. She died in New York City, at the age of 101.

CARRIE W. CLIFFORD (1862–1934)

Born and raised in Chillicothe, Ohio, and later educated in Columbus, Carrie Williams Clifford founded the Ohio Federation of Colored Women's Clubs. She served as editor of one of the federation's publications, *Sowing for Others to Reap: A Collection of Papers of Vital Importance to the Race,* which was designed to promote African-American self-awareness.

After her marriage to William H. Clifford, a lawyer and a Republican member of the Ohio state legislature, and the births of her two sons, she and her family moved to Washington, D.C. In Washington she became involved with a group of black intellectuals and literary artists that included such figures as Mary Church Terrell (q.v.), W. E. B. Du Bois, Alain Locke, and Georgia Douglas Johnson (q.v.). Clifford was also a member of the Niagara movement, from which the NAACP emerged.

Hand in hand with her involvement in advancing black causes were Clifford's efforts on behalf of women's rights. She was a suffragist and feminist, commenting in her writings especially on the injustices peculiar to women of color. Clifford published two volumes of poetry and contributed numerous short stories, articles, and poems to such periodicals as *Opportunity* and *The Crisis.*

ANITA SCOTT COLEMAN (1890–1960)

Raised in New Mexico, Anita Scott worked as a teacher until she married. She and her husband settled in Los Angeles, where they ran a boarding home for children.

Coleman wrote short stories, essays, and poetry filled with racial pride. In her poem "Black Faces" (*Opportunity,* October 1929) she wrote: "I love black faces . . . / They are full of smould'ring fire, / And Negro eyes, white—with white desire, / And Negro lips so soft and thick / Like rich velvet within / fine jewelry cases . . . / I love black faces." Between 1920 and 1939 her work appeared in *The Crisis, Opportunity, Half Century* and *The Messenger.* In a 1925 contest held by *The Crisis,* Coleman won second prize for "Unfinished Masterpieces," a prose piece, and third prize for another story.

ANNA J. COOPER (c. 1856–1964)

Anna Cooper, a towering intellect and a strong feminist, was born to a slave mother, Hannah Stanley, and her mother's master, George Washington Haywood. She attended St. Augustine Normal School and Collegiate Institute in Raleigh, North Carolina, and at age eleven became a student teacher there. While at St. Augustine, she met an Episcopalian divinity student, G. A. C. Cooper, whom she married in 1877. He died only two years later, and she never remarried.

Cooper graduated from Oberlin College in 1884, one of the first four black women to do so. One of her classmates, Mary Church Terrell (q.v.), was to remain her lifelong colleague in the struggle for racial equality. In 1887 she received her masters from Oberlin, after which she moved to Washington, D.C., to become a Latin teacher at Washington High School (later renamed M Street High School and, still later, Dunbar High School). She stayed at the school for thirty years, becoming its principal in 1901. Stressing high academic standards, she developed a college preparatory program at the school with some success; a few of her students were accepted into such institutions as Harvard, Yale, and Princeton.

In 1906 Cooper was asked to leave the school specifically because of her academic philosophy. The school board claimed that she pushed the students too hard and had them aspire too high for blacks. In 1910 she was invited back to the school, but in her previous capacity as Latin teacher.

Cooper applied to a doctoral program at the Sorbonne and in 1925 became the fourth black woman known to have received that degree. Returning to the United States, she became the second president of Frelinghuysen University, a night school for employed blacks, and she taught classes in her home because there were no funds for a proper building.

In 1892 Cooper published an essay which has come to be recognized as one of the early black feminist texts: *A Voice from the South—By a Black Woman of the South.*

Until her death at the age of 107, Anna Cooper continued to write and speak on racial and gender equality.

JOSEPHINE COPELAND (?–?)

Little is known about this author except what Arna Bontemps wrote of her in a biographical note in his anthology *Golden Slippers* (1941). Copeland, the fifth child in a family of six, was raised in Covington, Louisiana, then a small resort town just outside of New Orleans. She studied part-time at Dillard University, also in New Orleans, and completed a two-year teaching course. Before moving to Chicago she taught grades one to five in New Orleans from 1922 to 1929.

The poems we include in this volume are the only works by Copeland found thus far.

MAE V. COWDERY (1909–1953)

Mae Virginia Cowdery was the only child of Mr. and Mrs. Lemuel Cowdery of Philadelphia. Growing up in a black middle-class family, she attended Philadelphia High School for Girls, which was for scholastically talented students. In 1927, during her senior year of high school, three of her poems were published in *Black Opals,* the magazine of the Philadelphia black literary circle, which she later joined.

After graduating from high school, Cowdery moved to New York and attended the Pratt Institute. She was befriended by such Harlem Renaissance notables as Alain Locke and Langston Hughes, and she became involved in Harlem literary activities, occasionally publishing in *Opportunity* and *The Crisis* between 1927 and 1930.

In 1927 she won the Krigwa prize for her poem "Longings," and her photo appeared on the cover of the January 1928 issue of *The Crisis*. In 1936 she published a volume of her poetry entitled *We Lift Our Voices.* She took her own life in 1953.

MARION VERA CUTHBERT (1896–1989)

Marion Vera Cuthbert was born in St. Paul, Minnesota, and lived there until she entered college at Boston University. She received her bachelor's degree from that school in 1920, after which she became principal of the Burrel Normal School. In 1927 she was appointed dean of Talladega College in Alabama. In 1930 Cuthbert was awarded a Kent Fellowship to pursue graduate studies at Columbia University in New York. She received her master's degree there in 1931 and her doctorate in 1942. Her doctoral dissertation, "Education and Marginality: A Study of the Negro College Graduate," examines the political, social, and economic effects of education on the lives of African-American women. She published a volume of poetry in addition to essays that appeared in *Opportunity* and black educational journals.

CAROLINE BOND DAY (1889–1948)

Caroline Bond Day (originally Caroline Bond Stewart) was born in Alabama to Moses and Georgia Fagan Stewart. She studied at Tuskegee Institute and Atlanta University before attending Radcliffe College. There she received both her bachelor's and her master's degree, and she married Aaron Day, Jr., following her graduation in 1920. During her college years, she participated in philanthropic organizations including the YMCA and the Circle for Negro Relief.

While at Radcliffe, she began social science research on interracial families. This research was published in 1932 as *A Study of Some Negro-White Families in the United States.*

Day's constant advocacy for African-Americans is expressed in her plays and stories. She taught English and theater at the college and elementary-school levels, and in September 1925, *The Crisis* published her compilation of plays, "What Shall We Play?" the casting of which provided black actors with alternatives to both classical English drama and historical plays with racial themes. "The Pink Hat" won third prize in *Opportunity*'s 1926 contest.

CLARISSA SCOTT DELANY (1901–1927)

Clarissa Scott Delany was born to Emmett Jay and Eleanor Baker Scott of Tuskegee, Alabama, the third of their five children. Her father was secretary to Booker T. Washington, the founder of Tuskegee Institute, where she was raised until she was sent north for her education. Of her educational experiences she once wrote: "I was born at Tuskegee Institute, Alabama, in the twentieth century, and spent my early years in what is known as the 'Black Belt.' This was followed by seven years in New England (1916–1923), three at Bradford Academy, and four at Wellesley College, where my southern blood became tinged with something of the austerity of that section." She graduated Phi Beta Kappa from Wellesley in 1923.

After a post-college trip to Europe, Delany taught high school in Washington, D.C. Of this experience she wrote: "Three years of teaching in the Dunbar High School of Washington, D.C., convinced me that though the children were interesting, teaching was not my metier." During this time she also published poetry, book reviews, and an essay on her experiences in Europe. These pieces appeared in *Opportunity* and Countee Cullen's Harlem Renaissance anthology, *Caroling Dusk* (1927).

In October 1926, she married Hubert T. Delany, a young lawyer, in Washington, D.C. The couple moved to New York, where Clarissa did social work, helping the National Urban League and the Women's City Club of New York to collect information for their study of delinquent and neglected Negro children. Less than a year later, she died of a kidney infection. The only surviving member of the entire Scott family is Clarissa's niece, Elaine Brown (daughter of Clarissa's brother, Dr. Horace Scott), who became a leader in the Black Panther party during the 1950s (see Elaine Brown, *A Taste of Power: A Black Woman's Story* [New York: Pantheon, 1992]).

ALICE DUNBAR-NELSON (1875–1935)

One of the best-known black women writers of her time, Alice Dunbar-Nelson, born Alice Ruth Moore, attended a two-year teaching program at Straight College in New Orleans, graduating in 1892. She went on to further study at the University of Pennsylvania, Cornell University, and the School of Industrial Arts in Philadelphia. After marrying black poet laureate Paul Laurence Dunbar, who was many years her senior, she moved to Brooklyn and taught school. There she also served as secretary of the National Association of Colored Women.

The Dunbars separated in 1902, and in 1916 Alice married Robert John Nelson, the publisher of the *Wilmington Advocate*. She taught in a Wilmington, Delaware, high school until she was dismissed in 1920 for her political activism. She then quickly became associate editor of the *Advocate*, a weekly columnist for the *Washington Eagle*, and associate editor of the *A.M.E. Church Review*, a publication of the African Methodist Episcopal Church. She also helped to found a school for delinquent black girls and served as secretary of the American Interracial Peace Committee.

Dunbar-Nelson's writing career has gained recent scholarly attention thanks to the publication of her collected works in a volume edited by Gloria T. Hull (Oxford University Press, 1988). Dunbar-Nelson's diary, kept sporadically between 1921 and 1931, was also annotated and published by Hull, in 1984.

KATHERINE DUNHAM (1910–)

Katherine Dunham was born in Glen Ellyn, Illinois, and had her heart set on dancing from an early age. She is best known for her talent as a choreographer. She studied anthropology at the University of Chicago, concentrating on folklore and, more specifically, dance as social construct. While a student, she was invited to dance at the 1934 Chicago World's Fair. Dunham's studies in field techniques with distinguished anthropologist Melville Herskovitz sparked her interest in the Maroon (rebel slave) community of Accompong, Jamaica. Dunham did a year of field study in Jamaica funded by a Rosenwald Fellowship before returning to Chicago to receive her bachelor's degree. This experience resulted in the book *Journey to Accompong* (1946).

Dunham gave up completing a master's degree to serve as choreographer for her own dance troupe. With this company and on her own, she traveled to Senegal, Martinique, Cuba, Trinidad, Haiti, and Mexico, and she used those locales as backdrops for her writing.

ALOISE BARBOUR EPPERSON (?–c. 1954)

Aloise Barbour Epperson is a writer about whom little is known, save that her home was in Norfolk, Virginia. In a preface to Epperson's 1943 book of poetry, *Hills of Yesterday and Other Poems,* she is described as a very private woman for whom poetry functioned as a refuge from racism. Epperson describes herself, in her own introduction to the book, as feeling strongly "the infinite sadness of loving freedom and of forever being denied its full privilege because of racial barriers."

What little is known of Epperson's life comes from this preface, in which she refers to the death of an adored daughter, and from her dedication of a later book of antiwar and antiracist poems, *Unto My Heart and Other Poems* (1953), to her husband, James H. Epperson.

JESSIE FAUSET (1882–1961)

Jessie Redmon Fauset is one of the best known female writers of her era. As the literary editor of *The Crisis* from 1919 to 1926, she became, as Langston Hughes wrote in his autobiography (1940), "one of those who midwifed the so-called New Negro literature into being." As the author of four novels (including *The Chinaberry Tree: A Novel of American Life,* 1931), she was acclaimed by the distinguished black literary critic William Stanley Braithwaite as deserving a permanent place in the canon of black literature.

The seventh child of Anna Seamon and the Reverend Redmon Fauset of the African Methodist Episcopal (A.M.E.) Church, Jessie Fauset grew up in a Philadelphia family that was relatively privileged because of her father's position and because the family had been free since the eighteenth century. Her mother died when Jessie was very young. In 1900, when Fauset was denied admission to a local teachers' college and Bryn Mawr College was unsure whether to accept her as its first black student, her father urged her to apply to Cornell, where she was accepted. In 1905 she became the first black woman to graduate from Cornell and perhaps the first black woman to be elected to Phi Beta Kappa.

Despite her academic achievements, Fauset's attempts to find a teaching job in Philadelphia were unsuccessful. After teaching for a year in Baltimore, she began a fourteen-year tenure teaching French at M Street High School (later Dunbar High School) in Washington, D.C. She also began to publish articles in *The Crisis.* After Fauset received her master's degree in French, W. E. B. DuBois asked her to move to New York to become the literary editor of *The Crisis,* to which she herself contributed poems, stories, and essays. She opened her home as a literary salon for young writers. Fauset also edited *The Brownies' Book,* a magazine for black children founded by Du Bois, which was published from 1920 to 1921.

In 1927 Fauset began teaching French at DeWitt Clinton High School in New York City. Two years later, she married Herbert E. Harris, a businessman, and ten years later they moved to Montclair, New Jersey, though Fauset continued to teach in New York until her retirement in 1944. She came out of retirement once, in 1949, to teach English for one semester at the Hampton Institute (now Hampton University) in Hampton, Virginia.

SARAH COLLINS FERNANDIS (1863–1951)

A native of Baltimore, Maryland, Sarah Collins Fernandis graduated from the Virginia's Hampton Institute (now Hampton University) in 1882, after which she attended the New York School of Social Work. She then became a teacher, working in Tennessee, Florida, Baltimore, and at the Hampton Institute.

She married John A. Fernandis in June of 1902, and the couple moved to Bloodfield, one of the poorest black districts in Baltimore, to set up what would be a "model home," showing neighbors how to create an environment conducive to comfortable living. They helped Bloodfield to start kindergartens, libraries, and day nurseries, and actively participated in the community's renewal. The Fernandises then went on to do the same for "Scallop Town," a poor black neighborhood in East Greenwich, Rhode Island.

Many of Sarah Fernandis's poems and articles appeared between 1891 and 1936 in *Southern Workman,* which was published at her alma mater, the Hampton Institute. *Poems,* a volume of her work comprising mainly poems from *Southern Workman,* was published in 1925.

MERCEDES GILBERT (1889–1952)

Mercedes Gilbert was born in Jacksonville, Florida, where her parents were both in business. The family moved to Tampa, where she enrolled in a Catholic school and then graduated from Edward Waters College of Jacksonville. She then taught school in southern Florida for a few years before completing nursing school at the Brewster Hospital Nurses Training School.

In 1916 Gilbert moved to New York City, where she worked as a private duty nurse for a short time. At the suggestion of friends, she found a songwriter, Chris Smith, to collaborate with her in putting her poems to music. Several of her songs were recorded. Gilbert married Arthur J. Stevenson in July of 1922.

Then Gilbert launched a career in theater and movies. She performed in several Broadway and off-Broadway productions, including the two Broadway roles that brought her stardom: she played Zipporah, the wife of Moses, in *The Green Pastures,* which ran for five years and five months on Broadway, and for her performance in the leading female role in Langston Hughes's play *Mulatto* she received critical acclaim, playing on Broadway for a year and then touring for seven months. The *New York Amsterdam News* of August 8, 1936, called her performance "epochal." An interview with Gilbert in September 1936, describes her as "a golden personality, pleasant, unassuming, in spite of the glory that is rightfully hers for the stellar performances given daily by her in Langston Hughes' play 'Mulatto' [at the Ambassador Theater on West Forty-Ninth street.]"

In 1931 Gilbert's first book, a collection of poetry, comedy and drama, *Selected Gems,* was published by Christopher Publishing House. In 1938 she published a novel, *Aunt Sara's Wooden God* (1938).

EDYTHE MAE GORDON (1896–?)

Very little is known about Edythe Gordon. She was born Edith Chapman in Washington, D.C., and lived with her grandmother, Matilda Bicks, her mother, Mary Bicks, and her aunt, Elizabeth Bicks. In census records for 1900 Matilda Bicks is listed as a "laundress" without literacy skills. Her two daughters, Mary and Elizabeth (presumably Edith's mother and aunt) gave their occupations as "servants." In 1916 Edith married Eugene Gordon, a journalist and a member of the Communist Party who later became president of Boston's Saturday Evening Quill Club and the editor of its magazine, the *Saturday Evening Quill.* She began spelling her name "Edythe" around this time.

Several years after her marriage, Gordon enrolled at Boston University, earning a bachelor's degree and writing a master's thesis in 1935 entitled

"The Status of the Negro Woman in the United States from 1619–1865." She announces in it that hers is the first interdisciplinary study of black women to examine their legal, social, religious, economic, and educational status. By the time she received her master's degree, she and Eugene were living at separate addresses in Boston.

Gordon published fiction in the *Saturday Evening Quill;* the first volume of the magazine in 1928 included her short story "Subversion." This story was among that year's "distinguished short stories" named by the O. Henry Memorial Award Prize Committee. Gordon was also a contributor to the "illustrated feature" section, a tabloid supplement that appeared in many black newspapers. Only a small body of her work, including some twelve poems, is extant. In 1938 two of her poems appeared with a biographical note in an anthology edited by Washington, D.C., poet Beatrice M. Murphy. Nothing is known of her life after 1941, when her name ceases to appear in directories for the city of Boston.

OTTIE B. GRAHAM (1900–?)

The daughter of the Reverend W. Graham of Philadelphia, Ottie Beatrice Graham was born in Virginia and received her education at Howard and Columbia Universities. After college she settled in Philadelphia.

Graham began writing while at Howard University. "To a Wild Rose" was the prize story selected by the Delta Omega Chapter of the Alpha Kappa Alpha Sorority "for the best short story written by a Negro student." (The prize was fifty dollars.) The committee that awarded her the prize consisted of Arthur B. Spingarn, Jessie Fauset, and W. E. B. Du Bois. Their decision was unanimous.

SHIRLEY GRAHAM (1896–1977)

Shirley Lola Graham was born in Indianapolis to Etta Bell Graham, a Native American woman, and David Andrew Graham, a Methodist minister. Interviewed in 1975 at her home in Amherst, Massachusetts, by James V. Hatch and Camille Billops, Graham discussed her early life and called her father "a true shepherd of his flock" and a man imbued with a love for reading and study. Graham's family moved around the country quite often because of her father's ministry, and she grew up in New Orleans and on the West Coast. She graduated from Lewis and Clark High School in Spokane, Washington, and then married Shadrach T. McCanns, but they were divorced in the mid-1920s, and she was left with two baby sons.

Graham moved to Paris in 1926, where she remained until 1929, studying music and receiving a French certificate from the Sorbonne. Returning to the United States, she enrolled at Oberlin College, where she received a bachelor's in 1934 and a master's degree in 1935. There she also wrote her first musical play, which she soon expanded into an opera, *Tom-Tom: An Epic of Music and the Negro*. This work became the first all-black opera to be produced on a large scale with a professional cast.

Graham chaired the fine arts department at Tennessee Agricultural and Industrial State College and later directed the Chicago Negro Unit of the Works Progress Administration's Federal Theatre Project. In 1938 Graham enrolled in the Yale University School of Drama as a Julius Rosenwald Fellow, and several of her plays were performed there. She received her second master's degree in 1940, and over the next four years she served as the director of a YWCA theater group in Indianapolis, the head of the YWCA United Service Organization (USO) at Fort Huachuca, Arizona, and as a field secretary for the NAACP.

In 1951 Graham married her longtime friend and mentor, W. E. B. Du Bois, whom she had met at her parents' home. She took his name, becoming Shirley Graham Du Bois, and the two lived the last period of their lives as expatriates. W. E. B. Du Bois died in Ghana in 1963; Shirley Graham Du Bois died in Beijing in 1977.

ANGELINA WELD GRIMKÉ (1880–1958)

Angelina Weld Grimké was the only daughter of Sarah E. Stanley, a white Bostonian, and Archibald Henry Grimké, a former slave whose father was his owner. Archibald was also the nephew of Angelina Grimké Weld (Angelina's namesake) and Sarah M. Grimké, the famous Quaker abolitionists and feminists. In 1883 Grimké's parents separated. She lived with her mother until 1887, at which time she went to live with her father; her mother died in 1898, without having seen her daughter again. Grimké grew very close to her father, a successful lawyer and diplomat.

Grimké, a light-skinned girl, grew up in aristocratic Boston social circles and attended several schools where she was often the only African-American student: the Fairmount School in Hyde Park, Boston; Carleton Academy in Northfield, Minnesota; Cushing Academy in Ashburn, Massachusetts; and the Boston Normal School of Gymnastics. She graduated from the last in 1902 and began a teaching career in Washington, D.C. In 1916, after having taught at Armstrong Manual Training School for fourteen years, Grimké began teaching at Dunbar High School. Also in 1916, her play *Rachel* became the first staged play written by an African-American woman when it was produced by the NAACP and staged at Myrtill Normal School.

Grimké wrote verse throughout her life, and she published in many of the major magazines and anthologies of the Harlem Renaissance. Her poetry—categorized by her biographer Gloria T. Hull as elegies, love lyrics, nature lyrics, racial poems, or poems dealing with life and universal human experience—is strongly identified with women. Indeed, her strongest relationships were with women, including Clarissa Scott Delany (q.v.), Georgia Douglas Johnson (q.v.), and Mary Burrill.

In 1933 Grimké retired from teaching and moved to New York. There, she lived in semiseclusion until her death.

FLORENCE MARION HARMON (1880–1936)

The details of Florence Harmon's life remain elusive. What little is known of her is that she was born in the industrial city of Lynn, Massachusetts, north of Boston, and attended the nearby Gordon College of Theology and Missions. Her parents were Georgianna O'Brien Harmon of Lynn and Horace W. Harmon of Alabama. One of Harmon's stories was published in the 1924 Gordon yearbook. At the time of her death at the age of fifty-six, Harmon's occupation was listed as "dressmaker."

Harmon belonged to the Boston Saturday Evening Quill Club, of which she served as treasurer for a number of years. She also worked at the *Boston Post* newspaper. The two stories anthologized here (her only extant work besides the yearbook story) were published in the *Saturday Evening Quill*, the magazine of the Quill Club.

JUANITA V. HARRISON (c. 1891–?)

Juanita Harrison's biography is unlike that of any of the other writers in this volume. With only a few months of formal schooling in Mississippi before the age of ten, Harrison became a domestic, though she dreamed of traveling the globe. At the age of sixteen she began to work first in Cuba, where she learned some Spanish, then in California, where her employer helped her to invest her earnings.

At the age of thirty-six, Harrison realized her life's dream: she began an eight-year journey around the world that would take her to some twenty countries, all on the earnings she saved while working as a domestic. She visited Japan, Egypt, Burma, Thailand, Russia, Jerusalem, and several countries in Western Europe, working when she ran out of money and moving on whenever she felt like it. She traveled alone, though she met countless strangers of all races, nationalities, and classes.

While Harrison was working in Paris, her employer suggested that she publish the diaries that she had kept throughout her travels. In 1935 *The Atlantic Monthly* published two advance installments of her book, which was issued a year later. Her publisher decided to allow her writings to appear unedited, with many spelling and grammatical mistakes.

The last known information about Juanita Harrison is that, with her earnings from *The Atlantic Monthly,* she purchased a seven-by-seven-foot tent, which she set up on an abandoned lot near Waikiki Beach in Hawaii.

GLADYS CASELY HAYFORD (1904–1950)

Gladys Casely Hayford was born in Axim, the Gold Coast (now Ghana), to a prominent West African family. Her mother, Adelaide Smith Casely Hayford, was a renowned educator and the founder of the Girls' Vocational School in Sierra Leone. Her father, Joseph Casely Hayford, was a distinguished lawyer from the Gold Coast and an early leader in the Pan-African movement.

At an early age, Hayford was taken to England by her mother to treat a birth defect in one of her legs. There she learned English, though she continued to speak Fanti with her parents. She spent a total of five years in the British Isles, eventually attending college at Colwyn Bay, in Wales.

After college, Hayford joined a Berlin jazz troupe. Returning to Africa in 1926, Gladys taught African folklore and literature at her mother's Girls' Vocational School, fulfilling her conviction that, in her own words, "the first thing to do . . . was to imbue our own people with the idea of their own beauty, superiority and individuality, with a love and admiration for our own country, which has been systematically oppressed."

Gladys Casely Hayford's poems (sometimes written under the pseudonym Aquah Laluah) deserve a place in discussions of the Harlem Renaissance, though fewer than ten were published, because of her close connection with the Pan-African themes of that period. Hayford died in 1950, at the age of forty-six, after contracting black water fever (cholera).

ALVIRA HAZZARD (1899–1953)

Little is known about Alvirah Hazzard's life, but 1920 census records indicate that she was born in North Brookfield, Massachusetts, to John and Rosella Curry Hazzard, the oldest of six children. Her family was well established in New England, having lived there for several generations. After attending Massachusetts State Normal School at Worcester (now Worcester State College), Hazzard taught in the Boston public schools. On the graduation program at Massachusetts State Normal School, her name appears as "Marie Alvirah Hazzard." At the time of her death, she was a clerk at Boston City Hospital.

A member of the Saturday Evening Quill Club in Boston, Hazzard's writing appeared in the Quill Club's magazine, the *Saturday Evening Quill*. According to the *Quill*, Hazzard wrote for the *Boston Post*. Hazzard also appeared on the stage, in plays performed at the Allied Arts Center founded by black musicologist Maud Cuney-Hare.

ARIEL WILLIAMS HOLLOWAY (1905–1973)

Ariel Williams Holloway, formerly Lucy Ariel Williams, was born in Mobile, Alabama, to Fannie Brandon and Dr. H. Roger Williams. She received her bachelor's in music from Fisk University in 1926, and went on to receive a second bachelor's degree in music, with a major in piano and a minor in voice, from the Oberlin Conservatory of Music. After graduation she taught music and high school subjects at various public schools in North Carolina, Florida, and Alabama, and she served as the first supervisor of music for the Mobile public schools. She kept this job from 1939—while continuing to perform on the piano—until her death in 1973. After her death, an elementary school in Mobile was renamed for her. She was married to Joaquin M. Holloway, a letter carrier in Mobile, and their son Joaquin M. Holloway, Jr., was born in 1937.

From 1926 to 1935, Holloway published several poems in *Opportunity* magazine (under the name Williams), including "Northboun'," which won a prize in a 1926 *Opportunity* contest and was later included in Countee Cullen's classic anthology, *Caroling Dusk* (1927). A collection, *Shape Them into Dreams*, including works written many years before, was published by Exposition Press in 1955.

JANE EDNA HUNTER (1882–1971)

Born on a plantation in South Carolina, Jane Edna Hunter was raised by an aunt, and she later earned her room and board as a live-in domestic. As the founder of the Phyllis Wheatley Association, a training school and residence for young black women in Cleveland, Hunter sought to increase opportunities for young, single, migrant black women in urban areas.

Hunter worked her way through Ferguson Academy (later renamed Ferguson and Williams College) in Abbeville, South Carolina, and graduated in 1900. The end of a short-lived marriage to Edward Hunter (who was forty years her senior), which she broke off because the marriage was loveless, set her on her independent, nontraditional path.

Hunter began to work as a nurse in Charleston, South Carolina, and she was admitted to a training school for nurses at the Cannon Street Hospital and to an advanced training program at the Hampton Institute in Virginia. On the advice of friends, she moved to Cleveland in 1905.

Hunter founded the Wheatley Association in 1913, using Booker T. Washington's self-help philosophy, which often drew criticism. If most of the jobs available to black women were those of domestics, secretaries, or nurses, then, Hunter believed, young black women had to be trained for those jobs and not for anything else. She continued to run the Wheatley Association according to her principles until the age of sixty-six. As Adrienne Lash Jones has documented in her book *Jane Edna Hunter: A Case Study of Black Leadership, 1910–1950* (1990), thousands of women were housed and trained at the Phyllis Wheatley Association between 1913 and the early 1960s, and Hunter's legacy of more than half a million dollars, left in trust with a Cleveland bank, continues to benefit women.

ZORA NEALE HURSTON (1891–1960)

Zora Neale Hurston is perhaps the most prolific and well-known woman writer of the Harlem Renaissance. The novelist Alice Walker claims Hurston as a foremother and has written that "no other writer is as important" to her.

Hurston was born in the all-black, rural town of Eatonville, Florida, the daughter of John Hurston, a Baptist preacher and carpenter, and Lucy Potts. She was the seventh of eight children. She graduated from the Robert Hungerford Normal and Industrial School, which even today is 90 percent black. At Howard University she met Alain Locke, Georgia Douglas Johnson (q.v.), and May Miller (q.v.).

Hurston's first short story was published in 1921 in *Stylus,* a Howard literary magazine, when Hurston was thirty. After moving to New York to attend Barnard College of Columbia University, Hurston published in *Opportunity* and *Fire!!,* winning recognition in the *Opportunity* literary contests. She received a bachelor's degree from Barnard in 1928. At Columbia, she studied under Franz Boas, a renowned anthropologist, who encouraged her fieldwork among blacks, which she undertook beginning in 1927. Her anthropological work provided the base for much of her writing, including the novels *Mules and Men* (1936) and *Tell My Horse* (1939), as well as many articles and parts of other novels. From 1927 to 1932, her research was supported by Charlotte Osgood Mason, a wealthy patron of black arts.

Hurston's studies took her from New York to the Caribbean, and from New Orleans to Honduras. She also traveled the country with her musical reviews and worked at a college in North Carolina, at Paramount Studios in Hollywood, and in St. Augustine, Florida, during World War II.

In 1951 Hurston returned permanently to Florida. In dire straits financially, she took other jobs, such as substitute teaching, library work, and domestic service. Although while living in New York she had been very much a personality on the Harlem scene, in Florida she was forced to enter a welfare home in St. Lucie. She died there in 1960, the author of seven novels, several plays (one coauthored by Langston Hughes) and musicals, and numerous short stories and essays.

GEORGIA DOUGLAS JOHNSON (1877–1966)

One of the best known black women poets of the New Negro era, Georgia Douglas Johnson was the author of numerous lyrics and short stories, four volumes of verse, and several plays. She published in such periodicals as *The Crisis, The Messenger, Liberator, Opportunity, Palms,* and *Voice of the Negro.*

Johnson was born in September, 1877, the daughter of George and Laura Camp. She studied at Atlanta University, Oberlin Conservatory of Music, Cleveland College of Music, and Howard University. After completing her course in Cleveland, she returned to Atlanta to teach school, eventually serving as assistant principal. She married Henry Lincoln Johnson, a lawyer and politician, in 1903, and after moving to Washington, D.C., in 1909, the couple had two sons.

Her home was one of the primary meeting points for Washington's black intellectual circle and the city's black literary salon. In these two capacities she hosted such figures as W. E. B. Du Bois, Angelina Weld Grimké (q.v.), Zora Neale Hurston (q.v.), Countee Cullen, Clarissa Scott Delany (q.v.), Alice Dunbar-Nelson (q.v.), Jessie Fauset (q.v.), Langston Hughes, Alain Locke, and scores of other black writers and thinkers of the time. She was also involved with civil rights activities, politics, the Pan-African movement, women's issues, human rights organizations, the Congregational Church, the Republican Party, and various literary organizations.

Widowed in 1925, Johnson took government jobs to support herself and finance her sons' education. She published more than two hundred poems in four collections between 1918 and 1930.

HELENE JOHNSON (1906–1995)

Helene Johnson was named Helen at birth; an aunt later suggested she change to Helene because it was a "fancier" name. Under this name, she was published in many of the major periodicals and anthologies of the Harlem Renaissance. Born in Boston, Johnson never met her father; she lived with her mother, two maternal aunts, the husband of one of her aunts, and two female cousins. One of these cousins, Dorothy West (q.v.), also became a well-known writer. In fact West and Johnson moved to New York together in 1927, two years after Johnson had begun to make a literary name for herself by winning first honorable mention in an *Opportunity* literary contest for her poem "Fulfillment."

After moving to New York, Johnson published her poems in such magazines as *Vanity Fair, Opportunity, Fire!!, Harlem, Saturday Evening Quill, Challenge,* and *Palms.* Her work also appeared in several anthologies: *Readings from Negro Authors* (1931), Countee Cullen's *Caroling Dusk* (1927), Charles Johnson's *Ebony and Topaz* (1927), and, several years later, Arna Bontemps's *Golden Slippers* (1941).

While living in New York Johnson worked for the Fellowship for Reconciliation, an international organization that promoted pacifist resistance to war and violence and strove for interracial goodwill and justice.

After she married in the 1930s, Helene Johnson dropped out of the literary world. She had a daughter, Abigail Calachaly Hubbell, and worked full-time, which took time away from writing. Johnson moved back to Boston in the 1980s after separating from her husband, but returned to New York in the fall of 1986 to live with her daughter.

NELLA LARSEN (1891–1964)

Nella Larsen, born in Chicago, spent a difficult childhood and youth as the only dark-skinned child in her predominantly Scandinavian family. (See Thadious Davis, *Nella Larsen, Novelist of the Harlem Renaissance: A Woman's Life Unveiled,* Baton Rouge: Louisiana State University Press, 1994). In 1919 Larsen married Dr. Elmer S. Imes, a noted physicist, and became a socialite wife—a role that introduced her to some of the most celebrated figures of the Harlem literary scene. She was described by the *Amsterdam News* of May 23, 1928, as "a 'modern' woman who 'smokes, wears her dresses short, does not believe in religion, churches, and the like'" (Charles R. Larson, ed.,

An Intimation of Things Distant: The Collected Fiction of Nella Larsen, New York: Anchor Books, 1992, p. xii). Larsen was one of the few women writers of her time to sojourn abroad. In April of 1930 Larsen sailed for Europe under the auspices of a Guggenheim Foundation writing fellowship, returning to the United States in December of 1931.

She is best known for her novels *Quicksand* (1928) and *Passing* (1929). The publication in the January 1930 issue of *Forum* of her story "Sanctuary" prompted accusations that she had plagiarized the piece from a story entitled "Mrs. Adis" by Sheila Kaye-Smith, published in *Century* in January 1922. Larsen denied this, stating that she had never read the Kaye-Smith story, and she wrote a letter to *Forum* defending herself. In her letter, she states that the plot of "Sanctuary" was based on a tale told to her by one of her patients in a New York City hospital. But the negative publicity from the incident, as well as from her divorce from Imes, may have helped to bring an early end to her writing career.

ELISE JOHNSON McDOUGALD (1885–1971)

Elise Johnson McDougald was born Gertrude Elise Johnson, the daughter of Peter Johnson, a New York physician who was on the founding committee of the National Urban League, and Mary Whittle Johnson, a white English-woman. Her father was the third African-American admitted to practice medicine in New York City, and he was the founder of the McDonough Memorial Hospital. Elise married Cornelius McDougald in 1911.

McDougald studied at Hunter College, Columbia University, the College of the City of New York, and New York University, though she never received a degree. She began teaching in the New York City public school system in 1905, where she remained until 1954, with the exception of a leave of absence to raise her two children, Dr. Elizabeth McDougald and Cornelius McDougald, Jr. During her leave she also served as the head of the Women's Department of the U.S. Employment Bureau, as a counselor at the Henry Street Settlement, and in positions at the Manhattan Trade School and the New York branch of the U.S. Department of Labor.

In 1924 McDougald was chosen by competitive examination to be assistant principal of Public School 89. Twelve years later she was made full principal, the first black woman to attain such a position in a New York City public school.

Elise Johnson McDougland's writing appeared in *The Crisis, Opportunity,* and *Survey Graphic.*

MAY MILLER (1899–)

May Miller's father was the prominent sociologist and Howard University dean Kelly Miller. The Miller family was often host to such figures as Paul Laurence Dunbar, Georgia Douglas Johnson (q.v.), William Stanley Braithwaite, and W. E. B. Du Bois, and was close with the family of Emmet Scott, whose daughters Evelyn Scott and Clarissa Scott Delaney (q.v.) were Miller's friends.

Miller graduated from Dunbar High School in Washington, D.C., where she studied under Mary Burrill and Angelina Grimké (q.v.). She went on to Howard University, where she received a bachelor's degree in 1920 and also playwright's award for best play. She continued her studies at American University and Columbia University, specializing in poetry and drama. She then taught English, speech, drama, and dance at Frederick Douglass High School in Baltimore, and participated (as an actor and a playwright) in the Negro Little Theatre movement. In a 1972 interview with Cassandra Willis of the City College of New York, Miller stated that she used standard English in dramatic discourse "in order to mingle and compete in the mainstream" but also claimed the right to use dialect on occasion.

In the 1930s, Miller and Willis Richardson edited and published two volumes of plays and pageants, many of which were intended for children. One of her own plays won third prize in an *Opportunity* literary contest in 1925, and she won an honorable mention for another. *Riding the Goat,* a comedy, was her most popular play, and brought in many royalties from churches and schools. In 1940, Miller married John Sullivan.

During the 1920s and 1930s May Miller became friends with many of the important writers in Washington, D.C., especially Zora Neale Hurston (q.v.) and Georgia Douglas Johnson (q.v.). She was also appointed by Mayor Walter E. Washington to the District of Columbia Commission on the Arts and Humanities. She presently lives in Washington, D.C.

BRENDA RAY MORYCK (1894–1949)

Brenda Ray Moryck's writing career followed family tradition; her grandfather had been editor of a Boston newspaper from 1850 to 1860.

Moryck graduated from Wellesley College in 1916 and married Lucius Lee Jordan in 1917; he died later that same year. After moving to Newark, Moryck volunteered for the Newark Bureau of Associated Charities. In 1925 she took a job teaching at Armstrong Technical High School in Baltimore, where she remained until 1930.

In 1926, 1927, and 1928, Moryck won awards for her writing in both *The Crisis* and *Opportunity*, and she was a columnist for the *Baltimore Afro-American* and the *New Jersey Herald*. She lectured often on behalf of the various organizations she supported, which included the NAACP, the Women's Interracial Committee of the Federated Council of Churches, the National Negro Nurse's Association, the National Council of Negro Women, the South Harlem Community Welfare Association, and the Harlem YWCA, where she worked as a vocational guidance adviser.

In 1930 Moryck married Robert B. Francke, who was a lawyer and an attaché in the Haitian legation in Paris, but she kept her own name for professional reasons. The couple lived in Brooklyn. Moryck had one daughter, Betty Osborne.

PAULI MURRAY (1910–1985)

Pauli (born Anna Pauline) Murray—author, lawyer, civil rights activist, and legal scholar—grew up in Durham, North Carolina, in the home of her maternal grandparents and an aunt. Her grandfather had been a black Union soldier during the Civil War and had set up schools for freed blacks in Virginia and North Carolina. Her parents, Willam Henry and Agnes Georgiana Fitzgerald Murray, were middle class and of mixed ancestry. Murray's mother died when Pauli was four.

Murray received her bachelor's degree in English from Hunter College in New York City in 1933, and the next year her first poem, "The Song of the Highway," was published in Nancy Cunard's anthology *Negro: An Anthology*. At this time, Murray also found a friend and mentor in Pulitzer Prize–winning poet Steven Benet.

Murray was refused admission to the law school at the University of North Carolina because she was black; she went to Howard University instead, where she was first in her class and the only woman. When she applied again to law schools for an advanced law degree, she was refused admission to the law school at Harvard University because she was a woman; she went to the University of California at Berkeley instead.

Several of Murray's poems were published in the 1930s in *Opportunity.* Murray completed the poem "Dark Testament" in 1943 (the same year as the Harlem riot and Benet's death). It became the title poem in a collection of poetry (published in 1970) ranging in theme from racial issues to meditations on nature and humanity.

EFFIE LEE NEWSOME (1885–1979)

One of five children born to Benjamin Franklin Lee and Mary Elizabeth Ashe Lee, Effie Lee Newsome (originally Mary Effie Lee) spent her childhood years in Pennsylvania, Texas, and Ohio because her father, a bishop, was often transferred around the country. He eventually became the second president of Wilberforce University in Ohio.

Newsome attended Wilberforce University (1901–1904), Oberlin College (1904–1905), the Philadelphia Academy of Fine Arts (1907–1908), and the University of Pennsylvania (1911–1914). In 1920 she married Reverend Henry Nesby Newsome, and they apparently moved from Philadelphia to Birmingham, Alabama, where she founded the Boys of Birmingham Club in 1925. Eventually they moved back to Wilberforce, where she served as a librarian first at the elementary school at Central State College, and then at Wilberforce University until 1963.

Throughout her life, Newsome wrote poems, stories, and articles, mostly for children, and she edited a children's column for *Opportunity* and "The Little Page" in *The Crisis.* Under the pseudonym Johnson Ward, she won an honorable mention in the 1926 Krigwa contest sponsored by *The Crisis,* which published over a hundred of her poems from 1917 to 1934. Several of her poems also appeared in *The Brownies' Book,* W. E. B. Du Bois's magazine for black children.

ANN PETRY (1908–)

Ann Petry, born Ann Lane, was raised in Old Saybrook, a rural Connecticut town. She graduated from the Connecticut College of Pharmacy and, like her father, uncle, and aunt, was a pharmacist by profession. She worked in her family's drugstores in Old Saybrook and Old Lyme, Connecticut.

After marrying George David Petry in 1938, she moved to Harlem, where she worked for Harlem newspapers, writing stories and selling advertising space. She also acted in the American Negro Theatre. In November 1943 Petry's first short story, "On Saturday the Siren Sounds at Noon," was published in *The Crisis.* "Olaf and His Girl Friend" appeared in the May 1945 issue, and "Like a Winding Sheet" appeared in the November issue that same year. An editor at Houghton Mifflin who had read "On Saturday the Siren Sounds at Noon" encouraged Petry to submit a novel to the publishing company's fellowship competition, and Petry entered her manuscript for *The Street,* which won her the $2,400 fellowship prize for 1945. The book, which was inspired by her experiences during six years spent in Harlem, was published in 1946.

Ann Petry continues to live in Connecticut, where she moved around 1946. She has been prolific, writing many stories, novels, and children's books. Critic Bernard W. Bell praises her "faithfulness" to the complexity of black women's realities. Says Bell, "Ann Petry . . . moves beyond the naturalistic vision of Himes and Wright to a demythologizing of American culture and Afro-American character." Petry's daughter, Elizabeth Petry Gilbert, is an attorney.

ESTHER POPEL (1896–1958)

Living in Harrisburg, Pennsylvania, where her family had resided since 1826, Esther Popel commuted from her home to Dickinson College in Carlisle, Pennsylvania. She graduated Phi Beta Kappa from Dickinson with the class of 1919, and she was perhaps the first African-American woman to attend Dickinson. While at Dickinson she excelled in French, German, Latin, and Spanish.

After graduation, Popel worked for the War Risk Insurance Department, and taught for two years in Baltimore. She then moved to Washington, D.C., where she taught French and Spanish at Shaw Junior High School and Francis Junior High School. In addition to poetry, Popel wrote six plays for junior high school students, as well as essays on race relations, which she delivered as lectures at women's clubs throughout the Washington and New York areas.

Popel's poems were published with some regularity in *Opportunity* from 1925 to 1934. She was a frequent participant in the Washington literary salon held at the home of Georgia Douglas Johnson (q.v.), as Langston Hughes mentions in his autobiography, *The Big Sea* (1940).

FLORIDA RUFFIN RIDLEY (1861–1943)

Florida (originally Amelia) Ruffin was born in Boston to suffragist and civil rights activist Josephine St. Pierre Ruffin and George Lewis Ruffin, who was a judge in the Municipal Court of the Charlestown district of Boston and the first black judge in the North. After graduating from Boston Normal School and teaching in public schools, Florida married Ulysses Ridley, a tailor, with whom she had two children. They raised their children—Ulysses A. Ridley, Jr., and Constance J. Ridley—in Boston, living first on Charles Street on Beacon Hill and then in Brookline. (Her residence at 103 Charles Street is now a stop on the Women's Heritage Trail.)

Like her mother, Ridley was active in national and local organizations concerned with the status of blacks and women, and from 1894 to 1910 Ridley coedited and copublished *Woman's Era,* a monthly devoted to the interests of African-American women, with her mother. Ridley served as corresponding secretary both for the Women's Era Club and, later, the first national organization for black women, the National Federation of Afro-American Women. In 1923 she directed and promoted a Boston Public Library Exhibit about Negro achievement and abolition memorials.

W. E. B. Du Bois mentions Josephine Ruffin and her daughter (whom he calls "Birdie") as having hosted him and other black students at Harvard. He describes Josephine as "an aristocratic lady, with olive skin and high-piled masses of white hair." He also mentions her as publisher of the *Courant,* a weekly paper in which he published many of his Harvard daily themes (W. E. B. Du Bois, "A Negro Student at Harvard," in *Black and White in American Culture: An Anthology from the "Massachusetts Review,"* ed. Jules Chametzky and Sidney Kaplan, Amherst: University of Massachusetts Press, 1969, p. 123).

It was not until she was in her sixties that Ridley's short stories and essays—approximately six pieces are extant—began to appear in two of the journals of the Harlem Renaissance era, *Saturday Evening Quill* and *Opportunity.*

ESLANDA GOODE ROBESON (1896–1965)

Eslanda Goode Robeson's career as writer, anthropologist, and political activist has been overshadowed by that of her famous husband, the internationally known actor, singer, football player, and lawyer Paul Robeson. Originally named Eslanda Cardoza Goode, Robeson was born into a Washington, D.C., family whose ancestry was Spanish, English, Scottish, Jewish, Native American, and African-American. Her father, born into slavery, worked in the War Department as a clerk, and her mother, Eslanda Cardoza, was from a prominent Sephardic Jewish family. Robeson's grandfather, Francis Lewis Cardozo (the spelling varies), was a statesman who had been South Carolina's secretary of state and secretary of the treasury, and was a pioneer in education for blacks.

In 1905 Robeson's father died of alcoholism, and with her mother and two brothers she moved to New York, away from Washington's segregated schooling. Living in Harlem, the family witnessed and experienced the beginnings of the Harlem Renaissance. Eslanda studied chemistry at Columbia University Teachers' College. In 1920 she met the young Paul Robeson, a college football hero and one of the few black men at Columbia Law School. They were married in 1921. Eslanda received her bachelor's degree in 1923, after which she entered medical school.

Two years later, Robeson left medical school to promote her husband's burgeoning career. She wrote a biography of him, *Paul Robeson, Negro,* which was published in 1930. In 1928 the Robeson family—the couple and their son, Paul Jr.—moved to London. Inspired by the Bolshevik Revolution and friendships with such American leftists as John Reed, Robeson became politically active and deeply committed to social change. She influenced her husband in this direction as well, and in 1934 the Robesons traveled to the Soviet Union, which they viewed as a model society. According to Robert E. Skinner, "the fact that Paul literally sacrificed his fortunes and career to the cause of equality dramatically illustrates how much he came to share in his wife's beliefs and goals" (Barbara Sicherman and Carol Hurd Green, eds., with Ilene Kantrov and Harriette Walker, *Notable American Women,* Cambridge: The Belknap Press of Harvard University Press, 1980, p. 943).

In 1938 Robeson and her son went on a six-month trip to Africa, chronicled in her second book, *African Journey* (1945). As she explored the political, economic, and ethnic realities of Africa, she became convinced that the key to defeating racism lay in global solidarity.

IDA ROWLAND (1904–)

Ida Rowland was born into a Texas family of Native American, black, and European descent in 1904. Her family moved to Oklahoma when Rowland was thirteen, where she returned after receiving a bachelor's degree in sociology with minors in philosophy and english from the University of Nebraska–Omaha, a master's degree from the University of Nebraska, and a doctorate in social sciences from the French-language Laval University in Quebec. Rowland was the first black woman in Oklahoma to hold a Ph.D. For many years, Rowland taught social sciences at Arkansas A,M&N (now the University of Arkansas at Pine Bluffs), and currently she owns her own company, Bell Enterprises, which publishes instructional books on blacks for young people.

The poems included here come from her single volume of verse, *Lisping Leaves,* dedicated to her parents and published in Philadelphia in 1939, the same year she received her master's degree.

GERTRUDE SCHALK (1906–?)

Born Lillian Schalk in Boston in 1906 to Mary Wilkerson Schalk and Theodore O. Schalk, Schalk changed her first name to Gertrude, and it was under this name that her writings—four short stories—appeared in the *Saturday Evening Quill.* She also used the nickname Toki. She studied journalism at Boston University, taking courses in 1924 and 1925.

In 1946 Schalk married John V. Johnson. That same year she became editor of a women's page in *The Pittsburgh Courier,* and she also published in *Love Story Magazine,* the *New York Mirror,* the *Boston Post* and the "illustrated feature" section, a tabloid supplement in many black newspapers.

No information has been found about her life or career after 1946.

ANNE SPENCER (1882–1976)

The only child of parents who later divorced, Anne Spencer (born Anne Scales) received no formal education until she was eleven years old. She was sent from her native West Virginia to a boarding school for blacks in Lynchburg, Virginia, where she graduated in 1899 as class valedictorian. Two years later, she married Edward Spencer, whom she had met through an exchange of tutoring. The couple remained in Lynchburg, where Edward became the first black parcel postman in that city.

Spencer spent her time taking care of her three children, reading, writing, and tending her elaborate garden. Her husband built her a one-room cottage at the edge of the garden, where she did most of her writing. Spencer resisted Jim Crow laws in Lynchburg by refusing to use—or to let any of her children use—segregated public transportation. She also worked to have black teachers hired in place of whites, and she initiated the opening of Lynchburg's first black library, of which she was librarian from 1923 to 1945.

Spencer's first published poem appeared in *The Crisis* in 1920, when she was almost forty years old. James Weldon Johnson, who, like many other important black figures of the time, stayed at the Spencers' house during his travels from North to South (because black travelers were banned from most hotels), brought the poem to the magazine's attention. From that time on, Spencer's poetry was published in *Opportunity, Palms, The Crisis,* and *Survey Graphic,* and her work was included in most of the major anthologies of black writing published during the 1920s.

After Anne Spencer died in 1975, her home and garden were designated a Virginia Historic Landmark. They are also recognized in the National Register of Historic Places.

ELLEN TARRY (1906–)

The eldest of three children of John Barber and Eula Meadows Tarry of Birmingham, Alabama, Ellen Tarry attended State Normal School (later Alabama State University). After a succession of teaching positions in the Birmingham schools and at the Knights of Columbus Evening School, she served as a columnist and editorialist for the *Birmingham Truth* from 1927 to 1929 and wrote the column "Negroes of Note." Writing for children became important to her when she saw black children in Birmingham "who could only imagine becoming cooks, drivers, or maids." As she said in a 1992 interview, "I had always been able to dream. It bothered me that these children couldn't dream."

Born an Episcopalian, Tarry became increasingly interested in Catholicism, and she converted in 1922. Her faith has shaped her career as a writer and lecturer, and many of her writings have been published in Catholic periodicals.

In 1929 Tarry moved to New York, where she joined the Negro Writers'

Guild, a group that included Sterling Brown and Claude McKay. From 1937 to 1939, with a scholarship from the Bureau of Educational Experiments (later Bank Street College), she attended the Cooperative School for Student Teachers, specializing in children's literature. These studies, combined with her involvement with Friendship House, a Harlem Catholic Center, began for Tarry a career of research, public speaking, and writing.

Tarry's essay included in this volume, "Native Daughter," was one of the first articles she was able to sell to a major periodical (it appeared in *Commonweal* in 1940). Her autobiography, *The Third Door* (1995), has been reissued by University of Alabama Press (1992). The book party was held at the same public library where Ellen Tarry had been denied entry as a little girl because she was black.

Tarry presently lives in Manhattan.

MARY CHURCH TERRELL (1863–1954)

Mary Church Terrell, known to her friends as "Mollie," is one of the best known black women activists of the early twentieth century. From her home in Memphis—her father, Robert Reed Church, was a millionaire—Mary Church was sent north for her secondary and higher education. She received her bachelor's degree from Oberlin College in 1884. She then became a teacher at Wilberforce University in Ohio, later moving to Washington, D.C., to teach Latin and German at Colored High School. In Washington, she met and married Robert H. Terrell, an 1884 graduate of Harvard Law School who went on to have a distinguished career as a municipal judge in Washington. Marriage brought her teaching career to a close—married women were not permitted to teach in District of Columbia schools.

In 1895 Terrell was appointed to the District of Columbia Board of Education, the first black woman in the country to hold such a position. She is best known for her role as a leader in the civil rights, women's rights, and world peace movements. A contemporary of Booker T. Washington, she was more outspoken than he on discrimination; she believed in crossing Jim Crow lines at every opportunity. She joined many black women's suffrage organizations (doing "club work") and knew Susan B. Anthony. Her husband, too, believed ardently that women should have the vote, at a time when few men took that stand. She articulated in no uncertain terms what she saw as the double jeopardy of black women seeking careers: "It is as easy for a colored woman to secure [nondomestic positions] as it is to catch greased lightning in a bottle. I might walk up and down the streets of almost any city or town in this country without being able to get employment either as a typist or a stenographer in spite of my college education. My degrees of A.B. and A.M. would avail me nothing at all" (unpublished manuscript, Moorland-Spingarn Collection, Howard University).

The Terrells' first daughter, Phyllis, named after Phyllis Wheatley, the early American black poet, was born in 1898. In 1905 they adopted a second daughter, Terrell's niece Mary Church.

Terrell wrote prolifically for newspapers and magazines and was a prominent lecturer on civil and women's rights. For many years Mary Terrell hoped to become a "successful [fiction] writer," but the *Washington Post* was the only newspaper in which one of her stories appeared. As she writes in her autobiography, "my very first ["Venus and the Night Doctors," 1901] was also my last which managed to burst into print" (*A Colored Woman in a White World,* 1940, p. 224).

ELOISE BIBB THOMPSON (1878–1928)

Eloise Bibb Thompson, playwright, poet, and short story writer, was born and raised in New Orleans, Louisiana. There she published her first book, *Poems* (1895), at age seventeen. After two years at Oberlin Academy, a preparatory school, Thompson entered Howard University, graduating from its Teacher's College in 1908. After her marriage to Noah D. Thompson, the couple moved to Los Angeles, where they became members of the Los Angeles–based literary group the Ink Slingers. According to a letter published by Gwendolyn Bennett (q.v.) in her "Ebony Flute" column in a 1926 issue of *Opportunity,* this group came into existence with the help of Charles S. Johnson.

The most controversial of Thompson's writings was a 1915 play entitled *A Reply to the Clansman.* It was written in response to D. W. Griffith's film *Birth of a Nation,* which was based on a novel glorifying the Ku Klux Klan and demeaning African-Americans. Thompson's play was reviewed by nine theatrical and film professionals (including Griffith and Cecil B. DeMille). The play was purchased by them but never produced; Thompson had to go to court to retrieve it. In addition to writing plays, many of which remain unpublished, Thompson published short stories in *Opportunity* magazine and wrote for local periodicals, including the *Los Angeles Sunday Tribune.*

ERA BELL THOMPSON (1906–1986)

Era Bell Thompson, known as a successful journalist, especially with *Ebony* magazine, spent her early years in Des Moines, the only daughter among four children. The family moved to North Dakota where her father farmed and sometimes worked as a waiter, coal miner, or cook. Thompson lost her mother at an early age.

Thompson paid her own way through North Dakota State University in Grand Forks by doing housework and babysitting. She played on the basketball and soccer teams and established state records in track.

Thompson began writing while at North Dakota State, starting with articles for a class in rhetoric. She became women's sports editor for the university newspaper, beginning a career in journalism which would take her to newspapers and magazines in Chicago and Minneapolis, and eventually to Africa.

Thompson published her autobiography, *Amerian Daughter,* in 1946 with the support of a fellowship from Chicago's Newberry Library. In 1947 she went to work as an editor for the *Negro Digest,* and then for *Ebony.*

LUCY MAE TURNER (1884–?)

Lucy Mae Turner was born in Zanesville, Ohio, the granddaughter of the famous slave insurrectionist Nat Turner. She studied at Wilberforce University, from which she graduated in 1908. She then began teaching in East St. Louis, Illinois, buying a home with her sister, Fannie, and eventually living there with her mother as well. Turner continued to teach there until 1954.

Turner earned a bachelor's degree from Ohio State University in 1934 and a master's degree from the University of Illinois in 1942. After St. Louis

University opened the doors of its law school to blacks, Turner began taking courses toward a law degree, which she received in 1950.

In addition to her narrative of "The Family of Nat Turner," she also produced a book of poetry in dialect, published in 1938.

MARGARET WALKER (1915–)

The youngest writer in this anthology, Margaret Abigail Walker was born in Birmingham, Alabama, to Sigismund C. Walker, a Methodist minister and theologian, and Marion Dozier Walker, a music teacher. The family moved to New Orleans, where both parents were professionals at New Orleans University. Encouraged by Langston Hughes, who gave a reading at her school, Walker went on to Northwestern University. W. E. B. Du Bois published her poetry in *The Crisis*. In Chicago Walker joined the Federal Writers Program sponsored by the Works Progress Administration, which introduced her to Gwendolyn Brooks, Arna Bontemps, and Richard Wright. When funding for the project ended, Walker went to the University of Iowa for a master's degree. There she completed her first book of poetry, *For My People* (1942), which is regarded as a landmark in black literature.

After marrying Firnist James Alexander in 1943, Walker made a career of teaching in South Carolina and Mississippi. She had four children and supported her family financially when her husband became disabled. Walker received a Rosenwald Fellowship for writing in 1944.

IDA B. WELLS-BARNETT (1862–1931)

Ida B. Wells-Barnett, a crusading journalist and activist, was born into slavery in Holly Springs, Mississippi, the eldest of eight children of Lizzie Bell and James Wells. She attended Rust University, a high school and industrial school for freed people. In 1878 both of her parents and her youngest brother died in a yellow fever epidemic, and she took on the responsibility of caring for her remaining siblings. At the age of sixteen she passed the teacher's exam for the county schools and began to teach in Holly Springs; a year later she took her two youngest siblings to Memphis with her and began to teach in a school near that city.

In May 1884 Wells-Barnett began the pattern of activism and refusing to give in to racism that would inform her life. When her refusal to sit in the Jim Crow car of a train resulted in her being thrown off the train, she sued the railroad company and won, although the decision was overturned by the Tennessee State Supreme Court. She then began to publish articles condemning the inadequate education that was the lot of blacks in Mississippi and the rest of the South; this writing, done under the pen name of Iola, got her fired from her teaching job in 1891. Refusing to be silenced, however, she bought a part interest in a small Memphis newspaper of which she became editor and, eventually, sole owner.

In 1882 she published the names of the members of the mob that had lynched three of her colleagues, independent black business owners who had "dared" to compete with a white store, and she wrote an editorial questioning the popular misconception that most black men who were lynched had raped white women. She concluded that lynching was a racist device designed to eliminate financially independent African-Americans, and, furthermore, that it was possible that the "rapes" of white women covered up the possibility that white women could be attracted to black men. As a result of this editorial, her printing office was destroyed by an angry mob, and Wells, who was traveling out of the state at the time, was warned never to return to Memphis.

Wells-Barnett then settled in New York and began to write for *New Age,* where she continued to address lynching. Her renown spread internationally, and she was invited to go on a lecture tour in England in 1895, the same year in which she married Ferdinand Barnett, a Chicago lawyer and the editor of the *Chicago Conservator.* She moved to Chicago and had four children, all the while continuing to report on racial injustice. She took her children on lecture tours with her while she was nursing them.

Wells-Barnett was a member of the Committee of Forty, founded in New York in 1909, which was the predecessor of the NAACP, and in 1918 she was one of eleven blacks chosen by a group of 250 in Washington to serve as representatives to the Versailles Peace Conference—though the group was finally unable to go because they were denied passports.

Wells-Barnett was well known nationally and internationally for her philosophy on racial issues. She often sided with radical figures such as Marcus Garvey and W. E. B. Du Bois. Her autobiography, *Crusade For Justice,* was edited by her daughter, Alfreda M. Duster, and published in 1970.

DOROTHY WEST (1907–)

Dorothy West was born and raised in Boston, where she attended Girls' Latin School. With her cousin, the writer Helene Johnson (q.v.), she went to New York after winning a literary prize in the June 1926 literary contest sponsored by *Opportunity* magazine, for her story "The Typewriter." West and Johnson became part of the Harlem literary and social scenes. They were known for their association with such Harlem Renaissance greats as Langston Hughes, Wallace Thurman, Countee Cullen, and Zora Neale Hurston (q.v.).

In 1932 West traveled to Russia as part of a group of black artists, including Langston Hughes, to make a film about race relations in Alabama. Upon learning of her father's death, West returned early to the United States. She eventually settled in her family's summer cottage in Oak Bluffs, on the island of Martha's Vineyard in Massachusetts.

During the late 1920s, West's short stories were published often in the Boston-based *Saturday Evening Quill.* In 1934 she started her own magazine, *Challenge;* Richard Wright was her associate editor. Her first novel, *The Living Is Easy,* was published in 1948; her next, *The Wedding,* was published almost fifty years later, in 1995.

Since 1958, while living on Martha's Vineyard, West has contributed a social column, stories, and vignettes to the *Vineyard Gazette.* She has also lectured widely about the Harlem Renaissance era.

ZARA WRIGHT (?–?)

Little is known of Zara Wright save what she reveals through the preface and introduction to her novel, *Black and White Tangled Threads* and its sequel, *Kenneth,* which were published together in 1920. The books are dedicated to her "dear, departed husband J. Edward Wright" and bear an inscription indicating the hope that her book will inspire readers to act ethically and to love their fellow human beings. Wright praises her novels' heroine (who dedicates her life to educating disadvantaged blacks and to enlightening racist whites) as one who "sacrifices her principles of right and wrong to save those near and dear to her from imaginary shame and humiliation."

Black and White Tangled Threads received a favorable one-paragraph review in the *Chicago Defender,* which described it as a "realistic portrayal of individuals and events [that] lifts one to the heights of earthly ambitions" (December 1920, p. 8).

OCTAVIA B. WYNBUSH (1898–1972)

Born in Washington, Pennsylvania, to Abraham C. and Mary Sheppard Wynbush, Octavia Beatrice Wynbush attended Oberlin College, from which she graduated with a bachelor's degree in German in 1920. She went on to receive her master's in English from Columbia University in 1934, and she taught in various schools in Kansas, Louisiana, Arkansas, and Missouri until her retirement in 1964. She remained single most of her life, marrying Lewis Strong in 1963, at the age of sixty-seven.

Wynbush published eight short stories and several poems in *The Crisis* and *Opportunity.* Her stories take place mainly in the South, and most of her characters speak in dialect. Though she published often between 1931 and 1945, nothing is known of her literary career after 1945, when her last published story appeared in *The Crisis.* In a letter to the Alumni Office of Oberlin College dated November 3, 1945, Wynbush wrote: "I have hesitated to write anything about myself, because I have fallen so far short of my own expectations since having been graduated from Oberlin."

IDABELLE YEISER (c. 1897–?)

Idabelle Yeiser was active in one of Philadelphia's literary groups and published in *Black Opals,* Philadelphia's black literary magazine.

Much about Yeiser's life remains a mystery, including information about her parentage and her childhood. What is known, however, is that she grew up in a black middle-class home, and that, after graduating from Montclair State Normal School in New Jersey, she continued her studies at the University of Pennsylvania. Specializing in languages, she eventually received her doctorate in French from Columbia University, and after traveling abroad from 1925 to 1926, she returned to Philadelphia. In 1927 she won first prize for her personal experience sketch, "Letters," in *Opportunity,* and several of her poems were published in that magazine and in *The Crisis.*

Illustration Credits

Delilah Leontium Beasley: Courtesy of the Moorland-Spingarn Research Center, Howard University.

Gwendolyn B. Bennett: Courtesy of the Moorland-Spingarn Research Center, Howard University.

Hallie Quinn Brown: Courtesy of the Moorland-Spingarn Research Center, Howard University.

Ethel Caution Davis: From Wellesley College, *Legenda,* 1912; courtesy of Wellesley College.

Carrie W. Clifford: Courtesy of the Moorland-Spingarn Research Center, Howard University.

Anna J. Cooper: Courtesy of the Moorland-Spingarn Research Center, Howard University.

Clarissa Scott Delany: Courtesy of Wellesley College.

Katherine Dunham: Courtesy of the Moorland-Spingarn Research Center, Howard University.

Sarah Collins Fernandis: Courtesy of Hampton University Archives, Hampton, Virginia.

Mercedes Gilbert: Courtesy of the Moorland-Spingarn Research Center, Howard University.

Edythe Mae Gordon: Courtesy of Special Collections, Boston University.

Angelina Weld Grimké: Courtesy of the Moorland-Spingarn Research Center, Howard University.

Zora Neale Hurston: Courtesy of the Moorland-Spingarn Research Center, Howard University.

May Miller: Courtesy of May Miller.

Ann Petry: Courtesy of the Moorland-Spingarn Research Center, Howard University.

Esther Popel: From Dickinson College, *The Microcosm,* 1919; courtesy of Dickinson College.

Florida Ruffin Ridley: Courtesy of Maud Jenkins.

Anne Spencer: Courtesy of Chauncey Spencer.

Ellen Tarry: Courtesy of Ellen Tarry.

Mary Church Terrell: Courtesy of the Moorland-Spingarn Research Center, Howard University.

Era Bell Thompson: Courtesy of the Moorland-Spingarn Research Center, Howard University.

Margaret Walker: Courtesy of the Moorland-Spingarn Research Center, Howard University.

Ida B. Wells-Barnett: Courtesy of the Moorland-Spingarn Research Center, Howard University.

Dorothy West: Photo by Lorraine Elena Roses.

Octavia B. Wynbush: From Oberlin College yearbook, 1921; courtesy of Oberlin College.